Horace for
Students of Literature

Horace for
Students of Literature

THE "ARS POETICA" AND

ITS TRADITION

O. B. Hardison, Jr.
and Leon Golden

University Press of Florida
Gainesville / Tallahassee / Tampa / Boca Raton
Pensacola / Orlando / Miami / Jacksonville

Index by Mary Frances Hardison

00 99 98 97 96 95 6 5 4 3 2 1

Library of Congress Cataloging-in-Publication

Horace for students of literature: the "Ars poetica" and its
tradition / [edited by] O.B. Hardison Jr. and Leon Golden.
   p.   cm.
   Includes bibliographical references and index.
   Contents: Ars poetica / Horace — Poetria nova / Geoffrey of
Vinsauf — L'art poétique / Boileau — An essay on criticism / Pope
— English bards and Scotch reviewers / Byron — Notes toward a
supreme fiction / Stevens.
   ISBN 0-8130-1354-2 (alk. paper)
   1. Horace. Ars poetica. 2. Epistolary poetry, Latin — History and
criticism. 3. Literature — History and criticism — Theory, etc.
4. Aesthetics, Ancient — Poetry. 5. Horace — Influence. 6. Poetics —
Poetry. 7. Criticism. I. Hardison, O.B. II. Golden, Leon,
1930-
PA6393.H67   1995   95-2623
871.01—dc20

Contents

V. *English Bards and Scotch Reviewers*
and *Hints from Horace* by Lord Byron

VI. *Notes Toward a Supreme Fiction* by Wallace Stevens

Notes

Preface

This volume devoted to Horace's *Ars Poetica* and its tradition is a companion to *Aristotle's "Poetics," A Translation and Commentary for Students of Literature*. Like that volume, it is a collaboration. As in the earlier volume, the translation of the classical work, in this case the *Ars Poetica*, is by Leon Golden and the commentary by O.B. Hardison. Translations of the nonclassical works are by the authors indicated for each work.

Our debts to previous translators and commentators will be evident to anyone who is familiar with the territory. Of special value are the two most recent commentaries on Horace's *Art*: C.O. Brink's three-volume study (1963–82) and Niall Rudd's *Epistles Book II and Epistle to the Pisones* (1989).

The reader will also encounter several positions that have not been developed in previous studies. Among these are the analysis of the *Ars Poetica* as a dramatic monologue, the corollary analysis of the speaker as persona, comment on Horace's problematic attitudes to Augustan values, suggestions concerning the skeptical bent of the *Art* and the deeper meaning of the *carpe diem* motif in the *Odes*, the relevance of *convenientia* (Greek *akolouthia*) as a dominant theme of the work, the complex relations of the work to later imitations, and the varying facets of Horace's work revealed by these imitations. In a very real sense, the later texts included in the present volume are best understood as critical comments on the *Art*, and this is truest for the work that is least explicitly an "imitation"—Wallace Stevens's *Notes Toward a Supreme Fiction*.

We are grateful to many individuals for suggestions and encouragement. Our hope is that this volume will be as useful to the students of literature for whom it is intended as our *Aristotle's "Poetics"* has proved to be.

Second Preface

O.B. Hardison, Jr., died suddenly just after he had completed work on his commentary and notes for this book. On the model of our spirited discussions of Aristotle's *Poetics* several years earlier, it was his intention that we would engage in similar discussions of the works included here. His untimely death made that rewarding enterprise impossible. It was also impossible for him to make direct use of my translation in his references to the text of the *Ars Poetica* in the commentary. I do not think the reader will experience any serious problem because of slight variations between O.B.'s translations of Horatian passages and mine, and have decided that it is best not to make any alterations in O.B.'s text other than technical corrections.

This is O.B.'s book in design and execution. He imaginatively conceived of its scope and provided the insightful commentary. My principal task was to translate Horace's *Ars Poetica* and provide explanatory notes for that work. Sadly, that task has been enlarged to seeing the work through to its final publication on my own. I take on that responsibility as an act of *pietas* for a good and generous friend, for a brilliant scholar, and for an extraordinary teacher whose influence will be felt for generations to come.

In carrying out my responsibilities I am grateful to Professor George Kennedy for many valuable suggestions that have improved the text. I also thank George and Bobby Harper, close friends of O.B. Hardison and of mine for many years, for their important assistance in proofreading the original manuscript. In closing, I would like to express my gratitude to Matthew Hardison for his valuable assistance in locating and copying on disk the text of his father's manuscript.

Leon Golden

General Introduction

This is an era of dynamic, vigorous activity in the field of literary theory and criticism. New modes of analysis of literary form and function have stimulated intense interest in the nature and significance of artistic creation. While the focal point of critical theory has moved today some distance away from the center of attention of the great classical critics, the time-tested importance and ongoing influence of those critics is still easily recognized. The goal of this volume is to make available to the community of literary scholars and critics a demonstration of the strength and continuing validity of the Horatian tradition of literary criticism, which has been almost continuously present in our culture since the first century B.C. This is accomplished through the presentation of a series of texts, from the *Ars Poetica* itself to the twentieth-century masterpiece *Notes Toward a Supreme Fiction* by Wallace Stevens. The poet-critics included in this volume all reflect Horace's influence, sometimes in a direct and obvious way and sometimes in an indirect and subtle manner. What has lasted in Horace's poetic theory and what has been adapted from it by his successors as poet-critics across time are themes of permanent value to students of literature and criticism. History clearly attests to the fact that, whatever the developments and fashions of criticism at any given time, the Horatian tradition remains continuously operative as a significant instrument of literary analysis. In criticism, as in other areas of cultural experience, we benefit by exposure to the diversity of legitimate voices seeking our attention. In this volume the eloquent voice of the Horatian tradition, at some times more and at other times less influential in our culture, can, in a unique and effective way, be heard clearly.

In the *Ars Poetica* Horace maps out three critical directions that have been followed by later critics. One of these paths relates to form and style; another to methods of evaluating success and failure in poetry;

and a third investigates the essential purpose of poetic activity and the psychology of the creative artist. The impact of these investigations has been felt in different ways by the critics represented in this volume as well as by many others.

In the *Ars Poetica* we should note Horace's sharp focus on consistency, unity, and appropriateness as defining formal elements in a work of art. His emphasis also is on the difficult but necessary aesthetic goal of achieving both clarity and vigor in presentation and success in choosing an appropriate subject matter. Horace is both the preserver of tradition and the guarantor of the poet's right to change that tradition in terms of theme and diction. Horace also emphasizes the difficulty, the dignity, and the painfulness of the poet's craft.

For Horace "the foundation and source of literary excellence is wisdom," and he asserts that "the works written about Socrates are able to reveal the true subject matter of poetry." He urges later poets to look to the great Greek poets as models of the highest artistic achievement, and he castigates his contemporaries who will not work hard and sacrifice greatly to reach the highest standards of performance available to poets. Eloquently he denounces the corrosive power of materialism, which corrupts the soul of poetry, and states that when this rank materialism "has stained the human spirit can we really hope that poems will be written worth anointing and protecting with oil of cedar, and preserving in chests of polished cypress?" He shows in his famous line "poets wish to either benefit or delight us" that he considers poetry both illuminating and useful to the human condition. The unique demands and standards of poetry, in contrast to all other human activities, are seen in his comment that the field of law has room for practitioners of varying degrees of ability, but poetry, "if it misses true excellence by only a little, verges toward deepest failure." In line with this is his advice for poets to subject their work first to the harshest criticism available and then not to publish a word they have written "until the ninth year comes around" so that they can be certain that their work will genuinely have lasting value. Horace's commitment to excellence in poetry leads him to aim bitter and harsh criticism at mediocre poets who lack the energy and talent to attain the high standards he sets for poetic achievement.

For Horace, poetry has been an instrument for the dissemination of civilization, which requires the highest respect. The discipline of poetry, he emphasizes over and over again, is of great dignity and requires both significant natural ability and much hard work. Poetry's importance is such that it demands the most intense criticism because it is too important to be subverted by mediocrity. The final scene of the poem that describes the "mad" poet has been variously interpreted, but without doubt it affirms the unique total commitment of the poet to the craft of poetry in a way not matched by any other profession. To Horace we are indebted for an assessment of the poet's role in society as a skilled craftsman, teacher, and civilizing force whose communicated knowledge is of great importance to our culture.

The *Ars Poetica* was an important text during the medieval period although it was not equally well known at all times and places during this time. A large number of manuscripts of the poem from this period have been identified, and there exist many commentaries on it and imitations of it. The *Poetria Nova* of Geoffrey of Vinsauf, which is included in this volume, is one of the most important works written under the influence of the *Ars Poetica* and explicitly indicates its debt to that work. Like the *Ars Poetica*, the *Poetria Nova* aims to provide guidance in recognizing and creating poetic excellence. It does, however, go beyond the rhetorical analysis of poetry offered by Horace to provide a more comprehensive and systematic framework for discussion of stylistic elements in poetry. It attributes, as does the *Ars Poetica*, an elevated status to the poet but interprets that status in a rather different way than Horace. For these reasons and because it contains numerous paraphrases and reminiscences of the *Ars Poetica*, the *Poetria Nova* illustrates the forceful impact of Horace's treatise in the Middle Ages.

The direct influence of the *Ars Poetica* in the Renaissance and the seventeenth century was even greater than in the medieval period. Well over fifty printed editions of the works of Horace appeared in Europe before 1500, and numerous versified "arts of poetry" were written in the seventeenth and eighteenth centuries. One of the most important editions of this period was produced in the early sixteenth century by Iodocus Badius Ascensius for school use in literary analysis. In addition to editions of the Latin text, important translations were made of the *Ars Poetica* into Italian, French, and Spanish in the sixteenth century. After the recovery of Aristotle's *Poetics* attempts were made to fuse the Horatian and Aristotelian traditions into a powerful critical influence. During the Renaissance numerous, quite different, schools of criticism emerged, with each of them claiming Horace as its source. Horace's authority reached an extremely high level of influence in the seventeenth century, when the intellectual currents of scientific rationalism, neoclassicism, the *Poetics* of Aristotle, and the *Ars Poetica* were fused. Boileau's *L'Art poétique* (1674), represented in this collection in the Soames-Dryden translation, was one of the most important and influential results of the powerful Horatian influence during this period. It applied Horatian critical principles to French literature of the time. The Soames translation of this work (1680), revised by Dryden (1682), made use of examples from English literature in place of the French examples used by Boileau. Once again it is clear, as it was in the medieval period, that Horace's *Ars Poetica* was not just a subject of antiquarian research but a living influence and guide for poets and critics from the Renaissance to the eighteenth century.

The eighteenth century opened with another powerful testimony to the influence of Horace: Alexander Pope's *Essay on Criticism* (1711). Pope's focus was not on the rules for writing good poetry, as in the *Ars Poetica*, but, rather, on the standards for good criticism of poetry. This latter topic is, to be sure, an important theme in Horace's poem, but it is not the central theme, as it is in the *Essay on Criticism*. Under Horace's influence, Pope presents his own account of the errors that poets are liable to make, and it is here that we will most fully recognize Horatian influence.

The *Poetria Nova* of Geoffrey of Vinsauf and the edition of the *Ars Poetica* by Badius Ascensius were both textbooks for school use that helped train students to write well by the application of the rules for good writing that Horace presents. Boileau's *L'Art poétique* and Pope's *Essay on Criticism* were not designed as school texts but as guides for mature writers and readers. Increasingly, over time, the *Ars Poetica* moved out of the classroom and into the arena of scholarly debate. Significant scholarly resources were and are still being devoted to establishing the best possible text of the *Ars Poetica*, uncovering the various sources of its doctrines, and interpreting its meaning. Justification for the relevance of the work to artists and readers, however, was left to those poets who responded to its influence with their own adaptations of Horace's poem. Thomas Gray's *The Progress of Poesy* (1757) adapts important Horatian concepts to his own world view; James Beattie in *The Minstrel, or, The Progress of Genius* (1771) responds to the Horatian theme of nature as the source of poetry; and the Horatian discussion of the role of natural talent and artistic training in achieving excellence in poetry finds an important echo in Goethe's *Natur und Kunst*.

In 1809 Byron published *English Bards and Scotch Reviewers* and later a work entitled *Hints from Horace* (1811, not published until 1831), which appear to be the last poems to be written directly in a Horatian manner. In *English Bards and Scotch Reviewers* Byron adapts to his own time and place Horace's sharp criticism of mediocrity in poetry, and he extends that sharp criticism to an even more bitter evaluation of insensitive critics of poetry. *Hints from Horace* is an extremely skillful creative adaptation of the *Ars Poetica* that accurately interprets several of Horace's original insights by finding imaginative parallels in Byron's own literary world.

Although after Byron we find no poems directly imitating the *Ars Poetica*, we do find important works that are influenced by it. Horatian themes are found in Tennyson's *The Palace of Arts* (1832) and also in Paul Verlaine's *Art poétique* (1874), a poem showing the direct influence of Horace's discussion of meter, diction, and poetic purpose. Most important in Verlaine's adaptation is his acceptance of one of the most critical points in Horace's aesthetic theory—the requirement that poetry achieve the highest level of excellence or else fail in its essential purpose.

The final selection in this volume is Wallace Stevens's *Notes Toward a Supreme Fiction*. On the surface the poems of Horace and Stevens are vastly different in structure and tone. Yet at the deepest levels of meaning the *Ars Poetica* shares an important common ground with *Notes Toward a Supreme Fiction*. More than other works represented in this volume they celebrate the profound importance of poetry to human beings and the important contribution of poetry to civilization. In the *Ars Poetica* Horace speaks of the capacity of poetry to benefit and delight us; of the best of poetry that is "worth anointing and protecting with oil of cedar, and preserving in chests of polished cypress"; of poetry's almost impossibly high standards that make every artistic effort a failure that does not achieve "true excellence"; of the great poets of the past who led human beings to high civilization; and of the intense personal demands on the poet illustrated in the scene of the "mad" poet at the end of the poem. Stevens tells us that "the poem refreshes life so that we share, for a moment, the first idea"; that it is the task of the poet to express the inexpressible, to try "by a peculiar speech to speak the peculiar potency of the general, to compound the imagination's Latin with the lingua franca et jocundissima"; that it is the struggle of the poet "to find the real, to be stripped of every fiction except one, the fiction of an absolute"; that the poet, like the soldier, is at war, "a war

between the mind and the sky, between thought and day and night . . .
a war that never ends." Careful readers of the *Ars Poetica* and *Notes
Toward a Supreme Fiction* will note the common bond of intense seriousness and deep commitment to a most demanding discipline, which
is a central theme of both works.

Whoever writes a verse essay on poetry must do so with an eye on the
Ars Poetica, the first great work of this kind. Some of Horace's successors have consciously imitated specific aspects of the *Ars Poetica* while
others write in a spirit of deep artistic kinship with the great Roman
poet and critic. The Horatian influence is ever present in our culture
and can be viewed effectively in the works represented in this volume.

Leon Golden

I

Ars Poetica
by
Horace

Introduction

The *Ars Poetica* (*The Art of Poetry*) by Quintus Horatius Flaccus (65 B.C.–8 B.C.) is the only classical essay on literary criticism that has been known with something like continuity from the date of its composition to the present day. It was read and cited throughout the Middle Ages, although there are centuries without references and the work was better known in some areas of Europe than others. Its status was further enhanced by the revival of classical learning associated with the Renaissance. By the later fifteenth century it was widely considered the definitive guide to classical literary traditions and to the imitation of these traditions by modern authors. Elaborately annotated editions began to appear in Italy almost as soon as printing was introduced. From Italy, interest rapidly spread to France, England, Spain, Germany, and elsewhere.

When Aristotle's *Poetics* was rediscovered around 1535, it did not displace *The Art of Poetry*. In spite of what seem today obvious differences in theory and specific information, the two works were regarded as complementary, and where differences occurred that were impossible to paper over—as for example, the difference between Aristotle's theory of catharsis and Horace's idea that poetry should profit (or instruct) and delight—the problem was usually resolved by bending Aristotle's ideas to fit the more familiar ideas of Horace.

The belief that Horace and Aristotle were complementary allowed Horace to continue to reign supreme in the seventeenth and eighteenth centuries. During the neoclassical period, he was recognized as a prophet of reason, imitation, and "rules" in literary theory, and the form of *The Art of Poetry* was imitated in numerous verse essays on poetry in Latin, Italian, French, Spanish, and English. In the nineteenth century *The Art of Poetry* ceased to be a direct influence on the way poetry was written, but it continued to be quoted for its pithy observations about good and bad poetry and as a guide to understanding classical literature. Today, it remains central in the study of Latin literature and in the history of literary criticism. Although it is not usually consulted for its advice on how to write, it is familiar enough to have provided the model for at least one well-known comment on the state of twentieth-century American poetry, Karl Shapiro's *Essay on Rime*, published in 1945.

In spite of its influence on two thousand years of literary theory and practice, *The Art of Poetry* remains elusive. Readers who come to it for the first time are prepared for a work that sparkles and challenges in every line. Although they find lines that sparkle, they also find a work that seems to wander from subject to subject and that frequently discusses topics remote from modern interests.

The translation and commentary that follow are intended to assist these readers. They are based on three premises. First, much of *The Art of Poetry* is entirely understandable and immensely entertaining and still relevant to the understanding of literary art. Horace is a literary conservative, not an avant-garde artist, but his conservatism is the genial sort from which anyone can learn. Second, much of *The Art of Poetry* becomes clearer with an understanding of the background against which it was written. Its central ideas are variations, shaped by the social and intellectual conditions of Augustan Rome, of ideas about literary art that are still being debated. Third, because of its sustained popularity over the centuries, *The Art of Poetry* is a kind of critical litmus test. Each age has stressed different aspects and found different truths in it. To be familiar with it is to have a key for identifying the central critical ideas of different periods in the history of literature.

Most readers of *The Art of Poetry* will be interested in it primarily as criticism. However, Horace was a poet even more than a critic, and the *Art* is a poem as well as a presentation of critical theory. Although most commentaries struggle to present it as a formal treatise on literary art, and the present one will make its own gestures in that direction, it is actually a dramatic monologue in which the situation of the speaker (the term is preferable to "writer," even though the *Art* is technically a "letter") shapes what the speaker says.[1] Read in this way it becomes

---

[1]. O.B. Hardison's discussion of the character of the narrator in this introduction reflects what critics today would call "persona theory." Bernard Frischer, *Shifting Para-*

less like Aristotle's *Poetics* and more like some of the later works included with it in this volume in which social conditions decisively influence the speaker. In *English Bards and Scotch Reviewers*, for example, the prevailing literary culture encourages destructive attacks on new poets and the speaker lashes out against it. Again, the Second World War raging beyond the poet's study provides the context within which the speaker of Wallace Stevens's *Notes Toward a Supreme Fiction* fights his own war "between the mind and the sky."

These observations do not require an "either/or" understanding of the *Art*. The work does not have to be understood "either" as a treatise on poetry "or" as a dramatic monologue. It has elements of both. Literary theory supplies much of its content, but the character of the speaker determines the tone of the comments, the order in which they are made, and the lapses and omissions and contradictions and abrupt transitions; or, to put the matter in terms more appropriate to criticism, abrupt transitions and lapses and omissions and the like are the means whereby the poem represents the character of the speaker.

Finally, it may be noted that this way of presenting critical theory makes a modern and quite significant literary point. It is a commonplace today that each age reads its own predilections and taboos into the past. Thus the past is in part, at least, a mirror of the present rather than an otherness in which we find ideas different from the ones we hold. If this is so, no critical position can be called "objective," much less "true" in an absolute sense. Each position is relative to the circumstances that gave rise to it. A "treatise" falsifies this situation by pretending to be "objective analysis." This is precisely what the *Art* does not claim to be. Its use of the dramatic monologue enacts the truth that no critic is (or can be) objective. All critical theories—in fact, all theories—are shaped by the political and social and personal contexts within which they are developed. As the contexts change, they change.

---

digms: New Approaches to Horace's Ars Poetica (Atlanta: Scholars Press, 1991), makes an explicit application of "persona theory" to the interpretation of the *Ars Poetica* but with results that are quite different from those of Hardison. For Frischer the narrator in the poem does not give voice to Horace's own views but is, rather, the subject of a parody by the poet. For Hardison the narrator, while different from Horace, does represent, in a dramatic manner, a position more closely in harmony with Horace's own views.

Wallace Stevens agreed. He titled the second part of his *Notes Toward a Supreme Fiction* "It must change."

The interplay between critical theory and the voice of the speaker in the *Art* thus suggests skepticism about the possibility of absolute critical "truths." The suggestion is appropriate. Horace's general philosophy combines elements of Epicureanism and Stoicism, and the philosophy of Epicurus as presented in Lucretius's poem *De rerum natura*, which Horace knew well, questions many of the basic tenets of ancient religion. A more formal skepticism that questions the basis of knowledge itself was also current in Rome in the first century B.C. Shortly before Horace began writing, Cicero offered an exposition of the academic skepticism of Carneades in the first book of his *Academic Disputations*. Carneades argues that human knowledge is probable rather than certain. He is said to have delivered two brilliant orations during a visit to Rome in 156 B.C. In the first he praised justice as the source of order in human affairs. In the second he praised injustice as the only practical way of forcing order on irrational humans.

Arguments pro and con are one way to express a philosophy of doubt. They are also inherent in the dialogue form of works like Cicero's *Academic Disputations* because the form permits questions under discussion to remain unresolved. The speaker of *The Art of Poetry* frequently engages in pro and con debate with himself, but the most striking embodiment of the idea of doubt in the poem is the contrast between purportedly objective doctrine being presented and the emotion of the speaker presenting it. The effect is wonderfully effective and very much in accord with the dramatic monologue form.

Skepticism was reborn in Europe in the sixteenth century with Montaigne's *Essays* and was a powerful influence on seventeenth- and eighteenth-century thought. However, the popularity of *The Art of Poetry* during the Enlightenment rested on the idea that it stands for the norms of reason and nature and offers certainties in the form of "rules" rather than on its skepticism. Not until the romantic period do we find an imitation of Horace's *Art* in which the speaker is a distinct personality rather than an impersonal voice for official doctrine, and not until Wallace Stevens's *Notes Toward a Supreme Fiction* do we encounter a poet who is fully attuned to Horace by skeptical temperament as well as by an approach to criticism simultaneously playful, personal, and philosophical.

O. B. Hardison, Jr.

Ars Poetica

Translated by Leon Golden

1–13

If a painter were willing to join a horse's neck to a human head and spread on multicolored feathers, with different parts of the body brought in from anywhere and everywhere, so that what starts out above as a beautiful woman ends up horribly as a black fish, could you my friends, if you had been admitted to the spectacle, hold back your laughter? Believe me, dear Pisos, that very similar to such a painting would be a literary work in which meaningless images are fashioned, like the dreams of someone who is mentally ill, so that neither the foot nor the head can be attributed to a single form. "Painters and poets," someone objects, "have always had an equal right to dare to do whatever they wanted." We know it and we both seek this indulgence and grant it in turn. *But not to the degree that the savage mate with the gentle, nor that snakes be paired with birds, nor lambs with tigers.*[1]

14–23

Often, one or two purple patches are stitched onto works that have begun in high seriousness, and that profess important themes, so that they sparkle far and wide; as when the grove and altar of Diana and the circling of swiftly flowing waters through the pleasant fields or the Rhine river or the rainbow are described. *But this was not the place for such embellishments.* And perhaps you know how to draw a cypress tree. What does that matter if you have been paid to paint a desperate sailor swimming away from a shipwreck? You started out to make a wine-jar. Why, as the wheel turns, does it end up as a pitcher? In short, let the work be anything you like, but let it at least be one, single thing.

24-31

Most of us poets, o father and sons who are worthy of that father, deceive ourselves by an illusion of correct procedure. I work at achieving brevity; instead I become obscure. Striving for smoothness, vigor and spirit escape me. One poet, promising the sublime, delivers pomposity. Another creeps along the ground, overly cautious and too much frightened of the gale. Whoever wishes to vary a single subject in some strange and wonderful way, paints a dolphin into a forest and a boar onto the high seas. The avoidance of blame leads to error if there is an absence of art.

32-37

Near the gladiatorial school of Aemilius, a most incompetent craftsman will mold toenails and imitate soft hair in bronze but he is unsuccessful with his complete work because he does not know how to represent a whole figure. If I wished to compose something, I would no more wish to be him than to live with a crooked nose although highly regarded for my black eyes and black hair.

38-45

Pick a subject, writers, equal to your strength and take some time to consider what your shoulders should refuse and what they can bear. Neither eloquence nor clear organization will forsake one who has chosen a subject within his capabilities. Unless I am mistaken this will be the special excellence and delight of good organization—that the author of the promised poem, enamored of one subject and scornful of another, says now what ought to be said *now* and both postpones and omits a great deal for the present.

46-59

Also in linking words you will speak with exceptional subtlety and care if a skillful connection renders a well-known term with a new twist. If, by chance, it is necessary to explain obscure matters by means of new images it will turn out that you must devise words never heard by the kilted Cethegi, and license for this will be given if claimed with modesty.

Words that are new and recently coined will be received in good faith if they are sparingly diverted from a Greek source. Why then will the Roman grant to Caecilius and Plautus what is denied to Vergil and Varius? If I am capable of doing it, why am I grudged the acquisition of some few words when the tongue of Cato and Ennius enriched our ancestral language and revealed new names for things? It has always been permitted, and it always will be permitted to bring to light a name stamped with the mark of the present day.[2]

60–72

Just as forests change their leaves year by year and the first drop to the ground, so the old generation of words perishes, and new ones, like the rising tide of the young, flourish and grow strong. We, and everything that is ours, are destined to die; whether Neptune, hospitably received on land, keeps our fleets safe from the north winds, a task worthy of a king, or a marsh, barren for a long time, and suitable for oars, nourishes nearby cities and feels the heavy plough, or a river has changed its course that was hostile to crops and has discovered a better route to follow, all things mortal will perish; much less will the glory and grace of language remain alive. Many terms will be born again that by now have sunk into oblivion, and many that are now held in respect will die out if that is what *use* should dictate in whose power is the judgment and the law and the rule of speech.

73–88

Homer has demonstrated in what meter we should describe the deeds of kings and leaders as well as gloomy wars. Lament, first, was enclosed in unequally paired verses and later also our grateful thoughts for answered prayer. Scholars disagree about who originally published these brief elegiac verses, and it still is before the court as a matter of dispute. Fury armed Archilochus with his own iambus: both the comic sock and the grand tragic boot took possession of this foot, suited as it was for alternating dialogue and able to conquer the raucous shouts of the audience as well as naturally suited to action. The muse granted the lyre the task of reporting about the gods, the children of the gods, the victorious boxer, and the horse who was first in the race, as well as to record youthful anguish and wine's liberating influence. Why am I greeted as a poet if I have neither the ability nor the knowledge to preserve the variations and shades of the literary works that I have described? Why, perversely modest, do I prefer to be ignorant than to learn?

89-98

The subject matter of comedy does not wish to find expression in tragic verses. In the same way the feast of Thyestes is indignant at being represented through informal verses that are very nearly worthy of the comic sock. Let each genre keep to the appropriate place allotted to it. Sometimes, however, even comedy raises its voice and an angered Chremes declaims furiously in swollen utterances; and often the tragic figures of Telephus and Peleus grieve in pedestrian language when, as a pauper or exile, each of them, if he should care to touch the heart of the spectator with his complaint, abandons bombast and a sesquipedalian vocabulary.

99-113

It is not enough for poems to be "beautiful"; they must also yield delight and guide the listener's spirit wherever they wish. As human faces laugh with those who are laughing, so they weep[3] with those who are weeping. If you wish me to cry, you must first feel grief yourself, then your misfortunes, O Telephus or Peleus, will injure me. If you speak ineptly assigned words, I shall either sleep or laugh. Sad words are fitting for the gloomy face, words full of threats for the angry one, playful words for the amused face, serious words for the stern one. For Nature first forms us within so as to respond to every kind of fortune. She delights us or impels us to anger or knocks us to the ground and torments us with oppressive grief. Afterward she expresses the emotions of the spirit with language as their interpreter. If, however, there is discord between the words spoken and the fortune of the speaker, Romans, whether cavalry or infantry, will raise their voices in a raucous belly laugh.[4]

114-18

It will make a great difference whether a god is speaking or a hero, a mature old man or someone passionate and still in the full flower of youth, a powerful matron or a diligent nurse, an itinerant merchant or the cultivator of a prosperous field, a Colchian or an Assyrian, one raised in Thebes or in Argos.

119–52

Either follow tradition or devise harmonious actions. O writer, if you by chance describe once again honored Achilles, let him be weariless, quick to anger, stubborn, violent; let him deny that laws were made for him, let him claim everything by arms. Let Medea be wild and unconquerable, Ino doleful, Ixion treacherous, Io a wanderer in mind and body,[5] Orestes filled with sorrow. If you commit anything untested to the stage and you dare to fashion a novel character, let it be maintained to the end just as it emerged at the beginning and let it be consistent with itself. It is difficult to speak uniquely of common themes; and yet you will more properly spin the song of Troy into acts than if you are the first to bring to light what has not been known or recorded in literature. Material in the public domain will come under private jurisdiction if you do not loiter around the broad, common poetic cycle,[6] and do not strive, as a literal translator, to render texts word for word, and if you will not, as an imitator, leap down into a narrow space from where shame or the rules applying to the work forbid you to extricate your foot; nor should you begin your work as the cyclic poet once did: "Of Priam's fate and renowned war I shall sing." What might someone who makes this pledge bring forth that will be worthy of his big mouth? Mountains will go into labor, but an absurd mouse will be born. How much more skillful is the one who does not toil foolishly: "Tell me, O Muse, of the man, who, after the capture of Troy, viewed the customs and cities of many different peoples." He does not aim to extract smoke from the flaming light but rather light from the smoke, so that he might then describe spectacular marvels—Antiphates and the Scylla and Charybdis along with the Cyclops. Nor does he begin the return of Diomedes from the death of Meleager nor the Trojan War from the twin eggs. He always moves swiftly to the issue at hand and rushes his listener into the middle of the action just as if it were already known, and he abandons those subjects he does not think can glitter after he has treated them. Thus does he invent, thus does he mingle the false with the true that the middle is not inconsistent with the beginning, nor the end with the middle.

153-78

Listen to what I and the general public along with me desire, if indeed
you wish applauding listeners to wait for the final curtain and to remain seated until the singer says "Give us a hand now"; you must note
the characteristics of each stage of life and you must grant what is appropriate to changing natures and ages. A child who just now has learned
to repeat words and to stamp the ground with a firm footstep takes
great pleasure in playing with other children and heedlessly conceives[7]
and abandons anger as well as changes moods hour by hour. The beard-
less youth, with his guardian finally removed, rejoices in horses and
dogs and in the grass of the sunny Campus; supple as wax to be fashioned into vice, he is rude to those who give him advice, slow at providing for what is useful, extravagant with money, filled with lofty ideas
and passionate, but also swift to abandon the objects of his affection.
When one has reached manhood in age and spirit, the objects of his en-
thusiasm are altered, and he seeks wealth and connections, becomes a
slave to the trappings of honor, is hesitant to have set into motion what
he will soon struggle to change. Many troubles assail an old man,
whether because he seeks gain, and then wretchedly abstains from what
he possesses and is afraid to use it, or because he attends to all his
affairs feebly and timidly; a procrastinator, he is apathetic in his hopes
and expectations, sluggish and fearful of the future, obstinate, always
complaining; he devotes himself to praising times past, when he was a
boy, and to being the castigator and moral censor of the young. The
years, as they approach, bring many advantages with them; as they re-
cede, they take many away. To ensure that, by chance, roles appropriate
for old men are not assigned to the young and those designed for mature men are not given to children, you shall always spend time on the
traits that belong and are suitable to the age of a character.[8]

179-88

Either a scene is acted out on the stage or someone reports the events
that have occurred. Actions that have been admitted to our consciousness through our having heard them have less of an impact on our
minds than those that have been brought to our attention by our trusty
vision and for which the spectator himself is an eyewitness. You will
not, however, produce onstage actions that ought to be done offstage;

and you will remove many incidents from our eyes so that someone who was present might report those incidents; Medea should not slaughter her children in the presence of the people, nor abominable Atreus cook human organs publicly, nor Procne be turned into a bird, Cadmus into a snake. Whatever you show me like this, I detest and refuse to believe.

189-201

A play should not be shorter or longer than five acts if, once it has been seen, it wishes to remain in demand and be brought back for return engagements. Nor should any god intervene unless a knot show up that is worthy of such a liberator; nor should a fourth actor strive to speak.

Let the chorus sustain the role of an actor and the function of a man, and let it not sing anything between the acts that does not purposefully and aptly serve and unite with the action. It should favor the good and provide friendly counsel; it should control the wrathful and show its approval of those who fear to sin; it should praise modest meals, wholesome justice and laws, and peace with its open gates; it should conceal secrets and entreat and beg the gods that fortune return to the downtrodden and depart from the arrogant.

202-19

The double pipe not, as now, bound with brass and a rival of the trumpet, but thin and simple, with few holes, was sufficient to assist and support the chorus and to fill still uncrowded benches with its breath; where, indeed, the populace, easy to count since it was small in number, honest, pious, and modest came together. After a conquering nation began to extend its lands and a more extensive wall began to embrace the city,[9] we started to appease our guardian spirit[10] freely with daylight drinking on holidays, and then greater license arrived on the scene for rhythms and tunes. For what level of taste might an uneducated audience have, freed of toil and composed of a mixture of rustic and urban elements, of low life and aristocrats? Thus the flute player added bodily movement and excessive extravagance to the venerable art of past times and trailed a robe behind him as he wandered around the stage. So also the tonal range of the austere lyre increased, and a reckless fluency brought with it a strange eloquence whose thought, wise in matters of practical wisdom and prophetic of the future, was not out of tune with that of oracular Delphi.

220–50

The poet who contended in tragic song for the sake of an insignificant goat soon also stripped wild Satyrs of their clothes and in a rough manner, with his dignity unharmed, attempted jokes because it was only by enticements and pleasing novelty that the spectator, having performed the sacred rites and having become drunk and reckless, was going to remain in the audience. But it is appropriate to render the Satyrs agreeable in their laughter and mockery and to exchange the serious for the comic so that no god, no hero is brought on who, having just been seen in regal gold and purple, then moves into the humble hovel of low-class diction; or, while avoiding the lowly earth, reaches for empty clouds. Tragedy, indignant at spouting frivolous verses, like the matron who is asked to dance on a holiday, appears with some shame, among the impudent Satyrs. I shall not, O Pisos, were I a writer of Satyric drama, be fond only of unadorned and commonly used nouns and verbs; nor shall I strive so much to differ from the tone of tragedy that it makes no difference if Davus is speaking with audacious Pythias who, having swindled Simo, now has gained for herself a talent's worth of silver, or the speaker is Silenus, guardian and servant of his divine foster-child.[11] I shall aim at fashioning a poem from quite familiar elements so that anyone might anticipate doing as well, might sweat profusely at it, and yet labor in vain after having ventured to do what I have done: so great is the power of arrangement and linkage, so great is the grace that is added to words that are adapted from ordinary language. When Fauns of the forest are brought onstage, in my judgment, they should avoid behaving as if they had been born at the crossroads and were almost denizens of the forum or act ever as adolescents with their all-too-wanton[12] verses or rattle off their dirty and disgraceful jokes. That sort of thing gives offense to an audience of knights, respectable heads of households, and men with substantial fortunes, nor do they accept with a patient spirit, or bestow a crown on, whatever the consumer of roasted chick-peas and nuts approves.

251–62

A long syllable adjacent to a short one is called an Iambus, a "quick"
foot; for that reason Iambus commanded that the name trimeter be attached to the lines bearing his name although he delivers six beats a line
and from first to last is the spitting image of himself. Not so long ago,
in order that the trimeter reach the ears with somewhat greater dignity
and deliberation, Iambus admitted the stately spondee into his ancestral
rights, obligingly and tolerantly, but not so sociably as to withdraw
from the second and fourth foot of the line. This Iambus appears rarely
in the "noble" trimeters of Accius and, as for the verses of Ennius,
hurled onto the stage in their ponderous sluggishness, he pursues them
with the shameful charge of excessively hasty and slipshod workmanship or of sheer ignorance of the poet's craft.

263–74

It is not just any critic who will notice rhythmically flawed lines, and
indulgence, far more than is merited, has been granted to our Roman
poets. Because of that should I ramble around and write without any
discipline at all? Or should I consider that everyone is going to see my
faults and, warily playing it safe, remain within the hope of pardon? I
have then, in short, avoided blame, but I have not earned praise. Your
mandate is to hold Greek models before you by day and to hold them
before you by night. But (you say) your ancestors praised the meters and
wit of Plautus; well (I reply), they admired both with excessive tolerance, not to say stupidity—if you and I just know how to distinguish a
tasteless expression from an elegant one, and we have the skill to recognize the proper sound with our ears and fingers.

275–84

We are told that Thespis discovered the tragic muse's genre, which was
unknown until then, and hauled his verse dramas around in wagons;
these dramas, actors, their faces thoroughly smeared with wine-lees,
sang and performed. After him Aeschylus, the inventor of the mask and
the elegant robe, laid down a stage on modestly sized beams and taught
the art of grandiloquent speech and of treading the boards in the high

boot of the tragic actor. Old comedy followed in the footsteps of these tragic poets and not without much praise; but the license it assumed for itself descended into vice, and its force was justifiably tamed by law; the law was received with approval, and the chorus in disgrace became silent since its right to cause harm was abolished.

285-94

Our own poets have left nothing untried nor have they earned the least glory when they have dared to abandon the tracks of the Greeks and to celebrate domestic situations either by producing serious Roman dramas or native Roman comedies. Nor would Latium be more powerful in courage and in illustrious arms than in literature if the time-consuming effort required for a truly polished revision of the text did not give offense to every single one of our poets. O you, who are descendants of Pompilius, denounce any poem that many a day and many a correction has not carefully pruned and then improved ten times over to meet the test of the well-trimmed nail.[13]

295-308

Because Democritus believes that native talent is a more blessed thing than poor, miserable craftsmanship and excludes from Helicon, the home of the muses, rational poets, quite a number do not trouble to cut their nails or shave their beards; they seek out lonely spots; they avoid the baths. One will obtain the reward and the name of a poet if he never entrusts his head, incurable even by three times Anticyra's output of hellebore,[14] to the barber, Licinus. O what an unlucky fool I am! I have my bile purged just before spring arrives! No one else could write a better poem. But nothing is worth that effort! Instead, I shall serve in place of a whetstone that has the power to render iron sharp but itself lacks the ability to cut; while not writing anything myself, I will teach what nurtures and forms the poet, from what source his power springs, what his function and duty are, what is proper and what is not and in what direction poetic excellence leads and in what direction failure beckons.[15]

309-22

The foundation and source of literary excellence is wisdom. The works written about Socrates are able to reveal the true subject matter of poetry and, once the subject matter has been provided, words will freely follow. He who has learned what he owes to his country, what he owes to his friends, by what kind of love a parent, a brother, or a guest should be honored, what is the duty of a senator, what is the function of a judge, what is the role of a general sent into war—he, assuredly, knows how to represent what is appropriate for each character. I bid the artist, trained in representation, to reflect on exemplars of life and character and to bring us living voices from that source. Sometimes a tale that lacks stylistic elegance, grandeur, and skill but is adorned with impressive passages and characters who are accurately drawn is a greater source of pleasure and better holds the interest of an audience than verses that lack a vision of reality and are mere trifles to charm the ear.

323–32

To the Greeks, covetous of nothing except glory, the Muse granted inspired talent, to the Greeks she gave eloquence in full measure. Roman youths, on the other hand, learn by means of lengthy calculations how to divide a sum of money into a hundred parts. "You, there, Albinus's son, solve the following problem: If one-twelfth is subtracted from five-twelfths, how much is left? Come on, you should have given me the answer by now!" "It's one-third!" "Well done, my boy, you'll surely be able to protect your investments." "Now suppose that one-twelfth is added to five-twelfths, what does that make?" "I've got it—one-half!" When once this corruption and avid concern for material wealth has stained the human spirit, can we really hope that poems will be written worth anointing and protecting with oil of cedar, and preserving in chests of polished cypress?

333–46

Poets wish to either benefit or delight us, or, at one and the same time, to speak words that are both pleasing and useful for our lives. Whatever lessons you teach, let them be brief, so that receptive spirits will quickly perceive and faithfully retain what you have said. Everything superfluous seeps out of the well-stocked mind. In order to create pleasure, poetic fictions should approximate reality so that a play should not claim, on its own behalf, that anything it wishes must be believed nor should it extract a living child from the stomach of the ogress, Lamia, after she has dined. The centuries of elders drive away whatever is without serious value; the high and mighty Ramnes keep their distance from gloomy poems. He gets every vote who combines the useful with the pleasant, and who, at the same time he pleases the reader, also instructs him. That book will earn money for the Sosii, this one will cross the sea and extend immeasurably the life of a famous writer.[16]

347–60

There are, however, mistakes that we are willing to forgive. For the string does not always return the sound that the hand and mind desire, and although you seek a low note, it very often sends back a high one. Nor will the bow always strike whatever it threatens. But where many qualities sparkle in a poem, I will not find fault with a few blemishes, which either carelessness introduced or human nature, too little vigilant, did not avoid. What then? Just as the scribe who copies books, if he always makes the same mistake no matter how much he is warned, has no claim on our indulgence, and a lyre-player is mocked who always strikes the same false note, so the poet who is frequently found wanting turns into another Choerilus[17] who, amidst my scorn for his work, astonishes me the two or three times he is really good; I am also offended when great Homer falls asleep on us, but it is permitted for some drowsiness to creep into a long work.

361–65

Poetry resembles painting. Some works will captivate you when you stand very close to them and others if you are at a greater distance. This one prefers a darker vantage point, that one wants to be seen in the light since it feels no terror before the penetrating judgment of the critic. This pleases only once, that will give pleasure even if we go back to it ten times over.

366–78

And you, the older brother, although you have been molded by your father's voice to know what is correct and you are wise in your own right, take and hold in your memory this warning: only in certain activities are we justified in tolerating mediocrity and what is just passable.

A run-of-the mill expert in the law or pleader of cases is a long way from the skill of the eloquent Messala and doesn't know as much as Aulus Cascellius, but nevertheless he has a value.[18] But neither men nor gods nor booksellers have ever put their stamp of approval on mediocre poets. Just as at a gracious meal a discordant musical performance or a thick perfume or Sardinian honey on your poppy seeds give offense because the meal could have been put together without them; in the same way a poem that comes into existence and is created for the gratification of our mind and heart, if it misses true excellence by only a little, verges toward deepest failure.

379–84

The person who does not know how to play forgoes the athletic equipment in the Campus Martius, and someone who does not know anything about the ball, the discus, or the hoop stays away from the action in order to prevent the packed crowd of spectators from raising their voices in unrestrained laughter: But the person who has no idea how to create poetry still has the audacity to try. Why not? He is a free citizen, and was born that way, and especially because he is both rich (his property assessment places him in the equestrian class) and he has never been convicted of a crime.

385–90

Never will you say or do anything if Minerva, the goddess of wisdom, forbids it; you have good judgment, you have good sense. But if you shall, one day, write something let it first penetrate the ears of a critic like Maecius[19] or your father or myself; and then keep a lid on it until the ninth year comes around by storing your pages inside your house. You will always be able to destroy anything you haven't published; a word, once released, does not know how to return.

391–407

When men still roamed the forests, Orpheus, the priest and prophet of the gods, deterred them from slaughter and from an abominable way of life. On account of this he is said to have tamed savage tigers and lions. Amphion, the founder of the city of Thebes, also is said to have moved

stones wherever he wished by the sound of his lyre and his seductive en-
treaties. Once it was deemed wisdom to keep what was public separate
from what was private, what was sacred from what was not, to issue
prohibitions against promiscuity, to set down laws for those who are
married, to build towns, to inscribe laws on wooden tablets. In this
way honor and renown came to poets, inspired by the gods, and their
songs. After these, Homer achieved fame and Tyrtaeus, with his poems,
sharpened men's minds for the wars of Mars; oracles were given in
poetry, and the way of life was demonstrated, and the grace of kings
was tested by Pierian songs;[20] and entertainment was discovered, that
entertainment which brought to a close periods of extended labor. I say
this[21] so that you will not in any way feel shame for the skilled muse of
the lyre and the divine singer of songs, Apollo.

408–418

Is it nature or art, the question is put, that makes a poem praiseworthy:
I do not see what study, without a rich vein of natural ability, or raw
talent alone, would be able to accomplish. Each asks for assistance
from the other and swears a mutual oath of friendship. He who is eager
to reach the desired goal at the race-course has endured much and accomplished much as a boy. He has sweated and he has frozen; he has
abstained from sex and wine. The flute-player who plays the Pythian
piece[22] first learned his skill under a master he feared. Now it is enough
to say: "I fashion wonderful poems; may the mangy itch take the hindmost; it's a disgrace for me to be left behind and to admit that what I
did not learn, I simply do not know."

419–37

Just like the herald at an auction who collects a crowd in order to sell
his merchandise, the poet who is rich in lands, rich in money lent out
for interest, bids flatterers with an eye on profit to assemble. If in fact
he is someone who can properly serve up a lavish banquet and go bail
for a fickle, poverty-stricken client and can extricate someone from dis-
tressing lawsuits, I will be surprised if the blessed fellow can tell a liar
from a true friend. You, then, if you have given, or plan to give, a gift
to someone, must refuse to invite him, full of joyful gratitude, to a
reading of poems you have written. For he will shout, "Beautiful!"

"Great!" "Right on!" He will turn pale over them, he will even let dew drip from his friendly eyes, he will dance and pound the pavement with his foot. Just as hired mourners at a funeral almost say and do more than those who grieve from the heart, so a mocking critic will more easily be aroused than a *true* admirer. Kings are said to ply with many a cup and test with wine the person they strive to examine with regard to his worthiness of their friendship. If you plan to write poetry, the thoughts concealed within the fox should never deceive you.

438–52

If you ever read something to Quintilius,[23] he used to say, "Please correct this point and that." If you said that you could not improve them after two or three vain attempts, he would advise you to blot them out and to return the badly formed verses to the anvil. If you chose to defend your error rather than change it, he would expend not a word more nor waste any useless effort to stop you, alone, from loving your work and yourself without a rival. An honest and judicious man will be critical of dull verses and disapproving of harsh ones; next to those completely lacking in art he will smear a black line with a horizontal stroke of the pen;[24] he will excise pretentious decoration; he will compel you to shed light on what lacks clarity; he will expose the obscure phrase; he will note what must be changed and will turn out to be a veritable Aristarchus. He will not say, "Why should I displease a friend because of trivialities?" These "trivialities" will lead that friend into serious trouble once he has been greeted with unfavorable reviews and mocking laughter.

453–76

As when the evil itch or the disease of kings or the frenzied madness and wrath of Diana oppress someone, so sensible people are afraid to touch the mad poet, and run away from him. Inconsiderate children pursue and torment him. He, his head in the clouds, belches out his poems and loses his way; if, like a fowler whose attention is riveted on the blackbirds, he falls into a well or pit, no one will care to raise him up no matter how long he shouts, "Hey, fellow-citizens, look over here!" But if anyone takes the trouble to come to his aid and to lower a rope to him, I will say, "how do you know that he didn't throw himself

down there on purpose and doesn't want to be saved?" Then, I'll tell
the story of how the Sicilian poet perished. When Empedocles felt the
desire to be considered an immortal god, cool as a cucumber he leaped
into the burning fires of Aetna. Let the right be given, let permission be
granted for poets to die. Whoever saves someone against his will does
exactly the same thing as the person who murders him. Not just once
has he done this, and if he is extricated now he will not become a mere
mortal and put aside his infatuation with a death that will make him
famous. Nor is it sufficiently clear why he practices the poet's trade.
Did he sacrilegiously urinate on the ashes of his ancestors or disturb a
gloomy plot of consecrated land that had been struck by lightning?
Whatever the cause he is certainly mad and just like a bear—if he has
succeeded in smashing the restraining bars of his cage—his morose public recitations frighten off the educated and the ignorant alike; once he
gets his hands on a person, he doesn't let go until he kills him with his
reading—a leech who will not release the skin unless gorged with blood.

Life and Work of Horace

Horace was born in 65 B.C. in the provincial town of Venusia, about three-fourths of the way down the Italian peninsula and about halfway between the western and eastern seacoasts. Horace's father was apparently a freed slave who became a tax collector and acquired a small estate. He was prosperous enough to send his son to school in Rome. Around 46 B.C., after completing his Roman education, Horace traveled to Athens to study philosophy and literature.

Two years later the civil war between Brutus and Mark Anthony erupted. Horace was recruited into the army of Brutus. The fact that he was made a military tribune—an important office—in spite of his modest social station and lack of military experience suggests both Brutus's dire need for educated military administrators and the probability that Horace had already made some influential friends. Horace's military career came to a swift and inglorious end with the defeat of Brutus at Phillipi in 42 B.C. He admits freely that he was among those who fled the battlefield rather than courting death in defeat. By the following year he was back in Rome. His father had died, and his estate had been confiscated in reprisal for his support of Brutus.

Horace's immediate difficulties were solved by a job in Rome as a records clerk and scribe. He began writing poetry. To judge from his earliest poems, he saw a good deal of the dark underside of Roman society. He also met and became friends with Vergil, later the author of the *Aeneid*, and Varius, a prominent epic poet and tragedian whose works have been lost. In 39 B.C. he met Vergil's patron Maecenas, a wealthy and powerful adviser of Octavian. It was the beginning of a relationship that lasted throughout his life. Around 33 B.C. Maecenas gave Horace a small farm about twenty-five miles northeast of Rome. This "Sabine farm" became a favorite retreat, and Horace repeatedly celebrated it and the simple rural life it represented.

Horace's first publication was Book I of his *Satires* in 35 B.C. Book II followed in 30 B.C. and the *Epodes* in 29 B.C. All these works are characterized by racy diction, bohemian delight in wine and love affairs (both homosexual and heterosexual), and frequent glimpses of the unsavory aspects of life in the bustling, cynical, and corrupt city of Rome. The *Satires*, however, show that Horace gradually changed. The tone of the later satires is less sensational and more genial, and the suggestions of frequent dissipation give way to an interest in the pleasures of the simple life (II.2), the delights of the country in contrast to those of the city (II.6, which includes the fable of the town mouse and the country mouse), and the Stoic idea that only the philosopher is truly free (II.7).

Six years after the *Epodes*, in 23 B.C., Horace published three books of *Odes*. These lyric poems are among the loveliest and most finished lyrics in the Latin language. They treat various subjects, including love, the fondness of poets for wine, the virtuous life, the brevity of life, the ever-present shadow of death, and the greatness of Augustus and the new Roman state. Running through them is a haunting sense of the brevity of life. We must grasp the pleasures of life now because they will soon be gone. Poetry not only laments the swift passage of time but also celebrates those moments when life seems most real and most beautiful.

By 23 B.C. Horace had become friends with Octavian, now Augustus Caesar. Octavian was the great nephew and heir of Julius Caesar and the final winner in the wars that began with Caesar's assassination in 44 B.C. Although he carefully preserved the fiction of the importance of the Roman Senate, he had, in fact, become Rome's first emperor and had thus established the form of government that would continue until the fall of Rome. His assumption of the title "Augustus" ("Most High") and his tacit encouragement of the cult of emperor-worship were steps on the road to the imperial system.

The arts were enlisted in his program. Vergil's *Aeneid* contributed by popularizing the myth that the Julian clan (*gens Julia*), to which Augustus was related, descended from Aeneas, who came to Italy after escaping the massacre that followed the fall of Troy. Horace also celebrated the new order in lyrics (e.g., *Odes*, I.2, III.14), and, at the request of Augustus, in an official poem (*Carmen saeculare*) celebrating the "Secular Games" of 17 B.C. By dedicating a long verse epistle (II.1) on poetry to Augustus he publicized the emperor's literary interests. In other words, in spite of his protestations of love for the simple life and rural independence, Horace was a court poet dependent on the patronage of Maecenas and Augustus.

He seems to have managed his duties well, although readers have remarked on the fact that his official poems, and especially the *Carmen saeculare*, are sometimes all-too-obviously official. They suggest that even though Horace supported the new order of Augustus, he had deep reservations about it.

In 20 B.C. Horace turned from satires pure and simple to longer, more thoughtful poems that he called "epistles" or "letters." The second book of *Epistles*, which appeared in 14 B.C., is especially interesting for its extended treatment of the achievement of the "modern" Roman poets in contrast to the "ancients" and its summary of the history of drama (II.1). Horace also announces (II.2) that he has given up poetry for philosophy. The announcement was premature. A fourth book of *Odes* appeared in 13 B.C. This book concludes with a poem praising Augustus as the bringer of virtue and peace.

The date of *The Art of Poetry* is uncertain. It has sometimes been considered Horace's last poem, left incomplete, perhaps, at the time of his death in 8 B.C., or, at any rate, his poetic last will and testament to future generations. If so, the Pisos for whom it is written must be the family of the Lucius Piso who was consul in 15 B.C. and returned to Rome from a military campaign around 10 B.C. This is the identification made by Porphyrion, one of the earliest annotators of Horace's poetry. Many scholars, however, have preferred the Piso who was consul in 23 B.C. Current opinion is divided. C. O. Brink (*Prolegomena* [1963], 239–43) reviews several efforts to date the *Art* and concludes that none is clearly superior to the others. G. M. A. Grube (*The Greek and Roman Critics* [1965], 231) leans toward around 20 B.C. Niall Rudd (*Epistles Book II and Epistle to the Pisones* [1989], 19–20) argues for around 10 B.C. Fortunately, the date is unimportant for those interested in the *Art* primarily in relation to criticism.

The genre of the *Art* is also sometimes questioned, although here there is more agreement. It is in the same general form as the *Epistles* and is thus, like them, a modified form of Horatian satire. The fact that its treatment of literature is related to the treatment of literary themes in the first epistle of Book II supports the idea that its Horatian title was *Epistle to the Pisos*. Whatever else it does, the *Art* continues to use the device that Horace had developed in his *Satires*—the satiric persona.

Titles: Ars, satura, epistula

The usual title for the work is *Ars Poetica*. The term *ars* (Greek *techne*) means something like "handbook" or "statement of the principles of." Many ancient works titled *ars* are textbooks, as, for example, the *Ars Grammatica* of Donatus. Ovid's *Ars Amatoria* uses the term ironically. It is an "art of love"—that is, a "handbook of seduction." Other works that can be considered "arts" are philosophical and sophisticated. Although Aristotle's *Poetics* is not formally titled *ars*, it is most appropriately considered a philosophical treatise—that is, an *ars* or *techne*—on the principles of literary art.

The title *Ars Poetica* appears for the first time in the *Institute of Oratory* of the Roman rhetorician Quintilian ("Preface," 2; and VIII.3.60) about a century after Horace's death. It has encouraged readers to look for the logical organization, systematic coverage of the major topics, and combination of traditional theories with creative innovations that one would expect from a treatise on poetry written by a great poet. This understanding of the *Art* is implicit in the standard medieval title for the work—*Poetria*, meaning, roughly, "poetry manual." Between the sixteenth century and the end of the eighteenth century, the understanding of the work as a treatise hardened further. Readers tended to interpret it as a set of rules governing all aspects of poetry. This understanding is reflected in the formal and logical organization of the poems from the period that imitate it.

Roman tradition traces the term *satire* to *satura*—originally, a dish of mixed ingredients and later, a loosely organized work in poetry, prose, or a mixture of the two (Menippean satire) having a satiric, ironic, or didactic intent. Horace's model was the Roman poet Lucilius (180–103 B.C.), who is supposed to have written thirty books of satires. Judging from the fragments that have survived, they were roughly finished, lively, and colloquial. Many of them are recognizably satiric in the sense of being denunciations of human vice and folly; others, however, do not seem particularly satiric in this sense. They are chatty, descriptive, quasi-dramatic vignettes of everyday life. Horace borrowed the dactylic hexameter meter and an easygoing form from Lucilius. Surviving fragments of Lucilius show that Horace also imitated, and in some cases paraphrased, specific satires. There was probably a Lucilian model for the *Ars Poetica*. Horace felt that although Lucilius was lively, his workmanship was often crude. As he matured, he moved from the "muddy stream" of Lucilius (*Satires* I.10.50) toward a more polished style, but he continued to honor the earlier poet and even compares his faults to the occasional lapses in Homer.

The satires of Lucilius can be dialogues or monologues or straightforward descriptions of the passing scene, but they avoid formal organization. They move with the ebb and flow of conversation, the mood of the speaker, and chance incidents. Throughout, the personality of the speaker is important to the effect; or, to put the point more precisely, the selection of materials and the ebb and flow of mood objectify qualities of character. Horace felt that Lucilius was in the same tradition as the writers of "Old Comedy" (*Satires*, I.4.1–9). The obvious parallel is the ridicule of vice and folly, but the dramatic form is also important.

To the degree that *The Art of Poetry* is in the Lucilian tradition, its dramatic form and lack of clearcut logical organization are therefore not accidental but direct consequences of its genre. This does not mean that there is no organization under the apparently artless succession of its topics. Horace, himself, agreed that the highest achievement of art is to conceal art—*ars celare artem*.

Another term that Horace used to characterize his satires is *sermones*. *Sermo* means "speech." The term calls attention to the fact that Horatian satire avoids the formality of Vergilian verse and seeks instead the tone of living speech. Frequently it uses dialogue, and when formal dialogue is not used, the speaker is usually understood to be addressing a listener and interacting with him. As practiced by Lucilius (and in more polished verse by Horace) the language of the *sermo* is like the colloquial speech of Roman comedy and is explicitly contrasted by Horace (*Satires* I.10.30–40) to the elevated language of tragedy and epic.

In 23 B.C., Horace turned from satire to a closely related form that he called "letters" or "epistles" (*epistulae*). Like the satires that preceded them, the "letters" are colloquial in tone, informal in organization, and often humorous or ironic. Unlike the satires, they are longer, more thoughtful, and more even tempered. However, there is still a clearly identified speaker—supposed in the metaphor of "letters" to be addressing a correspondent—and the tone of the speaker's (or writer's) voice remains central to the effect created. Much attention is given in Book II of the *Epistles* to literary theory. The two poems in that book are usually called "literary epistles," and they share many interests with the *Ars Poetica*. The satirical edge of the first epistle in Book II is provided by the battle between admirers of older Roman authors and mod-

ern ones. Horace sees virtues on both sides of the argument. The old
writers were often noble but deficient in art. Much of the new, especially in drama, is cheap sensationalism. On the other hand, Vergil and
Varius (in the fields of epic and tragedy respectively) show the heights
to which the moderns can rise. As for Horace, he makes no claim to
elevated poetic status. He writes only "conversation pieces" (*sermones*)
"that crawl along the ground" (*Epistles* II.1.250–53).

The alternative title of *The Art of Poetry* is *Epistula ad Pisones*,
meaning "Letter to the Pisos." The Pisos are a father and two sons
who are directly addressed in the work and for whom it is supposed to
have been written. As noted during the discussion of the dating of the
Art, two families of Pisos, an earlier and a later one, have been proposed, and there is no way of deciding for sure which is intended.

Probably Horace, himself, thought of the poem as an "epistle." The
term accurately identifies the generally serious and didactic quality of
the poem, even though it has its waspish moments, especially in the last
hundred or so lines. In terms of organization, although the poem seems
to flow without a clear master plan, the sequence of its topics is often
quite logical, and most commentators agree that it has a fairly well
defined three-part structure. In terms of style, it is in the tradition of
the *sermo* in that it uses a standard rather than a poetically elevated vocabulary and often catches the living tones of colloquial speech. Whether
the protagonist is a "speaker" or "writer" of a letter is probably not
important, but for what the observation is worth, his relation to the
Pisos is so close that he seems to be speaking to them rather than
addressing them in a letter.

Context

The social context of *The Art of Poetry* is a moment that has always
been recognized as pivotal in the history of Western culture. Between
the fifth and the first century B.C. Rome was a republic. True, it was
governed by a patrician class and it accepted slavery, but within limits
Romans could (and did) take pride in the fact that after the expulsion
of the Tarquin kings, they had participated in shaping their own destiny. In the years before Horace's birth in 65 B.C. the republican order
began to disintegrate in a series of violent civil wars that ended with the
triumph of Julius Caesar in 44 B.C. Generally speaking, the republican
faction was conservative and patrician. It was unsympathetic to the

middle class, opposed to reform of an increasingly inequitable agricultural system, and committed to preserving the authority of the Senate, which was its power base. Its chief representative in the crucial period around 44 B.C. was Marcus Junius Brutus. Ranged against the republican party was what could be called a populist party, led until his assassination by Julius Caesar and afterward by Octavian, Caesar's great-nephew and heir. The populists called for economic and political reform and greater representation of the middle class, but they were carried irresistibly beyond political reform to revolution and from revolution to the establishment of an absolutist government.

For conservative Romans, the victory of Caesar over his political and military rivals was a tragedy. In the year of his triumph, 44 B.C., he was assassinated by republican conspirators. As everyone knows who has read Shakespeare's *Julius Caesar*, the conspirators were, in turn, defeated at Phillipi in 42 B.C. by a pro-Caesar faction led by Mark Anthony and Octavian. The brief peace that ensued was prelude to a new round of civil wars that ended with the defeat of Anthony by Octavian at the Battle of Actium in 31 B.C. At that point Octavian was the undisputed ruler of the Mediterranean world. He was also the military strongman of Rome.

Augustus brought peace, expansion, and economic prosperity. His reign was, from one point of view, a golden age symbolized by the closing of the doors of the Temple of Janus in 29 B.C. (They were kept open in time of war—cf. *Odes* IV.15.8-9, *Epistles* I.2.255.) But under the surface, tensions remained. Was Rome a free society or a well-run, extremely comfortable police state? Satirists claim in every age that the old days were better. Were the old values of independence, moderation, patriotism, and honor still valued in Augustan Rome, as the imperial propaganda machine claimed, or were they being replaced by avarice, the pursuit of power, and political manipulation?

Horace was the son of a freedman—a farmer and presumably a hard-working, honest public official. He never ceased praising the simple values of the country and contrasting them with the moral swamp of Rome. He was, however, a poet not a farmer, and his readers were sophisticated city-dwellers, not farmers. For most of his adult life he was dependent on the favor of patrons, including the Emperor. At the same time he was exposing the vices of the city, he was forced by his position to write propaganda celebrating the patriotism, piety, and honor of Rome's citizens, including the very citizens who were gradually undermining such republican institutions as had survived Phillipi. Publicly Horace lamented "civil strife" and praised the Emperor—how could he do otherwise? But he had been born during the republic, and he had defended it in the army of Brutus.

The dilemma must have been more wrenching because the case for the republic was weak. The Senate *had* proved unable to rise above factionalism in times of crisis. The civil wars *had* been devastating. Augustus had brought political unity and peace. Along with them, he *had* brought new territories and immense wealth to Rome. Are not peace and prosperity worth the sacrifice of a political institution of dubious value?

A deep conflict is evident in all of Horace's poetry. He praises the moderation of the old Romans and the simple delights of the country, but at the same time he writes poems describing his drinking contests, his enjoyment of fancy banquets, and his numerous love affairs. *Carpe diem*—"seize the day"—is an important theme in his lyrics (see *Odes* I.11.8). It implies that there are no higher values in life than the pleasures of the moment. The loss of belief in higher values—what has already been called Horace's skepticism—stems partly from philosophies of doubt that were circulating in Horace's Rome, but it must have been intensified by his repeatedly stated belief that Rome had sold out to the pragmatists. There is a parallel between Horace's celebration of the fleeting beauty of life and Wallace Stevens's insistence in *Notes Toward a Supreme Fiction* that the poet must be in love with the world because it is the only reality that humans can know. The parallel is obviously unintentional. It is a corollary of the fact that both poets confront their cultures at moments of crisis.

Like its age and its author, the *Ars Poetica* is ambivalent. It takes with one hand what it offers with the other. The speaker, for example, begins as a friendly and helpful member of the fraternity of poets. The Pisos have asked for advice about writing poetry, and as a professional, he will give it to them. Later, however, when the speaker considers the abuses of poetry in Augustan Rome, he vows to give up poetry and become a critic. At the same time, his tone changes from friendly to angry. He complains of being besieged by incompetent would-be poets, who, he says, are half-crazy and probably better off dead. The last image in the poem is that of a bore who has attached himself to the speaker like a bloodsucking leech. Is the speaker a genial mentor or an angry victim? Does he believe in the future of Rome or does he want to escape? Does he like the Pisos or consider them Philistines?

The ambivalence extends to the subjects treated. About three-fourths of the long comment on the history of poetry is devoted to epic and drama. Yet epic and drama are the two literary forms that Horace explicitly and repeatedly announced he would not write, while the forms he often boasts of having domesticated into Roman poetry—satire and lyric—are all but ignored. Commentators have suggested that Horace emphasizes drama because the Pisos (or the oldest son) planned to write a comedy (or a tragedy), but this is unpersuasive if only because the discussion treats epic as well as drama, and the discussion of drama includes Satyr Play along with comedy and tragedy.

A better explanation is suggested by the nature of the genres involved. The genres preferred by Horace himself are personal rather than public. The speaker in a typical satire is an outsider, a lonely critic or ridiculer of the vices of the times. Although Horace used satire, especially in the blander form of the epistle, to praise Augustus and the status quo, he is constantly being drawn back to the position of outsider and critic of things as they are. Lyric, Horace's other preferred genre, is not necessarily an outsider's form, but it *is* personal and introverted. Even though Horace wrote patriotic and moral lyrics, his typical themes are *carpe diem*, wine, and erotic pleasure. Like the comments of the "outsider" of satire, they are subversive of the official values professed by—among others—Horace himself.

Both satire and Horatian-style lyric would probably have seemed questionable to a former consul of Augustan Rome like the elder Piso. On the other hand, epic and drama are public and impersonal. Their formulas are well established, and Horace gives a rich sampling of the standard lore about them. Most important, epic and tragedy celebrate the history of the state and comedy mirrors its civic life. Horace's friend Vergil had shown how effective epic could be as propaganda for the regime's official values. Tragedy could also present great moments in history and could be equally noble in style. Epic and tragedy could also be understood as "useful" in the sense of teaching official morality. By concentrating on public genres like epic and drama and downplaying personal genres like satire and lyric, Horace's speaker is giving the Pisos what they want.

Another example of ambivalence in *The Art of Poetry* is the treatment of the ancient contrast, first explored in Plato's *Ion*, between inspiration and technique or "art." Roman criticism favored the idea that the poet is at times possessed by a force more powerful than rational calculation. Horace exclaimed of his Muse Melpomene (*Odes* IV.3), "O you, who taught the swan to sing . . . it is through you entirely that I am pointed out as the singer of the Roman lyre . . . That I breathe out my songs and please, if I please, is your doing." He later confessed of Apollo (*Odes* IV.6), "Phoebus inspired me; Phoebus gave me the name and the art of poet." There are four references to the Muse in *The Art of Poetry* (ll. 83, 141, 323, 407), and there are also references to the earliest poets as holy (l. 391) and as prophets (l. 400).

In spite of these references, Horace's *Art* emphasizes technique and learning and says little about inspiration. In other words, whatever Horace may have believed, the *Art* is an essentially rationalistic discussion of poetry. The speaker not only fails to give much credit to the positive contribution of inspiration to poetic creation (including the creation of Horace's odes) but suggests, like Socrates in the *Ion*, that poets who claim to be inspired are probably drunk or crazy.

Is the speaker rejecting the idea of an essential, though mysterious, source of true poetry? Or is he again giving the Pisos what they want—"how to do it" formulas? If he is simply giving the Pisos what they want, Horace's poem might be understood as a satire of the Philistine attitudes toward art implicitly held by the Pisos.

These observations lead back to the fact that Horace's speaker is a character—a persona. The root meaning of "persona" is "mask." The speaker is different from the poet. He is involved in a specific dramatic situation—he is speaking to the Pisos—and his attitude toward them and their implicit responses to him influence what he says. He says little about the genres that most interested Horace the poet. He is divided in his own mind about his status as an artist and about the society in which he lives, and he pointedly contrasts the artistic Greeks with the money-grubbing Romans. As the poem moves forward, he seems increasingly aware of his isolation from the society around him and increasingly baffled as to what should be done about the fact. Poetry civilizes, he says, but he vows to give up poetry in favor of criticism, and in the last episode of the poem he seems to reject even the critic's role.

In other words, Horace's speaker is a complex, fully developed character like the "Chaucer" who is a pilgrim in *The Canterbury Tales* and who is quite different from Chaucer the author. Yet the question of the relationship between the speaker and Horace remains more elusive than the relationship between Chaucer the pilgrim and Chaucer the author.

The psychological tensions exhibited by Horace's speaker are clearly tensions experienced by Horace himself. We have already noted, for example, that Horace was a veteran of Phillipi who wrote poems flattering the emperor; a praiser of the simple values of the countryside who wrote for a sophisticated Roman audience; a propagandist for official morality who expressed his skepticism about this morality by celebrating dissipation; and a consummate artist who felt he lived in a society that had little respect for art. Horace was, in short, a bundle of contradictions, and in this respect he closely resembles the speaker in *The Art of Poetry*.

One of the characteristics of the *Art* is that the speaker frequently doubles back on himself, qualifying and sometimes apparently contradicting statements almost as soon as he has made them. If the *Art* is read as a treatise, such moments are confusing even though they can occasionally be understood dialectically as the establishing of a position followed by qualifications intended to soften it. Conversely, if the *Art* is read as monologue intended to reveal the character of the speaker, the continual vacillation can be understood as a way of objectifying psychological ambivalence, or, alternately, a process of groping forward through uncertainties by a dialectical method of statement and counterstatement.

To preserve the distinction between poet and persona, in the commentary that follows the poet-critic of the poem will be referred to as "the speaker" rather than as "Horace."

Organization and Themes I: Decorum; "Fitting Together"

Opinions about the degree of organization of *The Art of Poetry* have varied considerably over the centuries. If it is a satire in the tradition of the Lucilian *satura*, there is no particular reason to look for formal organization. "There is a want of a system," wrote J. W. Duff (*Literary History* [1928], 532), "[which is] fitting enough in what is half epistolary, half didactic." G. M. A. Grube calls it "delightful but mystifying," adding that the mystery arises from "the absence—or apparent absence—of any systematic plan or structure" (*The Greek and Roman Critics* [1965], 239–40).

On the other hand, even though *The Art of Poetry* does not seem to be highly organized, important principles of organization may be concealed under its surface. The apparent lack of organization is partly the result of "gliding transitions," a term first used in 1906 by Paul Cauer, which tend to conceal rather than emphasize the movement from one topic to the next. Beneath the apparently free flow of ideas, Eduard Norden felt he had discovered a two-part structure according to which lines 1-294 are concerned with *ars*—the craft of poetry—while the remainder of the poem is concerned with *artifex*—the nature of the poet. More frequently, commentators have found a three-part structure in the *Art*. This is the position taken by the most detailed of recent commentaries, C. O. Brink's *Prolegomena to the Literary Epistles* (1963) and the *Ars Poetica* (1971), and it will be examined in more detail below.

One set of principles favored by early commentators was rhetorical. The topics have been examined frequently, most explicitly, perhaps, by George Fiske and Mary Grant (*Cicero's "Orator" and Horace's "Ars poetica"* [1924]; *Cicero's "De oratore" and Horace's "Ars poetica"* [1929]). The main divisions of ancient rhetoric are invention, organization, and style. To these Cicero added a strong emphasis on the topic of the training of the orator and an equal emphasis on decorum. Invention (*inventio*) is developing the material; organization (*dispositio*; Horace uses the term *ordo*) is presenting it in logical order; and style (*elocutio*) is expressing it in effective language.

Decorum (Greek *to prepon*, Latin *decorum*) normally means "that which is proper or becoming," as in Horace's famous observation "It is sweet and proper to die for one's country" (*Dulce et decorum est pro patria mori*). Decorum in this sense has moral overtones. Fiske and Grant argue that in one way or another decorum enters every part of Horace's *Art* from the introductory warning against mixing styles to the comments on Greek and Roman drama that end on line 294. The passage extending from line 295 to the end relates the standard rhetorical topics of the role of natural talent (*ingenium, natura, physis*), training (*exercitatio, melete*), and knowledge (*doctrina, episteme*) in the making of the orator to the making of the poet. Decorum is implicit in this passage because it is concerned with appropriateness of moral character and experience. On the other hand, there are different concepts of decorum. In general, Horace's concept was equated by Renaissance commentators with the moral-rhetorical kind discussed by Cicero. However, C. O. Brink argues that this concept is "a different thing altogether" (Brink, *Horace Poetry*, 80) from the concept developed by Horace, which emphasizes craftsmanship rather than moral values.

The late classical commentary of Porphyrion on *The Art of Poetry* includes a famous remark that Horace used "not all but the most significant" precepts in a treatise on poetry by a certain Neoptolemus of Parium. Much has been made of the organizational scheme of Neoptolemus, and that will be discussed below. The comment of Porphyrion on line 1 of the *Art* may be even more important, but less has been made of it. Porphyrion says that the first precept of Neoptolemus was about consistency, for which he used the Greek word *akolouthia*—"going with" (cf. Rudd, *Epistles Book II and Epistle to the Pisones*, 18). The Greek term is close etymologically to the Latin term Horace often uses for decorum—*convenientia*, which also means "going with" or "going together" and is equivalent to the English "fitting." Neoptolemus explains further that the good poet adds "harmony" (*harmonia*) and "continuousness" or "coherence" (*synecheia*) to even the longest poems.

In Horace's *Art, covenientia* is the effect achieved by bringing things together that are properly related either because they are related in nature or because the principles of art establish their relationship. It is achieved by craftsmanship—the conscious application of the rules of art to the materials of art. The idea is drawn from crafts like carpentry that depend for their success on the precise and elegant fitting of things together. A famous line in the *Art* refers to the overriding need for the art work to be "simple and unified" (l. 23). When things "fit," the result seems to a viewer to be "simple" and "unified," although the apparent simplicity may in fact be the result of a complex process, in which "art conceals art." A ship's hull, for example, looks simple, even inevitable, to an untrained observer, but anyone who understands shipbuilding knows how complex and elegant the shape actually is. A ship's hull is also a pleasing shape, and the pleasure it gives is aesthetic, so that workmanship and beauty seem related. Another term used in the *Art* for the effect of elegant "fitting together" is "harmony." It is the term used by Neoptolemus. Harmony is created by the proper fitting together of musical notes. It is inherently pleasing, and in this sense it is a metaphor for the aesthetic pleasure that art gives along with its useful teaching.

The *Art* begins with examples of violation of decorum. Each is an example of the disastrous result of "fitting together" two things that conflict either in nature or art—a man's head and a horse's body (natural conflict), a cypress tree in a seascape (also natural conflict), fine sculptural detail but poor overall plan (artistic conflict), and so forth. These things are unpleasant and grotesque—they arouse laughter, which is a response to "deformity," or abhorrence. Conversely, that which is fitting is also pleasing. Later in the *Art* character is treated as the proper "coming together" of circumstance (e.g., prosperous, tragic) and emotion or of circumstance and status (e.g., age, sex). Later still, genre is treated in terms of the proper "fitting together" of verse form (e.g., hexameter for epic) and subject (e.g., kings and generals), and, more specifically, the "fitting" of the characteristics of a single verse form (iambic trimeter) to the different conditions of tragedy and comedy.

Aesthetics enters the discussion of verse form and genre through observations that an improperly conceived character or verse form will "put the audience to sleep" or arouse laughter or (in the case of the characterization of Fauns) please the rabble but offend the educated. Revision too is related to the process of "fitting together." The famous advice to revise "to the fingernail" (*ad unguem* l. 294) is based on a metaphor from stoneworking. Acron, author of a late-classical commentary on the *Art*, explains that stoneworkers tested the closeness of the fit between two slabs of marble by trying to insert their fingernail in the joint. If it could not be pushed between the slabs, the joint was judged to be well made. Revision is thus like testing joints. Poetry is a "fitting together" and its success is to be judged by how perfectly the parts complement one another.

In sum, if decorum is a recurrent, perhaps a dominant theme in the *Art*, it is made specific and given content by the concept of "fitting together" or *convenientia*. The concept is somewhat different in implication from decorum in the sense of "the seemly or the becoming," which has moral overtones, and it appears to come from Neoptolemus. Decorum in this sense has a good claim to being the theme that unifies the first half (to l. 294) of the *Art*.

Organization II: Grammar, Rhetoric

Much of the material that Horace offers on proper diction, usage, literary genres, the relation between genre and verse form, and characteristics of iambic verse was discussed in ancient grammar. The section on poetry of a full-scale ancient grammar like Diomedes's *Three Books of Grammar* (*Ars grammatica libri III;* fourth century A.D.) was so detailed that it was given its own special label—*ars metrica* ("art of meter"). The *ars metrica* included treatment of literary genres, the relation of genre and verse form, the qualities of the standard meters, and the differences between tragic and comic iambic verse in much the same way, and in some cases in the same order, as Horace. Aristotle's *Poetics* shows that the *ars metrica* was flourishing in Greece at the time the *Poetics* was written, and two Greek treatises on the subject—by Hephaestion and Aristides Quintilian—have survived. Grammar has not generally been considered in relation to the *Art*, but in some areas the parallels are striking.

Rhetoric has been much more thoroughly explored. Two and perhaps three of the major divisions of rhetoric appear in the *Art*. Roughly the first hundred lines of the *Art* are concerned with matters essentially stylistic (*elocutio*). According to Fiske and Grant, the formal discussion of organization (*dispositio*) is limited to ll. 40–44, but parts of the discussion of genre also deal with organization. Invention (*inventio*) is treated explicitly in lines 38–41, but the topic is less easily defined than either style or organization. Character, emotion, and meter in different genres clearly relate to decorum but may also relate to poetic invention. Fiske and Grant argue persuasively that imitation (119–52) should be understood as a corollary of invention. The sections that relate to invention are identified in the subheadings of the present commentary.

Niall Rudd (*Epistles Book II and Epistle to the Pisones*, 22) offers one of the more ambitious applications of rhetoric to the analysis of the *Art*. A standard topic of rhetoric was subject matter (*res*) and words (*verba*). Cicero put these ideas into a formula for the training of an orator: "copiousness of subject matter and language" (*copia rerum ac verborum*). In Rudd's analysis the first third of the *Art* is a discussion of these two topics. After an introductory comment on the need for unity (ll. 1–41), the *Art* settles down to a discussion of language (*verba*, ll. 48–118), followed by a discussion of "material" (*res*, ll. 119–52). A discussion of drama follows (ll. 153–294), and after that, a section on "the poet."

Other standard rhetorical topics abound in the *Art*. Among them are the idea of unity, the idea of stylistic virtues and their cognate vices, the problem of pure diction (*Latinitas*), the concept of imitation in the sense of "following the best models," the value to the orator (or poet) of a solid grounding in philosophy, the usefulness of character stereotypes like "male" and "female" and "young," "middle-aged" and "old," and the social duty (*officium*) of the poet. C. O. Brink finds a detailed parallel between the chapter on decorum in Aristotle's *Rhetoric* (III.7) and the discussion of "appropriateness" in the *Art* (ll. 89-118). The parallel extends to the division of the subject in each work into appropriateness in relation to (1) situation (*Art*, pp. 89-98), (2) emotion (ll. 99-107), and (3) character (ll. 108-18). Taken with the rhetorical topics mentioned earlier these instances confirm the pervasive influence of rhetoric on the *Art*, though not, it should be stressed, the use of rhetorical concepts for its overall organization.

In general, rhetorical influence other than the idea of decorum is most evident in the earlier sections of the *Art* (roughly, lines 42-71), the discussion on character (ll. 153-78), the discussion of the "office" and training of the poet (ll. 304-60), and the problem of nature versus art (ll. 408-18). As for sources, the most often cited is Aristotle's *Rhetoric*. It is, however, not clear that Horace knew this work firsthand, so the claim for its influence is often qualified by the suggestion that there were intermediary, usually Alexandrian, sources in which Aristotle's rhetorical concepts were adapted to the discussion of poetry. Horace undoubtedly studied many Greek rhetoricians during his stay in Athens. However, rhetoric was studied intensely in the Roman schools, and Horace certainly knew Cicero's rhetorical works well. Parallels between the *Art* and Cicero's works, especially the *Orator* and the *De oratore*, are easy to find. Does Horace owe his largest debt to Aristotle's *Rhetoric* or to Alexandrian revisions or to Roman sources? The fact is that ancient rhetoric was standardized. Topics in one treatise appear in others. Although it is often easy to decide when Horace is drawing on rhetorical lore, it is often much harder to decide exactly where the lore comes from.

Neoptolemus of Parium

Consideration of Alexandrian influence on Horace reintroduces the subject of Neoptolemus of Parium. According to Porphyrion, Horace's *Art* "incorporated . . . the precepts of Neoptolemus of Parium about the art of poetry, though not all of them but only the most striking." Neoptolemus was known for centuries as a shadowy figure of the 3rd century B.C. who wrote a book on poetry that presumably combined some of Aristotle's ideas with theories of poetry common in Alexandria. In 1918 the German scholar Christian Jensen published fragments of a discussion of Neoptolemus in a papyrus of *On Poems* by Philodemus (fl. first century B.C.). According to these fragments, Neoptolemus divided the treatment of poetry into three parts—*poesis, poema,* and *poetes.*

Since Jensen there have been many discussions of how (and if) this triple division applies to Horace. Almost everyone agrees that the last section of the *Art* (ll. 295-476) treats "the poet." What about lines 1-294? Among recent scholars C.O. Brink and G.M.A. Grube believe that these lines are divided into two sections more or less corresponding to the first two divisions of Neoptolemeus. Conversely, Niall Rudd (*Epistles Book II and Epistle to the Pisones* [1989]) rejects the theory of Neoptolemus's influence, arguing that the *Art* is in two parts breaking at line 294. Rudd adds, however, the suggestion that the first part includes two subdivisions based on the rhetorical distinction between "words" and "things."

The simplest theory is that lines 1-118 treat *poesis,* by which is understood content, order, and style, and lines 119-294 treat *poema,* by which is meant "genres." These divisions overlap the rhetorical divisions already noted, including Rudd's division of parts of the first half of the poem into *verba* and *res.* The overlap is not surprising. It is a by-product of the conflation of poetic and rhetorical theory that was typical of Alexandrian literary scholarship and was, if anything, more emphatic in Roman than in Greek thought about literature.

Having summarized four systems of organization (*Prolegomena,* 31), Brink concludes that the commonly accepted labels for the first two topics should probably be reversed. His proposed outline is thus:

Introduction (Unity)	ll. 1-41
Poema	42-118
Poesis	119-294
Poeta	294-476

This is as good a presentation of Horace's use of Neoptolemus of Parium as is likely to be offered, short of new evidence. It will conclude our summary of theories of large-scale organization. In sum, most commentators favor a three-part structure, but there is by no means a consensus that the *Art* falls logically into more than two parts, and even those who argue for three parts disagree on what the labels of the parts should be and where they begin and end.

Aristotle's *Poetics*

Since the mid-sixteenth century it has been recognized that many ideas in Horace's *Art* are similar to ideas in Aristotle's *Poetics*. The question has always been how similar. Did Horace know Aristotle's text or did Aristotelian ideas find their way in much diluted and often distorted forms into *The Art of Poetry* via Alexandrian criticism?

The consensus today is that Horace did *not* know the *Poetics* firsthand and that the echoes of Aristotle in the *Art* come from Alexandrian intermediaries, among whom Neoptolemus may well have been especially important. There is really no way, given present knowledge, to improve on this conjecture. However, it will be helpful here to note that the similarities between the *Poetics* and the *Art* include the idea of unity, the difference between epics that seek unity by beginning "at the beginning" and those that are truly unified, the importance of consistency, the appropriateness of iambic meter for drama, the origin of tragedy and comedy in rural festivals, and the need for the poet (or the actor) to experience the emotions being represented in a play. Specifics of the Aristotelian influence will be presented below as they occur. Some passages in the *Art* are strikingly close to the *Poetics*; others are distant. In general the examples of probable influence are clustered in the section on literary genres (ll. 119–284).

Differences between Aristotle and Horace should also be noted. Aristotle is systematic and deductive. He relates poetry to three factors— means, method, and object of imitation. Horace has nothing like this. Both Aristotle and Horace value imitation, but Aristotle's imitation is best understood as "making plots," while Horace's is "following literary models," especially Greek models and "describing natural scenes." Aristotle argues that the purpose of tragedy is to produce catharsis. Horace argues that it is to "profit or delight" or to "mix utility with sweetness." The similarities make it clear that whether the Aristotelian influence was direct or indirect, it was important. The differences show clearly that Horace was following a path quite different from that taken by Aristotle.

The oldest manuscripts of *The Art of Poetry* are from the ninth century. Thereafter numerous manuscripts survive, especially in France and Germany. In spite of textual variants among the early manuscripts, the key readings of the *Art* are fairly well established. A few emendations are adopted in the present translation. These are identified in the notes. For the most part, however, the present text is conservative.

Epigrammatic Comments

The *Art* has always been a mine of quotations about poetic art. Most of these are effective in Latin but lose their flavor in English. Different readers will be struck by different phrases, but the following, given in Latin with English translation, are a sampling of the best known:

Line	Latin	English Translation
15–16	*purpureus pannus*	"purple patch"
23	*simplex duntaxet et unum*	"simple and single"
25–26	*brevis esse laboro,/ obscurus fio*	"I try to be brief and become obscure."
73	*res gestae regumque ducumque et tristia bella*	"Histories of kings and generals and the sorrows of war" (a characterization of epic).
102	*si vis me flere, dolendum est/ primum ipsi tibi*	"If you want me to weep, you must feel sorrow first."
139	*parturient montes, nascetur ridiculus mus*	"The mountains labor and bring forth a ridiculous mouse." (To describe inflated poetry.)
147–48	*ab ovo . . . in medias res*	"From the beginning . . . into the middle of the action." (Alternate ways to begin a long poem.)
268–69	*Vos exemplaria Graeca/ nocturna versate manu, versate diurna*	"Review the Greek models night and day."
309–10	*Scribendi recte sapere est principium et fons, rem tibi Socraticae poterunt ostendere cartae.*	"Knowing is the first principle and fountainhead of writing well;/ The writings of Socrates can teach the matter to you."
333	*aut prodesse volunt aut delectare poetae*	"Poets strive to either profit or delight." (Sometimes translated "both profit and delight.")
344	*miscit utili dulci*	"He [the poet] mixes the useful with the sweet."
359	*bonus dormitat Homerus*	"Even Homer nods."
361	*ut pictura poesis*	"A poem is like a picture."
372–73	*mediocris esse poetis/ non homines, non di, non concessere colmnae.*	"Not men nor gods nor the book-sellers allow poets to be mediocre."
471	*minxerit in patrios cineres*	"He urinated on his father's ashes."

Commentary

Lines 1–23: Simplicity and Unity
(Poetry as Description and as Imitation of Nature)

The *Art* begins with examples of failure of unity and sums up the conclusions to be drawn from the examples with a famous rule: "In short, whatever kind of poem you are creating let it be simple and unified." Two kinds of violation of this rule are mentioned—unnatural combinations and ornamental digressions. The first kind violates conditions that occur in the real world (nature); the second violates the rules of art. Under the heading of "unnatural combinations" are a human head on the neck of a horse and a lovely woman with the lower parts of a fish. Both of these sound like allusions to myth. The horse-man recalls centaurs and the fish-woman recalls both mermaids and the monster Scylla, whose lower parts were those of a sea-serpent.

Mythology is rich in such images. What is wrong with them? The answer is "nothing" except to someone who thinks they are fantastic and unnatural. Horace's speaker is obviously this kind of a person. He considers the images faulty because they are made up of disparate elements and thus are not "simple" in the special meaning of "homogeneous" that is appropriate to the rule offered on line 23 that poetry should be "simple and unified."

The speaker offers two judgments. In the first place, reasonable men will laugh at such images. He is recalling the idea, suggested in Aristotle's *Poetics* (V.1–8), that "the ridiculous . . . is a subdivision of deformity." The norm of reason appears frequently in the *Art*. It is allied to the norm of nature and the natural and is opposed to the idea that through poetic inspiration artists can depart from or rise above the merely "natural." The emphasis of the *Art* on reason and nature helps to explain its appeal during the seventeenth and eighteenth centuries,

often called the age of reason. The norm of reason also explains the
origin of humor. What reasonable men know is unnatural seems ridiculous and calls forth laughter.

In the second place, composite images resemble "idle fancies shaped
by a sick man's dreams." Here the speaker is repeating the suggestion,
found as early as Plato's *Ion*, that myths and other fantastic inventions
of poets are not inspired visions but the result of delirium or drunkenness. They are not only laughable but symptoms of mental disorder.
Horace's speaker is clearly on Plato's side, even though Horace, himself,
endorsed the idea of inspiration in the *Odes* and suggested in *Odes*
III.25 that drunkenness can contribute to inspiration—presumably by
creating something like an "altered mental state."

The theory that a mental faculty called fancy (*phantasia*) collects images but that the images are jumbled until properly united by reason
underlies Plato's position. When reason is not in charge, as in dreams or
drunkenness or madness or a delirium caused by a fever, the images get
mixed up, with the result, for example, that a man's head can be joined
to a horse's body even though such a combination cannot occur in nature. Lucretius states categorically (*De rerum natura* V.877-1010) that
such composite monsters cannot exist in nature. Centaurs and Scyllas—
fabulous creatures much like those evoked in Horace's opening lines—
are prime examples because "creatures with a double nature and a bi-
partite body created out of parts taken from different species cannot
be" (V. 877-80). A fabulous image is thus something unnatural and
lower than reason, not something supranatural and above reason.

In addition to calling for unity, the opening passage of the *Art* implies that the poet should stick to the real world—that is, nature. It anticipates the later advice that to please, fictions should be "close to
truth" (l. 338) and avoid monstrosities like a Lamia (serpent) giving
birth to a child. It also complements the final passage in the poem (ll.
453-76), which is a satirical description of the excesses of a mad poet.

On line 9 the speaker anticipates objections to his argument. Have
not poets always been allowed to invent freely by poetic license? Poetic
license is a valid principle, but it does not extend to blatant contradictions. Mixings of savage with tame or of one species with another go
too far and must be avoided. Quintilian cites the opening passage of the
Art in the *Institute of Oratory* (VIII.3.60) when condemning mixtures
of style: "The vice [I am discussing] is like mixing sublime with hum-

ble things, old with new, and poetic with prosy—like the monster Horace depicts in his book *Ars poetica* when he says, 'If you should join a man's head . . .'"

A different and essentially rhetorical violation of unity occurs when the poet is carried away by "noble beginnings and great promise." This sort of mood can lead to rhetorical excess—to ornamental passages that have no necessary relation to the work. They are identified as "purple patches." "Purple" suggests royalty and thus elevation; "patch" suggests something obviously different from the fabric to which it is attached. The examples cited are elegant but digressive passages of description—a sketch of Diana's grove or of the Rhine River or a rainbow. They recall the harmful effect on poetry of school exercises in formal description (*ekphrasis*) and ornament. By corollary they identify the speaker as an advocate of artistic restraint. In this respect, the position taken in the *Art* in reference to poetry resembles the position of moderate advocates of the "Attic" style of oratory in contrast to the highly ornamental "Asiatic" style. The merits of the Attic and Asiatic styles had been much discussed in Rome, with Cicero (*Orator* 23-32) and Quintilian (*Institute* XII.10.12-14) strongly defending the Attic style.

Two other examples follow: a painter who includes a cypress tree (a symbol of mourning) in a picture of a sailor swimming from a sinking ship, and a potter who begins to make a wine jar and ends with a pitcher. The first probably refers to a painter of "votive pictures," which were created as thanks to the gods for the event they depicted (in this case, escape from a shipwreck). The second is more problematic. The emphasis may be on size: the potter begins with a large project, an amphora, and ends with something anticlimactic—a small pitcher. More probably, according to C. O. Brink, the reference is to function, as though a blacksmith should begin to make a pump handle and end with a crowbar. The first possibility suggests a poet who begins to write an epic and settles for the story of a preliminary skirmish, the second, a poet who begins to write an epic and settles for an elegant description of the walls of a city. In either case something has happened to the art work in the process of being created. It lacks unity because it began as one thing and ended as another.

The concluding advice emphasizes two aesthetic criteria. The term "simple" implies uniformity or homogeneity rather than lack of complexity. A woman should be entirely female, and a tiger must not mate with a lamb. "Unified" means that everything should fit together. Aristotle argues strongly for unity in *Poetics* VIII and defines it as a situation in which "if any one part is transposed or removed, the whole will be disordered and disunified" (VIII.21–23). The idea obviously applies to the cypress tree in the picture of the shipwreck. It can be removed without loss; and, in fact, if it is removed, the picture will be improved.

Aristotle is thinking in the *Poetics* of unity of action. Horace's speaker seems to have this description in mind throughout and thus to be considering rhetorical and stylistic elements in the art work. The similarity of doctrine is significant, but the differences illustrate the danger of reading too much Aristotelian influence into the *Art*. The point is evident in another way. The passage in question includes a sustained comparison between painting and poetry. The comparison is important for the *Art*. It is loosely associated with the later observation (l. 361) "a poem is like a picture," although that comment is not about style. A poet who believes poetry is like painting will think of "imitation" in terms of verbal descriptions of things that exist in the world rather than action, and description is exactly what the examples given in lines 1–23 suggest the speaker has in mind.

"Unity" is a much favored word in twentieth-century criticism. The opening passage of the *Art* has received considerable attention because it deals with unity. Is this emphasis appropriate? That is, does Horace or his speaker intend to make unity the basic rule for the entire *Art*? Or is unity merely the first of a succession of topics treated—one desirable trait among many? It is tempting to take the former position, but the reader of the *Art* should recognize that the second has many supporters. A corollary of this issue is the question of how unity is to be achieved. Here the answer is a bit easier. The emphasis of the first twenty-three lines is on reason and imitation of things as they are. It follows that unity is achieved by the imitation of nature, which is always properly "fitted together," and by the application of reason to composition, which is the use of the rules of art to "fit together" things that are not found in nature. Horace's poet is first and foremost a craftsman. If the question is raised, "Craftsman of what?" the answer must be that the *Art* will explain this as it proceeds. In any case, the concept of "fitting together" is fundamental to the theory of art being developed.

A final word should be said about the speaker as he appears at the beginning of the *Art*. He begins abruptly. The implication is that he has been discussing artistic questions with the Pisos for so long that no preliminaries are necessary. His tone is assured and superior. He is an authority, and he is confident of his position. He also regards the Pisos as members of his own circle. Like him they are "reasonable men," and he knows they will laugh at the same things that amuse him. His comments are pithy and flow easily. The only break in the stream comes when he mentions poetic license. Poetic license conflicts with the norm of reason. The speaker dismisses the problem with the observation that even poetic license must be used in a reasonable way.

Lines 24–45: Rhetorical Unity; Organization

The discussion of unity is now extended to specifically rhetorical topics. They are presented through examples of error—being deceived "by the appearance of doing the right thing." An author seeks a desirable effect and slips into an allied error: the poet who tries to be brief becomes obscure; the poet who aims at an easy style becomes flat; the heroic poet becomes bombastic. The speaker is drawing on the well-worn rhetorical topic of virtues of style and cognate vices. His examples include all three of the styles normally discussed in rhetoric. "Smoothness" (l. 26) is associated with the "middle" style, "grandeur" (l. 27) with the "elevated" style, and "over-cautious" with the "plain" or "humble" style. The topic had often been treated in similar terms in Roman rhetoric—for example, in the *Rhetorica ad Herennium* (IV.5)—and Horace had no difficulty adapting it to poetry.

A new quality—"wholeness"—enters the discussion in the reference to the sculptor who is good at details but does not know how to deal with the work as a whole (ll. 34–35). The speaker remarks, "I would no more want to be like that artist" than have attractive eyes but a crooked nose. Again the emphasis is on elements that do not "fit together."

The section is followed by direct advice in the plural—evidently to the Pisos. "Consider your talent," the speaker advises, "and choose a subject fitted to it." If you do, you will find that style and organization (*ordo*) follow easily. The latter remark is a "sliding transition." It refers to the discussion of unity and also forward to the discussion of organization. As for the advice to relate subject to talent, it is best illustrated by what later became the proverbial example of Vergil. Vergil began his artistic career by writing the *Eclogues* about shepherds in a mostly humble style, moved to the middle style of the *Georgics*, four poems about farming, and only then attempted the elevated style and noble subject matter of the *Aeneid*.

The speaker concentrates on subject-matter and observes that with the right choice, clear organization (*ordo*) and pleasing style will follow. Organization per se is confined to lines 42–45. In spite of the fact that the subject usually received extended treatment in manuals of rhetoric, Horace's speaker is brief and general. His main point is that the poet should say what is appropriate for the moment and avoid saying everything at the beginning. Early commentators on the *Art* explained that Vergil, for example, said little about Aeneas building ships in Book III of the *Aeneid*, when the ships were actually being constructed, but included a passage on the subject in Book IX in connection with the burning of the ships by Turnus (*Aeneid* IX.77ff.). The oblique treatment of organization is bound to disappoint anyone who wants to find a disguised full-scale treatment of rhetoric in the *Art*. It does not lead to a detailed comment on strategies of introducing, developing, and ending a poem but to a change of subject from organization to style.

Lines 46–72: Diction

Style has been introduced by the separation of subject matter into "organization" and "pleasing style" (ll. 40–41). The first aspect of "pleasing style" is diction. This section is associated by Niall Rudd with the *verba* part of the *res et verba* formula of rhetoric. It might just as well be associated with grammar, since discussions of diction were a regular part of full-scale ancient grammars.

Greek and Roman rhetoric was much concerned with what would today be called usage. Among treatments that may be relevant to the *Art* are those by Aristotle (*Rhetoric* III.2–8), Cicero (*De oratore* 149ff.), and Varro (*De lingua Latina* 9). Should vocabulary be limited to current words or should authors be allowed to revive old ones and coin new ones by borrowing from other languages? The topic was considered under the term *Latinitas*, meaning something like "pure Latinity." According to Varro, the foremost authority on the subject during Horace's lifetime, good usage depends on nature, analogy, custom, and authority. Nature is essentially what is correct according to characteristics of the language. "Analogy" is what is correct according to variations on simple and direct expression permitted by the rules of grammar. "Custom" is what is correct according to the way language is actually used by reasonably well-educated speakers, including generally accepted variations from nature and analogy. "Authority" is the authority given to certain words because they have been used by great—hence authoritative—authors. Words justified by authority include archaisms, neologisms (coinages), and borrowings from foreign languages, which, for Latin, means words taken from Greek. It was proverbial that "authority" to innovate was granted freely to early writers. Later writers had less authority and felt unable to experiment as freely as they wanted.

The speaker sympathizes with the moderns. The best strategy is to use familiar words so skillfully that they seem fresh. However, if a new word or a borrowing is essential, license (*licentia*, l. 51) will be granted, especially if the word is derived from Greek. Since the old writers—Plautus, for example—were permitted to do this, moderns like Vergil should have the same right. The speaker now enlarges the scope of the comment. Addressing those who, apparently, oppose new terms, he argues that language is like a great tree that is constantly shedding and renewing its leaves. The same is true of even the most impressive human endeavors like creating a new port or draining swamps or straightening the course of a river. All three of these allusions to public works have been interpreted as references to projects undertaken by Augustus, but there are historical inconsistencies in this interpretation. Probably the allusions are simply to monumental human projects and have no specific reference. Even monumental projects are subject to time. Since language is human, it, too, is constantly dying and renewing itself, and usage (*usus*, l. 71) is the final "law and norm" of speech.

Lines 73–98: Genre and Meter
(Decorum)

There is now an abrupt move from style to meter, or, more properly, to the relation between style, meter, and genre. A typical ancient grammar had a well-defined progression from parts of speech and inflections to stylistic matters, including diction, to poetry, beginning with meter. The metrical section of an ancient grammar, the *ars metrica*, explained the concept of a metrical foot, the regular meters and their uses, and the irregular meters used in lyric stanzas.

The discussion usually included a brief note on the history of each meter and explained which meters were appropriate for which genres.

This was not a matter only of convention. Certain meters were felt to be intrinsically suited to certain purposes. The meter "created" the reality objectified by the subject matter in the sense of making it emotionally credible. This idea is a heritage of the time when poetry was associated with music because it was sung. Homer and Vergil recall this heritage when they begin their epics with a command to the Muse to "sing." The underlying reason for the ancient association between music, meter, and the constitutive power of poetry is the belief that specific musical modes create specific psychological effects—Dorian music, for example, makes listeners warlike while Lydian music makes them sensuous and erotic. Since it explains which meters are constitutive of which subjects, the *ars metrica* is the key to making poetic realities convincing. Horace's speaker draws heavily on the lore of the *ars metrica*, and he returns to it when considering the relation of iambic meter to drama (ll. 251ff.). His position is based on decorum. A poem becomes excellent when the right meter is "fitted" to the right subject and presented in the right language.

The noblest of ancient meters was dactylic hexameter. This is the meter used by Homer in the *Iliad* and the *Odyssey*, and the speaker credits him with having been the first to use it for epic. A classical dactylic foot consists of one long and two short syllables (-ᵕᵕ). The combination is striking and also artificial—it is rare in everyday speech. Six feet in a line create a hexameter. The speaker describes the subjects of epic poems as "the exploits of kings and generals and the grim events of war." Dactylic hexameter was considered intrinsically elevated and sonorous and thus well adapted to objectifying these subjects. Aristotle called it "the stateliest and most dignified meter" (*Poetics*, XXIV.25).

A dactylic hexameter line linked with a shorter (pentameter) line was used in antiquity for the kind of poem called elegy. Originally an elegy was any poem sung to the accompaniment of the flute; in Latin literature, for example in Ovid, Propertius, and Tibullus, it came to be identified with love poetry.

An iambic foot is one short followed by one long syllable (ᵕ-). It was used in lines of six iambic feet in the bitter satires of the Greek poet Archilochus (ca. 650 B.C.). Horace's speaker now compresses into a few lines a long and complex history that is presented more clearly in Chapter IV of Aristotle's *Poetics* and also, with more details, in Horace's *Satires* (I.10) and *Epistles* (II.2). Iambic meter was felt to be inherently "conversational," and critics from Aristotle on were fond of remarking that people use iambs in everyday speech without even being aware of the fact. Since iambic meter was associated with satire and also resembled everyday speech, it was used by the early writers of comedy. Aristotle says that tragedy originally used trochaic meter, which was also used by Satyr Plays, but changed to iambic because of the appropriateness of iambic meter for dialogue.

Of this considerable tradition, Horace's speaker notes three elements: (1) iambic meter is used in both tragedy and comedy because it is suited to dialogue; (2) it can be heard easily; and (3) it is "fit for action." Presumably the fact that iambic meter can be heard easily is related to the fact that it does not distort normal speech patterns. Some early commentators claim that its "beat" is strong and thus stands out in a din. Being "fit for action" is a little less obvious. "Action" may be simply a synonym for "acting" or "actions that occur in the course of a play." Later, for example, the speaker remarks (l. 179) that the story of a play is "either acted out on the stage or the acts are reported." If that meaning is assumed, the phrase further develops the idea that iambic meter sounds natural and is easy to understand in dialogue. Conversely, "action" may be a reference to the Aristotelian idea that a drama is an imitation of an action (*praxis*) that is whole and has a beginning, middle, and end. Aristotle calls iambic meter "actionlike" (*praktikon, Poetics*, XXIV.40). If this interpretation is correct, the speaker may be drawing attention to the relationship between iambic meter, dialogue, and the Aristotelian basis of drama in "action."

Drama is followed by lyric poetry, which is traditionally sung to the lyre. It is interesting that the speaker couples "lyric poetry" with the influence of a Muse. The allusion may be conventional, but it appears to admit the importance of something higher than reason in at least one kind of poetry, which is also the kind of poetry cultivated by Horace. Ancient lyrics were written in complex metrical forms. The initial list of lyric topics shows that the speaker thinks first of ornate and formal lyrics like those of Pindar (ca. 500 B.C.), whose poems celebrate athletic contests and praise the gods. The speaker then moves on to love and wine, themes common in later Greek poetry and common in the lyrics written by Horace.

The summary of the *ars metrica* ends with a series of rhetorical questions that underscore its importance to a would-be Roman poet. The key lesson is that meter and content are complementary. They are "fitting" in the sense that they fit together in an expressive and aesthetically pleasing way. This is another way of saying the poet must observe a decorum of meter to be successful. The speaker remarks that if he has not mastered this lesson he does not deserve the name of poet.

He adds an interesting and unanticipated observation. Nominally, tragedy and comedy are in the same (iambic) verse form, but the form is treated differently in the two genres. What is omitted from this comment is a familiar tradition that comic verse is so colloquial and so riddled with exceptions to metrical rules that it is close to everyday speech (e.g., Cicero, *Orator* 184), whereas tragic verse, though keeping to the norm of speech, is more formal in meter and in diction. The difference stems from the different subject matters of the two genres. Comedy treats the actions of low- and middle-class people, whereas tragedy treats the actions and destinies, usually fatal, of kings and princes. The story of Thyestes, who was tricked by Atreus into eating his own children, is a prime example. On the other hand, the rule differentiating comic and tragic verse cannot be applied mechanically. Comedy has its serious moments and tragedy is occasionally close to prose. The names Chremes, Telephus, and Peleus, who are mentioned here, appear in several plays. They may be referring to stock characters rather than to a specific drama. Surprisingly, he suggests that the moments when the tragic character speaks simply may be the most affecting. He also alludes playfully to the tendency of writers of tragic verse to inflate their style by using long compound words. The allusion makes it clear that the subject is still genre and meter rather than—say—style and emotion. *Sesquipedalia* (l. 97) does not have six "feet" but with six syllables it comes amusingly close.

The lesson is summarized in a very important rule: "Let each style keep the proper (*decens*) place allotted to it." *Decens* is related to *decorum*. As noted, the root meaning of this word, in contrast to *convenientia*, is "seemly." The idea seems to be that each style should "know its place." The idea of "fitting" style to subject is implicit but the language does not emphasize craftsmanship. We are closer here to Cicero's view of decorum than to *convenientia*.

If the passage from which this excerpt is taken is reviewed, decorum in both senses will be seen to run through it. The elements in the poem that have been mentioned and that must "fit together" include word choice, genre, subject matter, and meter. The relation of "fitting together" to the comments on unity at the beginning of the *Art* has already been noted. C.O. Brink remarks, "Among the basic axioms of the *Ars*, decorum ranks second only in importance to the basic distinction between style . . . and content" (*Prolegomena*, 228). Perhaps the "second only" phrase should be modified.

Brink considers the discussion of comedy and tragedy (ll. 89–98) the first part of a continuous discussion of decorum based directly or indirectly on chapter 7 of Book III of Aristotle's *Rhetoric*. Taking this position he reads the lines in question as a discussion of decorum based on situation. The second subject is decorum of emotion (ll. 99–107) and the third, decorum of character (ll. 108–18). This linkage to Aristotle is persuasive, but it requires lines 89–98 to be part of a "gliding transition" that carries forward the discussion of meter and genre while introducing the new topic of decorum of situation. The reading seems forced, and the position taken in the present commentary is that lines 89–98 are best understood as what they seem to be—a continuation of the discussion of ideas drawn from the *ars metrica*. As noted above, the playful reference to *sesquipedalia* (l. 98) seems to confirm the interpretation. This does not, of course, deny that the lines in question relate to the master topic of decorum or reject the idea that they are influenced by the discussion of "decorum of situation" in Aristotle's *Rhetoric*. They *do* relate to decorum, specifically to adjusting the "fitting together" of a single verse form (iambic trimeter) with two different genres (comedy and tragedy).

There has been no need to comment on the attitude of Horace's speaker since the introductory lines of the *Art*. He has remained self-confident and authoritative. In the present section, a suggestion of defensiveness enters the tone of his comments for the first time. The discussion of the *ars metrica* ends on a personal note. The speaker is no longer discussing rules objectively and sharing his insights with listeners who agree with him. Instead, he asks the listeners, and perhaps himself, "If I do not understand . . . these poetic forms, why should I be called a poet? Why . . . do I prefer to be ignorant rather than to learn?" The shift of mood is subtle but it is clearly marked by the personal reference and the rhetorical question. It is reinforced by observations that seem to undercut the very "laws" that have just been summarized: the simplest style is often the most affecting in tragedy in spite of the elevation of the form, and artificial diction (sesquipedalian words) leads to bombast, not elevation.

Lines 99–127: Emotion, Character, Invention
(Line 119: A New Section?)

The next few lines are a clear instance of "gliding transition." Discussion of meter has introduced the subject of emotion. Presumably, careful attention to meter gives a poem "beauty" (l. 99), which is a matter of observing the rules of art. Something more personal is needed to be "charming." To be charming is to captivate the audience, and to do this, the poet must feel the emotions being portrayed: "If you wish me to weep, you must feel sorrow yourself" (ll. 102–3). There is a similarity between this advice and the advice given in Aristotle's *Poetics* that "those are most persuasive who are involved in the emotions they imitate; for example one who is distressed conveys distress" (XVII.11–20). There is also a more general parallel between the discussion of emotion on the stage and the instructions in Aristotle's *Rhetoric* (II.1–11) on how the orator communicates emotion (Greek *pathos*) and the characteristics of various kinds of emotion. Most important, here and below there is the continuing parallel between the present material and Aristotle's chapter on decorum (*Rhetoric*, III.7).

The preceding interpretation seems straightforward, but it is complicated by the fact that the speaker has begun by addressing the listeners (or readers, presumably the Pisos) and then turns abruptly to address "Telephus and Peleus," who have just been cited above (l. 96) to illustrate the fact that tragic verse can be simple—almost prose—and yet still be affecting. The repetition of names emphasizes the transitional nature of the passage but confuses the reader. The Pisos seem to have disappeared. Is the speaker now giving indirect advice to those who will act the parts of Telephus and Peleus?

He is, at any rate, discussing the "fitting together" of emotion and circumstance, or, as Horace puts it, "fortune." Different circumstances cause us to experience different emotions like joy or anger or grief, and nature teaches us words appropriately fitted to our feelings. That is presumably how the poet invents emotionally convincing dialogue and how actors find the proper emotions to pour into the words when they are onstage.

Consideration of emotion leads the speaker to the circumstances that shape character and thus to the large and well defined topic of decorum of character based on gifts of nature and of fortune. Here some background will be useful. The word "character" is so common in modern

English that we assume, almost without thought, that we understand what it means. In fact, it is a complicated, mostly intuitive concept. Today we would probably emphasize psychological conditioning if asked to explain it. The Greeks and Romans took a different position. In *Poetics* XV Aristotle lists four requirements of character in tragedy. They are first, that character be "good"; second, that it be "appropriate"; third, that it be "like"; and fourth, that it be "consistent."

The requirement of goodness is related to Aristotle's idea that tragedy imitates "the better sort" of men and need not be examined further here since the *Art* contains no echo of it. The requirement that character be "appropriate" is more pertinent. Aristotle's word in the *Poetics* is "*harmottonta*," which is related to "harmony" and has the root meaning of "well joined," as in a carpenter's joint. It is probably this idea that is transmuted in Neoptolemus's remark about the need for harmony in a poetic composition (see above, p. 35). The requirement means that a "character" should be composed of traits that fit naturally together, as the notes in a musical chord fit together to form a harmony. The idea is the obverse of what Horace's speaker has in mind at the beginning of the *Art* when he warns against unnatural "mixes" and composites. Horace's speaker uses an overtly musical metaphor for the idea (ll. 112-13): if a character's words sound "discordant" (*absona*) the audience will "scoff."

Greeks and Romans tended to understand character in terms of standardized groups of traits related to large general categories. Female character, for example, is different from male character. Old people are different from young people. Kings are different from merchants, who are different from slaves. Categories are determined by nature or fortune. Being young, for example, is a matter of nature, since everyone must pass through youth. The specifics of one's life, however, are a matter of fortune. "By fortune," says Aristotle, "I mean birth, wealth, power, and their opposites—in fact, good fortune and ill fortune" (*Rhetoric*, II.12). Differences based on fortune include differences arising from geography and race (Cretan versus Athenian, Gaul versus Roman), social status (landowner versus beggar), profession (merchant versus sailor), ruling passion (miser, jealous husband), chance events (matron, widow), and the like.

In the *Rhetoric* (II.12-18; also III.7) Aristotle offers thumbnail sketches of several general character types, and his pupil Theophrastus invented a minor genre, the "character," which consists of sketches of specific types, usually with a witty or mildly satirical edge and made up essentially of lists of traits "appropriate" to the type being described. Such "characters" became stock types in Greek and later in Roman comedy. The speaker in the *Art* has this tradition in mind when he advises that the way a character speaks in a play must be consistent with his "fortunes" and adds by way of illustration brief references (ll. 114–17) to the characters of gods, heroes, old men, young men, noble ladies, a nurse, a merchant, an Assyrian, a Greek.

Aristotle notes in his discussion of character in the *Poetics* that a character should be "like." The question has always been "Like what?" The best explanation of the requirement is "like tradition" or "like life." "Like tradition" means like the character as presented in standard literary works. Penelope, for example, has a character that is well defined in the *Odyssey*. Penelope in a play about the suitors should be like Penelope in Homer. "Like life" means like people one knows. A Neapolitan in a play, for example, should be like Neapolitans one has met. Finally, there is the requirement that characters be consistent, which includes the suggestion that if they are inconsistent, they should be consistently inconsistent.

We now encounter a problem in interpretation. Line 119 is considered by many commentators the beginning of a new section of the *Art*. Typically, line 119 is identified as the transition from the section that Neoptolemus of Parium considers *poesis* (or in Brink's reading, *poema*) to the section on *poema* (or *poesis*). In plain language, the transition is from a discussion of general rules—unity, decorum, and the like—to a discussion of rules for specific genres.

This is not the position taken in the present commentary. The argument *against* regarding line 119 as the beginning of a new section is that the discussion of general rules for character development that precedes line 119 leads directly to the discussion of how the poet should follow the rules in lines 119–27. If this observation is valid, it strengthens the argument of Niall Rudd and others that the influence of Neoptolemus's three categories on the organization of the *Art* has been exaggerated. If a major transition is essential, it might be located at line 128, where there is a turn from character to plot, but this option is weakened by a later passage (ll. 153–78) that returns to characterization. Alternately, a major transition might be located at line 179, where there is a clear and emphatic turning from methods of creating plot and character to drama as a genre. This section is a likely candidate for Neoptolemus's *poema* if one is necessary.

The passage on character that begins on line 119 depends on and follows from the notions of appropriateness, likeness, and consistency. In line 119 the poet is given an option: follow tradition or invent. The poet (in this case, pretty clearly, the dramatist) who follows tradition is advised to stick to the characters as they have been established in earlier literature. This is an echo of Aristotle's requirement that characters be "like" the traditions established for them in earlier literature. A list of famous personages from Homer and mythology is included: Achilles, Medea, Ino, Ixion, Io, Orestes. Conversely, the poet who decides to invent is told to make his characters "self-consistent." The requirement echoes Aristotle's fourth requirement (consistency) and is related to the general emphasis of the *Art* on decorum. The idea is so important that it is repeated at the end of the passage (l. 127). No further advice is given, however, on the specifics of invention.

Lines 128–52: Invention versus Imitation
("Common Themes" and Universals)

Again there is something like a gliding transition. The discussion of traditional versus invented characters leads to the traditional versus the invented plot. Aristotle discusses invented plots in chapter IX of the *Poetics*. Poetry is "more philosophical than history" because it is concerned with universals rather than specifics. It can therefore create probable plots and assign names at will to the agents (the figures who act out the plot). This happens regularly in comedy, where the plots are freely invented and the agents are given "any names that happen to occur" to the poets. In tragedy the standard practice is to use a few well-known characters and myths, but there is no objection in principle to a purely fictional tragedy. Aristotle illustrates the point by citing the *Antheus* of Agathon, an entirely fictional tragedy.

There is a distant echo of this line of reasoning in the *Art*. The speaker remarks that "it is difficult to treat common themes in one's own way." "Common themes" (*communia*) is notoriously ambiguous. Does it mean "community property" or (as the *Ars* puts it) "public material" (l. 131)—that is, the myths that everybody uses? Evidently not, since the next clause suggests that to escape from "common themes," the poet can write about Troy, which is, of course, at the center of the "public" mythological material. What are "common themes" then? The best answer is that "common" means "universal." The speaker is saying that it is difficult to create plots based on universals—that is, fictional plots—and that it is much easier to write about the standard mythological topics. The term "universal" (Greek *katholou*) comes directly or indirectly from chapter IX of the *Poetics*. According to Horace's speaker, because of the difficulty of treating "common themes," the best formula for literary success is to treat well-known myths in new ways but to avoid imitation so close to the original that it is almost word-for-word translation.

The background here would seem to be the contrast between free and slavish imitation, and it is made relevant by the fact that earlier Roman poets imitated Greek originals so closely that their compositions were often essentially free translations. Their motive was to supply Latin literature with works as rich as those available to the Greeks. They were determined to transform Roman culture, and copying seemed to be acceptable in view of the urgency of the task. In more or less the same way, sixteenth-century English humanists undertook wholesale translations from Latin and Italian originals in order to enrich English culture. By Horace's time, however, the limits of imitation by copying were apparent. Vergil's *Aeneid* is the prime example of a work that "imitates" Homeric originals while, at the same time, remaining uniquely Roman and uniquely Vergilian.

Imitation in this sense is a compromise between following a model closely and inventing from whole cloth. Variations on the model's style or plot or list of characters or on the characters themselves require a certain degree of free invention.

The passage continues with illustrations of how to imitate while being original (in contrast to invention based entirely on "common themes"). It incorporates an Aristotelian precept from *Poetics* VIII: do not write your story "from the beginning." Concentrate instead on a single action and bring in other material later. Like Aristotle (again *Poetics* VIII), the *Art* cites the "cyclic poets" who wrote about the fall of Troy. It is clear that before and after Homer there were numerous epics that, put together, formed an informal "cycle" that told the whole story of the fall of Troy. In a similar way there are "cycles" of medieval stories and poems about King Arthur and "cycles" of folk ballads about the border wars between England and Scotland.

Aristotle's and Horace's speakers agree that unlike Homer, the cyclic poets began their stories at the beginning and promised to tell everything. A "cyclic" first line that includes Priam, his fate, and the whole Trojan War is contrasted by the speaker with a Latin translation of the first two lines of the *Odyssey*, which promise only a recounting of the travels of Ulysses after Troy's fall. A good beginning, he says, is like light shining in the darkness. Homer's beginning is modest (thus a kind of darkness), but it is the prelude to fabulous and wonderful stories (the light).

The speaker cites the story of Scylla to illustrate fabulous stories. It is an odd choice in view of the warning at the beginning of the *Art* against "mixed" images like a woman with a fish's extremities. In spite of the fact that such images are apparently part of the "light" shining from the heart of Homer's poems, the speaker does not seem to approve of them. He calls them "specious miracles" (*speciosa miracula*, l. 144), which is hardly complimentary. One justification for them may be that in a primitive work—and Homer is to a degree primitive in spite of his brilliance—fabulous monsters are acceptable in the same way that witches are acceptable in fairy tales but would be out of place in a realistic novel. At any rate, the fact that Homer conceals his "light" at the beginning returns the speaker to the subject of organization. The poet should not follow chronological order. If he is treating the material of Troy, he should not begin from the twin egg out of which Helen of Troy was born (*ab ovo*, l. 147) but should enter into the middle of the action (*in medias res*, l. 148).

The "twin egg" recalls the story that Leda was seduced by Zeus, who came to her in the form of a swan, and gave birth to an egg from which Helen appeared on the one hand and Castor and Polydeuces on the other. The myth symbolizes the temptation to push back the beginning of a story to its remotest beginnings. It is better to enter "into the middle of things." Homer does not tell the whole story of the fall of Troy, only the part of it related to "the wrath of Achilles." Likewise, his *Odyssey* begins with a Ulysses who has already been wandering for nine years after the fall of Troy and has been washed up on Calypso's island. In the same way Vergil's *Aeneid* begins with Aeneas and his crew washed up on the shores of Carthage. Largely because Horace's advice had become almost a law of epic by the seventeenth century, Milton began *Paradise Lost* with the bad angels in hell and only later (in Books V and

VI) does he have the angel Raphael tell how the bad angels were expelled from heaven.

We move from methods of beginning to the invention of episodes. Creating new variations on old stories and shaping the result into effective plots require "mixing the false with the true." Presumably the speaker means by "the false" what a poet adds to a received myth. It is "false" because it is not recorded in the source. In much the same way, Shakespeare invented Falstaff and added him to the English history that is presented in *Henry IV, Part I*. The process is called "lying" (l. 151). Plato had complained that poets lie, and this is one reason he banished them from his republic. Horace's speaker treats the process as a virtue. "Lying" here means something like "composing fiction." Aristotle had already offered more or less the same answer to Plato and even remarks at one point that Homer taught later poets the art of skillful lying (*Poetics* XXIV.65-70). Aristotle is also recalled (*Poetics* VII.1-10) in the observation that the skillful poet will produce a work with a beginning, middle, and end. Horace's speaker notes that the three should be blended together and not be "discordant." The reference recalls the early injunctions to avoid unnatural mixtures and to seek that which is "simple and unified." The ultimate source, doubtless modified by Alexandrian intermediaries, may be the rule that the beginning, middle, and end of any work should be related by probability or necessity (*Poetics* VII).

Lines 153-78: Character: Four Ages of Man

The *Art* now returns to an earlier topic—character. To be successful, the dramatic poet must make the speech of each character appropriate in the sense of well fitted to the character's status. Here "appropriateness" is specifically identified with decorum (l. 157), and status is interpreted in terms of age. Four characters typifying four ages of man (child, youth, mature man, old man) are sketched. Similar sketches are common in Greek and Roman rhetoric beginning with chapters 12-14 of the second book of Aristotle's *Rhetoric*, and the tradition was still sufficiently lively in the sixteenth century to produce the well-known speech on "the seven ages of man" by Jaques in Shakespeare's *As You Like It*. The present sketches consist essentially of lists of related ("well-fitted") traits that are associated with each general character type described. They are skillful, although they do not improve on the sketches of the three (or four) ages in Aristotle's *Rhetoric* and other ancient sources. The main problem is that they seem to add nothing to what has already been said about character (ll. 112–30). Why are they added here?

One difference between the present sketches and those given earlier (ll. 112–30) is the distinction between "traits based on nature," which are independent of the circumstances of the individual's life, and those based on "fortune," which vary with each individual's experiences. Here the emphasis is on nature. Everyone who is born goes through "youth," and anyone who lives long enough will experience "old age." The initial discussion of character included the option of inventing or following tradition. Since tradition supplies specifics about characters who appear in myths (e.g., Penelope was faithful; Achilles was temperamental and had a vulnerable heel), it allows characterization based on "gifts of fortune." Since "gifts of nature" are independent of fortune, they are like "common themes" and permit invention independent of tradition. If this line of analysis is valid, the discussion of the ages of man completes the topic of inventing characters introduced on line 119.

Lines 179–94: Characteristics and History of Drama

Over one hundred lines are devoted to drama. The sheer quantity of this material in comparison to the *Art* as a whole has led commentators to ask whether it is not included because the Pisos were especially interested in writing plays. This is possible, of course, but there is no way of knowing. All that we know from the *Art* is that they wanted advice about poetry in general. An odd aspect of this section on drama, however, is that in spite of its length and detail, it is devoted to a literary genre that Horace never cultivated, although he undoubtedly enjoyed going to plays and was pleased by the success of his friend Varius as a tragedian. Odder still is the long comment to the Pisos (ll. 234–50) implying that the speaker takes seriously the idea of writing a Satyr Play. If additional evidence were needed of the difference between Horace the poet and the speaker of the *Ars* this passage would supply it. There is not a shred of evidence anywhere else in his work that Horace was interested in writing Satyr Plays; and, in fact, the form was almost totally ignored by Augustan authors.

Most of the information included in the section on drama is handbook material. A good deal of it goes back in one way or another to Aristotle's *Poetics*, but here as elsewhere it has been modified by intermediate sources. Some of these are close in time to Aristotle, including Aristotle's own treatise "On Poets." Others are doubtless Alexandrian, including Neoptolemus of Parium. Direct Roman sources such as Varro's *On Poets* are also relevant, since much of the passage is concerned with specifically Roman dramatic forms. In sum, the passage is a mosaic of mostly standard information. This does not mean it is insignificant. No extant Roman discussion of drama before Horace is as comprehensive.

Lines 195–201: Various Tragic Rules

The passage begins with a tragic convention: Scenes of horror and of magic are narrated rather than acted out on the stage. The convention stems from the feeling that cruel and bloody events like Medea's murder of her children or Oedipus's self-blinding should be hidden from the audience. It is ironic that at the time tragedies were avoiding public violence, spectacles in the Roman arena involving mortal combat of gladiators and wild animals attacking humans were gaining popularity, but Horace's speaker has nothing to say on this score. Seneca (d. A.D. 65) observed the convention of offstage violence in his tragedies, and it became standard in neoclassical tragedy as written, for example, by Corneille and Racine. It is strikingly ignored in Shakespearean tragedy, in, for example, the assassination scene in *Julius Caesar* and the blinding scene in *King Lear*. In twentieth-century film and television, gratuitous and graphic violence is the rule rather than the exception. Refusal to stage magic scenes like the transformation of Procne into a nightingale may reflect the dislike, evident at the beginning of the *Art*, for mixing human and animal elements. However, the passage may be influenced less by feelings of propriety than by the difficulty of managing the effect onstage and the risk that a poor showing would be ludicrous.

Other rules are listed: plays should be five acts; the temptation to resolve the action by having a "god from a machine" intervene at the end should be avoided; no more than three speaking characters should be on the stage at one time. The list is miscellaneous. No principle unites the three rules. They are not explained but baldly asserted. A determined commentator might trace the five-act rule to a convention beginning with Aristotle's suggestion in *Poetics* VII that a tragedy should be reasonably compact ("have a certain magnitude") and add to this his discussion of the "quantitative parts" of drama (*Poetics* XII). However, the fact is that the five-act rule is late in Greek tradition and only intermittently valid for earlier Roman drama. It is observed by Seneca, who wrote after Horace, and it became a rule amounting to law for neoclassical drama. Whether Shakespeare observed it or not is a matter of dispute (the editions of the plays printed before 1623 usually have no act divisions); in general, however, his plays divide into five units, and most of the plays in the First Folio of 1623 are so divided. This evidence suggests that Horace's *Art* was a primary influence in establishing five acts as the normal length of a play.

The "god from the machine" rule can be traced quite specifically to Aristotle's insistence that in the best tragedies events are controlled from "within the plot" and should follow each other according to probability and necessity, a condition that is violated by divine intervention, as happens in the tragedy *Medea* (*Poetics* XV.25–35). The three-character rule is a reminiscence of an often-repeated tradition that Thespis invented the tragic protagonist, Aeschylus added a second character (making true dialogue possible), and Sophocles added a third, bringing tragedy, as Aristotle remarks (*Poetics* 4), to "its [proper] magnitude." The meaning of the rule is not that only three characters can be in the play—all extant Greek tragedies have more than three characters. It is, rather, that no more than three characters can have speaking parts in a given scene, although more can be onstage.

The chorus now catches the attention of Horace's speaker. Roman comedies no longer included a chorus. Tragedy, however, retained it. Ancient critics believed, probably rightly, that tragedy developed out of choral liturgies and that the chorus was older than drama itself. When drama had emerged, there was initially only one character, who carried on an antiphonal dialogue with the chorus. In the tragedies of Aeschylus, where two actors can be onstage at the same time, the chorus remains important and often speaks directly to one of the characters. In general, the early chorus speaks in passionate lyric tones and is deeply—almost liturgically—involved in the action.

Gradually the chorus was rationalized. Horace's speaker lists typical roles it played in later tragedy: giving advice, praising goodness, expressing shock over evil and grief over suffering, praying to the gods for salvation of the protagonist or of the city. His main point is that the chorus should behave like an actor, which is exactly the point made by Aristotle near the end of *Poetics* XVIII: "It is necessary to consider the chorus as one of the actors and as an integral part of the drama." Aristotle goes on to observe that the chorus is often superfluous and that choral songs are often inserted arbitrarily. The advice may be recalled in the remark by Horace's speaker that the chorus should not "sing" anything between acts that is not related to the plot.

Lines 202–19: Music

Mention of the chorus leads to the music that accompanied it. The comments here are partly historical, but the history is heavily influenced by the speaker's moral attitudes. Although historically the choruses of the earliest tragedies to survive (those written by Aeschylus) are anything but plain in diction, the speaker implies that florid diction and elaborate lyricism were late developments and associated with moral decline. Music reflects this situation. A sober and restrained form of music is "fitted to" a sober and restrained audience. A loud and florid music is "fitted to" a drunken and unruly audience and an inflated literary style. Associated with the decadent phase of drama are singers who move over the stage in fancy robes and actors who speak in proverbs and Delphic prophecies (ll. 215–18). Of interest in relation to the speaker's attitude toward the Augustan age is the fact that one of the causes of moral decline is said to be expansion by "a conquering race" (l. 208). Nominally the topic is early Greek drama, but the parallel to Augustan Rome is obvious and reinforced by the many references in Horace's satires to the decadence of Roman life.

Again, the speaker deserves attention. He is becoming less detached from his subject—less the friendly, self-assured mentor—and more involved in what he is describing. His history of drama is the story of movement from a morally upright rural community to an urban society more interested in drinking and "luxurious movement" (l. 214) than in serious drama. Neither Horace nor his speaker seem to have been anti-imperialists, but military expansion is explicitly cited (l. 208) as one of the factors that led to social corruption. As society became corrupt, drama followed, becoming loud, vulgar, and pretentious. Thus art, which is properly a civilizing force, became another means of spreading the general blight. The comments are about Greek drama, but the tone of moral judgment is the speaker's. He is an outsider peering in at society and unhappy with what he sees.

Lines 220–50: Satyr Play

The discussion of music is followed by a summary of the rise of the Satyr Play from village festivals. Aristotle includes some of the same details in *Poetics* IV.

The etymology of "tragedy" is *tragos* ("goat") and *ode* ("song"). The term is said to have originated because in village dramatic competitions the winning poet was awarded a goat as the prize. Horace's speaker associates these contests with Satyrs, and hence with comic raillery, rowdy behavior, and drunkenness. The short, generally rowdy form of drama known as "Satyr Play" was thought to be a remnant of this stage of the history of drama. A Satyr Play was regularly presented at the Greek dramatic festivals after three tragedies. Although the form was popular, only one complete example has survived, *The Cyclops* by Euripides. It was a minor, almost insignificant form in Rome. The early commentator Acron says that a writer named Pomponius wrote Satyr Plays, but the reference may be erroneous, and at any rate no Roman Satyr Play has survived. A typical Satyr Play included comic and serious elements. Roles were assigned to gods and heroes, and Horace's speaker warns that they should be treated respectfully and not degraded. According to Aristotle and other ancient historians of drama, the Satyr Play was a stage in the development of tragedy. Aristotle (*Poetics* IV) says that it used brief plots, absurd diction, and trochaic verse—a form more suited to dance than to speech. Horace's speaker agrees that tragedy had to separate itself from the Satyr Play's "trivial verses" (l. 231) in order to achieve its proper stature.

Having said all this, the speaker turns back to Satyr Plays as though they were the stock-in-trade of the Roman dramatist. Addressing the Pisos, he announces that if *he* writes a Satyr Play (implying that he very well might) he will use somewhat elevated diction, will differentiate in his dialogue between speakers who are essentially comic, like the stock characters Davus and Simo, and speakers who are noble or divine, like Silenus, the father of the Satyrs and, as the allusion to his having a divine charge recalls (l. 239), guardian of the young Dionysus. Silenus is a character in *The Cyclops* by Euripides. The play itself is brief and combines serious moments with the grotesque drunkenness of Polyphemus. Even when writing a Satyr Play, says the speaker, he will follow the rule of decorum. For example, a Faun (i.e., a forest-bred Satyr) will not behave like a city-bred punk. Even though the lower classes like crude behavior, better-educated spectators find it offensive. The idea that only the few are competent judges of art is implicit in much of the *Art*. It is, in fact, the unstated assumption behind the relationship between the speaker and the Pisos. It becomes overt here and later in the poem.

Lines 251–74: Versification; Iambic Trimeter

The speaker moves on to the verse form of comedy and tragedy. As we have already learned (ll. 80–82), the basic form is the iamb. Ancient dramatic verse was regarded as "dipodal." That is, two iambs were considered to make one foot. There were six iambs in a standard line of dramatic dialogue, so it was called "iambic trimeter"—three units of two iambs each. On the other hand the ictus occurs six times in an iambic trimeter line. (To make things more complicated, Romans, in contrast to Greeks, sometimes considered the trimeter line a line of six iambic feet called a *senarius*.)

Another feature of dramatic verse is that substitution was allowed in the predominantly iambic pattern. Very liberal substitution was allowed in the comic line—so much so that the line written by the Roman comic dramatist Terence was called by the grammarian Priscian "almost indistinguishable from prose." This line was thought to be close to colloquial speech and hence appropriate to the lower- and middle-class characters featured in ancient comedy. Substitution was also permitted in the tragic line. However, since tragedy is more elevated than comedy and features gods, heroes, and monarchs, its line should be more formal. The substitution of a spondee (two long syllables: --) for the first, third, or fifth iamb was considered "weighty" and therefore appropriate for tragedy.

Horace's speaker summarizes all of this lore (ll. 251–58) and relates it to the work of the two most famous of the older Roman tragedians. Accius (d. ca. 86 B.C.) wrote "noble" lines but seldom substituted a spondee. Ennius (d. 169 B.C.) wrote bombastic and careless verses. We never learn whether or not Ennius used spondees, but his carelessness leads the speaker to note that so many Romans are indifferent to prosody, Roman poets can be careless without fear of criticism. This makes him indignant and leads to rhetorical questions directed to the Pisos. "Should I do slipshod work, he says, merely because nobody will notice it?" The answer is obvious.

Turning to the Pisos, he advises them to study Greek models "night and day" (l. 269). The line is famous and is usually misunderstood. It is not a call for full-scale imitation of Greek literary forms. Although the speaker approves imitation of these forms and calls later (l. 310) for the study of Greek philosophy, the present line urges imitation of Greek versification, especially dramatic versification. Plautus, who wrote comedies (d. 184 B.C.), was among the most popular of all Roman writers. The Pisos claim (or the speaker thinks they will claim) that what was good enough for Plautus is good enough for them. Unfortunately, Plautus does not measure up. His wit is coarse and, more to the point, his verse is slipshod—an allusion to the freedom of comic versification.

The speaker again becomes a part of the statement. He explicitly criticizes the Romans for their indifference to artistry (in this case, artistic prosody). A defensive note can be heard in his rhetorical question about doing slipshod work. The comment calls attention to the indifference of most Romans to the effort of the artist on their behalf. Given this situation, it is understandable that the speaker should need to reassure himself that the Pisos, at least, agree with him.

Lines 275-94: Tragedy and Comedy; Roman Poets

There follows a curiously brief comment on the development of tragedy and comedy. Thespis (fl. 6th c. B.C.) is said to have invented tragedy when he changed the leader of the Dionysian chorus into an historical hero and, by extension, the liturgy of the god into plot about the hero's mythic or historical deeds. Horace's speaker implies this in the reference to discovering "the tragic Muse" (l. 275), but he concentrates on the tradition that the original Thespians carried their plays about on wagons and performed with their faces smeared with wine-lees. The latter detail, odd to a modern reader, depends on a false etymology of "tragedy" from *truges* ("wine-lees") and *ode* ("song").

Next in the tragic line comes Aeschylus. Aristotle (*Poetics* IV) notes that Aeschylus added a second actor, making true dialogue possible and reducing the importance of the chorus. Horace's speaker ignores the second actor and the chorus but mentions other innovations: the tragic mask, the flowing tragic robe (Greek *syrma*, Latin *pallium*), a wooden stage, and, most important, the magniloquence of great poetry. For some reason the history of tragedy ends here. Sophocles and Euripides are ignored. We turn directly to the form of comedy called Old Comedy.

In the handbooks Old Comedy is said to be characterized by bitter invective directed at real people. Aristophanes (d. 385 B.C.) is not mentioned although he is the only writer of Old Comedy whose plays have survived in more than fragments. His tone is flamboyant, often outrageous and ribald. Although the list of his characters includes gods, heroes, clouds, birds, and frogs, he also includes historical characters, most notoriously, perhaps, Socrates in *The Clouds*.

According to Greek tradition, which simplifies history in this case, Old Comedy grew so offensive that it was eventually replaced by New Comedy, which abandoned satire of specific individuals and turned instead to satirizing general types like the miser and the boasting soldier. The chief Greek writer in this form is Menander (d. ca. 291 B.C.). The Roman comedies of Plautus and Terence are based on Menander's work. None of these details is included in the *Art*. The single detail noted is that the New Comedy abandoned the chorus.

Turning to Rome the speaker boasts that native poets have tried all Greek forms. He makes clear in his comments what Horace puts into a memorable epigram in *Epistles* (II, 1): "Captured Greece, captured her savage victor and brought the arts to backward Italy." He has no difficulty admitting that Roman culture rests on Greek achievement. However, he is proud that Romans have invented forms of their own. Tragedies that deal with Roman history rather than Greek mythology are called *fabulae praetextae* (l. 288) because a Roman garment, the *toga praetexta*, was worn by the actors. By the same token, comedies on specifically Roman themes were called *fabulae togatae* because the actors wore togas. One problem remains. It has been mentioned in connection with Ennius (l. 259) and Plautus (ll. 270-71). Roman poets are inclined to be careless. Again the speaker turns to the Pisos to address them directly. They should, he says, reject any poem that has not been revised and polished "ten times" (l. 294) down to the finest detail ("to the fingernail," l. 294).

Lines 295-476: Overview—The Poet-Critic

Line 255 marks the beginning of a major new section of the *Art*. Almost all commentators have recognized it. Eduard Norden regards it as the second part of a treatise divided between art (*ars*) and artist (*artifex*). Since the arrival of Neoptolemus of Parium on the scene of Horatian criticism, the section has generally been identified with what Neoptolemus called "poet" (*poeta*). Etymologically, Greek *poeta* means "maker" and Latin *artifex* means "craftsman." The labels are so close that it is unnecessary to argue about them. They both recognize that the *Art* now turns from poetry to the preparation of the poet and the task of the critic. In the process, the focus shifts from the poet as creator to the poet as authority on poetic matters and therefore to the poet as critic.

The mood of the speaker also changes. In the first part of the *Art* it is neutral or friendly, with the speaker in the role of mentor or informal teacher. Occasionally, as in his remarks about writing Satyr Plays, he turns from art in general to his own artistic standards, and on such occasions a defensive note sometimes can be heard in his comments. At times, too, he becomes critical of Roman culture or of Roman artistic standards.

In the second half of the *Art* the speaker distances himself from his pupils. He becomes ironic, satirical, occasionally morose, and toward the end downright indignant. He becomes less the teacher in the sense of one who explains principles and encourages talent and more the critic in the sense of one who identifies errors and vices. He also becomes increasingly self-absorbed. Toward the end of the *Art* he expresses open contempt for those who seek his advice.

Are these changes part of the character of the speaker or are they comments by Horace the poet? The argument for a biographical interpretation is supported by the fact that Horace announced plans to give up poetry after the third book of his *Odes*, although he later changed his mind. In like manner, the poet-critic of the *Art* announces (ll. 305-6) that he has given up writing.

The decision to give up writing may well have been accompanied by, even caused by, a feeling of revulsion on Horace's part against the direction his art and life had taken. The *Art* might have been partly or wholly composed while this feeling was strong. However, it is impossible to say for sure what Horace the poet felt. It is therefore safest to note the change in the character of the speaker without insisting on biographical parallels. Whatever did or did not happen to Horace, the speaker of the *Art* unquestionably changes. His concept of art becomes exclusive and elitist: only the few who are truly creative appreciate art. It also becomes self-contradictory. If only the few who are truly creative can appreciate art and they appreciate it already, what is the point of becoming a critic? Who will the critic teach? By corollary, if only a few sensitive readers appreciate art, what difference can art make? Why make such sacrifices to create it? This question is especially relevant if the few sensitive readers of Augustan Rome are the same few who are systematically destroying the last vestiges of the republic and encouraging the mumbo-jumbo of emperor worship.

Lines 295–332: Talent versus Art; Learning

The section on the poet-critic begins with a tradition central to the idea of how the poet, himself, contributes to the creative process. In most primitive poetry, including the Hebrew psalms, the Homeric hymns, the odes of Pindar and the *Iliad* and *Odyssey*, the poet attributes the poem to a higher power called a Muse and equated, in general, with inspiration.

Related to inspiration is another, imponderable talent (Latin *ingenium*, sometimes translated "genius" or "wit"). Talent is something we are born with. It is a gift of nature and cannot be learned. Rhetoric and poetics teach that writing is an art—a technique that can be mastered by following rules. *The Art of Poetry* is in this tradition and reflects the fact by the profusion of rules that the speaker lays down. But what good are the rules if success depends on talent?

Another side of the argument about what the orator or poet needs to be successful debated the value of technical rules in contrast to general learning. The tradition that begins with Aristotle's *Rhetoric* emphasizes mastery of technical rules. These can be used for any specific subject or "content," and for that reason they are more important to the orator than mastery of content. Isocrates and Cicero opposed this position. They argued that general learning (or "doctrine") is essential to the orator. The learning should include history and poetry, but ethical and political philosophy are the most important subjects because the secret of great oratory is a large vision of human life. Cicero's *De oratore* is essentially a dialogue in which one speaker—Crassus—argues for general learning, and another—Antonius—argues for rules and technique. The debate is not resolved, but the balance is clearly in favor of learning, even though the value of rules and technique is recognized.

The terms used in Roman rhetoric to discuss these ideas are "talent" (*ingenium*), "art" (*ars*), and "doctrine" (*doctrina*). Two other relevant terms are "imitation" in the sense of imitating models (*imitatio*) and "exercise" (*exercitatio*), meaning experience gained from practice.

The treatment in the *Art* opens with the topic of talent versus art.

The Greek philosopher Democritus (d. ca. 370 B.C.) favored talent and associated poetry with a kind of delirium, thus excluding "healthy" poets (l. 296) from the highest artistic achievement. As the author of an "art" of poetry and a teacher of this art to the Pisos, Horace's speaker is distressed. Instead of refuting Democritus, he ridicules poets who believe this sort of thing. They are introverts; they never take baths; worst of all, they never have haircuts. The speaker, himself, rather pompously announces that he takes hellebore—a strong purgative drug—every spring to ensure a sweet and reasonable disposition. Hellebore was usually shipped to Rome from Anticyra on the Gulf of Corinth. The crazy poets the speaker is attacking could not be helped, he says, if they took hellebore from three Anticyras.

The speaker's reference to purgation may be ironic. He may be saying, "If you have to be mad to write poetry, I want none of it; in fact I purge myself every spring in order to be sure of staying sane." More probably, the speaker has become so upset that he has begun to talk about himself. He announces that he is a reasonable man: he purges himself of bile in the spring, and he writes good poems. But the effort to be reasonable adds up to nothing. Throughout the letter to the Pisos the speaker has been proclaiming the need of the would-be poet for rational artistry. Yet people still claim, like Democritus, that poetry is purely a matter of talent.

Recognition of the futility of his arguments in favor of reason pushes the speaker to a logical and emotional impasse. He exclaims despairingly, "It's not worthwhile!" (l. 304). The sentence expresses frustration. It is followed by a startling decision. The speaker announces he will give up poetry and become a critic of others. Specifically, he will correct prevalent errors by explaining the duty (*officium*, l. 306) of the poet and the kinds of learning the poet needs.

This is a dramatic moment in the *Art*. The interaction between the social conditions of Augustan Rome and the speaker's personality force the poem to veer in a new direction. The Pisos seem momentarily to be forgotten. If we take the speaker seriously, the moment is self-destructive: he rejects the roles of poet and mentor that have provided his identity up to this point in the poem. Should we take the speaker seriously? Different readers will have different answers, but the lines in question are striking in their content and style. They are surely more than a device to introduce a debate between the claims of talent and art.

The plan (ll. 306–8) to explain where the poet draws his sustenance includes four topics: the duty of the poet, the source of his materials, what nurtures him, and poetic flaws. These topics conform generally to standard rhetorical topics, supplemented in the case of "poetic flaws" by the discussion in *Poetics* XXV of artistic faults and their answers. The duty of the poet is defined as pleasure and utility (ll. 333ff.). The source of his materials is imitation (317ff.). Learning nurtures the poet (ll. 309ff.). Flaws are discussed in detail in lines 347ff. Additional topics with a rhetorical background are talent (or nature) versus art (323ff., 408ff.), the perfect poet (347ff.), and the civilizing power of art (391ff.). Decorum enters this list of topics on line 308, which speaks of teaching "what is appropriate" (*quid deceat*).

The first subject treated is the nurturing power of learning. Knowledge is the source and wellspring of good writing. The reference to "Socratic pages" (l. 310) makes it clear that the knowledge is philosophy and that it is "general philosophy" concerned with ethics and politics rather than technical subjects like logic. The speaker lists examples: patriotism, friendship, statesmanship, leadership. His position is much like that taken by Crassus regarding the kind of learning needed by the orator in Book I of Cicero's *De oratore*. Decorum also appears in the passage. A broad knowledge of philosophy allows the poet to achieve a proper "coming together" (*convenientia*) of traits and responsibilities in his characters. Note that the focus is still on drama, although the topic applies to poetry in general.

Still concentrating on drama, the speaker cites another kind of learning important to the poet. In addition to philosophy there is imitation. For the most part, imitation has been presented in the *Art* as imitation of other (usually Greek) literary works. Here the speaker returns to imitation of life or of nature, the kind of imitation suggested by his ridicule in the first few lines of unnatural combinations like a woman with the torso of a fish. Life is the great model (*exemplar*, l. 317) for the poet, and as such is the source of "living voices." The speaker agrees that a play drawing on life may please an audience—even though it lacks formal art (l. 320)—more than one that is studied and artificial.

The admission comes in the midst of a strong argument in favor of artistry. Perhaps the speaker is simply showing that he is broad-minded. Probably, however, he is setting up a contrast between nature and art in which nature has precedence but art remains essential. A like interpretation seems appropriate for the comments about the talent (*ingenium*, l. 323) of the Greeks. The idea of Democritus that talent is the key to po-

etic success was so repugnant to the speaker a few lines previously that
it led him to abandon poetry. Now, however, he seems to admit that
the talent of the Greeks was the basis of their artistic success.

To make matters worse, the source of Greek talent is said to be the
Muse. Which Muse, exactly, is left vague, but unquestionably some
Muse, and with the Muse comes the idea of inspiration. The talented
Greeks who seem to write by a divine gift are then contrasted to Romans who spend their time doing laborious arithmetic lessons. What
are arithmetic lessons if not a path to the mastery of an art? But the art
is accounting, symbolic of avarice. Roman money grubbing effectively
stifles the ability to create the kind of poetry that is preserved in a spe-
cially carved box—the Roman equivalent to a leather binding.

The discussion seems to favor nature and talent rather than art. Is
this the speaker's meaning or has he made such a strong case for art that
it is time to admit the opposing arguments are not entirely without
virtue? The precedent of Cicero's *De oratore* favors this idea. All of
Cicero's speakers have valid points to make, and there is no synthesis at
the end to tell the reader how much weight to give to any given position. Yet the main thrust of Cicero's argument is clear enough. No orator can be successful without native talent, nor can the orator ignore
nature. Talent and nature, however, are givens. Insofar as oratory can
be learned, it is an art. Horace's speaker seems to take a similar position. This interpretation is not entirely satisfying, but it makes the best
of a passage as difficult in its way as the discussion of the Satyr Play.

Two other observations are relevant. First, the reference to the talent
of the Greeks reflects the sense of cultural inferiority of Romans con-
fronting Greek culture. Quite apart from the massive direct debt of
Rome to Greece in every field from science to poetry, the best the Romans had been able to achieve was, by their own admission, based on
Greek models. Second, the sense of cultural inferiority is reflected in the
contrast between the noble achievements of the Greeks, symbolized by a
noble avarice for "nothing but fame," and the ignoble avarice (*cura pe-
culi*) of Romans for money.

Lines 333–46: Profit and Delight

The office of the orator, according to Cicero's *Orator* is to teach, to
please, and to persuade (*docere, delectare, movere*). Horace's speaker offers a similar goal for the poet: "the poet's task is to profit or delight"

(l. 333). It is a famous line. Although it is disjunctive (*"either* one *or* the other"), the discussion that follows shows that the best poetry does both, so the translation "profit . . . *and* delight" accords with the spirit of the passage as a whole. "Profit" is usually equated with moral teaching; delight with the pleasures of verse, metaphor, and story.

The interpretation is valid. The poet, we are told, should offer materials that are helpful. The process is interpreted as a kind of teaching (l. 335), and the teaching should be kept brief so that it is the more easily absorbed. Having commented on profit, the speaker turns to pleasure, which he equates with fiction. Just possibly, he is recalling the discussion of invented plots (ll. 119-39), since he advises that they be closer to truth rather than to "accepted myths." He is, at any rate, still talking about drama, and the topic brings him back to the image of the serpent Lamia giving birth to a child (l. 340). Some things, whether mythic or fictional, will not play. Qualified judges—another appeal to upper-class spectators (*Ramnes*, l. 342)—will reject them.

The idea that poetry should profit and delight was central in sixteenth- and seventeenth-century criticism. It seemed to fit neatly with Aristotle's suggestion in *Poetics* IX that poetry is "more serious and more philosophical" than history. A classic example of this line of thought is found in Sir Philip Sidney's *Defence of Poesie* (ca. 1585). Drawing on the *Poetics* and on standard interpretations of Horace, Sidney makes two points. First, poetry couples general moral truths drawn from philosophy with specific stories from mythology and history. If a story violates ethical norms—if, for example, a tyrant lives a long and happy life instead of suffering for his crimes—the poet changes it so that the outcome illustrates poetic justice. Tyrants suffer for their crimes, and virtuous characters are rewarded. Shakespeare's *Macbeth* is taken from legendary English history and in a very general sense shows how ambition leads to ruin. In Edmund Spenser's *Faerie Queene* (1590) the Redcross Knight (St. George) and Sir Guyon (distantly based on Sir Gawain) are drawn from mythic history, and their stories illustrate the triumph of virtue over adversity.

Sidney's second point is specifically Horatian. Philosophy offers useful moral truths. However, it is abstract and therefore lacks interest. Myth and history, conversely, offer marvelous stories and charming details, but are all too often devoid of moral truth. In this analysis, philosophy corresponds to the "profit" part of Horace's formula and history to the "delight" part.

The interpretation neatly reconciles the literary theories of Aristotle and Horace. It also gives literature a unique function. Because poetry combines the useful and the delightful it does more than teach, it persuades. Sidney remarks that the object of poetry is not *gnosis* (knowledge) but *praxis* (action). When we see the bad results of ambition in *Macbeth*, we shun ambition in our own lives. Likewise, when we see the rewards of holiness in Spenser's Redcross Knight, we strive to become holy in our own lives. Sidney's *Defence* not only reconciles Aristotle and Horace, it also makes the duty (*officium*) of the poet identical with that of the orator. In the *Defence* rhetoric and poetic are thus two sides of the same coin. It is a neat trick, though by no means original with Sidney, and it is fairly typical of mainstream European poetic theory for a century after the *Defence*.

Horace's speaker now returns to his original point. The best poet delights and instructs at the same time. A work that does this is sure to make money for Socius and company (Roman booksellers). It will also make the author's reputation abroad and among future generations. The comment on making a reputation abroad reflects the desire of Roman authors to become known outside Italy, especially in Greece. In the same way, nineteenth-century American authors were especially eager to become known in Europe. The reference to future reputation reflects a yearning for immortality through art also evident in Horace's famous ode beginning "I have created a monument more enduring than bronze" (III.30). It is a note often sounded in Renaissance poetry, as in Shakespeare's sonnet 55: "Not marble nor the gilded monuments/ Of princes shall outlive this powerful rhyme."

Lines 347–90: Flaws in Art

Flaws in art are permissible. The imagery in which this idea is put is musical. The musician seeks harmony—a perfect fitting together of notes—but sometimes slips. Error is pardonable if a poem is filled with compensating pleasures. The comment flows easily until it is stopped short with a question: "What about this?" (l. 353) Emphasis now shifts from minor flaws to the fact that some artists blunder constantly, like a harp player who always hits the wrong string. An obscure poet—perhaps a made-up name but probably a court poet of Alexander the Great (ca. 330 B.C.)—is mentioned. Choerilus was so bad that people laughed in delight whenever he did something right. But even the blemishes that occur when Homer nods off are painful.

The problem of flaws in art leads to recognition that critical judgments are, to a degree, relative. It is in this context that one of the famous observations in the *Art* is made: "A poem is like a picture." The comparison between poetry and painting was introduced in the opening lines of the *Art*. One of its implications was that poetry is more an art of verbal description and (perhaps) vivid images than an art of making fictions or of versification. This is a fair interpretation and not surprising in view of that fact that Horace wrote lyrics and conversational poems and avoided drama and narrative poetry. However, the observation that poetry is like a picture has nothing to do with descriptions or visual imagery. You see a picture differently from every perspective, says the speaker. What you see depends on where you are. By the same token, you will see a poem differently depending on what you look for. One poem may please only at the first reading while another will repay ten readings.

The speaker turns to the elder son of the Piso family. He will offer advice about what to aim for in composition. The elder son has already learned that no one demands a poem to be perfect. Minor slips are tolerable in a good poem, and even Homer makes them. On the other hand, they are irritating even in Homer. A lawyer can be mediocre and still be useful. He may not be as great as the famous Messalla (d. A.D. 8) who fought with Octavian at Actium and later became a patron of literature, but he can do many jobs. Nobody, however—not men, not gods, not booksellers—is willing to tolerate a mediocre poet.

The passage continues with a series of images of things that do not fit together: the orchestra is out of tune, the perfume ointment is tacky, the poppy seeds are served with bitter honey. Poems have to be put together in just the right way. They are created to delight the mind, and if they don't, they are useless. Other images are introduced. Don't try fencing if you can't use a sword. Stay out of the game if you can't play ball. Yet, says the speaker, in spite of this obvious rule, people who know nothing about writing will set about making verses. They think that because they are well born they can't go wrong. Obviously, the speaker thinks they are hopelessly mistaken, and his comments are laced with irony. In earlier passages he has appealed to the upper-class audience as the best judge of poetic merit; here he expresses a little of the rancor against the privileged class that might be expected of a freedman whose father was a slave and who fought with Brutus to save the Republic.

The speaker turns back to the oldest son of the Pisos. You know better, he says, than to go "against Minerva." The phrase "against Minerva" (l. 385) has the force of "against your own character." The son will never do something as uncharacteristic as claiming one of his poems is good just because he is from one of Rome's best families. If the son *does* write a poem, says the speaker, he should submit it first to a critic like Maecius, the author and friend of Cicero, then to his father and then to the speaker. Even after it has been scrutinized three times, the poem should not be published. It should be filed away for nine years. A work in a drawer can always be burned, but when it has been published, it is out there for good. The nine-year rule is famous and doubtless very useful, but few writers, if any, have observed it.

Lines 391–407: The Civilizing Power of Poetry

The requirement that poetry profit as well as delight is initially defined in terms of teaching. The definition is enlarged in a sustained lyrical passage on the civilizing power of poetry. Along with reminiscences of the early poets (*prisci poetae*) come suggestions that they were divinely inspired. The passage is what is called a "topos"—a standard topic handled by many writers and used for many different purposes. A version of the topos appears at the beginning of Cicero's youthful rhetorical treatise *De Inventione* (I.2ff.) adapted, of course, to demonstrate that rhetoric was the force that brought civilization to primitive man. In the present case, poetry is the civilizing force. The speaker recognizes that the early poets achieved their goals with divine assistance. They are called "prophet-poets" (*vatibus*, l. 400), and the importance of the inspiring Muse is acknowledged (l. 407). The emphasis on divine aid is understandable given the material, which is shrouded in myth, and the miraculous nature of the deeds ascribed to the earliest poets. For that very reason, it may be taken with a grain of salt. It goes with the topos and the lyrical, almost romantic tone of the passage and does not necessarily reflect the opinion of the speaker.

Two significant features of the passage are less characteristic of the topos. In the first place, the object of the early poets was clearly rational. They wanted to civilize previously uncultivated men. They do this by establishing norms of behavior, creating orderly cities, imposing laws, and the like. Their accomplishments are described in miraculous terms, but properly understood the miracles are allegories for the civilizing process. In the second place, the divine inspiration that assisted them was entirely benign. At no point does the speaker mention poetic frenzy or fantastic images.

Another significant aspect of the passage is its emphasis on music. The earliest poets accompanied themselves on the lyre. Harmony—the "fitting together of musical notes and words"—caused the miracles to happen, and the ultimate inspiration of the early poets was Apollo, called "the singer" (l. 407). The allusion to harmony that runs through the section is allegorical. Harmony symbolizes the aesthetic charms of art, which arise from its elegant "fitting together" of elements. Art does not perform overt miracles like those attributed by myths to Orpheus, but because of its charm it performs quiet miracles that are no less effective. The proof of this is the humanizing effect poetry has had on the Greeks. And, of course, the unspoken hope of the passage is that poetry will have the same effect on the Romans.

Orpheus is mentioned first. He is called a prophet (*interpres*) of the gods. According to the myth, the music of Orpheus was so beautiful that it tamed wild animals. An interpretation of the myth is offered: when men still lived in the woods (like animals) Orpheus tamed them in the sense of bringing them together and teaching them social behavior. Amphion is said to have played music so powerful that he moved stones and caused them to come together in the walls of Thebes. This too is an allegory, although the speaker does not pause to explain it: the power of poetry is so great that it persuaded men to come together in cities. More generally, the early poets taught the difference between public and private, sacred and profane, marriage and single life. They established the organization of life in towns and formulated codes of law. Here the speaker is thinking of Solon (ca. 600 B.C.), the poet and lawgiver of Athens whose laws were inscribed on wooden tablets.

Because of their civilizing achievements the early poets became famous and their poetry was considered divine—a hint that it gained this reputation from its good effects rather than because it was inspired. Homer and Tyrtaeus are mentioned next. Both were military poets—Homer of the Trojan War and Tyrtaeus (? seventh century B.C.) of Spartan marching songs. Other sorts of poetry began to flourish. Oracles were delivered in verse and poems were written showing how to live an ordinary life—the speaker may have Hesiod's *Works and Days*, an agricultural poem, in mind here. The Pierian spring was associated with the Muses and especially with lyric poetry. The speaker recalls the two kinds of traditional lyric, one that celebrated the deeds of the mighty, as in the odes of Pindar, and the other that provided recreation and celebrated ordinary pleasures. From Orpheus to the poets of ordinary pleasures, poetry is shown to be profitable and useful in the sense of advancing the cause of civilization and making everyday life more enjoyable.

The tone of the passage is remarkable. It is lush, brilliantly figured, and flowing. The speaker is obviously moved by what he is describing. It is as though he has momentarily recovered his belief in the value of art. However, the passage soon ends and the speaker returns to the problems created by the antipoetic culture that surrounds him.

Lines 408–18: Nature and Art

The transition from the power of poetry to the sources of successful poetry is abrupt. The only link in evidence is the emphasis on inspiration in the earlier passage. The first "source" treated is nature in the sense of "natural talent." This subject is not really new since it was implicit in the earlier debate about talent versus art (ll. 295–308). "Art" is here equated with "study," meaning study of the rules of art rather than study of philosophy. Nature is also clearly defined. It is "natural talent" (*ingenium*). Study and talent are both necessary, although all the examples given are of study: jockeys prepare arduously for their races, and musicians study their instruments for years before they are ready to perform at important public occasions like the Pythian Games. The speaker satirizes those who think they can write without study. He paraphrases a line used by boys playing tag (l. 417): "[I'm out in front]; a pox on those in the rear." Untrained poets are like the boys who say that. They refuse to admit they don't know how, and, at the same time, they don't want to be left behind.

Lines 419–52: The Critic

Perhaps untrained poets are that way because there are so few honest critics. The speaker has already mentioned the need for honest critics (ll. 387–88), and he has announced that he is about to become a critic (ll. 304–5). Now he has to face the difficulties of the profession he has chosen. Poets who are rich and powerful or who can give a fine dinner or lend money will have a hard time finding honest critics. Those who advise them will praise their work, even seem to weep over it, but they will be no more sincere than hired mourners at a funeral. The funeral is a nice touch. It suggests the dismal quality of the poetry being "criticized." Borrowing from Aesop's fable of the crow tricked by the fox into dropping a piece of cheese, the speaker warns the would-be poet to watch his wallet in the presence of a flattering critic. Horace had ample opportunity to watch the interplay between poet, critic, and patron, so it is not surprising that the tone of his speaker is slightly sour.

The false critic is now contrasted to Quintilius—probably Quintilius Varus (d. 23 B.C.), a friend of Vergil—who was a model of honesty, even when it hurt. The speaker seems to be recalling personal experiences when he remarks that when you asked him to look over a poem, he would give advice freely. If, however, you did not take the advice, he would step aside and leave you to yourself. The point is generalized: an honest critic will point out inert lines, criticize harsh-sounding ones, cancel sloppy ones, and weed out overly ornamental ones. The list moves from the sound of the verse to syntax to the use of ornaments like metaphors and similes. It continues with the observation that the good critic will force the poet to clarify obscure lines, will censure an ambiguous phrase, and will, in general, be as conscientious as Aristarchus (second century B.C.), a Homeric scholar and a proverbially exacting critic. Such a critic is a true friend because if a poem that has blemishes is published, the reputation of the poet will be permanently injured.

The idea of the false and true critic outlined in this passage was destined to have enormous influence. The passage implies that the true critic will have clearly defined standards and use them to expose flaws in the works he judges. What does "criticism" mean if not "finding fault"? The idea of the critic as fault-finder and of criticism as an essentially negative task is one of the less attractive legacies of Horace's *Art*. It is widespread in European criticism of the seventeenth century. During the eighteenth century it began to give way to more philosophical ideas of what the critic should do, including the idea that the critic's job is to understand the conditions that make art possible and its aesthetic and social effects. The change is evident in Germany in works like Lessing's *Laokoön* and Schiller's *On Naive and Sentimental Poetry*, largely because of the stimulating influence of philosophy on eighteenth-century German critical theory. In England, Wordsworth and Coleridge confronted an implacably hostile group of critics who were dedicated to neoclassical—including what they considered Horatian—standards of art and who mercilessly condemned the new art because they felt it violated those standards.

The situation led critics in the later eighteenth century to propose a new kind of criticism. Samuel Taylor Coleridge called it "genial criticism" in the *Biographia Literaria* (1817). The object of such criticism is not to find fault but to understand the author's intention and criticize the work in terms of that intention. Although the idea seems reasonable enough today, it was not popular among reviewers who wrote in the early nineteenth century. When Byron began publishing, his work was attacked with as little mercy as had been shown Wordsworth and Coleridge. Instead of passively accepting the critical verdict, Byron fought back, and the result was his violent counterblast titled *English Bards and Scotch Reviewers*. This work is a powerful attack on the idea of reviewing as fault-finding. It is entirely different in spirit from Horace's *Art*, but its intellectual toughness, wit, and rootedness in the issues of its day have obvious parallels to the earlier work.

Lines 453–76: Conclusion—the Mad Poet

The *Art* ends with the image of the mad poet. It is a satirical image, and the satire is etched in acid. The speaker has just observed that some people insist writing is all "nature" and set out to write poems in spite of their lack of knowledge of art. Their refusal to face up to a reasonable truth is a kind of madness. Suddenly we are face-to-face with the mad poet himself. The speaker is amused but the amusement is laced with contempt.

Madness is also associated with poetic inspiration. The speaker has remarked that Democritus excluded sane authors from the ranks of the best poets because they were not inspired. He has also recognized divine inspiration and the aid of the Muse during the mythic age of poetry. However, even if the description of the early poets is taken at face value, it stresses the reasonable ends to which inspiration worked and makes no reference to the divine frenzy so often linked with inspiration.

The mad poet has no useful social purpose (hence his poetry cannot "profit") and is mad in a destructive way. His madness consists not in inspired vision but in his refusal to recognize that he is incompetent.

The speaker compares him to someone who is diseased or afflicted by Diana's malady—lunacy.

Men are afraid of him, and children laugh at him. He may fall into a hole. If he does, he should be left there. He is like Empedocles the Greek philosopher (d. ca. 433 B.C.), who threw himself into the volcano on Mt. Aetna thinking that he was immortal. Let poets who seek to destroy themselves do so, says the speaker; it is wrong to save someone against his will. Presumably the speaker is using suicide metaphorically for the willfully self-destructive act of publishing bad poetry.

Horace suggests that the mad poet is so depraved because he urinated on the urn containing his father's ashes. (Funerary urns were kept at the entrances of Roman houses where they could be properly revered by loving survivors.) He is an animal that is all passion and no reason—a bear. His urge to read his verses to a critic is like the effort of the bear to break out of its cage. The final image is what happens if the mad poet gets his way. He fastens himself to his victim like a leech and stays there until filled with the victim's blood.

It is an unpleasant image, and nothing follows. The last we hear of the speaker is a complaint about being trapped by poets who insist on reading to the critic even though they are despised. If a parallel to this situation is helpful, it is easy to find in the portrait of the bore in Horace's satire "I happened to be strolling along the Via Sacra" (*Ibam forte Via Sacra, Satires*, I.9). There, however, the situation is much more fully developed, and the humor is lighter. The point of "I happened to be strolling" is simply to describe the bore in an amusing fashion. The point of the episode at the end of the *Art* is to illustrate how unpleasant mad poets are.

Why end with a mad poet? One answer is that the concluding image balances the poem's opening image of a poet with such bad judgment that the images he produces are like the fantasies of someone delirious with fever. The beginning and end thus act as brackets. The point of the brackets is the master lesson of the poem: without art poetry is ridiculous and painful.

We have noted that the speaker is a character as well as a voice delivering rules of art. If we concentrate on the speaker, he is seen at the end in his most unflattering pose. He is not giving advice to the Pisos. He has evidently forgotten them in his concern for himself. Nor does he end on a positive note. Quite the contrary. He has given up poetry to become a critic, but the final image of the poem is an illustration of the futility of the critic's work. At the end the speaker feels trapped and wants only to escape.

In the course of the *Art* the speaker moves from being a self-assured and friendly teacher of the principles of art to satirizing those who violate those principles. Disgusted with the philistinism of Roman society and convinced of the futility of trying to write poetry, he has turned to criticism. He soon realizes, however, that honest criticism is as difficult as writing poetry. Most people do not want honest criticism. Worst of all, having proclaimed himself a critic, he is sought out by precisely those artists—the mad poet kind—whom he most despises. In the final image the mad poet is compared to a leech. The final image of the speaker is that of a victim in full flight from the responsibilities he himself has chosen.

If we turn from the speaker to the *Art* as a critical document, the ending is understandable even though surprising. The speaker has been discussing the good critic. This is an appropriate concluding topic—the penultimate chapter of Aristotle's *Poetics*, for example, deals with artistic flaws and their answers. Horace considers the question of nature and art. Nature is beyond the help of criticism, and if nature is the only requirement for successful poetry the critic is useless. In fact, nature is not the only requirement, but some poets refuse to recognize this fact. This observation leads to the poet who is beyond help because he refuses to learn the principles of art. The refusal is a kind of madness. That it is madness in the negative sense, not inspiration, is shown by the poet's antisocial behavior. Not even the deranged poet, however, can resist the temptation to seek out critics. He fastens on the critic like a leech. In the end, the speaker concludes that the critic's job is as impossible as the poet's. It is a sentiment that will be understood by anyone who reviews books. It is also a way of ending a poem about the nature of art even though it may not be the way we expected.

Ars Poetica—Medieval Phase

The medieval history of the *Ars Poetica* is well documented in its larger outlines. Many details remain obscure, however; and further insights can be expected as the manuscripts and commentaries continue to be explored. Studies by Max Manitius (1893) and Grant Showerman (1925) have provided a very rough first approximation of the diffusion of manuscripts and allusions during the period, and these are supplemented by a rough census by Hilda Buttenwieser (1941). Some 250 manuscripts of Horace's works can be dated between the Carolingian period and 1300, not counting excerpts in numerous florilegia and extended quotations in critical works like the *Documentum de Modo et Arte Dictandi et Versificandi* of Geoffrey of Vinsauf and the *Metalogicon* of John of Salisbury. Of the manuscripts one-fourth are German and one hundred French. There are relatively fewer Italian manuscripts, but, in Buttenwieser's words, they are "far from infrequent." Not all the manuscripts contain *The Art of Poetry*, although most do. After 1300 the number of manuscripts increases so rapidly and the diffusion is so broad that no census exists and perhaps none is needed, although better information about manuscript diffusion would clarify several questions about Horatian influence.

Beyond manuscripts and quotations, evidence for the medieval influence of *The Art of Poetry* consists of works that comment on the *Art* or imitate it. Again the record is relatively clear. The *Art* was well known in the late classical–early medieval period. Its influence waned between the fifth and the eighth centuries but revived during the Carolingian period. Between the Carolingian period and the "twelfth-century Renaissance" the *Art* was widely but irregularly known and used. This situation persisted until the fifteenth century, when the *Art* came to be recognized throughout Europe as the central explanation of classical literary theory.

The period between the third and the fifth century A.D. was one of cultural transition. Those who cared about ancient culture undertook a review of its accomplishments, almost as though they had decided consciously to save the best of them. The effort is a striking instance of the cultural nostalgia—the yearning for roots—that is common during periods of rapid cultural change. The result was an impressive number of commentaries, summaries, paraphrases, handbooks, and summaries of background information dealing with literary works of golden-age Roman culture. Many of them are mechanical and elementary, but just these qualities made them invaluable during a period that lacked a sophisticated understanding of classical culture.

The most characteristic of these late classical works are grammar textbooks and commentaries. The object of grammar was said to be correct speaking and writing and the reading and interpretation of the poets. Correctness required mastering spelling, syllabification, parts of speech, rules of inflection, and the like. Interpreting the poets involved reading a select group of literary classics, which were then interpreted and imitated in the students' own compositions. The modern idea of a literary canon developed out of the list of classical works normally included in the grammar curriculum. Imitation in the sense of imitating literary models was encouraged by the practice of applying lessons learned in reading to original compositions.

Late classical grammar textbooks range from elementary, like the *Ars minor* of Aelius Donatus, to advanced and sometimes quite challenging treatments of grammar from a linguistic point of view like the three books of the the *Ars major* of the same Donatus and Priscian's *Grammar* (sixth century) in eighteen books. Complementing such works were more focused discussions of specific authors and poems. Essays on the meters of Terence and of Horace were popular. Horatian influence is apparent in two brief essays (fourth century) "On Drama" by Euanthius and "On Comedy" by Donatus. Both essays treat the history of drama and dramatic conventions summarized in Horace's *Art*, and the second quotes the passage (ll. 274-88) tracing drama from its invention by Thespis to experiments by Roman poets in native forms. Both essays had a long afterlife. They were excerpted and quoted in encyclopedias and collections of quotations and incorporated with or without credit in discussions of drama. When editions of Plautus and Terence began to be published during the Renaissance, the essays were often included or paraphrased in the introductory material. In this way an indirect as well as a direct Horatian influence on the European understanding of drama can be traced from late antiquity to the sixteenth century.

Detailed treatments of grammar regularly treated usage, including *Latinitas*, ornamentation, including "figures of diction" and "figures of thought," and poetry, including meter, the major literary genres, and specialized lyric forms. In the *Three Books of the Art of Grammar* (*Ars grammatica libri III*, fourth century), Diomedes devoted all of the last book to the *ars metrica*. His dominant theme is Horatian—the importance of decorum—and there is ample evidence that he had read *The Art of Poetry* carefully. Evidently, in late antiquity it was considered an authoritative outline of critical theory.

Glosses (also called *scholia*) and commentaries are characteristic products of the grammar curriculum. They were created to assist "reading and interpreting the poets." A gloss is essentially a series of notes (*scholia*) to individual words. The notes explain archaic words, difficult points of grammar, learned allusions, ambiguous statements, obscure metaphors, and the like. Much of what is included in a typical gloss is taken from standard reference works, but there is always an interpretative element. The object is to "explain" the meaning of the work being glossed. For a work as complex as Horace's *Art of Poetry*, interpretations differ, and any given "explanation" is likely to be a disguised argument in favor of one interpretation and against alternatives.

Unlike a gloss, a commentary is interpretation from the beginning. It is an essay or group of essays on the text rather than a series of footnotes. It seeks to explain the larger ideas of the text, and it does so by relating them to the biography of the author, the history of the times, philosophical or literary ideas embodied in the text, and the like.

Two glosses survive for *The Art of Poetry* from the late classical period. The first is by Porphyrion and the second is by Acron or (since the name has been challenged) pseudo-Acron. Both are essentially collections of footnotes. There is a good deal of overlap between them plus some important variation. The most influential single point in these glosses is Porphyrion's observation that *The Art of Poetry* draws on a treatise by Neoptolemus of Parium that proposed treating poetry under the headings of *poesis, poema, poeta*.

The two glosses demonstrate interest in the *Art* in the late classical period. However, they are not purely and simply late classical works. The manuscripts in which they survive are from the Carolingian period (ninth–tenth centuries), and the original texts have been enlarged over the centuries. The earliest surviving manuscripts of the *Art* are also Carolingian.

No manuscripts or commentaries on the *Art* survive from the fifth to the eighth century, and references to and quotations from it are rare. The period was extremely turbulent, and the decline in Horace's fortunes can be attributed in part to the fact that poetry was less important than survival during these years. Obviously, however, something survived, otherwise there would have been no manuscripts to copy. One of the important ninth-century manuscripts of Horace, now at Berne, Switzerland, came originally from Ireland, and the key role of Irish monks in preserving ancient learning between the fifth and the eighth century is well documented. Quite possibly Irish learning was an important link between the late classical Horace and the reawakening of interest in him during the "revival of learning" in Europe that occurred during the reign of Charlemagne (d. 814). The fact that glosses of Acron and Porphyrion were recopied along with the text of Horace's poems during the Carolingian period shows that once again he had become a school author.

There is also at least one semi-original Carolingian work on the *Art*. Its title is *Vienna Scholia on Horace's Art of Poetry (Scholia Vindobonensia ad Horatii Artem Poeticam)*, and it was edited in 1877 by Joseph Zechmeister. It is attributed to "Albinus," a common name for Alcuin of York, who was Charlemagne's chief adviser on educational matters. The attribution is dubious, but the range of classical knowledge in the work suggests an author "in the school" of Alcuin and a date of composition in the early tenth century. Although the work is titled *Scholia*, its discussions of individual points are often so detailed as to approximate a formal commentary.

The author knows that many ideas in the *Art* are best understood in relation to ancient rhetoric. Since Horace frequently adopts rhetorical lore, emphasis of the *Scholia* on rhetoric is appropriate. The debt is discussed repeatedly, and in this respect the *Scholia* foreshadow the tendency of certain kinds of medieval criticism to use so many rhetorical ideas that they seem at first glance to be little more than rhetoric textbooks illustrated by quotations in verse.

Modern commentaries dealing with rhetorical influence on the *Art* tend to cite Aristotle's *Rhetoric* and its Hellenistic descendants or sophisticated Roman rhetorics like Cicero's *De oratore*. The author of the *Scholia* has lost touch with these works. He turns instead to the so-called *Rhetoric to Herennius (Rhetorica ad Herennium)* for his rhetorical theory and many of his specifics. The *Rhetoric to Herennius* is not a brilliant work, but it is comprehensive, simply written, and filled with easy-to-understand examples. It is exactly what medieval theorists needed, and its prestige was enhanced by the fact that during the Middle Ages it was attributed (wrongly) to Cicero.

The *Vienna Scholia* is about halfway between gloss and commentary. Many items are essentially footnotes, but others amount to brief essays on Horace's use of rhetorical theory, mythology, prosodic conventions, and the like. The comment on Horace's initial image of a man-horse, for example, explains that the art of poetry is "the art of fiction" and that Horace wrote the *Art* for the Pisos, "whose oldest son wrote comedies. . . . They asked Horace to give them rules for the art of poetry, which he, as the grammarian Victorinus says, gave twice, saying first, what to avoid and second, what to seek. And he used an analogy with painters (since poets and orators use analogies when they speak)." This is more than a gloss. It identifies the function of poetry as fiction (an un-Horatian idea), explains who the Pisos were (drawing its information from Acron), paraphrases an interpretation by a late classical grammarian (Victorinus), and notes that poets and orators use analogies.

A few lines later the *Vienna Scholia* explain that the monsters sketched by Horace symbolize failure to observe decorum of style. The author means the low, middle, and elevated style, and he explains these styles and relates them to cognate vices by referring to the *Rhetoric to Herennius*. Again the interpretation is un-Horatian—an aesthetic comment in the *Art* is explained by the *Scholia* in rhetorical terms.

"Style" is a narrower concept in the *Scholia* than in ancient rhetoric. It is understood as word choice. The *Scholia* explain that in the low style a lamp is called a pot (*testam*), in the middle style a lantern (*lucerna*), and in the elevated style chandelier (*lychnus*, a fancy Greek term for lamp). Styles should not normally be mixed, but exceptions are allowed based on good cause and rhetorical principles. The comment shapes the interpretation of the initial images of Horace's *Art* in a much more rhetorical way than a modern commentary would do, and it prepares the reader for rhetorical interpretations of later passages. The famous advice to observe simplicity and unity (*Art* l. 23), for example, is interpreted as an extension of what has come earlier. "Simple" in "simple and unified" is said to mean "without mixture of styles," and "unified" means "consistent in subject matter."

Enough has been said about the *Vienna Scholia* to suggest their quality. They are intelligent, helpful, and quite well informed, although their author was unfamiliar with many sources that were known in antiquity. They are clearly part of the "reading and interpreting the poets" part of grammar, but they draw so extensively on rhetoric that they could easily be considered a "rhetorical interpretation" of Horace's *Art*. The technical discussion in the *Scholia* of the *ars metrica* is explicitly grammatical but adds little to what Horace, himself, says. Absent from the commentary are discussions of nature, reason, and imitation—three terms of great interest during the Renaissance.

From the Carolingian period on, there is a continuous manuscript tradition of the *Art*. The number of manuscripts varies widely, however, from country to country. If manuscripts are a valid measure, interest was higher in France and England than in Germany and higher in Germany than in Italy. The thirteenth and fourteenth centuries are paradoxical. In Italy, where the first stirrings of the Renaissance can be felt

in Dante's *On Vernacular Eloquence* (*De vulgari eloquentia*, ca. 1305),
there are few references to the *Art*, even in documents that discuss literary questions with great sophistication. Dante mentions it only once in
On Vulgar Eloquence (IV.4). There are two references in the *Letter to
Can Grande* explaining the *Divine Comedy*, but the *Letter* is probably
not by Dante. Petrarch knew the *Art*, but he made little use of it when
discussing literary theory. His "Letter to Horace" shows more interest
in the *Odes* and *Satires* than the *Art*. Boccaccio is equally indifferent to
the *Art* and refers to it only once (XV.4) in the last two books of his
Genealogy of the Gods, which are a formal "defense of poetry."

On the other hand, northern European authors, who might be considered more backward culturally than the Italians, refer frequently to the
Art. It was, for example, often included in the lists of curriculum works
in medieval collections of essays having the generic title *Introduction to
the Authors* (*Accessus ad auctores*). Conrad of Hirsau (d. ?1150; cf.
R.B. Huygens, *Dialogus super auctores* [1955]) begins his treatment of
Horace with a little essay on the *Art of Poetry*. He teaches that *poetria*—
the term he uses for the work—is a female symbol for subject matter,
and the work itself is an explanation of the rules that govern the proper
coordination of technique and subject matter. Knowledge of *The Art* in
France and England during the high Middle Ages is further confirmed
by numerous quotations in, for example, the *Commentary on the first
Six Books of Vergil's Aeneid* (twelfth century) attributed to Bernard
Sylvestris, and John of Salisbury's *Metalogicon* (ca. 1170). The *Art* is
quoted no less than twenty-two times and at length by the author of
the *Document Concerning the Mode Art of Versifying* (*Documentum de
modo et arte versificandi*, ca. 1210), a prose treatise usually attributed
to Geoffrey of Vinsauf and preserved in several English and French
manuscripts.

II

Poetria Nova
by
Geoffrey of Vinsauf

Introduction

Mention of Geoffrey of Vinsauf leads to one of the most interesting of the medieval works that draw on the *Art*. The *Poetria Nova* (*New Art of Poetry*), also attributed to Geoffrey, probably dates from around 1202.

Geoffrey was an Englishman who lived in the latter part of the twelfth and the early part of the thirteenth century. He is the reputed author of three other works, the prose *Documentum* (already mentioned), a *Summa de coloribus rhetoricis*, and a short poem, *Causa magistri Guafredi Vinesauf*. He studied at Paris, taught in England, and once made a trip to Rome. The *Poetria* is dedicated to Pope Innocent III although Geoffrey had obviously never met him. A second dedication at the end is offered to "William," who is identified in some early manuscripts as William, Bishop of London, and in others as William of Wrotham, a prominent government official.

The best current guess about the date of the *Poetria* is between 1200 and 1205. The work exists in some fifty manuscripts, of which twenty are English. There are numerous textual problems, and the text on which the translation given below is based is the one developed by Margaret F. Nims. Her translation was published by the Pontifical Institute of the University of Toronto in 1967 and is used here with the kind permission of Professor Nims and the president of the Pontifical Institute of Medieval Studies of the University of Toronto.

The work is written in Latin dactylic hexameter verses, the same measure used in Horace's *Art*. A nagging problem is created by the differences between the *Poetria* and the *Documentum de Modo et Arte Dictandi et Versificandi*. They suggest that the *Poetria* is offered as an original composition while the *Documentum* is intended as a summary of "standard doctrine." Probably the *Documentum* was composed after the *Poetria*, but this too is conjectural. It is possible, for example, that the *Documentum* was composed first but was circulated, with revisions, only after the *Poetria* became popular.

The *Poetria* is one of several treatises on the art of poetry that were produced in the twelfth and thirteenth century. The most important are the twelfth-century *Ars Versificatoria* of Matthew of Vendome, and, in the thirteenth century, the *Poetria* and *Documentum* of Geoffrey, the *Laborintus* of Eberhard (Evardus) the German, the *Ars Poetica* of Gervase of Melkley, and the *Parisiana poetria* of John of Garland. The works of Matthew, Geoffrey, and Eberhard were collected in 1924 by Edmond Faral (*Les Arts poétiques du XIIe et XIIIe siècle*). The *Parisiana poetria* has been superbly edited with facing English translation by Traugott Lawlor (1974).

Many readers have found these treatises more or less indistinguishable. Closer examination reveals significant differences. Geoffrey's *Poetria* is marked by Platonic idealism and a high estimate of the poet as creator. Gervase of Melkley's *Ars* is distinguished by its precise scholastic classification of the figures. All the treaties are to some degree written in the shadow of Horace, but Geoffrey's is the only one that announces in its title the ambition to outdo *The Art of Poetry*.

Poetria Nova

Translated by Margaret F. Nims

Holy Father, wonder of the world, if I say Pope Nocent I shall give you a name without a head; but if I add the head, your name will be at odds with the metre. That name seeks to resemble you: it will no more be confined by metre than your great virtue by the shackles of measure. There is no standard by which I may measure your virtue; it transcends the measures of men. But divide the name—divide the name thus: set down first "In," then add "nocent" and it will be in friendly accord with the metre. In the same way your excellence, if it is divided up, is equalled by many, but taken in its wholeness it is equalled by none. In illustrious lineage you compare with Bartholomew; in gentle heart, with Andrew; in precious youth, with John; in firm faith, with Peter; in perfect knowledge, with Paul. In these qualities taken together, there is no one with whom to compare you. One of your gifts remains to be mentioned which heaven allows no one to approach: the grace of your eloquence. Silence, Augustine! Pope Leo, be still! Cease, John! Gregory, stay your speech! Why should I specify all these? Granted that one man or another may be golden-tongued and brilliant in discourse, yet his speech is inferior to yours, and the gold of your eloquence sets its own precedent. You quite transcend the human condition: where will physical youthfulness like yours be found in a man of such age, or where a heart so mature implanted in one so young? What strange conflict in the nature of things: a youth of ripe age! Although, when the era of faith began, the Lord set John above Peter in love, yet he chose to set Peter above John in the papacy. In you, Holy Father, an unheard-of thing has now, in our days, come to pass: a pope who is Peter the elder, and a pope who is John the youth. Your retinue—fit men for a man so great— radiate and glow round the pope as stars round the sun. You alone are like the world's sun, they like its stars, Rome like the heavens. England sent me to Rome as from earth to heaven; it sent me to you as from darkness to light. General light of this world, deign to shed your lustre upon me. Most gracious of men, share your graciousness with one who is yours. Only you can and must, only you desire and know how to give with munificence: know how to, in that you are prudent; wish to, in that you are gracious; must, in that you are high-born; can, in that you are pope. Since you are so good and so great, here has my mind come to rest after journeying far and wide; in giving what it has to offer it prefers you alone to all others; it dedicates to you all it is capable of. Receive, great men, this little work, brief in form, vast in power.

I. General Remarks on Poetry
Divisions of the Present Treatise

If a man has a house to build, his impetuous hand does not rush into action. The measuring line of his mind first lays out the work, and he mentally outlines the successive steps in a definite order. The mind's hand shapes the entire house before the body's hand builds it. Its mode of being is archetypal before it is actual. Poetic art may see in this analogy the law to be given to poets: let the poet's hand not be swift to take up the pen, nor his tongue be impatient to speak; trust neither hand nor tongue to the guidance of fortune. To ensure greater success for the work, let the discriminating mind, as a prelude to action, defer the operation of hand and tongue, and ponder long on the subject matter. Let the mind's interior compass first circle the whole extent of the material. Let a definite order chart in advance at what point the pen will take up its course, or where it will fix its Cadiz. As a prudent workman, construct the whole fabric within the mind's citadel; let it exist in the mind before it is on the lips.

When due order has arranged the material in the hidden chamber of the mind, let poetic art come forward to clothe the matter with words. Since poetry comes to serve, however, let it make

due preparation for attendance upon its mistress. Let it take heed
lest a head with tousled locks, or a body in rumpled garments,
or any final details prove displeasing, and lest in adorning one   65
part it should in some way disfigure another. If any part is ill-
groomed, the work as a whole incurs censure from that one part.
A touch of gall makes all the honey bitter; a single blemish dis-
figures the entire face. Give careful thought to the material, there-   70
fore, that there may be no possible grounds for reproach.

Let the poem's beginning, like a courteous attendant, introduce the subject with grace. Let the main section, like a diligent
host, make provision for its worthy reception. Let the conclusion, like a herald when the race is over, dismiss it honourably.
In all of its parts let the whole method of presentation bring   75
credit upon the poem, lest it falter in any section, lest its brightness suffer eclipse.

In order that the pen may know what a skilful ordering of
material requires, the treatise to follow begins its course with a
discussion of order. Since the following treatise begins its course
with a discussion of order, its first concern is the path that the   80
ordering of material should follow. Its second care: with what
scales to establish a delicate balance if meaning is to be given the
weight appropriate to it. The third task is to see that the body
of words is not boorishly crude but urbane. The final concern is
to ensure that a well-modulated voice enters the ears and feeds   85
the hearing, a voice seasoned with the two spices of facial expression and gesture.

II. Ordering the Material

The material's order may follow two possible courses: at one
time it advances along the pathway of art, at another it travels
the smooth road of nature. Nature's smooth road points the way
when "things" and "words" follow the same sequence, and the
order of discourse does not depart from the order of occurrence.   90
The poem travels the pathway of art if a more effective order
presents first what was later in time, and defers the appearance
of what was actually earlier. Now, when the natural order is
thus transposed, later events incur no censure by their early appearance, nor do early events by their late introduction. Without   95

contention, indeed, they willingly assume each other's place, and
gracefully yield to each other with ready consent. Deft artistry
inverts things in such a way that it does not pervert them; in
transposing it disposes the material to better effect. The order of
art is more elegant than natural order, and in excellence far ahead,   100
even though it puts last things first.

The first branch of order has no offshoots; the second is prolific: from its marvelous stock, bough branches out into boughs,
the single shoot into many, the one into eight. The air in this region of art may seem murky and the pathway rugged, the doors   105
locked and the theory itself entangled with knots. Since that is
so, the words that follow will serve as physicians for that disorder. Scan them well: here you will find a light to dispel the
darkness, safe footing to traverse rugged ground, a key to unlock
the doors, a finger to loose the knots. The way is thrown open;   110
guide the reins of your mind as the nature of your course demands.

Let that part of the material which is first in the order of nature wait outside the gates of the work. Let the end, as a worthy
precursor, be first to enter and take up its place in advance, as a
guest of more honourable rank, or even as master. Nature has   115
placed the end last in order, but art respectfully defers to it,
leads it from its humble position and accords it to the place of
honour.

The place of honour at the beginning of a work does not re-
serve its lustre for the end of the material only; rather, two parts
share the glory: the end of the material and the middle. Art   120
draws from either of these a graceful beginning. Art plays, as it
were, the conjurer: causes the last to be first, the future to be
present, the oblique to be straight, the remote to be near; what is
rustic becomes urbane, what is old becomes new, public things
are made private, black things white, and worthless things are   125
made precious.

If a still more brilliant beginning is desired (while leaving the
sequence of the material unchanged) make use of a proverb, ensur-
ing that it may not sink to a purely specific relevance, but raise
its head high to some general truth. See that, while prizing the
charm of the unusual, it may not concentrate its attention on the   130
particular subject, but refuse, as if in disdain, to remain within
its bosom. Let it take a stand above the given subject, but look

with direct glance towards it. Let it say nothing directly about
the subject, but derive its inspiration therefrom.

This kind of beginning is threefold, springing up from three
shoots. The shoots are the first, the middle, and the last parts of   135
the theme. From their stem a sprig, as it were, bursts forth, and
is thus wont to be born, one might say, of three mothers. It remains in hiding, however, and when summoned it refuses to
hear. It does not as a rule come forward when the mind bids it;   140
it is of a somewhat haughty nature, and does not present itself
readily nor to all. It is reluctant to appear, unless, indeed, it is
compelled to do so.

Proverbs, in this way, add distinction to a poem. No less appropriately do exempla occupy a position at the beginning of a
work. The same quality, indeed, shines forth from exempla and
proverbs, and the distinction conferred by the two is of equal
value. In stylistic elegance, proverbs alone are on a par with ex   145
empla. Artistic theory has advanced other techniques [for the
poem's beginning] but prefers these two; they have greater prestige. The others are of less worth and more recent appearance;
the sanction of time favours the two forms mentioned. Thus the
way that lies open is more restricted, its use more appropriate,   150
its art superior, as we see both from artistic principle and from
practice.

Three branches of [artistic] beginning have thus been discovered by careful search: end, middle, and proverbs. A fourth branch
is the exemplum; but this one, too, like the one before it, rises
up in three shoots. In these eight branches the pen itself takes
pride.

That your eyes may see as witness what we have said to your   155
ears, consider the brief story that has as its first part Minos, its
second the death of his son, its conclusion the thwarting of Scylla.

Natural order begins the story in some way like this:

Aside from the bounty of Fortune, whose lavish gifts flow
forth as from a torrent, Nature, with other splendour, prospers   160
the glory of Minos. She arms his body with exceptional strength
and adorns his limbs with rare beauty. She refines alike the gold
of his mind and the silver of his tongue. She polishes each detail
to perfection, infusing a marvelous charm of manner. Such grace   165
as befits a king is reflected alike in every part of his nature.

Art draws a beginning for the poem from the end of the story thus:

By the treason of Scylla was Scylla betrayed; she was wounded by the very weapon with which she inflicted a wound. She who   170 *was false to her father failed in her longing; because she condemned, she incurred like condemnation. Fit vengeance recoiled on the source of deceit in deceit of like measure.*

From the middle of the story we may fashion a beginning like this:

Spying into the mind and years of Androgeos, Envy sees in his   175 *years a boy, in his mind an old man; for, endowed with the mind of age, the boy has nothing boyish about him. From his very triumphs arise his misfortune. Since his praise soars aloft he is dashed from that height. Since his lustre is great, he labours to his own destruction, and exerts his man's mind to the doom of his youthful years.*

The following general statement is appropriate for the first   180 part of the story:

What is more desirable is more evanescent. All things augur decline, and prosperity is prompter to ruin. Ever blandly, fierce chance lays its snares, and happier fortune swiftly anticipates flight.

For the middle, this generalization is relevant: 185

Envy, vilest of things, wholly a mortal poison, good only for evil, malign only towards good, silently plots all malign counsel, and spreads abroad to the world whatever bitter thing it conceives.

The end of the story suggests a proverb of this sort: 190

Just is the law that strikes guile with grief; that turns grief back on the head whence it issued.

This illustrative image may serve for the beginning of the story:

Suddenly the grim gale rages under a joyous sky; the murky air pours rain after a sun serene.   195

You may choose an exemplum like this to illustrate the middle of the story:

Upon the sown seed, foster child of nursing earth, the gloomy darnel vents its rancour; it blocks the seed's will to be born, and closing its gates maliciously grudges the seed's rising.

So too, in a similar way, you may prelude the end of the story: 200

*Often the arrow learns to rebound on the archer; and the stroke,
turned aside, to recoil on the striker.*

III. Amplification and Abbreviation

For the opening of the poem, the principles of art outlined above
have offered a variety of paths. The poem's development now
invites you onward. Keeping to our image, direct your steps   205
further along the road's course.

The way continues along two routes: there will be either a
wide path or a narrow, either a river or a brook. You may advance at a leisurely pace or leap swiftly ahead. You may report
the matter with brevity or draw it out in a lengthy discourse.
The footing on either path is not without effort; if you wish to   210
be wisely guided, entrust yourself to a reliable guide. Reflect
upon the precepts below; they will guide your pen and teach the
essentials for each path. The material to be moulded, like the
moulding of wax, is at first hard to the touch. If intense concentration enkindle native ability, the material is soon made pliant   215
by the mind's fire, and submits to the hand in whatever way it
requires, malleable to any form. The hand of the mind controls
it, either to amplify or curtail.

A. Amplification

If you choose an amplified form, proceed first of all by this step: 220
although the meaning is one, let it not come content with one
set of apparel. Let it vary its robes and assume different raiment.
Let it take up again in other words what has already been said;
let it reiterate, in a number of clauses, a single thought. Let one
and the same thing be concealed under multiple forms—be varied and yet the same.   225

Since a word, a short sound, passes swiftly through the ears, a
step onward is taken when an expression made up of a long and
leisurely sequence of sounds is substituted for a word. In order to
amplify the poem, avoid calling things by their names; use other
designations for them. Do not unveil the thing fully but suggest   230
it by hints. Do not let your words move straight onward through
the subject, but, circling it, take a long and winding path around

what you were going to say briefly. Retard the tempo by thus increasing the number of words. This device lengthens brief forms   235
of expression, since a short word abdicates in order that an extended sequence may be its heir. Since a concept is confined in
one of three strongholds—in a noun, or a verb, or a combination
of both—do not let the noun or verb or combination of both
render the concept explicit, but let an amplified form stand in   240
place of verb or noun or both.

In order that you may travel the more spacious route, let apos-
A third step is comparison, made in accord with one of two
laws—either in a hidden or in an overt manner. Notice that
some things are joined deftly enough, but certain signs reveal the
point of juncture. A comparison which is made overtly presents
a resemblance which signs explicitly point out. These signs are   245
three: the words *more, less, equally.* A comparison that is made
in a hidden way is introduced with no sign to point it out. It is
introduced not under its own aspect but with dissembled mien,
as if there were no comparison there at all, but the taking on,   250
one might say, of a new form marvelously engrafted, where the
new element fits as securely into the context as if it were born of
the theme. The new term is, indeed, taken from elsewhere, but it
seems to be taken from there; it is from outside and does not
appear outside; it makes an appearance within and is not within;
so it fluctuates inside and out, here and there, far and near; it   255
stands apart, and yet is at hand. It is a kind of plant; if it is
planted in the garden of the material the handling of the subject
will be pleasanter. Here is the flowing water of a well-spring,
where the source runs purer; here is the formula for a skilful
juncture, where the elements joined flow together and touch each   260
other as if they were not contiguous but continuous; as if the
hand of nature had joined them rather than the hand of art. This
type of comparison is more artistic; its use is much more distinguished.

In order that you may travel the more spacious route, let apostrophe be a fourth mode of delay. By it you may cause the sub-   265
ject to linger on its way, and in it you may stroll for an hour.
Take delight in apostrophe; without it the feast would be ample
enough, but with it the courses of an excellent cuisine are mul-
tiplied. The splendour of dishes arriving in rich profusion and
the leisured delay at the table are festive signs. With a variety of   270

courses we feed the ear for a longer time and more lavishly. Here
is food indeed for the ear when it arrives delicious and fragrant
and costly. Example may serve to complement theory: the eye is
a surer arbiter than the ear. One example is not enough; there
will be an ample number; from this ample evidence learn what   275
occasion suitably introduces apostrophe, what object it addresses,
and in what form.

Rise up, apostrophe, before the man whose mind soars too
high in prosperity, and rebuke him thus:

Why does joy so intense excite your spirit? Curb jubilation
with due restraint and extend not its limits beyond what is meet.   280
O soul, heedless of misfortune to come, imitate Janus: look to
past and to future; if your venture has prospered, regard not be-
ginnings but issues. From the sun's setting appraise the day, not
from its rising. To be fully secure, fear the future. When you
think that you have done all, the serpent lurks in the grass. Keep   285
in mind, as example, the sirens; learn from them in a happier
time ever to beware an unhappy. There is nothing stable in things
of this world: after honey comes poison; dark night brings the
day to a close, and clouds end calm weather. Though happily all   290
man's affairs are subject to change, misfortune is wont to return
with greater alacrity.

If vaunting presumption impudently puffs up a man, pour the
oil of mild words on his swelling pride:

Let your eyes go ahead of your footsteps; take stock of your
mind and measure your strength. If you are strong, dare great   295
things; if you are weak, lay lighter burdens upon your shoulders;
if your strength is but moderate, love what is moderate. Assume
nothing which you are presumptuous in assuming. In all things
virtue is one: to heed your true measure. Firmly imprint on your
mind: although you are greater than others, feign yourself less,   300
and deceive yourself in your own regard. Do not thus hurl others
down to the depths, nor rate yourself above the heavens. Let
deeds surpass words; boasting diminishes fame.

If the timid man should give free rein to fear in time of adversity, come to his aid with this potent resource of words: 305

Fear not. If perchance you do fear, assume the spirit of one
temporarily fearful, not of one habitually timid. Let fear be a
guest when it enters the gates of the mind, not a permanent resi-

dent. Learn how to fear: if you fear, fear without witness, and   310
let not your countenance know the fear of your mind; for if fear
in your heart feeds on and wastes your features, a happier spirit
fosters and fattens your enemy; and the grief that is sucking your
limbs dry heaps up joy for your foe. More advisedly, therefore, if
fear casts down your spirit, let a happy deceit lift up your head,   315
and with the shield of brave features succour your fear; so, if the
mind is afraid, the countenance may will to be feared. Nay, rather,
will to be hopeful; and let it be shame, for one who is fearing,
to grow pale with mean-spirited dread. If it is possible, dilate
the soul that is straitened. If the body is weak, let the spirit be
strong; take care to supplement limited physical strength with   320
great hope. An easy deed is made heavy for one who rebels against
it, and a heavy deed becomes light for the willing mind. Will it,
therefore, and to have no fears will be easy.

In time of success, time of auspicious fortune, you may say   325
these words as presage of grief to come:

Queen of kingdoms while King Richard lives, England, whose
glory spreads afar a mighty name, you to whom is left the world's
dominion, your position is secure under so great a helmsman.   330
Your king is the mirror in which, seeing yourself, you take pride;
the star, with whose radiance you shine; the pillar, whose sup-
port gives you strength; the lightning which you send against
foes; the glory by which you almost attain the height of the
gods. But why do I mention details? Nature could not have made   335
one greater than he, and willed not to make his peer. But let no
reliance at all be placed in human strength; death breaks what is
brave. Have no faith in your omens; if they have shone briefly
upon you, soon stormy fate will bring to a close the calm day,
and the shadows of twilight will usher in night. Soon now will   340
be shattered that mirror which it is your glory to view; that star
will suffer eclipse by whose light you shine; that pillar will shud-
der and crash whence you now draw your strength; that light-
ning will cease to flash which now makes your enemies tremble;
and you who are queen will be slave. Happy omens are about to
bid you farewell: you are at ease now, soon you will toil; now   345
you laugh, you will weep; you are wealthy, you will be in need;
now you are flourishing, soon you will wither; you have being
now, you will scarcely even have that. But how will you know

it? What will you do? Will your ear interpret the singing of birds—or their movements your eye? Will you question the fates of Apollo? Away with astrologers! Deaf is the augur, the sooth- 350 sayer blind, and the prophet mad. To know present things is permitted to man; God alone knows the future. Let augury's ancient error return to its native place—its home is not here; and let the heathen father of falsehood feed what he begot; for sound 355 faith removes from the light of the Church the tripods of Phoebus and the throne of the Sibyl. You can foreknow this one thing: that no power can be lasting; that fortune ordains short life for prosperity. If you wish examples, consider the fates of your elders. The flowering prosperity of earlier times has with- 360 ered away: Minos overthrew Athens; the son of Atreus, Ilium; Scipio, the forts of great Carthage; and many a man conquered Rome. Fate's game of chance was reversed in short order. Short is the space between happy omens and sad; night is the neighbor 365 of day. The fates of others teach this, but your own fates will teach you.

In time of grief, express your grief with these words:

Once defended by King Richard's shield, now undefended, O England, bear witness to your woe in the gestures of sorrow. Let 370 *your eyes flood with tears, and pale grief waste your features. Let writhing anguish twist your fingers, and woe make your heart within bleed. Let your cry strike the heavens. Your whole being dies in his death; the death was not his but yours. Death's rise was not in one place only but general. O tearful day of Venus! O bitter star! That day was your night; and that Venus your ven-* 375 *om. That day inflicted the wound; but the worst of all days was that other—the day after the eleventh—which, cruel stepfather to life, destroyed life. Either day, with strange tyranny, was a murderer. The besieged one pierced the besieger; the sheltered* 380 *one, him without cover; the cautious one pierced the incautious; the well-equipped soldier pierced an unarmed man—his own king! O soldier, why, treacherous soldier, soldier of treachery, shame of the world and sole dishonour of warfare; O soldier, his own army's creature, why did you dare this against him? Why did* 385 *you dare this crime, this hideous crime? O sorrow! O greater than sorrow! O death! O truculent death! Would you were dead, O death! Bold agent of a deed so vile, how dare you recall it?*

You were pleased to remove our sun, and condemn day to dark-
ness. Do you realize whom you snatched from us? To our eyes he   390
was light; to our ears, melody; to our minds an amazement. Do
you realize, impious death, whom you snatched from us? He was
the lord of warriors, the glory of kings, the delight of the world.
Nature knew not how to add any further perfection; he was the
utmost she could achieve. But that was the reason you snatched
him away: you seize precious things, and vile things you leave as   395
if in disdain. And Nature, of you I complain; for were you not,
when the world was still young, when you lay new-born in your
cradle, giving zealous attention to him? And that zeal did not
flag before your old age. Why did such strenuous effort bring   400
this wonder into the world, if so short an hour stole the pride of
that effort away? You were pleased to extend your hand to the
world and then to withdraw it; to give thus, and then to recall
your gift. Why have you vexed the world? Either give back to us
him who is buried, or give us one like him in excellence. But you   405
have not resources for that; whatever you had that was won-
drous or precious was expended on him. On him were exhausted
your stores of delight. You were made most wealthy by this crea-
ture you made; you see yourself, in his fall, most impoverished.
If you were happy before, in proportion to happiness then is   410
your misery now. If heaven allow it, I chide even God. O God,
most excellent of beings, why do you fail in your nature here?
Why, as an enemy would, do you strike down a friend? If you
recall, your own Joppa gives evidence for the king—alone he de-
fended it, opposed by so many thousands. Acre, too, gives evi-   415
dence—his power restored it to you. The enemies of the cross
add their witness—all of them Richard, in life, inspired with
such terror that he is still feared now he is dead. He was a man
under whom your interests were safe. If, O God, you are, as
befits your nature to be, faithful and free of malice, just and
true, why then did you shorten his days? You could have shown   420
mercy to the world; the world was in need of him. But you
choose to have him with you, and not with the world; you would
rather favour heaven than the world. O Lord, if it is permissible
to say it, let me say—with your leave—you could have done this   425
more graciously, and with less haste, if he had bridled the foe at
least (and there would have been no delay to that end; he was on

the verge of success). He could have departed more worthily then
to remain with you. But by this lesson you have made us know   430
how brief is the laughter of earth, how long are its tears.

If you wish to rise up in full strength against the ridiculous,
assail them in this form of speech: offer praise, but in a facetious
manner; reprove, but with wit and grace; have recourse to gestures but let these be consistently fitting. Give your speech teeth;
attack with biting force—but let your manner rather than your   435
lips devour the absurd. Lo, what was hidden in darkness will be
revealed in full light. A lively theme is under discussion: *"Boys*
are raised up and made masters." Let their "masterly status"
evoke laughter:

Now he sits, loftily graced with the title of master, who up   440
to now was fit for the rod. For laymen, the cap on his head guar-
antees him authentic; as do the cut of his robes, the gold on his
fingers, his seat at the head, and the crowd in his study.

You can laugh at the absurd situation; it is indeed a ridiculous
thing:

By his own and by popular verdict this is a learned man.

But you perceive the same thing that I do: he is a very ape   445
among scholars. I said that in a whisper, let no one hear it aloud.
He boasts of himself indeed, and rattling on, promises marvels.
Hurry up, one and all; now the mountain's in labour, but its offspring will be only a mouse. Going before him, bid the master   450
good day; but smile, too, at times, with a sidelong glance. Mock
him with the ciconia's sign of derision; or pull a wry mouth, or
draw in your nostrils: for such expressions of ridicule it is fitting
to use not the mouth but the nose.

Apostrophe varies its countenance thus: with the mien of a   455
magistrate it rebukes vicious error; or it languishes in tearful
complain against all that is harsh; or is roused to wrath over
some great crime; or appears with derisive force in attacking buffoons. When evoked by causes such as these, apostrophe contrib-   460
utes both adornment and amplification.

Fifth aid, personification, come forward to lengthen our route
yet further. Give power of speech to that which has in itself no
such power—let poetic license confer a tongue. So the earth,
feeling Phaeton's heat, complained to Jove; so Rome, with di-   465
shevelled hair, bewailed in tearful voice the death of Caesar. If

an original example is acceptable, consider this one; here, employing personification, is the complaint of the holy cross:

I, the ravished cross, make my complaint, seized by violent
and brutish hands and defiled by the touch of curs. Shamefully　470
was I seized long ago, and I am not yet wrested back, not yet re-
deemed by the sword. Tell me, O man, did I not grow tall for
you? Was I not made fruitful for you? Did I not bear sweet fruit
for you, did I not bear salvation? Tell me, tell me, O man—tell
me, you who were lost, you whom I redeemed, did I deserve to
be thus seized without an avenger? To perish thus? No hostile　475
power, but your own sin had made possible my seizure from
you. Since I saw your numerous crimes, when seized I willed to
be seized. It was less shame to be held at naught in an alien
camp than to be so held in my own. If your vileness was con-　480
cealed from the world, yet he who sees all things saw you. God
fully knows your whole being, both inside and out; and he took
me from you. In accord with rigorous law, grave vengeance ought
to have fallen upon you: death without end. But I have come,
says the merciful one, to have mercy on those who are miserable,
not to insist on judgment. I have come to spare, not to punish.　485
Take heed! Come to your senses! Turn back at last lest you per-
ish, O Sunamite! If you but turn, I shall turn to you, and return
with fervour to your returned heart. Rise up at once, make haste,
the hour compels and impels you. Why do you sleep? Awake! If　490
the holy cross has redeemed you, redeem the cross by the sword;
become thereby the redeemer of that by which you were redeemed.
What sane man fails to respond to what is for his benefit? Our
Lord toiled on the cross; does the servant rest? Take up your own
cross; he took up his. He tasted the bitter chalice; you do　495
the same! Surely consideration for the servant will not surpass
that for his Lord? If you wish to be his disciple, you must follow
his sufferings with yours. Heaven is not reached by delights.
Render therefore to God that death you must needs pay to na-
ture: die in him. Since escape from death is impossible, make of　500
necessity a virtue. Let my cause be martial for you, even though
it be mortal. If you are vanquished, by that very defeat you are
victor; for indeed to be vanquished is more than to vanquish; the
victor enjoys the mere hope of the crown, the vanquished enjoys
its possession. Burst asunder delays, then; silence the body's pro-　505

test; set aside your pleasures; and let the ready hand be swift to take arms, and the winged will chafe at delays.

A second example of the effective use of personification will be helpful: if, for instance, a tablecloth now worn out should say:

I was once the pride of the table, while my youth was in its 510 *first flower and my face knew no blemish. But since I am old, and my visage is marred, I do not wish to appear. I withdraw from you, table; farewell!*

In this way, personification employs two tones: at one time its speech is serious, at another jocose.

If this early example is not sufficient, here is a recent one. A 515 proud fortress, rising up on the brow of a hill, seemed to speak thus to the French:

Why, O France, do you brag? What grounds for the menace and pride of your speech? Away with your arrogance! Unlearn your threatening gestures! Why the shields at your side, or the 520 *spears, or the swords? Womanish rabble, abandon your manly maneuvers, that your bearing may accord with your deeds. Strip off the shield and the helmet's cone. It becomes your ilk to spin the weighed wool and to empty the distaff. Why, then, or of what do you boast? Put a curb on your tongue; fear to utter your* *520 *insolent words. I will bridle your jaws, and throw chains on your neck, and in a short time I will make you a slave. I am engaged in a mere trifle when I meet you, the would-be minion of Mars! Let other foes rise, any number you please; they are not equal to me; I am rather a cause of fear to them, I who am fash-* 525 *ioned to the model of King Richard's heart.*

If it is desirable to amplify the treatise yet more fully, go outside the bounds of the subject and withdraw from it a little; let the pen digress, but not so widely that it will be difficult to find the way back. This technique demands a talent marked by re- 530 straint, lest the bypath be longer than decorum allows. A kind of digression is made when I turn aside from the material at hand, bringing in first what is actually remote and altering the natural order. For sometimes, as I advance along the way, I leave the middle of the road, and with a kind of leap I fly off to the side, as it were; then I return to the point whence I had digressed. Lest 535 this matter of digression be veiled in obscurity, I offer the following example:

The bond of a single love bound together two hearts; a strange
cause divided them one from the other. But before they were   540
parted, lips pressed kisses on lips; a mutual embrace holds and
enfolds them both. From the fount of their eyes, tears flow down
their cheeks, and sobs alternate with farewells. Love is a spur to
grief, and grief a witness to the strength of love. Winter yields to
spring. The air unclasps its robe of cloud, and heaven caresses the   545
earth. Moist and warm, air sports with earth, and the feminine
earth feels the masculine power of the air. A flower, earth's child,
bursts forth into the breeze and smiles at its mother. Their first
foliage adorns the tips of the trees; seeds that were dead spring   550
up into life; the promise of harvest to come lives first in the ten-
der blade. Now is the season in which birds delight. This hour of
time found the lovers apart, who yet through their love were not
parted.

Description, pregnant with words, follows as a seventh means
of amplifying the work. But although the path of description is   555
wide, let it also be wise, let it be both lengthy and lovely. See that
the words with due ceremony are wedded to the subject. If description is to be the food and ample refreshment of the mind,
avoid too curt a brevity as well as trite conventionality. Examples of description, accompanied by novel figures, will be varied,   560
that eye and ear may roam amid a variety of subjects.

If you wish to describe, in amplified form, a woman's beauty:
Let the compass of Nature first fashion a sphere for her head;
let the colour of gold give a glow to her hair, and lilies bloom   565
high on her brow. Let her eyebrows resemble in dark beauty the
blackberry, and a lovely and milk-white path separate their twin
arches. Let her nose be straight, of moderate length, not too long
nor too short for perfection. Let her eyes, those watch-fires of
her brow, be radiant with emerald light, or with the brightness of 570
stars. Let her countenance emulate dawn: not red, nor yet white—
but at once neither of those colours and both. Let her mouth be
bright, small in shape—as it were, a half-circle. Let her lips be
rounded and full, but moderately so; let them glow, aflame, but   575
with gentle fire. Let her teeth be snowy, regular, all of one size,
and her breath like the fragrance of incense. Smoother than pol-
ished marble let Nature fashion her chin—Nature, so potent a
sculptor. Let her neck be a precious column of milk-white beauty,   580

holding high the perfection of her countenance. From her crystal
throat let radiance gleam, to enchant the eye of the viewer and
enslave his heart. Let her shoulders, conforming to beauty's law,
not slope in unlovely descent, nor jut out with an awkward rise; 585
rather, let them be gracefully straight. Let her arms be a joy to
behold, charming in their grace and their length. Let soft and
slim loveliness, a form shapely and white, a line long and straight,
flow into her slender fingers. Let her beautiful hands take pride 590
in those fingers. Let her breast, the image of snow, show side by
side its twin virginal gems. Let her waist be close girt, and so
slim that a hand may encircle it. For the other parts I am silent—
here the mind's speech is more apt than the tongue's. Let her leg 595
be of graceful length and her wonderfully tiny foot dance with
joy at its smallness.
So let the radiant description descend from the top of her head
to her toe, and the whole be polished to perfection.
If you wish to add to the loveliness thus pictured an account 600
of attire:
Let her hair, braided and bound at her back, bind in its gold;
let a circlet of gold gleam on her ivory brow. Let her face be free
of adornment, lovely in its natural hue. Have a starry chain en-
circle her milk-white neck. Let the border of her robe gleam with 605
fine linen; with gold let her mantle blaze. Let a zone, richly set
with bright gems, bind her waist, and bracelets enrich her arms.
Have gold encircle her slender fingers, and a jewel more splendid
than gold shed its brilliant rays. Let artistry vie with materials in
her fair attire; let no skill of hand or invention of mind be able 610
to add aught to that apparel. But her beauty will be of more worth
than richness of vesture. Who, in this torch, is unaware of the
fires? Who does not find the flame? If Jupiter in those days of
old had seen her, he would not, in Amphitryon's shape, have de-
luded Alcmena; nor assumed the face of Diana to defraud you, 615
Callisto, of your flower nor would he have betrayed Io in the
form of a cloud, nor Antiope in the shape of a satyr, nor the daugh-
ter of Agenor as a bull, nor you, Mnemosyne, as a shepherd; nor
the daughter of Asopo in the guise of fire; nor you, Deo's daugh-
ter, in the form of a serpent; nor Leda as a swan; nor Danae in 620
a shower of gold. This maiden alone would he cherish, and see
all others in her.

But since the description of beauty is an old and even trite theme,
let the following lines serve as model for a less common subject:
When the festal couch welcomes kings and powerful princes,   625
the image of milk is first of the table's delights: Ceres is honoured.
Aged Bacchus grows young in goblets of gold; alone there, or min-
gled with fragrant nectar, he condescends to depart from his ele-
gance and be merry. A royal procession of dishes parades in on
platters of gold; courses and gold marvel at themselves and each   630
other. The guests note above all the paragon of the table: his
countenance vies with Paris, his youth with Parthenopeus, with
Croesus his wealth, his lineage with Caesar. If you would note
other details of his person, his linen vies with the snow, his pur-
ple with flame, his jewel with a star. You would observe that cer-   635
tain details give greater pleasure according as they cater to the
taste of the guests. The mime has diverse attractions to woo both
the eye and the ear. His manner of entertaining is not the same
for all; each man to his taste. A varied programme has greater
appeal. The ringing sistra fly, feeding the eyes of kings; they pass   640
from hand to hand, and sistrum flies up to meet sistrum. They
vanish and reappear, and repeatedly rise and fall. They feign threats,
and conduct what looks like a sportive battle; they fly from each
other and pursue each other. While the twin castanets are play-   645
ing in the two hands of a second mime, song plays on his lips;
nor are his feet idle—they move gracefully forward and back and
around with the same light step. Voice is the dance's partner;
song strikes the skies, the castanets clash together, sound makes
joyous assault on the ear. A third man, agile in tumbling, whirls
over in somersaults; takes a flying leap; or with graceful bound   650
springs erect from a supine position; or arches his supple limbs
with his neck bent back towards his ankles. Or he raises the point
of his sword and leaps sure-footed amidst treacherous blades.
You would marvel at every exploit; but still more enjoyable than   655
these, now the sound of wrestling arises: now in sport and skill
fingers are locked together; now the hand, hooked back, curves
the arm into an arc at the side, and with swift maneuver de-
prives the shoulders of movement. You could see musical instru-   660
ments follow the sport, each with its own way of pleasing: the
feminine flute, the masculine trumpet, the hollow drum, the clear
bright cymbals, the mellow symphonia, the sweet-sounding pipe,

*the cithera sleep-inducing, and the merry fiddle. Warmly the guests
applaud the whole entertainment; and whatever delights are appropriate for the banquets of kings while away the hours.* 665

In this way you may celebrate the feasts of kings and the joys
of the feast. In this way we amplify by a long description the
brief matter proposed.

There remains yet another means of fostering the amplified style:
any statement at all may assume two forms: one form makes a
positive assertion, the other negates its opposite. The two modes 670
harmonize in a single meaning; and thus two streams of sound
flow forth, each flowing along with the other. Words flow in abundance from the two streams. Consider this example: *"That
young man is wise."* Affirm the youthfulness of his countenance 675
and deny its age: *"His is the appearance of youth and not of old
age."* Affirm the maturity of his mind and deny its youthfulness:
"His is the mind of mature age and not of youth." The account
may perhaps continue along the same line: *"His is not the cheek
of age but of youth; his is not the mind of youth but of age."* 680
Or, choosing details closely related to the theme, you may travel
a rather long path, thus:

*His face is not wrinkled, nor is his skin dry; his heart is not
stricken with age, nor is his breath laboured; his loins are not
stiff, nor is his back bowed; physically he is a young man, men-* 685
tally he is in advanced maturity.

In this way, plentiful harvest springs from a little seed; great
rivers draw their source from a tiny spring; from a slender twig a
great tree rises and spreads.

B. Abbreviation

If you wish to be brief, first prune away those devices mentioned 690
above which contribute to an elaborate style; let the entire theme
be confined within narrow limits. Compress it in accordance with
the following formula. Let *emphasis* be spokesman, saying much
in few words. Let *articulus*, with staccato speech, cut short a 695
lengthy account. The *ablative*, when it appears alone without a
pilot, effects a certain compression. Give no quarter to *repetition*. Let skilful *implication* convey the unsaid in the said. Introduce no *conjunction* as a link between clauses—let them proceed
uncoupled. Let the craftsman's skill effect a *fusion of many* 700

concepts in one, so that many may be seen in a single glance of the mind. By such concision you may gird up a lengthy theme; in this bark you may cross a sea. This form of expression is preferable for a factual account, in order not to enshroud facts discreetly in mist, but rather to clear away mist and usher in sunlight. Combine these devices, therefore, when occasion warrants: emphasis, articulus, ablative absolute, deft implication of one thing in the rest, omission of conjunctions between clauses, fusion of many concepts in one, avoidance of repetition. Draw on all of these, or at least on such as the subject allows. Here is a model of abbreviation; the whole technique is reflected in it:

> Her husband abroad improving his fortunes, an adulterous wife bears a child. On his return after long delay, she pretends it begotten of snow. Deceit is mutual. Slyly he waits. He whisks off, sells, and—reporting to the mother a like ridiculous tale—pretends the child melted by sun.

If a concise account is to be kept within very narrow limits, be especially careful to let every general statement lie dormant. Do not be concerned about verbs; rather, write down with the pen of the mind only the nouns; the whole force of a theme resides in the nouns. Once this has been done, follow, as it were, the technique of the metal-worker. Transfer the iron of the material, refined in the fire of the understanding, to the anvil of the study. Let the hammer of the intellect make it pliable; let repeated blows of that hammer fashion from the unformed mass the most suitable words. Let the bellows of the mind afterwards fuse those words, adding others to accompany them, fusing nouns with verbs, and verbs with nouns, to express the whole theme. The glory of a brief work consists in this: it says nothing either more or less than is fitting. The exercise of an unusual brevity may be yet more pointed; the following concise lines serve as illustration:

> A husband, selling him whom the adulterous mother feigns begotten of snow, in turn feigns him melted by sun. Since his wife feigns her offspring begotten of snow, the husband sells him, and likewise feigns he was melted by sun.

IV. Ornaments of Style

Whether it be brief or long, a discourse should always have both

internal and external adornment, but with a distinction of ornament reflecting the distinction between the two orders. First
examine the mind of a word, and only then its face; do not trust   740
the adornment of its face alone. If internal ornament is not in
harmony with external, a sense of propriety is lacking. Adorning
the face of a word is painting a worthless picture: it is a false thing,
its beauty fictitious; the word is a white-washed wall and a hyp-
ocrite, pretending to be something whereas it is nothing. Its fair   745
form conceals its deformity; it makes a brave outward show, but
has nothing within. It is a picture that charms one who stands at
a distance, but displeases the viewer who stands at close range.
Take care, then, not to be hasty, but be Argus in relation to   750
what you have said, and Argus-eyed, examine the words in relation to the meaning proposed. If the meaning has dignity, let
that dignity be preserved; see that no vulgar word may debase it.
That all may be guided by precept: let rich meaning be honoured
by rich diction, lest a noble lady blush in pauper's rags.   755
    In order that meaning may wear a precious garment, if a word
is old, be its physician and give to the old a new vigour. Do not
let the word invariably reside on its native soil—such residence
dishonours it. Let it avoid its natural location, travel about else-   760
where, and take up a pleasant abode on the estate of another.
There let it stay as a novel guest, and give pleasure by its very
strangeness. If you provide this remedy, you will give to the word's
face a new youth.

1. Difficult Ornament

The method suggested above affords guidance in the artistic   765
transposition of words. If an observation is to be made about
man, I turn to an object which clearly resembles man [in the
quality or state of being I wish to attribute to him]. When I see
what that object's power vesture is, in the aspect similar to man's,
I borrow it, and fashion for myself a new garment in place of
the old. For example, taking the words in their literal sense, gold   770
is said to be yellow; milk, white; a rose, very red; honey, sweet-
flowing; flames, glowing; snow, white. Say therefore: *snowy* teeth,
flaming lips, *honied* taste, *rosy* countenance, *milky* brow, *golden*
hair. These word pairs are well suited to each other: teeth, snow;   775
lips, flames; taste, honey; countenance, rose; brow, milk; hair,

gold. And since here the linking of aspects that are similar sheds
a pleasing light, if the subject of your discourse is not man, turn
the reins of your mind to the human realm. With artistic tact,
transpose a word which, in its literal sense, applies to man in an   780
analogous situation. For example, if you should wish to say:
"Springtime makes the earth beautiful; the first flowers grow up;
the weather turns mild; storms cease; the sea is calm, its motion
without violence; the vales are deep, the mountains lofty"; con-   785
sider what words, in a literal sense, express the analogous situation in our human life. When you adorn something, you *paint*;
when you enter on existence, you *are born*; affable in discourse,
you *placate*; withdrawing from all activity, you *sleep*; motion-
less, you *stand on fixed foot*; sinking down, you *lie*; lifted into   790
the air, you *rise*. The wording is a source of pleasure, then, if
you say:

Springtime paints the earth with flowers: the first blossoms are
born; the mild weather soothes; storms, dying down, slumber;
the sea stands still, as if without movement; the valleys lie deep; the   795
mountains rise aloft.

When you transpose a word whose literal meaning is proper to
man, it affords greater pleasure, since it comes from what is your
own. Such a metaphor serves you as mirror, for you see yourself
in it and recognize your own sheep in another's field. Consider
several examples of this kind. If, for instance, we wish to de-   800
scribe the malignity of winter, introducing this trope:

Winter ever threatens with mouth agape, harsher than harsh
tyrants. At its command, storm clouds spread gloom through the
sky; darkness blinds the eye of day; the air gives birth to tem-
pests; snow closes the roadways; hoar frost pierces one's marrow;   805
hail lashes the earth; ice imprisons the waves.

Or, if we would speak of weather favourable for navigation:

The north wind does not chide the waters, nor the south wind
inebriate the air; but the rays of the sun, like a broom in the
murky sky, sweep clean the heavens; and with placid mien the   810
season fawns on the deep; the secret murmuring of a breeze stills
the water and quickens the sails.

Or if, in similar strain, we would speak of the metal-smith's
work:

Flames waken in response to the bellows; the crude metal is

buried in fire; tongs transfer the heated mass directly from fire to 815
forge; the mallet, as master, deals blow after blow, and with
hard strokes chastises the metal; and so it does what he wishes:
it draws forth a rounded helmet, useful counsellor for the head;
or it generates a sword, legitimate fellow for the side; or a cui-
rass makes its appearance, friend of the body; together with these 820
are born a greave, for the leg to don as shield, and a spur to in-
cite the horse, which the ankle adopts as its own; and other
shapes of iron which the craftsman's skill fashions as armour.
Objects so unlike in appearance, arms of such varied shape, ex- 825
haust the iron. The mallet curbs its blow; the forges regain their
breath, their course accomplished; the work comes to rest at its
goal, and completes the task prescribed.

You may transpose verbs very effectively in this way; verbs so 830
transposed will be readily visible to the mind's eye; to transpose
them so, however, requires both labour and skill. This mode of
expression is at once difficult and easy: finding the word is difficult; its relevance, once it is found, is easy. Thus contrary qualities mingle, but they promise peace, and, enemies once, they stay 835
on as friends. There is a certain balance required here: the word
must not be trivial, crude, or awkward; it derives charm and
value from its seriousness of meaning. Its seriousness, however,
must not be pompous or obscure; easiness of comprehension renders it luminous and checks bombast. Each quality must temper 840
the other. Let this be your mode of expression then: combine seriousness and easiness in such a way that the one does not de-
tract from the other; let them be in accord with each other and
enjoy the same dwelling; let harmonious discord reconcile their
differences.

In order that a transposed verb may be introduced with more
finished art, see that it does not enter accompanied by a noun 845
alone. Provide it with an adjective as well, and let the adjective
be such that it affords all possible aid in clearing away any obscurity there may be in the verb. If there is no obscurity, then let
the adjective elucidate the verb's meaning still more fully by shedding clear light upon it. For example, if, employing this manner 850
of speech, I make some such statement as: *the laws relax*, or *the
laws stiffen*, the metaphor is not yet sufficiently clear. The transposed verb hides its meaning, as it were, under a cloud; and since

a verb so introduced remains in darkness, let an adjective come
to its aid and shed light upon it. Say rather: *the modified laws* 855
relax, or *the stringent laws stiffen*. Now the adjective adds meaning to the verb, for stringency suggests rigour and rigid laws;
kindly modification tempers and mitigates laws.

But what if a transposed verb is perfectly clear in itself? Even
so, let an adjective reinforce it, so that its own clarity may be 860
doubled by that of the adjective. Granted that I speak gracefully
enough if I say: *Earth quaffed more of heaven's dew than was*
right, and a shower lavishly dispensed it; yet the expression will
be apter and more effective if you say: *The intoxicated earth* 865
quaffed more dew than was right, and a prodigal shower lavishly
dispensed it; for adjective and verb act as partners and cling together like ivy, as if they could not endure to be torn asunder;
rather they swear a pact of unity and are friends of one mind.
Discrimination of this sort has imparted a fine polish to the 870
words, removing any trace of obscurity.

An even more effective figure, surpassing the rhetorical colour
just mentioned, results when the noun [or adjective] is at strife
with the verb, and they clash on the surface, but beneath there is
friendly and harmonious accord. Here is an illustration: *The mu-* 875
nificent man gives lavishly, but in pouring out wealth he regains
it; never is his hand weary except when it rests. And this: *Before*
the face of God, devout silence cries out. Consider other areas of
experience and observe that the same thing is true: when lovers 880
quarrel, with mutual recrimination, harmony of spirit grows while
tongues are at war; love is built on this estrangement. So, too,
in the examples given above, the words are basically in accord,
although on the surface they are at variance. There is opposition
in the words themselves, but the meaning of the words allays all 885
opposition.

A metaphorical word glows with a different radiance when it
is employed in a figurative and in a literal sense at the same time,
as in this example: *That ancient practical wisdom of Rome armed*
tongues with laws and bodies with iron, that it might prepare
tongues and bodies alike for warfare. Or take this example, since 890
brevity has greater zest: *Faith arms their hearts, iron their bodies*.

A verb is susceptible of metaphorical meaning, so is an adjective, so is a noun. Transposition of a verb, however, is made in

various ways: either in relation to its subject, or to its comple- 895
ment, or to both at once. It is metaphorical in relation to its subject, as in this example: *In springtime clouds are at rest, the air
grows gentle, the breeze is still; birds, chirping to each other, are
merry; the sea slumbers, brooks play, boughs don the raiment of* 900
youth, fields are painted, the earth rejoices. In relation to its complement as here: *The pope, potent in words, scatters seed from
his lips when he speaks; he feeds the eyes thereby, and gives drink
to the ears, and satisfies in abundance the whole mind.* In relation to both, as in lines such as these: *When the lips of the pope* 905
*provide a feast of sweet words, attentive ears, while he speaks,
drink in words from the speaker's lips, and what is heard rest-
fully soothes the mind.*

An adjective is also transposed according to a threefold relationship: either in relation to its noun, which it modifies in a figurative sense, as in this example: *Consider the character of a discourse,* 910
*whether it is raw or overdone, whether succulent or dry, shaggy or
trim, rough or polished, impoverished or sumptuous.* Or in relation to its complement, as in the following: *What will our king
do, unarmed in policy, girt round with hostility, divested of* 915
friends? Or in relation to both at once, as when one says a man
skilled in speech is *flowering* in eloquence; an old man is *wasted*
in years; a poor man *slender* in means.

We have still to consider the transposed use of a noun. If the
noun that is transposed is common, it confers upon diction rhe- 920
torical adornment of this sort: *The thundering of the populace
roused the city*; or: *a trumpet of thunder, the fury of the blast,
the quarreling of the winds, the crashing of the sea, the rage of
the storm.* If the noun is proper, it is transposed either with a
view to praising or censuring by the name alone (you may praise
with such names as this: *He is a Paris*, or you may censure in a 925
similar way: *He is a Thersites*), or with a view to suggesting some
analogy, as for instance in an expression of this kind: *That captain rules the ship and is our Tiphys*, or: *That country fellow
rules the chariot, our guide and our Automedon.* Or I may transpose a proper noun for another reason: that the likeness suggested
may be not a true one, but by contrast a kind of ridicule, as 930
when I call a man deformed in body a *Paris*, or one cruel in heart
an *Aeneas*, one of slight strength a *Pyrrhus*, one rude in speech a

Cicero, or one who is wanton *Hippolytus*. Altered meaning   935
of this kind gives new vitality to a word.

A simple metaphor transposes one word. Sometimes several
words are transposed, as in the following figure: *Shepherds rob
the sheep*; here you transpose two nouns, *shepherds* and *sheep*;
you apply the name of *shepherd* to those in authority, and the   940
name of *sheep* to those who are subject. An entire sentence may
be metaphorical, and no part of it literal, as a sentence of this
kind illustrates: *He plows the shore, washes brick, beats the air.*
These are some of the ways in which metaphor lends adornment
to words.

Transpose words in the ways outlined above. Be moderate,   945
however, not bombastic or pompous. Two elements combine here,
the laudable and the laborious; to transpose a word aptly is laborious, to succeed in transposing it aptly is laudable.

When meaning comes clad in such apparel, the sound of words   950
is pleasant to the happy ear, and delight in what is unusual
stimulates the mind. *Transfero, permuto, pronomino, nomino,*
these verbs form from themselves verbal nouns which are the
names of figures. The one term *transsumptio* includes them all.   955
Take pains to provide dishes like these, together with these
draughts; such feasting satisfies the ear, such draughts slake its
thirst.

Art has woven other garments of less price, yet they, too, have
a dignified and appropriate use. There are in all ten tropes, six in
this group, four mentioned above. This decade of figures adorns   960
expression in a way we term *difficult* in that a word is taken
only in its figurative and not in its literal sense. All the tropes
are of one general class, distinguished by the figurative status of
the words and the uncommon meaning assigned them. Lest understanding be uncertain and hesitant here, the following examples   965
will ensure confidence.

Consider a statement of this kind: *The sick man seeks a physician; the grieving man, solace; the poor man, aid.* Expression attains a fuller flowering in this trope: *Illness is in need of a
physician; grief is in need of solace; poverty is in need of aid.*   970
There is a natural charm in this use of the abstract for the con-
crete, and so in the change of *sick man* to *sickness*, *grieving man*
to *grief*, *poor man* to *poverty*.

What does fear produce? Pallor. What does anger cause? A flush. Or what, the vice of pride? A swelling up. We refashion the statement thus: *Fear grows pale, anger flushes; pride swells.* 975 There is greater pleasure and satisfaction for the ear when I attribute to the cause what the effect claims as its own.

Let the comb's action groom the hair after the head has been washed. Let scissors trim away from the hair whatever is exces- 980 sive, and let a razor give freshness to the face. In this way, art teaches us to attribute to the instrument, by a happy turn of expression, what is proper to the one who uses it. So from the resources of art springs a means of avoiding worn-out paths and of travelling a more distinguished route.

Again, a statement expressed in the following way adds lustre to style: *We have robbed their bodies of steel, their coffers of* 985 *silver, their fingers of gold.* The point here is not that zeugma adorns the words with its own figure of speech, but that when I am about to mention something, I withhold its form completely and mention only the material. Whereas a less elegant style mentions both, art is silent about one, and conveys both by a single term. This device brings with it three advantages: it curtails the 990 number of words required, it constitutes a poetic adornment, and it is helpful to the metre. It curtails the number of words in that a single term is more succinct than a word-group; it constitutes a poetic adornment in that an expression of this kind is artistically more skilful; and it is helpful to the metre if an oblique case, 995 whose form the metre rejects, requires such help. This is clear from the following example: *The finger rejoices in gold. Gold* is a shorter sound, *a ring of gold* is longer; the latter form names the object itself, the former conveys it more artfully; in the former [*aurum*] the metre admits of oblique cases, in the latter [*an-* 1000 *nulus auri*] it rejects them.

Instead of the thing contained, name that which contains it, choosing the word judiciously whether it be noun or adjective. Introduce a noun in this way: *tippling England; weaving Flanders; bragging Normandy.* Try out an adjective thus: *clamorous* 1005 *marketplaces; silent cloisters; lamenting prison; jubilant house; quiet night; laborious day.* Seek turns of expression like the following: *In time of sickness Salerno, with its medical skill, cures those who are ill. In civil causes Bologna arms the defenseless with* 1010

*laws. Paris, in the arts, dispenses bread to feed the strong. Or-
leans, in its cradle, rears tender youth on the milk of the authors.*

Give hyperbole rein, but see that its discourse does not run
ineptly hither and yon. Let reason keep it in check, and its moderate use by a source of pleasure, that neither mind nor ear may   1015
shrink from excess. For example, employing this trope: *A rain of
darts lashes the foe like hail; the shattered array of spears resembles a forest; a tide of blood flows like a wave of the sea, and
bodies clog the valleys.* This mode of expression diminishes or   1020
heightens eulogy to a remarkable degree; and exaggeration is a
source of pleasure when both ear and good usage commend it.

If you intend to say: *I studied for three years,* you may, with
happier effect, adorn the statement. The wording above is inelegant and trite; you may refine the inelegant, your file may renew
the trite in this way: *The third summer came upon me in study;*   1025
*the third autumn found me engaged; the third winter embroiled
me in cares; in study I passed through three spring times.* I word
the statement more skillfully when, suppressing the whole, I imply that whole from the parts, in the way just exemplified. Part
of the year may be wet: *The year is wet;* part may be dry: *The*   1030
year is dry; part may be hot: *The year is hot;* part may be mild:
The year is mild. I attribute to the whole what characterizes a
part of it. By this same mode of reckoning, you, Gion, will be
accounted turbid and clear, narrow and broad, brackish and sweet,   1035
because of some varied part of your course. Again, by the same
figure, a day is to be accounted dry and yet rainy because of a
part of it. Since both forms of this figure are pleasing, you may
give pleasure by either form.

There is likewise an urbane imprecision of diction when a word
is chosen which is neither literal nor precise in its context, but
which is related to the literal word. For example, if one proposes   1040
to say: *The strength of the Ithacan is slight, but yet he has a
mind of great wisdom,* let catachresis alter the wording thus:
Strength in Ulysses is short, wisdom in his heart is long, for
there is a certain affinity between the words *long* and *great,* as   1045
between *short* and *slight.*

In the figures given above there is a common element of adornment and weightiness, arising from the fact that an object does
not come before us with unveiled face, and accompanied by its

natural voice; rather, an alien voice attends it, and so it shrouds 1050
itself in mist, as it were, but in a luminous mist.

A certain weightiness of style results also from the order of
words alone, when units grammatically related are separated by
their position, so that an inversion of this sort occurs: *rege sub
ipso; tempus ad illud; ea de causa; rebus in illis* [under the king
himself; until that time; for this reason; in those matters]; or a 1055
transposed order of this sort: *Dura creavit pestiferam fortuna
famem* [harsh fortune produced a pestilent famine]; *Letalis ege-
nam gente fames spoliavit humum* [deadly famine robbed the
destitute soil of produce]. Here words related grammatically are
separated by their position in the sentence. Juxtaposition of related words conveys the sense more readily, but their moderate
separation sounds better to the ear and has greater elegance. 1060

If you wish to speed onward by means of the weighty style,
have recourse to these sails, occupy this harbour, cast the mind's
anchor here. Yet be weighty in such a manner that your subject
is not hidden under a cloud; rather let the words pay fealty to 1065
their rightful lord. Words are instruments to unlock the closed
mind; they are keys, as it were, of the mind. One who seeks to
open what is closed does not set out to draw a cloud over his
words. If indeed he has done so, he has done an injury to the
words, for he has made a lock out of a key. Be the bearer of a
key, then; open up the subject readily by your words; for if what 1070
is said enters through the ears into the mind's gaze without light,
it is pouring water into a river, planting in dry soil, beating in
the air, drawing a plow in sterile sand. If, therefore, you introduce any words that are strange or recondite, you are displaying
your own virtuosity thereby and not observing the rules of dis- 1075
course. The straying tongue must draw back from this fault and
set up barriers against obscure words. Take counsel: it may be
you know all things—you are greater than others in this—still,
in your mode of expression be one of those others. Be of average, 1080
not lofty, eloquence. The precept of the ancients is clear: speak
as the many, think as the few. You do not demean yourself by
observing this precept; you can be at once elegant and easy in
discourse. Regard not your own capacities, therefore, but rather 1085
his with whom you are speaking. Give to your words weight suited
to his shoulders, and adapt your speech to the subject. When you

are teaching the arts, let your speech be native to each art; each
delights in its own idiom. But see that its idiom is kept within
its own borders; when you come out into the common market-
place it is desirable to use the common idiom. In a common   1090
matter, let the style be common; in specialized matters let the
style be proper to each. Let the distinctive quality of each subject
be respected: in the use of words this is a very commendable
practice.

2. Easy Ornament

If a mode of expression both easy and adorned is desired, set   1095
aside all the techniques of the dignified style and have recourse
to means that are simple, but of a simplicity that does not shock
the ear by its rudeness. Here are the rhetorical colours with which
to adorn your style:

*Deed so evil! Deed more evil than others! Deed most evil of all
deeds! O apple! Wretched apple! Miserable apple! Why did it*   1100
*affect you, that tasting of Adam? Why do we all weep for the
fault of that one man, Adam? That taste of the apple* [māli] *was
the general cause of evil* [măli]. *The father* [pater], *to us so cruel
a foe, showed himself not to be father* [patrem]. *He who was rich
became poor; he who was happy, wretched; he who enjoyed such
radiance was thrust back into darkness. Where now is Paradise,*   1105
*and that joy of which you were lord? I ask you, most powerful
of creatures, whence sprang your great crime? You sin by approving in spirit the deed of your wife, by tasting forbidden fruit, by
defending your actions in speech. Approving, tasting, defending,* 1110
*do you not then merit your fall? Tell me, why did you touch
fruit so harmful? My wife offered it me. But why did you taste
it? She was persuasive. Knowing the deed pernicious, why did
you approve? I was afraid of making her angry. After the deed,
why were you slow to repent your guilt by petitioning God for*   1115
*pardon? Say, in this deed of death, what reason was found? There
was only delusion for reason.*

*He is free who is not a slave to vice. But since that man was a
slave, shall we enjoy freedom? If he who was strong in great
virtue did not resist the foe, how shall we who are frail resist?* 1120
The fall began with the enemy, and by his cunning we fell, and

corrupt as we are we cannot live without falling. Of avail to the
fallen is aid of this kind: tears, fasting, psalms.

The unclean spirit does not harm him for whom God is more
powerful than the world. He who places no hope in the foe— 1125
whence can he fear the foe? If the foe is wont to be grievously
harmful only to those who are his, benevolent law does not suffer
us to be of his tribe. Lest perchance tempests by their violence
overwhelm us, let us preserve honour and reject evil. For virtue is 1130
most excellent [optima] *of all things, vice* [vitium] *is the worst*
[pessima] *of things—nothing is so pernicious* [perniciosum].

This he had proved [expertus], *this he pitied* [misertus]—*he*
who, deigning to be born [nasci], *came to be reborn* [renasci] *from*
death; the man who could be [potuit]—*he alone—the being who*
brought good [profuit] *to all. Here in flesh* [carne] *without flaw*
[carie], *not caught in fault's* [criminis] *net* [hamo], *a man* [homo] 1135
simple and suppliant [simplex, supplex], *he set at naught* [lusit],
the insidious serpent who deceived us [elusit], *and, made a hos-*
tage [hostia], *he destroyed the hostile one* [hostem] *and by his*
dying dismayed him [moriendo, remordit].

Serpent of envy and foe of our race, why did you seek Christ's
death on the cross? Did he deserve it? But he was free of all 1140
guilt. Did you think his body a phantom? But he assumed true
flesh of a virgin. Did you think him mere man? But by his power
he proved himself God. Deservedly, therefore, are you condemned.
Remember, the servant who condemns his master will be con- 1145
demned by him. So condemnation justly came to a close with
him from whom it began. For the enemy had first condemned
Eve; Eve, secondly, condemned her husband; her husband, thirdly,
condemned all his offspring; the offspring, fourthly, condemned
God; God, last of all, condemned the enemy whose cause of 1150
death he was—he was, and so to the world he brought good; he
brought good, and it was made free; it was made free because he
redeemed all things. If he contended by his own power and ef-
fortlessly, he would have saved all things. For his might is a virtue
almighty, and his is the power to do all things by a nod or a
word or simply by willing. You see that he could do this; in the 1155
sequel you will hear why this was not his will. Here is his rea-
soning: if open violence were offered the foe, God could be—

nay, would be—not acting in accord with strict justice in this.
The demands of justice decreed—but I pass this by as well
known—that as the enemy brought death to mankind through   1160
treacherous means, so man by subtle maneuver should bring death
to the enemy, taken captive in the toils of divinity. For this rea-
son, to dwell with us in true flesh God came; marked with the
stain of our flesh he could not be; and at length those who were   1165
his in his own blood he washed. Lord of life and death as he
was, death he rent asunder and life—rent life asunder by dying,
and death by rising again; not by the life he first assumed, but
by that same life resumed his own he redeemed.

Betrayer of human nature—betrayer, I say, where is now your
strength? Where is your strength? Death has broken your bonds;   1170
his death with wondrous power has broken your bonds. Death
how happy! How happy a death! That death our redemption! This
death of his healed the wounds of our soul; washed the unclean;
removed guilt. O how holy the grace of Christ! How gracious   1175
the holiness! To you, fount of holiness, I wholly dedicate myself
from this time. Confer, take away; scourge, spare; command,
forbid; do whichever you wish; lo, I am your servant, Lord; use
your servant just as you please; whatever you do, I give thanks.
O Jesus so good, what shall I call you? If I call you holy, or   1180
holiness itself, or fountain of holiness, or add still more, you are
greater yet. This being so great willed to become so small. Com-
ing in the form of a servant, he came to recover the sheep he had
lost, sheep which would be snatched by violence from the enemy,   1185
not by judgment, unless perchance he defeated the foe just as
man had before been defeated. But such a one had to be a pure
man, or an angel, or God. A pure man he could not be, for pure
man straightway was impure and could easily fall into sin. Angel
you could not be, for since the angelic nature had fallen you   1190
would not stand firm in ours. Yet let it be so! Let it be granted
that one or the other had stood strong in virtue and wrought our
redemption. To be created is certainly less than to be redeemed.
Redeemed man would be less bound, then, to the creator and   1195
more to him who redeemed; and so there would have been need
of one greater than his creator. It was necessary, therefore, that
God become man—God whose fullness of wisdom controlled
human faculties with the reins of divinity. To him alone the

world owed both its creation and its redemption; and to God   1200
alone it gave worship. As the need had directed, so was its ful-
filment in act. For other persons there remains a single nature;
the Son united himself to ours, enclosed in the womb of a virgin.
Her womb enclosed him whom the world could not contain; he   1205
had a beginning in time who existed before time was. True man,
true God, he experienced all that is proper to us, sin only ex-
cepted. Enduring mockery, he was silent; beaten with stripes, he
passed through the bonds of death; his gentle body hung on the
fearful cross; his spirit, sent forth, came as rare guest to the   1210
realms below; after three days he returned to life, victorious by
his own power. Thus the shepherd led back to the fold the sheep
that had been drawn astray. How great an event was this! And
what . . . but I let the word pass, for no word can be found ade-
quate to so great a marvel. Therefore since they could not be re-   1215
deemed unless God was made man, and unless, once made man,
he determined to conquer death, the conquering of death redeemed
those who were his from death.

The exercise given above has gathered together the flowers of
diction; in these figures there is both easy intelligibility and a literal use of words. No figure is missing from the number, and the   1220
usual order of the colours is retained. If occasionally I have given
words a metaphorical sense, it has been in accord with good taste
to combine difficult ornaments with easy so that the easy style,
although it affords pleasure by the sweetness of its own manner,
might give still greater pleasure if seasoned with the flavour
of difficult figures. In this way, then, let the mind's finger pluck   1225
its blooms in the field of rhetoric. But see that your style blossoms sparingly with such figures, and with a variety, not a clus-
ter of the same kind. From varied flowers a sweeter fragrance
rises; faulty excess renders insipid what is full of flavour.

There are other figures to adorn the meaning of words. All of   1230
these I include in the following brief treatment: when meaning is
adorned, this is the standard procedure. *Distributio* assigns specific roles to various things or among various persons. At times,
licentia, fairly and lawfully, chides masters or friends, offending   1235
no one with its words. At times, *diminutio* implies more in the
subject than is expressed in words, and makes its point by under-
statement, though with moderation. So, too, *descriptio* presents

consequences, and the eventualities that can ensue from a given
situation. It gives a full and lucid account with a certain dignity   1240
of presentation. Or again, *disjunctio* distinguishes alternatives,
accompanying each with a reason, and, bringing both to a conclusion. Or single details are brought together, and *frequentatio*
gathers up points that had been scattered through the work. By
turning a subject over repeatedly and varying the figure, I seem   1245
to be saying a number of things whereas I am actually dwelling
on one thing, in order to give it a finer polish and impart a
smooth finish by repeated applications of the file, one might say.
This is done in two ways: either by saying the same thing with
variations, or by elaborating upon the same thing. We may say
the same thing with variations in three ways; we may elaborate   1250
upon the same thing with variations in seven ways. You may read
about all of these at greater length in Cicero. [By *commoratio*] I
go deeply into one point and linger on in the same place; or [by
contentio] I institute a comparison in which the positions set
forth are antithetical to each other. Often from an object basically dissimilar I draw forth a point of resemblance. Or I present   1255
as *exemplum*, with the name of a definite authority, some statement he has made or some deed he has performed. Or I pass over
the figures just mentioned, and, as another figure comes to the
fore, I introduce a comparison of one thing with a similar thing
by means of an appropriate image. Or there is a figure allied to   1260
this last one, whereby I depict or represent corporeal appearance,
in so far as is requisite. Again, I set down certain distinguishing
marks—very definite signs, as it were—by which I describe clearly
the character of a man; this is a better and more effective figure.
There is another figure whereby a speech is adapted to the person   1265
speaking, and what is said gives the very tone and manner of the
speaker. Again, adorning the subject with a different kind of freshness, at one time I fashion a new person by giving the power of
speech where nature has denied it; at another, I leave to suspi-   1270
cion more than I actually put into words; again, I compress the
entire subject into a few words—those which are essential to it
and no others. At another time the subject is revealed so vividly
that it seems to be present to the eyes; this effect will be perfectly achieved by five means: if I show what precedes, what con-

stitutes, and what follows the event itself, what circumstances 1275
attend it, and what consequences follow upon it.

You may read, in the passage given above, the list of figures of
thought, their number (twice ten, if you subtract one), and the
sequence they observe. Since the order I followed above will not
be varied, I have rendered the subject clear by offering examples.

To proclaim sacred laws is the pope's prerogative; to observe 1280
the form of law prescribed is the part of lesser men. But very
many go astray, and that straying judges you, holy Father. You
spare, and do not punish, those who seek shameful gain. They
buy and sell what is illicit, with no one to avenge their guilt.
Powerful Father, you whose power is by no means brief, be mind- 1285
ful of vengeance. Gentle Father, unsheathe at some time the
sword's point. If vengeance sleeps, the guilty will range like a
wolf crouched to spring, or a fox lurking in wait for the doe. In
one place he will bring to completion, in another he will medi-
tate crimes; in one instance under cover, in another out in the 1290
open, replete with malice in both. His evils are two: the fraud of
simony, the coldness of avarice. He embraces both the one and
the other, and does not abhor them. But I labour with futile voice;
whatever I may say against him, I am washing brick. If I give 1295
my approval, that is not what he deserves; if I condemn, his
crime does not move him. Note what bitter poison he bears: he
will be seen as a flatterer face to face, a detractor when out of
sight; an apparent friend, a secret enemy; an avaricious owner, a
cruel extortioner; an oppressive plunderer, an ingratiating huck-
ster; an illicit buyer, swift to the evil of simony, now so com- 1300
mon. Most excellent Father, avenger of crimes, extend your hand
to destroy this evil. The wisdom of the pope wishes to suppress
what is wicked, and it is his duty to do so. Neither the task nor
the will is alien to a prudent pope. As a good pope, ponder thus 1305
in your heart very often: "O how marvelous the virtue of God!
How mighty his power! How great I now am! How insignificant
I once was! From a small stock I have grown in a trice to a mighty
cedar. He who is God of gods has magnified his own work; he
has willed me in the flower of youth to be the head of old men. 1310
O wonderful gift! He gives to a young man the keys of the
heavenly kingdom and authority over the world. Not much time

*has passed since my heart was a novice in knowledge; my speech
was unpolished, my power slight. Now he has so raised up my
heart and my lips and my power, and so placed them in this* 1315
*office above others, that I am the world's sole wonder. This is
not the doing of man; the grace of the Highest has set me highest; no praise is due me in this, but thanks is due him from
whose fullness we have received all things. Hence I am bound
more firmly, and more strictly obliged to him to put down what* 1320
*he wills to put down, to raise up what he wills to raise, to wish
what he wishes, to hate what he hates. And I desire to be so
bound; and I will put down all he has ordered put down, I will
raise what he ordered raised, solicitous for one thing alone: to
will what he wills, to hate what he hates." Who is so void of* 1325
*wit, so destitute of soul, so distracted, that he would not praise
this work, that he would not judge it to be the work of a prudent nature? So a prudent pope bases all his efforts on this, and
because of this, that such great power has accrued to him for this
end: to take away the sins of the world, to make the world clean,* 1330
*in order to lead it by the straight path to heaven. Since God has
raised him up to this work, it is his concern to accomplish the
task allotted. Therefore if he is remiss in this, he is fountain and
source of two wrongs: for he is his own enemy and the public
enemy as well. Is it better to injure the world by torpid sleep* 1335
*than to promote its interests by vigilant care? Take heed and re-
member: the pope like a good shepherd guards his fold from the
jaws of the wolf; or, as a physician cures bodies, so he, as physician and shepherd, heals souls and their wounds. Our God, making* 1340
*all things whole, laid down his life for his sheep. So it is evident,
by force of both reason and example, that the sins of the world
must be taken away. Suppress wickedness, then, holy Father, suc-
cessor of Peter; and with his Simon let simony be brought to destruction. His own sordid gain gratifies each man; the general* 1345
*depravity oppresses you only. This one sin is corrupting all men.
It may be that no mortal thing disturbs them, yet while this
stands against them the death of the soul results from one sin as
well as from many: just as a ship is engulfed in the rising seas
because of one crack no less than of many—both dangers have* 1350
*the same destructive effect. Yet it can hardly be that a man may
live without fault, whence Cato the moralist says: "No one lives*

without fault." That spirit of nature malign, the general foe,
swoops round man on hidden wings, with tortured desire to win   1355
back the one whom he lost. That great champion of ours snatched
man away with the mighty power of a lion, the cunning of a serpent, and the simplicity of a dove. Who is he? He is, indeed, of two
natures. Free of all blemish, somewhat ruddy of countenance, pleas-   1360
ant to view, paragon of angels, a form beautiful above the forms
of men, special image of the Father; he, the second Adam, who
opened for us the gates of life with the key of his death. Called
as we are to those joys, what do we do? We are apathetic, in the   1365
image of the lazy man. Do you know the procrastination of the
lazy man? If he is called in the morning he refuses to hear. If he
is summoned repeatedly, with insistent voice, he snores loudly
through his nose, although he is awake. Forced at length by the
shouts, but sluggish of speech, he gets his tongue moving and
"What do you want with me," he says.—"Get up! Come on   1370
now!"—"It's night, let me sleep."—"No, it's daytime; get up!"—
"Ye gods! Look—I am getting up. Go ahead; I'll be there." But
he doesn't follow the man he's fooling; and then: "Aren't you
coming?"—"I'd have been there by now, but I'm looking for my
clothes and can't find them."—"It's no use—I know you, Birria.   1375
Get up at once!"—"Sir, I'm right with you." But he isn't; rather
he turns his head to this side and that, or scratches his arms, or
stretches his limbs. So he looks for any excuse for delay. With his
lips, he is always coming—but not with his feet. So, coming, he
never arrives—not he. Driven to it, perhaps, he drags his steps as   1380
he moves, matching a turtle's pace. We, when called to true joys,
are the very image of this man. Enchanted by pleasures of many
kinds, we close up the ears of our heart; or, if our ears are open,
we still put off coming to those joys. Or if we come, unwillingly
drawn perhaps, we move at the pace of a tortoise. Reckless of our   1385
welfare, we neglect our Lord for the foe. Ah wretched men! Why
will we not remember the day of counsel, on which his hand redeemed us from the claws of the enemy; remember, indeed, what
things he endured, what manner of things, what great things, in   1390
torments, in mocking words? The servant of the high priest maliciously denounced the replies of our Lord, and striking him
said: "Do you answer the high priest thus?" He gently responded:
"Friend, if I have spoken anything ill, tell me in what. If well,

why do you strike me?" To you also, Pilate, resisting as far as   1395
you could, Judea thundered, howling, "Crucify him!"—taking
up the cry and roaring again, "Crucify him!" As they struck him
with blows, another added these mocking words: "Prophesy,
Christ, who is it that struck you?" Insolently another continued: 1400
"Others he saved, in his own cause he's a failure. He hoped in
the Lord, let the Lord, if he wills, release him." He willed to be
treated thus with contempt, he who was scourged with rods,
hung on the wood of the cross, given vinegar to drink, pierced
with a lance, struck with a reed, his head crowned with sharp   1405
thorns; enduring all sorrows, he ended deaths so varied in one
death. [Spittle, the lash, threats, reproaches, nails, the lance,
thorns—in his blessed death, these are the goal to which our fall
led. By these delights, O man, by this craft of the cross, he re-
deemed you, strongly weak while he destroyed death by dying].   1410
When he suffered death, nature said: "I must needs suffer; my
Lord is suffering. Lament with me, all manner of things; heaven,
hide your lights; grow darkling, O air; seas, roar aloud; tremble,
O earth; all elements weep together." Nature shuddered in lam-   1415
entation and was rent apart wholly. All manner of things gave
forth signs: heaven hiding her lights, the air growing dark, the
sea roaring aloud, earth trembling, all the elements in tears. That
did not happen in accord with the natural sequence of things,   1420
but because the Lord of nature had suffered the violence of death.
Nature suffered that violence with you, compelled by your sor-
row. Only a people perverse scoffed at the dying God; their sub-
sequent history bears the shame. Treacherous race! Stiff-necked
generation! Learn to soften that heart so hardened; remember the   1425
fearful destruction of cruel Pharaoh. Learn how to be blessed;
search out each detail about Christ; you will see with clear eyes.
Ought not Christ to have suffered thus? According to the in-
scription there written, the Lord reigned from the cross and won   1430
there the victory, repelled the enemy and redeemed the world.
Thus a man fought for mankind, but that man was God; a com-
batant then, now wielding a royal sceptre, and, in time to come,
judge. That the saviour of man had to be God and no other, the
Son, not the Father or Holy Spirit, conclude from these few re-   1435
marks. When the angelic choirs were created at heaven's birth,
Lucifer, peerless in radiance, drew from the creator's radiance

more light than others; therefore he grew presumptuous. Then,
swelling with pride, he began to aspire towards the ultimate   1440
light. For he saw Light begotten of Light, the Word of the Fa-
ther; he saw, too, the Holy Spirit proceeding from both; he saw
the same nature in all three; he saw they were three distinct per-
sons. He envied the one sole Word, and he who was creature   1445
wished to be equal to the one begotten of the Father: "I propose
to settle in the regions of the north," he said, "and to seem like
to the most high." Thus he willed sin to become an inhabitant
of heaven; but its residence was brief, for heaven could not en-
dure what was sinful. Lucifer straightway fell there as he had   1450
risen, and his dawn was swiftly changed into dusk, his goodness
to evil, his apex to nadir; saint became demon. He had been of
two forms in one hour: bright and dark, good and evil, high and
lowest, angel and devil. He who suffered that fall dragged down   1455
to the depths a tenth part of all the angelic orders and brought
on each one alike its own ruin. After a space of five days, the
sixth day fashioned Adam; it formed Eve as well—citizens of
your realm, Paradise. To them their creator said: "Taste every   1460
kind of fruit, both of good and of evil; touch not the tree of
knowledge." Moreover, he added the cause: lest by tasting they
die the death. And what of Satan? He saw them, saw them fash-
ioned for this purpose: to make up the number of the angelic
host that had fallen, and to enjoy those delights which the angel 1465
lost. Then, pondering what he might do, taking the form of a
serpent, advancing straight and erect, he came in secret to Eve,
not daring to speak to Adam: "Why," he said, "are you forbid-
den to eat of that tree which was mentioned?" She replied, "For
this reason, indeed: lest perchance through it we die." At that   1470
"perchance" he saw her unstable in faith; and then, gaining as-
surance, he overcame her with this: "Not so," he said, "on the
contrary, eat; and thus you can be, as the gods are, expert in
good and evil." Vain hope of a promise so great puffed her up;   1475
she tasted what was forbidden; and her husband, lest he distress
her—although with full knowledge—did likewise. That was the
primal sin; but their second fault was more grievous: to be un-
willing to repent their guilt and implore God's pardon by prayer.
Indeed, he even cast the crime back on his wife's initiative. And 1480
what of the wife? She in turn cast it back on the serpent's guile.

This defense of their guilt was the source of a greater offense.
Thus they fell from your throne, Paradise, each one condemned.
So the human race perished. Neither natural nor legal right, nor   1485
power of any kind, was of avail to the race to prevent Tartarus
from swallowing all souls. Great was the wrath that thundered
as so many thousands of years rolled by, and still the fierce storm
was not quelled. Therefore the Son of God pondered: "Because
Lucifer presumed against me, he fell and was lost. That fall of   1490
his was the root of this one. So I am, as it were, a remote cause
of this plight: I shall be the cause of a kindred salvation. If I
choose to contend by my own strength, the enemy will easily
fall. But if I conquer in that way, I shall be using strength and
not judgment. Therefore since the cunning of the enemy over-   1495
came man, it follows necessarily, by the order of reason, that it
should be man who overcomes him; that he who slipped and fell
should rise up and strongly tear himself free from the claws of
Satan; that he who bore the yoke of a slave should walk freely   1500
with head erect; that he who perished in misery should live on in
joy. But that man must be God: only if God assumed flesh would
man's power overthrow his enemy, for thus human power be-
came one with the power of God.·It is therefore necessary that,   1505
as the enemy hurled man down, he be hurled down by man; as
he overcame by means of a tree, so by a tree he be overcome;
that he be taken in the very snare which he laid." So spoke the
Son. The Paraclete was author of his conception, and with his
own hand fashioned human attire for the one who descended in   1510
secret into a virgin's womb through closed gates; and went forth
from that virgin's womb, again through closed gates. A marvel-
ous thing every way: marvelous the ingress, marvelous the egress,
and marvelous the whole progress of his life. In him the enemy
found nothing to claim as his own. Yet he attacked a being not   1515
his; condemning him, condemned by him, he condemned him to
the death of the cross. He bore our sins on the cross, not his own.
He washed away our crimes there; and discharged a debt that
he had not incurred. But death itself did not evade him when it   1520
thus invaded his life. When it would swallow the man, it was
intercepted by the hook of his divinity; and so it thought to de-
feat what it swallowed, but was struck aghast to be defeated, for
his spirit robbed Tartarus of its due, and transformed the dark-

ness of grief into raptures of light for his friends. Those whom   1525
the region of death held, his grace alone thus redeemed; so wrath
was at an end, because of him on whose account it began.

If you examine these rhetorical figures carefully, in all of them
the meaning clearly reveals its content. You will find only two   1530
where it does not present the content in a readily apparent manner.

If this statement is proposed—*my power is not slight, my dig-*
nity not insignificant, I am implying more than I say, and the
actual situation is of greater consequence than the words indi-
cate. If I happen to be speaking on behalf of my friends, or on
my own behalf, this manner of speech is in good taste, and I show   1535
becoming modesty in employing such an expression. In this way,
the meaning makes its appearance veiled; the true situation is not
clearly apparent; there is more consequence in the actual fact
than the expression of it indicates.

From the numerous and great resources left by his father, the
squanderer of wealth has not enough to conceal his poverty with   1540
a covering, nor even an earthen jug in which to beg a fire. Here I
speak in excessive terms about a thing that is in itself excessive; I
chide immoderately what is not moderate; there is moderation
neither in the actual situation nor in my expression of it. If the
situation is more moderate than my words, still the excessive
language does suggest that there is less excess in the fact itself.

That peerless man: the word means *most excellent;* but *most*   1545
vicious glances at us obliquely: this is its meaning. The word belies its appearance, or else our perception errs. In such ambigui-
ties, the actual fact is veiled and the mockery is obvious.

The boy's ruddy colour fled his cheeks when he saw the rods,
and his countenance was bloodless. Such pallor indicates that he   1550
was afraid. *A blush had spread over the maiden's face;* her appearance indicates that she was ashamed. *The stroller went saun-*
tering on with hair adorned; the manner of expression suggests
dissolute conduct. Note the signs that accompany a given cir-   1555
cumstance. Present the facts, but do not present them as such;
rather, reveal only signs of the facts: show fear by pallor, sensu-
ality by adornment, and shame by a sudden blush; show the
thing itself by its definite signs, what is prior by what is conse-
quent upon it: this complexion, this sex, this age, that form.

Recently in another's chamber . . . but I will not say it. In this   1560

way I break off my words, and I do not say *that man*, but *a man
of such-and-such an age*, or *of a certain appearance*.

*You are great, and the world supplicates you on bent knee. Al-
though you have power to vent your rage, do not do so; remember*   1565
Nero. After introducing an analogy in this way, I add nothing
further. Or here I offer a different example contained in the following story:

*When Alexander the Great declared war on Athens, no terms
for restoration of peace were acceptable unless perchance the sages
of the city were surrendered as pledge. One of the wise men re-*   1570
*plied to the proposal in these words: "It happened that a wolf
declared war on a shepherd. Terms of peace were discussed between them, but no covenant of peace was agreeable to the wolf
unless as a pledge and warrant of amity the guardian of the flock
was handed over to him. When this was done, the enemy who
before had been cautious then became more assured." After say-*   1575
ing this much, he ceased.

He did not wish to apply the analogy between the proposal
and the exemplum, for he wisely gave part to the ears and left
part to the understanding. This is the method of a skilled speaker,
to include the whole force of a remark in half a remark.

Thought, finding excellent adornment in such devices, does   1580
not appear unveiled, but makes itself known by signs. It shines
with an oblique ray and chooses not to advance directly into the
light. There are five species [of *significatio*], but all are forms of
the same device.

Bring together flowers of diction and thought, that the field of   1585
discourse may blossom with both sorts of flowers, for a mingled
fragrance, blending adornment of both kinds, rises and spreads
its sweetness.

3. Theory of Conversions

You know what is fitting, and you say the fitting thing, yet you
may be guided by chance, not by a principle of art. You do not
understand what to look for in a subject at first glance, and on   1590
what aspect to concentrate your attention; at what point you
should begin applying your efforts, and what source gives rise to
the adornment of words. Your mind wanders over one part after
another, and your aimless steps betray a mind unsure of itself,

like the steps of a blind man feeling out where or what his way 1595
is—one whose staff is his eye and whose guide is fortune. What
then? By the precepts of art you may curb your mind so it will
not wander like a buffoon. Begin at a definite place. There are
only three places: first, a word inflected by tense; secondly, a
word inflected by case; finally, a word that remains unchanged. 1600
The method of approach is as follows.

Let us take the first place: consider the verb. Change it into a
noun—one which derives from the same verb, or from one syn-
onymous with it, or from one similar to it by reason of some 1605
obvious likeness. A noun derives from its verb as a branch grows
from its trunk and retains the life of its root. Now, since the
noun does this, and is not itself sufficient for our purpose, the
fire as a whole will be built up from this spark by the keen dis- 1610
cernment of the mind as it adds other words. Maneuver the subject about in this way, concentrating intently upon it: change the
noun about into any case at all, and adapt to it, in each of its
cases, a related series of words which may adequately express the
proposed statement. To this end, you will struggle with the whole
force of your mind. Hammer it out with a will on the forge of 1615
the understanding, pound it again and again, and at last pound
out what is suitable. Now, the method of procedure is this: first,
bring together in your mind all the grammatical forms; next,
choose the most effective one—that case through which meaning
enters the ear most delightfully. A discerning judge must be at
work here; he must see with discernment. To be discerning, you 1620
need both theory and practice. Precept may be clarified here by
example; take the following brief theme: *I am grieving over this
matter.* Now apply the principle just established: *From this fountain grief flows over me. Hence the root (or the seed, or the* 1625
*fount, or the source) of grief rises within me. This affair is mat-
ter and cause for grief. It sows (or gives birth to, or piles up)
grief. With cruel wounds, tormenting grief, you rage against me.
My mind, as it were, lies prostrate, injured and ill with grief.* 1630
So, from the verb *grieve,* take the noun *grief;* change it around
into any case; add to it, in whatever case it may be, a related sequence of words to suit the subject. Or, again, take a noun not
from that same verb, but from a similar verb suggesting grief— 1635
for example: *sigh, complain, groan, weep.* The nouns from these

verbs are: *tears, groans, sighs, complaints.* Nouns, in this way, express the force of the verbs: *Sighs rise from my soul, complaints from my lips; tears flow down my cheeks; I utter continual groans.* Now say it more elegantly thus: *Sighs break forth from the depths of my heart; heaven rings with my complaints; the found of my eyes floods forth tears; groans rend asunder my spirit.* Metaphor, in this way, binds nouns to verbs with, one might say, the knot of artistic skill. Grace of expression is, indeed, pleasant when words are used literally, but the accompanying pleasure is greater when they are skilfully converted to metaphor.

A word inflected by case may follow two methods: one is valid for an adjective, the other for a noun. You study one apart from the other, but in this present formulation consider the adjective first.

The directive given above for the conversion of a verb is valid in an analogous way for the conversion of an adjective. Proceed by the same steps here as you did there, for the two paths follow the same route. This is clearly evident in the following example: *Her countenance is radiant.* Change the adjective, observing the rule given above: *Radiance brightens her countenance. It glows with the beam (or with the light) of radiance. Her visage is wedded to radiance. Her chin wears a radiance like the sun's. Dawn breaks on the world from the radiance of her cheek alone.* This is an effective method; when employed with hyperbole it intensifies or diminishes eulogy or denunciation to a marked degree. Denunciation and panegyric offer suitable occasions for this technique. Thus you will take *radiance* from *radiant,* to find a more effective means of expression by trying the various cases. Or again, take a noun not from the adjective *radiant* but from one that resembles it: *snowy;* and, deriving a noun from the adjective— that is, *snow*—follow this sequence: *Snow and her cheek are not remote in beauty. Radiance glows in her face with a light as intense as if it were rival of snow. Her features in their radiance are likened to snow. In its natural brilliance her visage resembled the snow. Confident of victory, her features contend with the snow.* I am omitting the fifth case, which is to be used when apostrophe requires it.

In the way just described, you may change an adjective into a noun derived from it, or from another adjective like it; and the

164 0

164 5

165 0

165 5

166 0

166

167 0

167

skilful writer will devise other words, giving elegance to their grouping, so that the combination of words added to the noun will retain the meaning of the original statement while varying the rhetorical colour; and will say the same thing without sounding the same.

For a noun, follow this process: if the noun is appropriate as it   1680
stands, it does not need the craftsman's attention. If it is not appropriate in its present case, change it from case to case, and try to weave together a texture of words in such a way that a plain statement assumes a robe of novelty and beauty. Here is the un-   1685
adorned face of a theme: *I have done the evil deed on purpose.*
Now I give freshness to the face of the word: *My purpose was the spur to action*, or: *was instigator of the evil deed*. Or: *The prompting of a vicious purpose offered itself* or *came forward as an argument for crime*. Or try the word in this case: *The deed*   1690
was in accord with the purpose, or *A villainous hand was accomplice to the purpose*. Or suggest a wording like this: *A criminal hand extended purpose to action*. Again, if anyone should offer you this "raw" statement, so to speak: *Everyone talks of this deed*, dress the word thus: *This deed is the cry of the people*;   1695
or: *Common gossip is witness of the deed*; or: *No tongue gives the nay to the deed, but the people's voice, one and all, proclaims it.*

Shall I offer further examples? To what end? Meaning rejects   1700
no grammatical case; one and the same meaning may be adjusted to all cases. Cultivate an ability to find the way: it lies open to discovery, if only you are able to discover it. If the way is not clear to anyone, that is not the way's fault, but his who lacks an understanding of art and has no skilled colleague to consult. Three things perfect a work: artistic theory by whose law you   1705
may be guided; experience, which you may foster by practice; and superior writers, whom you may imitate. Theory makes the craftsman sure; experience makes him ready; imitation makes him versatile; the three together produce the greatest craftsmen.

The unchanging array of words which do not admit of inflec-   1710
tion, although permissible in discourse, are well set aside. Their tribe will often, and preferably, withdraw from the hall, to be presented under some different form. The new form should be this: see what such a word signifies, then express by a noun or a

verb the concept signified, so that a new verbal structure results, more effective than the original one. Take this brief theme: *Then* 1715 *he will come. Then* is a sign of time. Express that time by a noun, while preserving the same general meaning: *That day will bring him.* If this is your theme: *He will come hither,* the following expression will add grace to your words: *This place will* 1720 *welcome his coming, or will be host to his arrival, host of a year or a day.* If you prefer a more ornate style, elaborate on the theme. If you intend to say: *Once (or twice, or frequently) I am at fault,* say rather: *This is the sole (or second, or habitual) trans-* 1725 *gression of my spirit;* or; *Felony takes its rise (or returns, or grows habitual) within me.* Follow the same directive when *iste* or *ille, alter* and *alteruter* are used (if the disjunction is minor, use *alteruter;* if it is definite, use *alter*). Do not introduce a remark of this kind: *If that man* [ille] *comes, this one* [iste] *will* 1730 *depart.* Say rather: *That man* [ille] *will make his arrival the occasion of this one's* [istius] *departure.* The former wording was the manner of inexperience; the second, the manner of art. Here is another instance of the same sort: *The people run completely around the city—the people round the city's circuit on swift foot. He is justly punished for his crime—his crime is the ample* 1735 *reason for his punishment.*

Lest examples weary anyone, I include many under a few, and the others under these I have given. If you wish to know the force of more numerous examples, consider a few; the many are as the few. Study these few; the law that holds good for them 1740 holds good for the greater number. The author adds in the *Topics*: by gazing at fewer things we make greater progress. Lest I meander in lengthy examples, let many points, by a sounder principle, be covered in a single brief illustration: You are an annoy- 1745 ing debt-collector; your refrain is: *You're trying to hold out.* [My reply:] *You want things on the dot. I need time; I have to think my way through. You're too persistent a dun. I can't make it today. Be patient. Tomorrow can do what today cannot.*

This skill does not come easily and without effort; but when 1750 the mind concentrates upon it, it is as eager as a wrestler to enter the combat. Its struggle, indeed, is with itself. It seeks its own counsel and does not find it. It tries again, and is rebuffed a second time. It presses on with greater energy, and yet continues to

resist itself. Tormented by its labours, it is in anguish; and at
last, by violent effort, it wrings out from itself what it wishes. 1755
So it exults, victor over itself and self-vanquished. If you wish to
enjoy this happy victory, amplify what is slight, prune what is
redundant, groom what is shaggy, clarify what is obscure, correct
what is faulty. Every aspect of the work will be sound because of 1760
your careful efforts.

4. Theory of Determinations

Add this to the precepts above: since a word that is uttered alone
is, as it were, the raw material of discourse—a thing rough and
shapeless, so to speak—give it a companion. This addition will
confer shapeliness.

Let metaphor grace the period to brighten its charm, when 1765
two words join in a partnership like this: *the meadow smiles*, or
study flowers. Or join closely related words, several pairs of them,
in a series of this sort: *There appeared, to the table's disgrace, a
soiled covering, bran bread, rough food, bitter drink, a slatternly* 1770
attendant. Or we may double the adjective thus: *The table was
poor and small, its covering old and threadbare, the food poorly
cooked and rough, the drink sour and brackish, the table's attendant gross and awkward. The whole was utterly lacking in
grace.* Or a noun may determine another noun, in this way: *You* 1775
*are Cato in intelligence, Tully in eloquence, Paris in beauty, Pyr-
rhus in strength.* Again, you may employ the second noun as
metaphor, thus: *the rose of her countenance, the lily of her brow,
the ivory of her teeth, the fire of her lips, the balsam of her
breath.* Or again, in a figurative but commendable style, say: 1780
Love's Tiphys, Samson's Delila, Cato's Martia.

A noun may determine an adjective in much the same way as
it determines another noun. Thus a noun in the genitive case
may determine an adjective: if, for instance, in the following
words a miser is said to be *full of riches, empty of virtues, most* 1785
*avid of possessions, prodigal of another's property, sparing and
retentive of his own.* Or a noun in the dative case may determine
an adjective—as here, if I am describing Nero: *His mind is detest-
able for its many vices, formed hostile to strangers, worse still
to his followers, worst of all to himself, helpful to no one, de-* 1790
structive to all. Or here are the other cases: *Disgusting in all his*

conversation at table, always ready with avid gluttony for excess, not approving the wines unless they flow freely, quaffed unto nausea. He is wont to make banquets vile, breathing out filth, belching wine, and pouring out poison. This last example is in 1795 Sidonius' manner. An adjective is, indeed, accompanied more effectively by two nouns, as is apparent in this example: *The table cover wins approval, lovely in its newness and whiteness; the food prepared with costliness and skill; the drink delicious in its* 1800 *wine as in nectar; the attendant notable in manner and apparel. Graciousness in giving, and the countenance of the giver constitute the double glory of a feast.*

By a similar principle, I join nouns in the nominative case with verbs, thus: *Now my skin shrivels, my heart palpitates, my lungs gasp for breath, my loins stiffen, my back curves, my body* 1805 *trembles, and death stands at the threshold.* Or I join a nominative case with a verb in the following way: *He comprehends like Cato, speaks like Cicero, acts vigorously like Pyrrhus, shines like Paris, dares like Capaneus, loves like Theseus, makes music like Orpheus.* Or again, you may use oblique cases of the noun, thus: 1810 *He blazes with anger, terrifies with a look, thunders in speech, threatens with his sword, rages in his gestures.* Or multiply clauses in this way: *Divine goodness, pitying the contrite heart, forgives trespasses, remits sin, implants love of itself, and promises the* 1815 *joys of true life; but man loses this unless he perseveres in his love.* Or you may find appropriate adverbs for verbs, thus: *The actor gorges early, drinks avidly, spends recklessly, lives shamefully.* Or again, try a variety of determinations in this way: *He gathers the dice swiftly, examines them shrewdly, shakes them* 1820 *deftly, throws them vigorously, cajoles them amicably, waits the outcome composedly. When they are favourably cast he remains placidly cool, he smiles at unlucky throws; in neither case is his temper disturbed, in the one and the other he is philosophic.* This is the usual style of Sidonius; the extended series of clauses 1825 is an excellent technique. To extend them thus is appropriate for verse in two instances: panegyric and denunciation. In panegyric, multiple clauses heighten the praise, and in denunciation they act as a mallet to strike repeated blows. The pen of Sidonius claims 1830 as its distinctive mark this practice of amplifying verse by introducing numerous clauses. The very different style of Seneca is far removed from the practice of Sidonius: *He is free who serves not vice; rich, who finds what he has sufficient; poor, who desires more.* This is Seneca's manner, bringing his line to a swift conclusion. Both authors, it is true, deserve honour; but which should I follow, the former or the latter? Since freshness is a source of greater pleasure, and sameness of manner wearies us, I shall not be like the latter, nor yet like the former; I shall not be exclusively either diffuse or concise; rather, I shall be both concise and diffuse, becoming both of these authors by being neither.

5. Various Prescriptions

If you heed the directives carefully and suit words to content, you will speak with precise appropriateness in this way. If mention has perhaps arisen of an object, sex, age, condition, event, place, or time, it is regard for its distinctive quality that the object, sex, age, condition, event, time, or place claims as its due. Felicity in this matter is an admirable thing, for when I make an apt use of qualifying words [*determino*] I give the whole theme a finished completeness [*termino*]. An object described [*condĭta*] in its entirety is a dish well-seasoned [*condīta*]. Note this prescription and heed its tenor; it is a prescription that is valid for prose as well as for verse. The same principle of art holds good for both, although in a different way.

Metre is straitened by laws, but prose roams along a freer way, for the public road of prose admits here and there wagons and carts, whereas the narrow path of a line of verse does not allow of things so inelegant. Verse wishes its very words to be graceful in appearance, lest the rustic form of a word embarrass by its ungainliness, and bring shame to the line. Metre desires to appear as a handmaid with hair adorned, with shining cheek, slim body, and peerless form. The charming gracefulness of verse cannot find a group of words of equal sweetness to the ear. A line of prose is a coarser thing; it favours all words, observing no distinction except in the case of those which it keeps for the end of periods: such words are those whose penultimate syllable carries the accent. It is not desirable that other words hold this final position. Aulus Gellius reaches the same conclusion and subjoins his reason: lest otherwise the number of syllables be weak and insufficient to bring the line to a close. If the last word of a pe-

1835

1840

1845

1850

1855

1860

1865

riod should be, as it frequently is, of a different cursus, nevertheless the one suggested above is preferable in as much as sounder opinion supports it—and my authority here is Aulus Gellius. For the rest, the method of prose and verse does not differ; rather, the principles of art remain the same, whether in a composition bound by the laws of metre or in one independent of those laws, although what depends upon the principles of art is not always the same. In both prose and verse see that diction is controlled in such a way that words do not enter as dry things, but let their meaning confer a juicy savour upon them, and let them arrive succulent and rare. Let them say nothing in a childish way; see that they have dignity but not pomposity, lest what should be honourable becomes onerous. Do not let them enter with unsightly mien; rather, see that there is both internal and external adornment. Let the hand of artistic skill provide colours of both kinds. 1870 1875 1880

Yet there are times when adornment consists in avoiding ornaments, except such as ordinary speech employs and colloquial use allows. A comic subject rejects diction that has been artfully laboured over; it demands plain words only. The following comic tale makes this clear in a few lines: 1885

Three of us are sharing expenses and we have no servant. We lay down this rule, that we are to prepare our own meals, each man in his turn. After the other two have had their turn to serve, the third day comes round and meal time calls me. I use my breath for bellows to make the fire. The water supply is down and demands replenishing. I grab a jug and look for the spring. There is a stone in my path; my foot slips; the jug is broken. Now two things are lacking—a jug and water. What am I to do? While I'm thinking it over, I go into the market. A man is sitting there with jugs all around him. As I'm turning over in my hands and examining jugs I have picked up he, seeing I am poor, fears a theft and shouts at me in rough language. I go off, embarrassed, come upon a friend, and tell him my story. "I'll go back to him," I say, "and you follow me and announce the death of my father." I disguise myself and go back to the place. I pick up a jug in one hand, a second jug in the other. My friend calls out and says: "What are you doing? Whatever are you do- 1890 1895 1900 1905

ing here? Poor fellow, your father, who was sick, has died—and
are you hanging around here, you dolt?" At that "had died" my
grip, as I clasp my hands together, smashes the jugs. I run away.
I confound the boorish fellow who shamed me, and pay back his
insulting words in this way.

A comic discourse is marked with the character of lightness in   1910
the following ways: levity of spirit is the source of comedy; comedy is an immature form, attractive to green years. Moreover,
the subject of comedy is light; to such a subject the sportive period of youth readily devotes itself. See to it that the third element is light. Let all aspects, then, be light: the whole is in per-   1915
fect harmony if the spirit is light, and the subject light, and the
expression light.

If you are treating of serious matters, let the style be serious
and the spirit serious, the thought mature and the expression
mature. Adorn both thought and expression in the ways prescribed
above.

It is, however, of primary importance to clear away from the   1920
poem what is unsightly, and to root out what is faulty. Recall
briefly what things, what kind of things, and how many things
render the flow of discourse faulty. *Ecce deae aethereae advenere*:
the hiatus of sound in this sequence of words is appalling. Artistic theory has given as a law to vowels that there be no concentrated sequence of them. It tolerates a sequence, but forbids a   1925
concentrated sequence; and the particular grouping of vowels
above, because it is concentrated, is ugly, and constitutes an extreme example of hiatus.

Tu, Tite, tuta te virtute tuente tueris: the graceless and too frequent repetition of a single letter is a cause for censure, whereas   1930
tactful repetition is a grace.

Cum non sit ratio rationis de ratione, hinc non est ratio prae-
bere fidem rationi: a word is cheapened when it is repeated so
frequently and inanely. The moderate repetition of words is an
adornment; whatever is excessive is a thing remote from adorn-   1935
ment.

Repetition of the same word-endings is sometimes a grace; an
excessive number of such sounds is graceless: *infantes, stantes,*
lacrimantes, vociferantes. These four defects result in a faulty

style. There is a fifth defect when too long a period is held in
suspension. A sixth is added to these when the transposed order   194c
of a word appears incongruous, as here: *Luci misimus Aeli.*

Now, I have provided a comb: if they are groomed with it,
compositions, whether in prose or verse, will gleam with elegance.
But whether or not you make good use of the comb, you will be
able to discern beauty of form clearly in this mirror.   1945

When you examine the appearance of a word to see whether
some lurking blemish may mar it, do not let the ear be the sole
judge, nor the mind be sole judge; let a triple judgement of mind
and ear and usage decide the matter. This is my method when I
am labouring to polish words: I chide my mind, lest it linger in   195c
one place, for the quiet of standing water makes it stagnant.
Rather, with unflagging energy I turn now in one direction, now
in another, and I adorn the subject now with one figure, now
with another. I do not turn it over in my mind once only; rather,
I reconsider it many times. At last the active mind, when it has   1955
completed its circuit, chooses one form out of many. It breathes
freely at what it considers a flawless position. But in many cases,
the augur is mistaken; as long as words lie buried deep in the
understanding, many seem good to the mind which the ear, on
its part, fails to approve.

See to it that an expression, as it wins the mind's approval,   196c
may likewise charm the ear, and the two approve the same thing.
Even that is not sufficient, and I still do not trust it unless I
reflect upon it again. A first examination discerns neither well
nor fully. As I revolve the subject, I evolve more. If the topic is
malodorous, its unpleasantness is intensified as it is moved about 1965
more; if it is full of savour, the taste is more delightful through
repeated testing. See, then, that there are three judges of the proposed expression: let the mind be the first judge, the ear the second, and usage the third and final one to conclude the whole.

V. Memory

If you wish to remember all that reason invents, or order dis-   197
poses, or adornment refines, keep in mind this counsel, valuable
though brief: the little cell that remembers is a cell of delights,
and it craves what is delightful, not what is boring. Do you wish

to gratify it? Do not burden it. It desires to be treated kindly,　1975
not hard pressed. Because memory is a slippery thing, and is not
capable of dealing with a throng of objects, feed it in the following way. When you appease hunger, do not be so sated with
food that you can have nothing further set before you. Be more
than half, but less than fully satisfied. Give to your stomach not
as much as it can hold, but as much as is beneficial; nature is to　1980
be nourished, not overburdened. To remain between satiety and
hunger is the wiser practice. So, too, in drinking, you moderate
drink in accordance with reason. Sip, do not swill; let drink be
taken in an honourable [*honori*], not an onerous [*oneri*], fashion.　1985
Drink as a temperate man, not a tippler. The abstemious man
arraigns wine with better grace than the drunkard refutes him.
Knowledge, which is the food and drink of the mind, should be
tasted in accordance with the same rule. Let it feed the mind in
such a way that it is offered as a delight, not a burden to it.
Suppose you are to learn this entire discourse: divide it into very　1990
small parts. Do not take several at once; rather, take one at a
time, a very short section, much shorter than your shoulders are
capable and desirous of bearing. In this way there will be pleasure, and nothing burdensome in the burden. Let practice come
as companion; while the matter is fresh and new go over it fre-　1995
quently and repeat it; then stop, rest for a little while, take a
breathing space. After a short delay has intervened, another piece
may be summoned up; when it has been memorized in the same
way, let practice join both parts together in the cell mentioned
above, let it consolidate them and cement them together. Join a　2000
third part to these two with a similar bond, and a fourth part to
the other three. But, in following through these steps, you make
a mistake if you do not consistently proceed in such a way that
you stop short of weariness. This advice holds good for all the
faculties of sense; it sharpens those that are dull, makes pliable　2005
those that are rigid, and raises to greater heights of excellence
those that are acute and flexible. Whatever attempts more than
these precepts accomplishes less. Therefore let this sound principle adapt to each man the weight he can bear, and be the one
model for all.

To these methods add others which I make use of—and which
it is expedient to use. When I wish to recall things I have seen,　2010

or heard, or memorized before, or engaged in before, I ponder
thus: I saw, I heard, I considered, I acted in such or such a way,
either at that time or in that place: places, times, images, or
other similar signposts are for me a sure path which leads me to
the things themselves. Through these signs I arrive at active   2015
knowledge. Such and such a thing was so, and I picture to myself such and such a thing.

Cicero relies on unusual images as a technique for training the
memory; but he is teaching himself; and let the subtle teacher, as
it were in solitude, address his subtlety to himself alone. But my
own subtlety may be pleasing to me and not to him. It is benefi-   2020
cial to one whom it suits, for enjoyment alone makes the power
of memory strong. Therefore have no faith in these or in other
signposts if they are difficult for you, or if they are unacceptable.
But if you wish to proceed with greater security, fashion signs
for yourself, whatever kind your own inclination suggests. As long   2025
as they give you pleasure, you may be taught through their means.
There are some men who wish to know, but not to make an
effort, nor to endure the concentration and pain of learning. That
is the way of the cat; it wants the fish, but not the fishing. I am
not addressing myself to such men, but to those who delight in   2030
knowing, and also in the effort of acquiring knowledge.

VI. Delivery

In reciting aloud, let three tongues speak: let the first be that of
the mouth, the second that of the speaker's countenance, and the
third that of gesture. The voice has its own laws, and you should
observe them in this way: the period that is spoken should observe its natural pauses, and the word its accent. Separate those   2035
words which the sense separates, join those that sense joins.
Modulate your voice in such a way that it is in harmony with
the subject; and take care that voice does not advance along a
path different from that which the subject follows. Let the two
go together; let the voice be, as it were, a reflection of the subject. As the nature of your subject is, so let your voice be when   2040
you rehearse it: let us recognize them as one.

Anger, child of fire and mother of fury, springing up from the
very bellows, poisons the heart and soul. It stings with its bel-

lows, sears with its fire, convulses with its fury. Under its emotion, a caustic voice speaks; an inflamed countenance and turbu- 2045
lent gestures accompany it. The outward emotion corresponds
with the inward; outer and inner man are affected alike. If you
act the part of this man, what, as reciter, will you do? Imitate
genuine fury, but do not be furious. Be affected in part as he is, 2050
but not deeply so. Let your manner be the same in every respect,
but not so extreme; yet suggest, as is fitting, the emotion itself.
You can represent the manner of a rustic and still be graceful: let
your voice represent his voice; your facial expression, his own;
and your gesture his gesture—by recognizable signs. This is a
carefully tempered skill; this method is attractive in the tongue 2055
that recites, and this food is a delight to the ear. Therefore, let a
voice controlled by good taste, seasoned with the two spices of
facial expression and gesture, be borne to the ears to feed the
hearing. Strength issues from the tongue, for death and life depend upon the powers of the tongue, if haply it is aided by the 2060
tempering principles of facial expression and gesture. So, then,
let all be in harmony: suitable invention, flowing expression,
polished development, firm retention in memory. If discourses
are delivered ineptly, there are no more to be praised than is a 2065
recitation charmingly delivered but without the other requirements mentioned.

Epilogue

Now I have crossed the sea; I have fixed my Cadiz on the shore.
And I resolve upon you as my goal, you who, greatest of creatures, are neither God nor yet man. You are neither—yet some-
where between the two: one whom God has chosen as his partner.
He deals with you as an associate, sharing the world with you. It 2070
was not his will to possess all things—he alone; rather, he willed
earth to be yours and heaven his own. What better thing could
he do, what greater? For what better or what greater man? I put
it more moderately, for what man as great, or what man like to
you? Therefore, Father, vicar of Christ, I commend myself wholly 2075
to you, you whose wisdom is like a full-flowing fountain, whose
keenness of mind is like a fire throwing out sparks, whose ready
eloquence is a swift-flowing torrent, and whose grace is a mar-

vel. Transcending all that is human, I would wish to speak freely,   2080
but the reality is far richer than speech.

Crown of the empire, you whom Rome, capitol of the world,
serves with bent knee; you who, rich in the sweet nectar of the
muses, give forth fragrance tempered with the perfume of your
manners, with your leave I shall speak, and briefly. Although
you are able to do most things, be pleased to retain only the   2085
power to do them. Take care to imprint on your mind: although
you can inflict injury, do not wish to; the power to injure is already injury enough. Do nothing which you would afterwards
wish undone, but let deliberation be the cautious prelude to action. Do you not see, if you regard the true qualities of our
prince, that he has become the soldier of the cross and of Christ,   2090
and sword of the entire church? Devotion so great calls for love,
not for hatred; for praise, not reproach; for rewards and not pen-
alties. Therefore, you who conquer all else, allow yourself to be
conquered here. Be pleased to turn, and desire the king to return.
Flower and crown of the clergy, with wonted sweetness the rich-   2095
est honeycombs drop their dew from your heart [grant me a
share of your honey's sweetness]. I plead for our prince. I am
least of men, you are greatest; yet be receptive, and let him fare
better in his role of suppliant.

Accept, O flower of the kingdom, this special gift of a little
book which I have written for the pope. Receive the highest hon-   2100
our this private work offers. And take not the book alone, William, man of gold, but with it I give you all that I am; I am
wholly yours as a votive offering. Your heart, generous in all
things, is not ensnared by trifles, but ever aspires on high. Nobility in giving, which men of this age do not know, is inborn in   2105
you, jewel of donors, who alone so give that in giving no hand is
more lavish, no mind happier, no hesitation so brief. You are the
man upon whom alone God has bestowed every gift that is fitting, as on one with a mind of great wisdom—one on whose   2110
mind the minds of kings are wont to rely in carrying on the
affairs of the kingdom. You are great in giving, prudent in doing, modest in bearing, inflexible in law, in everything faithful;
and divine power, going before you, ever fosters your success,
and you ever rise towards the heights. But if every peak of hon-   2115
our should rise higher for you, you could not rise in honour as
much as you justly deserve.

Commentary

Although the *Poetria Nova* is closely related to the *Documentum de Modo et Arte Dictandi et Versificandi* and there is considerable overlap between the two works, there are two striking differences. First, the *Poetria* is verse while the *Documentum* is prose. Second, although the *Poetria* has numerous paraphrases and playful reminiscences of Horace's *Art*, there is not a single direct quotation in it from the *Art* or any other work by Horace, and Horace's name is never mentioned. The few references to other authors in the *Poetria* look almost like oversights: Sidonius (a Christian poet), Seneca, and Aulus Gellius are mentioned, and "Tully" (i.e., Cicero) appears because he was thought to be the author of the *Rhetoric to Herennius*. The examples of figurative language and other literary devices in the *Poetria Nova* are not quoted from classical authors but are invented by Geoffrey. Conversely, the illustrations in the *Documentum* tend to be from established authors including Vergil, Ovid, Lucan, and Statius.

An explanation of this peculiar state of affairs is suggested by the title *Poetria Nova*, which may not have been the author's but is the title usually given to the work. By the thirteenth century, the *Rhetoric to Herennius* had been joined in the schools by an early treatise by Cicero titled *On Invention (De inventione)*. *On Invention* seemed incomplete when compared to its rival. It was was called "the old rhetoric" (*rhetorica vetus*) because it covered some of the same territory as the *Rhetoric to Herennius* but was less comprehensive and less schematic in its organization. Being more comprehensive, the *Herennius* was called "the new rhetoric" (*rhetorica nova*). Horace's *Art of Poetry*, which was considered the standard treatise on poetry by Geoffrey and his contemporaries, was usually called *Poetria*, a title used as early as the commentary of Acron. The title *Poetria Nova* therefore announces that the work it identifies is like Horace's *Art* but carries Horace's ideas forward in the same way that the *Rhetoric to Herennius* carries forward ideas first sketched by Cicero in *On Invention*. The decision not to refer to Horace directly in the *Poetria Nova* or quote from other established authors is a corollary of the claim of the work to being "new." The author is not simply paraphrasing Horace and illustrating him with familiar quotations but is rethinking everything. Conversely, the *Documentum de Modo et Arte Dictandi et Versificandi* asserts that it is *not* new by quoting extensively from the *Art* and illustrating various figures with passages from well-known Latin authors.

What then is "new" about the *Poetria Nova?* For a reader of the *Art* three elements stand out. First, the *Poetria* is organized as a comprehensive treatise. Excluding dedication and epilogue, which are addressed to patrons, it treats six topics—general remarks on poetry, organization, amplification and abbreviation, figures, memory, and delivery. This scheme doubtless seemed to the author to resemble in its logical elegance the scheme embodied in the *Rhetoric to Herennius*. Second, as the list of parts makes clear, the work is essentially a development of the five traditional departments of rhetoric—invention, organization, style, memory and delivery, with style divided into amplification-abbreviation and figures. The rhetorical bias in literary theory, already evident in the *Vienna Glosses*, has become so powerful that it has all but replaced topics specifically related to poetry. Moreover, within rhetoric, style in the sense of the lore of ornamental figures has all but overwhelmed the other departments. At least four-fifths of the *Poetria Nova* is devoted to figures of speech and thought taken from the *Rhetoric to Herennius*. Third, and qualifying the debt to rhetoric, the *Poetria* begins with comments about the conception of the artwork that contrast strikingly with the opening lines of the *Art*, although both openings emphasize the need for unity.

In sum, the *Poetria* can claim to be new: (1) because it adheres much more closely than *The Art of Poetry* to the logical and comprehensive organization proper for an "art," (2) because it presents rhetorical materials explicitly and in detail rather than alluding to them so obliquely that a commentary is needed to make the significance of the allusions clear, and (3) because of the opening comments about the conception of the artwork. The author has learned from Horace but is prepared to go further. One element, however, does not change. In spite of its heavy debt to rhetoric, the *Poetria* remains what the *Art* was in the high Middle Ages—a work used as an aid in "reading and interpretation of the poets." The purpose of the work is also related to grammar. By learning its definitions and imitating its examples, students gain skill in making their own compositions.

There is little in the text of the *Poetria Nova* that is difficult in the sense that Horace's *Art* is difficult. The figures of speech and thought will be unfamiliar to anyone who does not know ancient rhetoric, but they are defined and illustrated in the text itself. The doctrines of "conversion" and "determination" are technical but they are not obscure.

The Poet as Creator

The most suggestive part of the work is its introduction. The "general remarks" begin with a comparison between a poet and an architect. Both must plan the work in the mind before giving it a material existence. The mental plan is called an "archetype." It is created by an act like drawing a circle with a compass around the "material" (l. 55). Then the material is "clothed" with words. As this is happening, care should be taken that every part is harmonious with the others: "If any part is ill-groomed, the work as a whole incurs censure from that one part" (ll. 66–67). Beginning, middle, and end should follow one another gracefully. There follows a formal partition—an outline of the main parts in the work—moving from organization to style to delivery.

The preceding summary looks simple enough and in one sense it is. The author is simply saying that a poet should plan before beginning a work. However, the background for the comment is complex. The *Poetria Nova* was written during the high point of a revival of Neoplatonic theorizing about the nature of creation. Central to much of this theorizing is the image of God as "fabricator" and "architect" that goes back to Plato's *Timaeus* and that seemed to Christian writers to illuminate the biblical image of God as creator in Genesis and in passages that describe him ordering "all things in number and weight" (*Wisdom* 11.21) and as an *artifex* ("maker"; compare the ancient division of a poetic treatise into *ars* and *artifex*; e.g., *Wisdom* 13.1, Hebrews 11.10). All these images have echoes in the passage on the poet as creator that begins the *Poetria Nova*. Geoffrey's artist is an *artifex*. He creates the idea of the work before he "materializes" it. The reference to the compass is an explicit allusion to the image of God circumscribing creation with a compass (or "circuit"), which comes from the book of *Wisdom* (8.27). Geoffrey's poet clothes unformed matter (*res*) with words (*verba*) in a manner that recalls the passage in Genesis (3.21) where God is said to put "garments" on creation. The result is a work of art as beautiful and as coherent in its small way as creation itself.

The commonplace nature of these motifs is evident from twelfth-century comments on divine creation. Alanus de Insulis, for example, compares God the Creator to an *artifex*: "God . . . [is] like an elegant architect . . . an artful artifex of a wonderful artifice" (Ed. T. Wright, *Anglo-Latin Satirical Poets* [1872], II, 468). The *artifex*-God creates ideas that are archetypes of the material world in exactly the same way that the *Poetria* advises the poet to shape "the entire house" before "the body's hand builds it." A twelfth-century comment on Boethius's *Consolation of Philosophy* uses exactly these concepts: "Those who have discoursed on the construction of the world . . . have asserted there are two worlds. One is called the archetype (*archetypum*), the other the sensible world. . . . They call the archetypal world the conception and mental image of the sensible world, which was in the divine mind before the world came to be. For before God created this sensible world in corporeality, he saw it just as it is present now because he was conceiving it in his mind" (quoted in B. Stock, *Myth and Science* [1972], 91).

In short, the newest feature of the *Poetria Nova* is its sustained comparison of artistic creation to divine creation as rationalized in neo-Platonic interpretations of Genesis. The comparison ramifies in the work many ways. The poet's creative power is like the divine power that shaped creation. The poem is a little world being brought to life by the poet. Images of light associated with the divine are applied by Geoffrey to artistic creation. The material of artistic creation is like unformed matter and is shaped by words just as unformed matter was shaped by the divine ideas. Words are compared to garments, and artful style is described in images suggesting fertility.

On the other hand, after the introduction, emphasis shifts to more conventional topics. Many were suggested by Horace's *Art*. This is true, for example, of the references in the introduction to the need for the work to be harmonious as a whole and for the beginning to be consistent with the middle and end. In the second section, the distinction between art and nature leads to a distinction between beginning "in the middle" on the one hand and "at the beginning" on the other. The latter discussion replaces Horace's distinction with one that depends on a typically medieval contrast between what is "artificial"—i.e., done using rules of art—and what comes "naturally" and does not need rules.

An allusion to Horace is combined with the Genesis motif when Geoffrey claims that his explanation of the different kinds of artificial beginning will provide "light to dispel the darkness" (l. 108; *Art*, l. 143).

Echoes of Genesis can also be heard in the comparison of different methods of beginning to sprouting branches. The discussion of the swift and leisurely styles reshapes Horace's remarks on different styles in terms of the rhetorical topics of diminution and amplification. It also introduces another image with Platonic overtones. The poet's material is like wax that talent (*ingenium*) warms and then shapes—again with "the hand of the mind." Amplification is like placing "garments" on things that are otherwise plain. Geoffrey's illustration of the way to use amplification in a lament leads to his famous lines on the death of Richard the Lion Hearted. Richard was wounded by a longbow on Friday (the day sacred to Venus) March 26, 1199. Chaucer's Nun's Priest recalls these lines when he asks for words to express his shock over the kidnapping of Chauntecleer in *The Nun's Priest's Tale* (ll. 527–31):

> O Gaufred, deere maister soverayn,
> That what thy worthy kyng Richard was slayn
> With shot, compleynedest his deeth so soore,
> Why ne hadde I now thy sentence and thy loore
> The Friday for to chide, as diden ye?

Another form of amplification—dispraise—is illustrated by a satirical sketch of a boy-scholar. In the midst of this un-Horatian context the author brings in a famous Horatian tag: "now the mountain's in labour, but its offspring will be only a mouse" (l. 449). Yet another passage applies Horace's comments on lyric poetry to an amplified description of dancing (ll. 624–66; *Art*, ll. 83–85).

Ornaments of style are divided into difficult and easy. They are compared in general to pictures, and the author recalls Horace's advice that poetry should be "like a picture" (*Art*, l. 361) in the sense that one picture pleases close up and another does so farther off. The true excellence of poetry is an inner quality—meaning. When there is an appropriate meaning, it can and should be ornamented so that its outward and visible part expresses its inward excellence. The sentiment is Platonic. It is related here (ll. 756ff.) to Horace's comments about diction, since a key element in ornamentation is word choice.

Difficult ornaments require transpositions of meaning. The "transpositions" are repeatedly said to be "garments," carrying forward the idea that words are the covering of the poet's material. The common rhetorical label for figures of this type is "tropes," which are usually contrasted to "schemes" or "figures" of the sort classified as "easy" by Geoffrey. They are given standard rhetorical labels—metaphor, allegory, metonymy, hyperbole, and the rest. Obscurity is to be avoided, and the style should vary from "common" to elevated in accordance with the subject. Geoffrey is drawing directly from the discussion of figurative language in the *Rhetoric to Herennius* (IV.31–34).

Incidentally, if the reader is unsure at this point of the distinction between tropes, or "difficult figures," and "figures of diction and of thought," that is because the systems used in ancient rhetoric for classifying figurative language were inconsistent and the inconsistencies were passed on to the Middle Ages. The system used in the *Poetria* is imperfect but as good as most others.

The easy ornaments are subdivided into figures (or "schemes") of diction and of thought (Latin, *figurae verborum* and *figurae sententiae*; Greek, *schemata lexeos, schemata dianoias*). These are treated in detail in Book IV of *Herennius* (figures of diction, IV.19–46; thought, IV.47–56). They are included in handbooks of grammar as well as rhetoric books. Borrowing a metaphor from *Herennius* (IV.16) Geoffrey calls them "colors" (l. 1097) and "flowers" (l. 1217). The metaphor relates poetry to painting. It also carries forward the light imagery that runs through the *Poetria*: ornament in a literary work is like light in creation and the varied colors of flowers in the created world.

Figures of diction involve modifications of word order that create effective sound patterns and shades of emphasis but do not "transpose" the meanings of words. They are illustrated in a single long passage that includes them all (ll. 1098ff.). Figures of thought involve changes of emphasis and thus of concept. To some degree they overlap the "difficult figures." They, too, are treated in a comprehensive passage (ll. 1280ff.).

The discussion of "conversions" and of "determinations" that follows is essentially an explanation of ways to make language appropriate and elegant. It is based on grammatical theory of the twelfth century rather than on classical ideas of decorum. "Conversions" occur when words are "converted" from their normal grammatical functions. Nouns, for example, can be made out of verbs and vice versa. Nouns can also be "converted" by using functions associated with their Latin "cases"—possessive, dative, accusative, and ablative. For example, the ablative case, which is usually expressed by a prepositional phrase in English, can be used to give a noun an adverbial function ("He was wounded *by the sword*"). Additional rules permit conversion of adjectives into nouns and the like. The meanings of uninflected words like adverbs can be expressed (hence "converted") by using nouns or verbs. For example, instead of saying "*Then* he will come" (l. 1716), the poet can say "*That day* will bring him." The theory of conversions is a kind of machine for producing variations on standard expressions. Skill is attained (l. 1705) by combining theory (*ars*) with practice (*exercitatio*).

"Determination" is the technique of qualifying words. Nouns are "determined" in this sense by adjectives or other nouns. Adjectives can be "determined" by nouns in special cases (e.g., genitive, as in "full *of riches*") or by adverbs, and so forth.

The *Poetria* now returns to familiar territory. Decorum is recommended in terms of character (ll. 1842ff.) and meter (ll. 1853ff.), with an additional comment on prose rhythm (ll. 1865ff.). The passage is Horatian, although Horace does not discuss prose. Further comments are offered on the adjustment of diction to genre—in this case, comedy. Since rhythm and meter involve sound, this is a good place for the author to advise against unpleasant sound effects like hiatus or the repetition of a letter or word. The general rule is that as an expression "wins the mind's approval, may [it] likewise charm the ear" (ll. 1960–61).

The last two major sections of the *Poetria* are taken directly from rhetoric, and there is nothing comparable to them in Horace's *Art* (for memory, *Herennius*, III.16.28–24.40; delivery, III.9.19–15.27). Longer compositions are normally written out even when they will be delivered orally as, for example, orations or sermons. However, the fiction persisted at least until the late Renaissance that rhetoric is an art of speaking rather than writing. Because speakers were considered more effective when they spoke without notes, "memory," meaning "the art of memory," was regularly included as a topic in manuals of rhetoric. Delivery is the technique of reinforcing oral presentation with gestures, facial expressions, and body language. It too was a standard part of rhetoric and a corollary of the fiction that rhetorical compositions are normally spoken.

A last reminiscence of Horace's *Art* occurs in the passage (ll. 2041ff.) stating that the reciter of a poem should feel the emotions of the characters. But the passage is also tinged with Platonic distrust of emotion. Horace says, "If you want me to weep you must weep too" (ll. 102–3).

The author of the *Poetria* recognizes the importance of emotion but emphasizes the need for restraint: "Imitate genuine fury but do not be furious. Be affected . . . but not deeply so" (ll. 2048–50). The *Poetria* ends in approved rhetorical fashion with a restatement of the major topics of the work: invention, style, development, memory. All of these (l. 2062) should be in harmony, and the delivery should be apt, an echo of the Horatian concept of decorum as proper "fitting together" of elements.

III

~~~~~

L'Art poétique
by
Nicolas Boileau-Despréaux

Introduction and Commentary

Renaissance and Seventeenth Century:
Badius Ascensius, Heinsius, Boileau

The history of *The Art of Poetry* in the Renaissance is rich and diverse, varying not only from period to period but also from country to country. For present purposes only a very broad outline of the subject will be possible.

In Italy the *Art* was oddly neglected during the age of Dante, Petrarch, and Boccaccio. For Dante, the key literary topics were set by the heritage of ancient grammar and rhetoric and by the tradition of poetry as allegory that had developed out of biblical exegesis. For Petrarch the central topics of the debate about poetry were its moral utility, its ability to stimulate national pride, and its ability to confer immortal fame on the poet and his subjects. Boccaccio emphasized the moral utility and prophetic insights of poetry with special emphasis on the value of the myths and other fabulous material used by pagan poets.

The discussion of poetry became more self-consciously classical in the fifteenth century. The humanists of this period sought to recover the ancient theory of poetry from the best ancient sources available. Horace's *The Art of Poetry* is the only work to survive from the golden age of Latin literature that is explicitly a work of literary criticism. Before Aristotle's *Poetics* became widely known in the early sixteenth century, it was the only available ancient work of formal critical—in contrast to grammatical or rhetorical—theory in Greek or Latin. Two important poems on poetry that can be considered free imitations of Horace date from this period—the *Nutricia* of Angelo Poliziano (1486), a treatment of poetry as the "nurse" of human civilization, and the *De arte poetica* of Girolamo Vida (1527). The *Nutricia* is essentially a 780-line enlargement of the passage in Horace's *Art* on the civilizing power of poetry (ll. 391–407). Vida's *De arte* is a formal treatise in three books on the major topics of poetry and the first of many versified "arts of poetry" of the seventeenth and eighteenth century.

Complementing such works were numerous annotated editions of the *Art*. Grant Showerman counts forty-four printed editions of the *Works* of Horace in Italy before 1500, with ten more in Germany and four in France (*Horace and His Influence* [1922], 110). The first edition appeared in Milan in 1470. It was followed in 1476 by the first edition to include the commentaries of Acron and Porphyrion. In 1482 Christoforo Landino published an edition with the ancient commentaries plus his own modern observations, and in 1492 Antonio Mancinelli issued a similar edition with *his* commentary. Editions with all four commentaries were popular in the sixteenth century and were known as Horace "with the four commentaries" (*cum quattuor commentariis*).

Badius Ascensius

Although the *Art* was already a central work of criticism in Italy by 1500, the most important edition of the early sixteenth century was published in Paris in 1503. It is the work of Iodocus Badius Ascensius (Josse Bade, 1461–1535). Dedicated to the "excellent boys" (*adolescentes optimi*) of the grammar school at Lyons, it was intended to assist students encountering the work for the first time and their masters, and it was an immediate success. A Paris edition of 1519 boasts that it concludes "the four commentaries," and in it, the Badius commentary has replaced Landino's. At least twenty-one reprints were issued between 1500 and 1590, many of them from the Venetian press of Giovanni Maria Bonelli.

The Badius commentary is typical of elaborately annotated editions of the classics in the early sixteenth century and important in its own right. Horace was, after all, the principal source of information about ancient poetry. Generations of schoolchildren gained their knowledge of ancient poetry from the *Art* and the accompanying Badius commentary. They used this information when they interpreted other classical works and when they composed their own Latin and vernacular poems.

Badius divides the *Art* into five units (*particulae*), which are, in turn, subdivided into twenty-four sections of two to fifteen lines each. Each section is followed by a summary reducing it to one or more "rules." The range of reference is broad, but most of the authors cited were known at least intermittently during the Middle Ages. The chief sources are the commentaries of Acron and Porphyrion and the *Artis grammaticae libri III* of Diomedes (fourth century). These are supplemented by materials from rhetoric and from a grab-bag of late classical and early medieval sources, including essays on drama by Euanthius and Donatus, topics from the *accessus ad auctores* tradition, and prosodic commonplaces from the *ars metrica*. The mix retains a medieval flavor, and Bernard Weinberg has remarked that the Badius edition is less a groundbreaking new work than a channel whereby medieval ideas were transmitted to the sixteenth century. There are, however, new elements. One of them is the inclusion of authors either not known, or if known not often cited, in the Middle Ages: Quintilian, Cicero's *De oratore*, Valerius Maximus, Plato, Dionysius of Halicarnassus, Demetrius, Hermogenes.

To say that the Badius commentary is "medieval" is to miss the point. Most sixteenth-century readers would have regarded its eclectic and traditional quality as appropriate. They considered *The Art of Poetry* a classic, the repository of eternal verities. The Badius commentary reflects its understanding of this fact by avoiding novel interpretations. The novelty, such as it is, is not in the authors cited or in the main lines of interpretation but in tone and emphasis.

The commentary begins with a group of topics that had been considered essential since the Middle Ages for an introduction (*accessus*) to the work of a major author. These are the life of the author, the title of the work, its "quality" (that is, its verse form), its intention, the number of books, and an explanation of the work itself. Badius omits the life of Horace in his edition of the *Art* volume since it has already been printed in his edition of Horace's *Odes*.

In a passage borrowed from Diomedes, poetry is defined as "metrical composition of fictional or true narrative . . . intended for utility and pleasure." The assumption that poetry is versified language is a heritage from *ars metrica* and is common in medieval criticism. It is implicit in all that follows. In the later sixteenth century it was attacked by those who believed with Aristotle that a poem is an imitation of an action and that the soul of poetry is plot, but it was reasserted in the extremely influential *Seven Books of Poetics* (*Poetices libri septem*, 1561) of Julius Caesar Scaliger, and it remained influential in the seventeenth century.

Badius agrees with Porphyrion that the *Art* has three parts. They are *poetice*, *poemata*, and *poesi*. Following Diomedes (rather than Porphyrion), he explains that *poetice* is the theory of poetry, *poemata* poetic genre (i.e., tragedy), and *poesi* the work itself—for example, the *Iliad* or the *Odyssey*.

Badius next identifies three fundamental poetic genres—narrative, dramatic, and mixed. The classification is based on whether the poet speaks entirely in his own person (narrative) or through his characters (dramatic) or sometimes directly and sometimes through characters (mixed). Essentially the same distinction is made in chapter III of the *Poetics* by Aristotle, where it is related to "manner" of imitation. The narrative genres are defined as sententious, didactic, and historic. The dramatic are tragedy, comedy, satire, and mime. The mixed are epic, lyric, and elegy. Badius also lists three styles, subjects, and qualities (i.e., prosodic patterns). The styles are high (*sublimis* or *altisonus*), middle (*mediocris*), and low (*humilis*), and the subjects are upper, middle, and lower class. Applying the resulting system to *The Art of Poetry* Badius concludes that it is "didactic" in genre, "middle" in style, and hexameter in "quality."

The concept of a "triple decorum" of style, subject, and character is fundamental to the Badius commentary and to the bias of Horatian classicism in the sixteeenth century. It recurs frequently and always in the same form: great subjects and noble characters require the high style and elevated verse forms. These include dactylic hexameter (epic), dignified iambic trimeter (tragedy), and elaborate stanza forms (Pindaric lyric).

Badius offers the following outline of *The Art of Poetry*:

(1) Poetic blemishes (*vitia*)
(2) Decorum of language
(3) Decorum of subject, character, verse form
(4) Actors and acting
(5) The need to revise.

The subjects assigned to the first three sections are familiar. They recall the progression of subjects in a typical late classical grammar from: (1) errors of style, to (2) purity of language, to (3) meter and verse. The parallel is significant. Almost half the *Art* in the Badius reading is taken up with topics that were taught in the grammar curriculum.

In the first section ("blemishes") Badius explains that the man-horse described by Horace is "monstrous" and "unnatural" because it "departs from nature." The appeal to nature is already present in the *Art*, so it cannot be considered original with Badius, but Badius has emphasized a topic that would be increasingly important during the next two centuries. The norm of nature would be invoked in controversies over fantastic romances like Ariosto's *Orlando Furioso* and allegories like the *Divine Comedy*.

Avoiding blemishes requires a concept of the whole work. Badius uses the image of the poet as architect (minus its Platonic overtones) so prominent in the *Poetria Nova*. Such a poet will be careful to avoid mixing not only images but "arguments." Epic subjects, for example, should not be mingled with comic or elegiac matter. Badius does not point to specific works that mix "arguments," but his position is the germ of the argument against mixed genres that would become intense a century later, as, for example, in the controversy over Guarino's tragi-comedy *Pastor Fido* and in English arguments about the propriety of mixing clowns and kings in Shakespeare's plays. Another rule announced by Badius is that the poet should seek clarity and vividness (*perspicuitas*), a position that anticipates the seventeenth-century argument in favor of simple and direct language and against tortured metaphors and conceits. The prosodic sections in part III of the Badius commentary are especially rich in materials carried over from late antiquity, and the second section of part III (discussing *Art* ll. 251–62) ends with no less than twenty-seven "rules."

The Later Sixteenth Century

In spite of Horace's popularity there are surprisingly few translations of the Art during the sixteenth century, but the number is sufficiently large—and the editions sufficiently important—to deserve notice. In Italy Ludovico Dolce translated the *Art* into Italian blank verse (*versi sciolti*) in 1535 and issued a revised version in 1559. In France a translation by Grandischan was published in 1541, but it is unimportant compared to the free translation by Jacques Peletier in 1544/45. This was a significant literary event. It did much to encourage Du Bellay to publish the *Défense et illustration de la langue française* and thus to launch the *Pléiade*. Horace's injunction to study Greek sources night and day was regularly understood in the sixteenth century to refer to versification, and Du Bellay quotes it in the chapter of the *Défense* denouncing French medieval verse. Ronsard, the greatest of the French poets of the age, chose Horace's praise of philosophy (*scribendi recte sapere est principium et fons*) as the motto for his *Abrégé de l'art poétique français.*

No Spanish translations of the *Art* appeared until the end of the century (1591, 1592), and although the *Satires* were published in German in 1502, the *Art* was not translated until the seventeenth century.

The impact of the *Art* was less significant in England than in France simply because no important changes in literary climate can be traced to it. Nevertheless, four translations were made before 1650. The first was by Thomas Drant, who translated all of Horace into fourteeners in 1567. In 1586 William Webbe reduced the *Art* to forty-one "canons" in his *Discourse of English Poetrie.* Around 1590, a partial translation of the *Art* was made by no less a figure than Queen Elizabeth I. Ben Jonson's translation survives in two versions. It was first published in the 1640 edition of Jonson's *Works.*

Except for the Badius edition, the most important commentaries on Horace's *Art* before 1600 are all Italian. These include the commentaries on the *Art* by Aulo Parrasio (1531), Francesco Robortello (1548), Giovanni Pigna (1561), and Antonio Riccoboni (1591, 1599). An abrupt enlargement of source material can be observed in the Horace commentaries after the Latin translation of Aristotle's *Poetics* by Alessandro Pazzi in 1536. The rediscovery of the *Poetics* did not, however, change the basic orientation of the commentaries. Marvin T. Herrick has shown (*The Fusion of Horatian and Aristotelian Criticism, 1531–1555* [1946]) that Horatian criticism formed a broad and well entrenched tradition and that when Aristotle appeared, the first impulse of the critics was to find ways to make Aristotle's ideas compatible with Horace's. Conversely, Horatian ideas were read into Aristotle. In this way much of the impact of Aristotle's theory of poetry was blunted. Bernard Weinberg (*A History of Literary Criticism in the Italian Renaissance* [1961], I, 71–249) distinguishes four "phases" in the influence of the *Art* in the sixteenth century: (1) commentaries, (2) conflation with Aristotle's *Poetics,* (3) practical criticism, and (4) return to theory. The conclusions Weinberg draws from his review are much like Herrick's: "It would not be possible, I believe, to state that any general change in the interpretation of Horace takes place" (I, 154).

As Weinberg recognizes, certain elements do emerge more clearly as the century progresses. Emphasis on decorum is continuous from the earliest commentaries, but interest in decorum of genre increases. Here

Aristotle's attempt to derive the nature of epic and tragedy from the means, object, and manner of imitation unquestionably enriched interpretations of Horace. In general, too, discussion becomes more literary and less rhetorical. Imitation becomes a topic of interest in itself, although it tends to be understood in the traditional rhetorical way as following literary models. According to Weinberg (I, 248) there is also an increasing tendency to regard poetry as "expression in verse," which is an idea drawn from the *ars metrica* and popularized by Julius Caesar Scaliger and quite different from Aristotle's idea that poetry is "making" or "imitation of an action." On the other hand, the idea that poetry is expression in verse is as old as the *ars metrica*, which predates Aristotle's *Poetics*, and is repeated at the beginning of the Badius commentary.

Three genuinely new elements can be found in Horace's interpretations in the period in question. In the first place, Riccoboni is only the most promient of several interpreters who express dissatisfaction with the organization of the *Art*. His solution was to reorganize the work along more logical lines. This has the effect of making it into the sort of *techne* or *ars* that commentators had always assumed it to be. In fact, Riccoboni manages to change it into a more or less conventional late sixteenth-century manual on poetry. But something else is evident in his analysis. He has treated the *Art* not as a source of inspiration for poets but as a scholarly problem. A split has developed between the analysis of problems inherent in the *Art* itself and the use of the *Art* as a guide for writing poetry. After the sixteenth century, commentaries on the *Art* are increasingly oriented toward its internal problems. Those who want to preserve it as a living influence on the creation of literature write Horatian poems about poetry, not commentaries.

In the second place, several late sixteenth-century discussions of poetry, including those by Giulio Cortese (1588) and Camillo Pelegrino (1598), consider diction and figures of speech (here, "conceits"—*concetti*) the central elements of poetry and develop this line of thought into a new view of poetry called *concettismo*, illustrated in Italian literature by the work of Giambattista Marino.

"Conceits" are figures that surprise and delight by their unlikely combination of disparate elements or their clever elaboration of simple concepts. They depend heavily on the faculties of "wit" and "genius," which are common seventeenth-century ways of translating Latin *inge-*

nium. The appearance of the term *ingenium* in the *Art* encouraged advocates of "conceits" to claim Horace as one of their own, a point that their opponents would vehemently deny.

The poetry of wit is primarily a linguistic construct. It aims more at pleasure than profit, and at the same time that it dazzles with its ingenuities, it risks seeming willfully obscure. Italian *concettismo* is related to what is called "Gongorism" in Spanish literature, *préciosité* in French, and "metaphysical poetry" in English. It flourished in the first half of the seventeenth century, but its popularity declined in the face of charges by neoclassical critics that it is obscure, trivial, and—worst of all—unnatural.

The third new development in Horatian criticism is more prominent in France than in Italy. Beginning with the Badius commentary, it was common to divide the *Art* into sections and to discover one or more "rules" in each section. In France, the *Art* was increasingly looked on as a source of such rules, complemented, especially in drama, by Aristotle's *Poetics.* In the seventeenth century, this view hardened.

It was an age that valued clarity and nature and distrusted medieval allegories and romances with their magicians and monsters and wild voyages to the underworld. The justification for the doctrine of imitating nature was "verisimilitude" (French *vraisemblance*), meaning being "like truth" or "like nature." Although the term is not used in Horace's *Art*, the concept can easily be found by those who look for it. The passage on the man-horse at the beginning of the *Art* can be considerd a warning against failure to observe verisimilitude, while Horace's denunciation of monstrosities and his satirical portrait of the mad poet in *The Art of Poetry* seem to speak effectively against those who favor fantastic romances and obscure diction. Alexander Pope combines reminiscences of Horace with a sense of the awesomely powerful image of nature revealed by Sir Isaac Newton and other pioneers of science in *An Essay on Criticism* (1711):

> First follow NATURE, and your subject frame
> By her just standard, which is still the same:
> Unerring nature! still divinely bright,
> One clear, unchanged, and universal light,
> Life, force, and beauty must to all impart,
> At once the source, and end, and test of art. (ll. 68–73)

It was also an age that prided itself on being "rational" and "scientific." In accord with this trend, literature sought guidance from rationally demonstrable rules, comparable to scientific laws. Examples include the need to avoid mixed styles, the need to report acts of violence rather than acting them onstage, and the unities of time, place, and action. Seventeenth-century critics felt the important rules had already been discovered by Horace and Aristotle—did not the best commentaries on *The Art of Poetry* include lists of rules after each major section? Pope wrote (*Essay*, I, 87-91):

> Those RULES of old discovered, not devised,
> Are nature still, but nature methodized:
> Nature like liberty is but restrained
> By the same laws which first herself ordained.

Complementing the rules were the models provided by the great ancient writers. The doctrine of imitation recognizes that the poet needs "exercise" as well as talent and art. Pope describes Vergil preparing to write the *Aeneid*. He might have drawn from "nature's fountains," but he decided to imitate Homer because when he examined the *Iliad* and the *Odyssey*, "Nature and Homer were, he found, the same" (*Essay on Criticism* I.135).

Finally, the seventeenth century also valued clarity and simplicity in expression. Rationalists considered the literature of *concettismo* and *préciosité* perverse. Horace pointed in the right direction when he warned against laboring to be brief and becoming obscure and advocated purity of diction and decorum in all things. The ideal of clarity is evident in the generally successful efforts of François de Malherbe (d. 1628) to purify the French language. Malherbe was in a sense the ideal Horatian critic. He was at his best not in grand generalizations but in the detailed work of criticizing word choice, metrical license, enjambed lines, sound effects, and the like. His ideal for French generally parallels the Horatian ideal of direct, standard, and graceful Latin. It was complemented in the seventeenth century by the project of creating a French Academy to oversee the French language and to publish an authoritative French dictionary. Malherbe's linguistic program has its philosophical complement in the doctrine of René Descartes (*Discourse on Method; Discours de la méthode*, 1637) that "clear and distinct ideas" are evidence of truth. If ideas should be clear and distinct, language should be too. The concept is continuous with the ancient dispute about the relative importance of things (*res*) and words (*verba*). Nature (equivalent here to "things") is simple and orderly. Should not the words that represent nature follow suit, avoiding inflated rhetoric and false ornament? Thomas Sprat, Secretary to the Royal Society, states the principle as it was understood by seventeenth-century British philosophers of science: "They [the members of the Royal Society] have therefore been most rigorous in putting in execution . . . a constant Resolution, to reject all the amplifications, digressions, and swellings of style; to return back to the primitive purity, and shortness, when *men* deliver'd so many *things* in almost an equal number of *words*. They have exacted from all their members, a close, naked, natural way of speaking: positive expressions; clear senses; a native easiness: bringing all things as near to Mathematical plainness, as they can" (*History of the Royal Society* [1667], in J. Spingarn, *Critical Essays of the Seventeenth Century* [1957], II, 117-18).

Julius Caesar Scaliger's *Seven Books of Poetics* (*Poetices libri septem*) was published in 1561. Although he had rivals who seem in retrospect to be more original and—finally—more interesting, his prestige grew throughout the sixteenth century and by the seventeenth he was recognized as one of the chief prophets of the new rationalist poetics. He did not write a commentary on Horace's *Art*, although he quoted it with easy familiarity.

The creation of a text and commentary "in the school of" Scaliger was the work of Dutch scholar Daniel Heinsius, who published it in 1610. Heinsius was concerned with logical organization in both poetry and poetic theory and he accepted Riccoboni's theory that Horace's text was orderly, if only the lines could be rearranged to make their order clear. The reason for the disorder of the received text, he decided, was the negligence and stupidity of the medieval scribes who transmitted it to the modern age. Although he did not dare, finally, to rearrange the text itself, he included proposed rearrangements in the notes to his edition.

Heinsius was a moralist and a literary conservative, and he makes this clear in his discussion of comedy. The rowdiness of the Old Comedy is wrong. Comedy should refine and amuse rather than move to unruly laughter. Old Comedy lacks restraint; proper literature should be seemly. Old Comedy delights in grotesque characterizations; the skilled poet should avoid inhumanity and be true to life—that is, imitate nature. When imitation is not based directly on nature it should be based on proper models, especially classical models. Plautus is an inferior and Terence a superior model because the latter represents character in a more natural way. Unity of time and place are essential for both tragedy and comedy, and unity of action is commended, although subordinate actions can be included in a larger, unified story line. Improbabilities are to be avoided. In his more youthful criticism Heinsius had insisted on the importance of inspiration. He was probably led in this direction by his reading of the work of the *Pléiade*. In his commentary on Horace's *Art* imagination is all but ignored. What is important is artistry in the sense of *ars* or *techne*—the rational application of rationally derived rules to the creation of literary works.

In the words of the most detailed study of the Heinsius commentary, the result is "an intellectualistic classicism" (J.H. Meter, *The Literary Theories of Daniel Heinsius* [1984], 131). It is important because Heinsius exerted considerable influence in France and England. He did not by any means "invent" neoclassicism, but he helped to shape its development. His edition of the *Art* was used by Ben Jonson for his translation (publ. 1640) and Jonson returned to Heinsius (*De tragoediae constitutione*, 1611) for a long passage on tragedy in his *Timber, or Discoveries* (1620–35). The influence of Heinsius in England is reviewed by Paul Sellin, *Daniel Heinsius and Stuart England* (1968), and in France by Edith Kern in *The Influence of Heinsius and Vossius upon French Dramatic Theory* (1943).

In a study of Horace's influence during the Renaissance (*La formación de la teoría literaria moderna: La tópica horaciana en Europa* [1977]), Antonio Garcia-Berrio notes that each of the critical schools of the Renaissance claimed Horace as its own. Horace is thus the "patron" of many literary movements rather than the father of one: "The Horace with whom we are dealing has little to do for the most part with the real Horace. We are dealing, rather, with a 'value' that is changeable and flexible, interpolated and mutilated, or adapted precisely to corroborate the most irreconcilable theories: in sum, a renaissance invention . . . a 'patron' of accommodation" (16). For Garcia-Berrio Horace's own theory of poetry is a variant of a classical theory that verse is constitutive of reality and that gave way in the Renaissance to view that art imitates a pre-existing nature or literary models and gives "priority in the causal order to the natural objectivity of themes, characters, and the social quality of style rather than to structural and rhythmic-formal considerations" (82).

The position is striking and persuasive. However, it is unique to Garcia-Berrio and is not found in any ancient, medieval, or Renaissance commentary on Horace's *Art*. If Horace *did* have a constitutive view of poetry, that fact is by no means clear, and, conversely, there is much in Horace that seems to accord fully with sixteenth- and seventeenth-century theory.

The seventeenth century rediscovered in the battle of the ancients and the moderns a topic that greatly interested Horace but did not seem especially important in the sixteenth century. Horace saw himself as a "modern" in contrast to the "ancients" of the first great age of Latin literature, the age of Ennius, Lucilius, Plautus, and the rest. He defended the moderns in the tenth satire of Book I of the *Satires* and the *Epistle to Augustus* (II.1), and his feeling that literature improves progressively is evident in several places in the *Art*, although he also recognizes that it can decay.

All European countries experienced "anxiety of influence," to use Harold Bloom's phrase, in the seventeenth century. The ancients—meaning the great poets of Greece and Rome—were models so perfect that they could never, it seemed, be surpassed. Are the moderns condemned to write inferior imitations and to experiment with verse forms that can never be more than trivial? Or do new times bring new insights and opportunities? Can Petrarch be considered comparable to Catullus? Ronsard to Horace? Shakespeare or Ben Jonson to Sophocles or Terence? A representative English contribution to this debate is John Dryden's *Essay of Dramatic Poesy* (1687), in which the different points of view are offered in a dialogue in which Crites represents the ancients and Neander the moderns. The French version of the debate began earlier and lasted longer than the English version. The terms were much the same, and, in fact, the French influenced the English, but the debate had deeper ramifications in France.

The marvelous, for example, is accepted with reservations by both Aristotle and Horace. It violates "nature" and verisimilitude, but it is found, nevertheless, in many of the great models, most obviously, Homer's *Odyssey*. Evidently it is acceptable when it is based on myth (cf. *Art*, ll. 143–47). In 1669 Desmartes de Saint-Sorlin suggested in the preface to his play *Marie-Magdeleine* that the Christian marvelous is more acceptable than pagan myth because people believe it to be true. His friend Charles Perrault carried the argument forward in a defense (1678) of Torquato Tasso's magic-filled romance about the crusades, *Jerusalem Delivered*. Several other writers took up the theme, all of them arguing that the moderns are superior because they use the marvelous in believable and morally uplifting ways. The counterattack began in 1687 and continued to the end of the century. Opponents argued that the miracles of faith should not be mingled with profane fictions and myths and tales of love. The quarrel rapidly moved beyond the issue of the Christian marvelous, but that issue was not abandoned. It had the effect of driving a wedge between "polite literature," understood as fiction intended chiefly for enjoyment, and truth understood as subject matter too sacred to be debased.

This position extended to arguments for and against inspiration. As has been noted, Horace generally ignores inspiration in the *Art* or equates it with madness and delirium. Seventeenth-century rationalists agreed. Inspiration is an excuse to be sloppy or evidence of mental derangement. It is irrational and unnatural. On the other hand, neither the argument against Christian themes nor the argument against inspiration was quite as conclusive as it seemed. The idea of inspiration (Greek *enthousiasmos*) goes back at least to Plato's *Phaedrus* and was revived during the Renaissance in neo-Platonic defenses of poetry, including Books XIV and XV of Boccaccio's *Genealogy of the Gods*, Du Bellay's *Défense et illustration* and Sir Philip Sidney's *Defence of Poesie*. In the seventeenth century, it was associated by devotional poets with the indwelling guidance of the Holy Spirit. The defining example of the century is John Milton's *Paradise Lost*, which ignores neoclassical prohibitions against the "Christian marvelous" and announces in each of its four invocations that it is a work of inspiration: "And chiefly Thou O Spirit, that doest prefer/ Before all Temples th'upright heart and pure,/ Instruct me, for Thou know'st" (ll. 17–19).

The quarrel between the ancients and moderns extended into the eighteenth century. It was a quarrel the ancients could not win. Neoclassical standards continued to be urged, and the ancients continued to be held up as models for imitation, but throughout the eighteenth century new literary forms and topics appeared. Examples include the bourgeois novel, the importance of the undefinable quality called "taste," the power of momentary and inexplicable flashes of insight of the sort described in Longinus's *On the Sublime*, and new styles, some of them re-

viving the techniques of *concettismo* and some of them looking forward
to romantic poetry.

The Later Seventeenth Century: Boileau

The period from 1650 to 1725 might with some justification be described as "Horace triumphant." The synthesis between scientific rationalism, neoclassicism, the *Poetics* of Aristotle, and *The Art of Poetry*
was complete. In spite of the many valid points made by Garcia-Berrio,
it is a synthesis that seems close to the spirit of *The Art of Poetry*. And
in spite of the continued vitality of poetry celebrating Christian miracles, the sufferings of martyrs, and the mysterious inspiration of the
Spirit, the dominant thrust of the age was secular.

The age is rich in poetic imitations of the *Art*. In England, for example, Rochester published his *Allusion to the Tenth Satire of Horace*
(1680), Soames his translation of Boileau (1682), Mulgrave his *Essay
upon Poetry* (1682), Roscommon his translation of Horace's *Art* (1684)
and his *Essay on Translated Verse* (1684), Samuel Wesley his *Epistle to
a Friend*, Granville his *Essay on Unnatural Flights of Poetry* (1701),
and, as the climax of the series, Pope his *Essay on Criticism* (1711).

Nicolas Boileau-Despréaux was born in 1636, the year when Corneille presented his tragedy *The Cid*. Since that play ignited a famous
controversy over the three unities, it was a propitious year for a critic
destined to write the definitive explanation of French neoclassicism.
Boileau came to know Racine, Molière, and La Fontaine well. Like
them, he became part of the court circle of Louis XIV, which had
achieved almost a monopoly on French *belles lettres* by the second half
of the seventeenth century. He regarded Louis as a modern Augustus
and himself as a modern Horace, and the king seems to have agreed. In
gratitude for Boileau's services, Louis saw that he was elected to the
French Academy. Like Horace, Boileau claimed to speak only the truth
to his royal patron, even as he flattered him. Not surprisingly, Boileau
writes for the court class, and he instinctively understood Horace's appeal in the *Art* to the judgment of the select few.

His principal youthful work was a series of vigorous and biting satires. During his middle years he composed the *Art of Poetry*, a group of
less peppery satires, and a mock epic about a reading desk titled *Le Lu-
trin*. Later he composed "epistles" modeled on Horace and carried on a
series of literary disputes, including his contribution to the quarrel be-

tween the ancients and the moderns. Of special interest is the fact that in the same year (1674) that he published *L'Art poétique*, Boileau published a translation of *On the Sublime* by Longinus, which discusses the inexplicable leap of imagination that produces the truest poetic moments. Boileau's interest in *On the Sublime* parallels the interest of René Rapin (*Réflexions sur la poétique* [1672]) in a *je ne sais quoi*—an "I don't know what"—that produces moments of true poetic intensity but cannot be explained. Both critics, in other words, contributed significantly to the neoclassical poetic, but both expressed dissatisfaction with it—a feeling that it was too reasonable, that it left something out—by invoking effects that are beyond the power to reason, to control or define. The seeds of the destruction (or perhaps deconstruction) of neoclassicism are evident in the work of its foremost spokesmen.

Boileau's *Art of Poetry* was recognized as an important statement of neoclassicism as soon as it appeared. The translation reprinted here was made in 1680 by Sir William Soames, and revised in 1682 by John Dryden, who replaced the examples from French literature used by Boileau with examples from English literature. The revision is an attempt to find a pattern in English literature between, roughly, 1600 and 1680 similar to the pattern found by Boileau in French literature of the same period. The careful reader will note both similarities and distortions as the history of English poetry is bent to fit the French model. There is also, of course, a good deal of distortion in the French model, itself, as illustrated by the fact that Boileau finds no French literature of lasting significance before Malherbe: *Enfin Malherbe vint* reads the French. Underlying the understanding of both French and English literary history is a deeper layer of interpretation; namely, Horace's understanding of the history of Roman literature.

Boileau's *Art* reflects a rising interest, fed by the quarrel between the ancients and the moderns, in literary history and a search for models useful in interpreting the modern historical experience. It also includes many themes and concerns that are part of the tradition of Horace's *Art*: the norms of nature and reason, the importance of decorum, the proper content and ranking of genres, the place of the marvelous and the irrational in literature, the critic as mentor and judge.

Two points stand out. First, in spite of the tendency of scholarship to treat Horace's *Art* as an object of research, Boileau takes it as a living document. The considerable influence of his updating testifies to the fact that contemporaries were impressed by his achievement. Second, Boileau understands Horace's poem to be an "art" or *techne*. His updating is as neatly organized as Geoffrey of Vinsauf's *Poetria* or Girolamo Vida's *De arte poetica*. The first canto introduces the rule of reason. The second reviews the minor genres. The third considers tragedy, epic, and comedy. And the fourth treats the duties of the critic and the civilizing power of poetry.

In general the detail of Boileau's *Art* is Horatian, but there are also new elements. Although Boileau disapproved of *préciosité*, only a poem sensitized to its claims would begin with the un-Horatian point that "genius" is the essential element in poetry and without it the poet will find Apollo "deaf" (l. 6). Having said this, Boileau immediately assures the reader that genius does not overreach nature but springs from nature and allows the poet to imitate nature. Since genius is essential and different poets have different abilities, Boileau paraphrases Horace's advice that the poet should assume tasks suited to his talent (Horace, *Art*, l. 38).

Reason is allied to nature, and the poet is advised, "Love reason then; and let whate'er you write/ Borrow from her its beauty, force, and light" (ll. 37–38). Again the seventeenth-century topic leads back to Horace. The reasonable poet will not engage in pretty but boring digressions—a reminiscence of Horace's advice about the purple patch—and will take care to avoid vices allied to the stylistic virtues he is seeking. A crowd of minor authors is summoned up to illustrate crudities of style, the most important being Samuel Butler, author of the excellent mock epic *Hudibras* (1663), which is praised, and DuBartas, author of a long poem (*Divine Weeks* in the English translation of Joshua Sylvester) expanding the biblical account of creation in Genesis.

Horace glances back over the early history of Roman poetry on several occasions (e.g., *Art*, ll. 55–59, 285–91). Boileau devotes a formal section to early French poetry, and the section is provided with English examples by Dryden. Beginning with Du Bellay, it had become conventional for French critics to dismiss medieval French poetry as crude and trivial. Boileau traces the first stirrings of French genius to François Villon (d. ca. 1490) and Clément Marot (d. 1544). Dryden substitutes Edward Fairfax (l. 115), translator of Tasso's *Gerusalem Liberated* (1600) and Edmund Spenser, who celebrated Rosalind in *The Shepheardes Calendar* (1579). The substitutions do not seem very apt; evidently he is not interested in the transition from medieval to Renaissance but from Renaissance to neoclassical. William D'Avenant (l. 121) is the now-forgotten author of an English epic in quatrains titled *Gondibert* (1650). Malherbe, who is mentioned next by Boileau, is the dominant critic of seventeenth-centry France. Dryden substitutes Edmund Waller (d. 1687), a minor mid-century English poet who wrote in a plain and metrically regular form ("easy words and pleasing numbers," l. 136) that anticipated the plain lyric style approved later in the century. The unstated implication of the survey, whether in French or in English, is that the true system of poetry has been understood for only fifty years. Now that it has been explained, however, poetry is improving rapidly. The canto concludes with advice about revision and criticism that echoes Horace's *Art*: Revise and polish a hundred times until the work is a perfect whole (ll. 173–80). Here and in the comments on fantastic wits (l. 185) the claims of inspiration and of *préciosité* are briefly noted and dismissed. The observation leads to a Horatian comment on the critic's need for honesty (*Art*, ll. 419–52).

The second canto is a summary of standard classical prescriptions for minor classical genres. Only one "modern" genre receives serious treatment—the sonnet. The summary is formal because although the classical genres were still being imitated—and would be for the next century—the conviction was going out of them. The discussion of lyric is generally consistent with Horace until line 312, where the sonnet is treated. Even here the description is artificial since the sonnet had ceased to be a major lyric form in France and Engand since the early seventeenth century. The comment on epigram is surprisingly detailed. The explanation is that Boileau associated it with *préciosité*. It became such a fad, he grumbles, that lawyers adorned their speeches with "conceits" and preachers with "quibbles" (ll. 347–48). The fad came to grief when "affronted reason looked about/ And from all serious matters shut them out" (ll. 349–50). The reference here is to the rejection of *préciosité* and metaphysical poetry in favor of the plainer, simpler, and metrically regular poetry of Malherbe and Waller.

Tacked to the end of the discussion of epigram are references to popular folk forms—the round and the ballad. Here the English is misleading since the French equivalents are formal song-forms—*rondeau, ballade,* and madrigal, and these forms are associated in France with the Middle Ages and the early Renaissance. Satire brings up the rear of the parade of minor genres. It was the characteristic genre of the age of reason. Dryden makes Chaucer (l. 395) a distant prophet of modern satire, equivalent perhaps to Lucilius in Rome and parallel to Mathurin Régnier

(d. 1613), the French author cited by Boileau at this point. The "David Logan" mentioned in the last line is an English engraver of the time.

Canto III begins with tragedy. Boileau discusses the paradox of the pleasure derived from watching painful events and continues with comments on tragic emotions. The unities are identified as "reason's rules" (l. 472), and Horace's advice to narrate violent events rather than present them on the stage is repeated. The history of ancient tragedy is summarized—more cogently, it may be added, than by Horace—and a review of the modern tragedy is offered.

The earliest modern drama was religious and to Boileau (perhaps to Soames and Dryden, too) plays that present "angels, God, the Virgin, and the saints" (l. 512) are "scandalous." Eventually "right reason" prevailed, and modern tragedy emerged. Boileau is thinking of the replacement of the miracle plays and saints' plays of the later Middle Ages by formal tragedies imitating the tragedies of Seneca. Dryden would have thought of the replacement of the medieval theater by Shakespeare and his contemporaries, but the main point would have been the same. The medieval theater was not only crude, it also verged on blasphemy.

The dominant modern tragic theme is love. The plots are to be taken from the Homeric myths, and decorum of character, understood much as in Horace's *Art* (ll. 119–27), is required. Only one modern tragedian is mentioned. Boileau names La Gautier Coste de la Calprenède (d. 1633), author of historical romances and tragedies. Dryden chooses George Chapman (l. 556; d. 1634), author of the tragedy *Bussy Dambois*, rather than Shakespeare or Ben Jonson. Being a playwright, Dryden must have felt keenly the truth of the concluding lines on tragedy: "An author cannot easily puchase fame;/ Critics are always apt to hiss, and blame" (ll. 574–75).

Epic makes personified gods out of virtues like prudence and beauty. The concept is rationalistic and a bow to Renaissance explanations of the Horatian rule that literature must profit as well as delight, but it suggests a bloodless and ultmately sterile view of heroic poetry. The standard pagan themes are listed, and the poet is advised to avoid the Christian marvelous because it will be debased in a frivolous secular context: "The mysteries which Christians must believe,/ Disdain such shifting pageants to receive" (ll. 626–27). Tasso is cited as an exception (Dryden might have added Milton, whose *Paradise Lost* had been published in 1667), but the true source of Tasso's popularity is said to be his description of the love of Tancred and Armida rather than his Christian theme.

What follows is interesting because it is a call for pure fiction and another illustration of the way that the separation of "myth" and Christian "truth" trivialized literature. The old myths please because they are pure imagination in the sense of being fairy tales having no basis in truth. Conversely, if the poet includes Christian truths in profane fictions he will "Of the true God create a god of lies" (l. 663). Is Boileau equating "pleasure" in Horace's "profit-pleasure" formula with make-believe? Apparently so. The same suggestion is evident in the elegantly trivial paintings, often with thinly disguised erotic overtones, of classical gods and goddesses by French Enlightenment painters. If this is the case, however, what has happened to the idea of imitating nature and observing the rule of reason? A crack seems to open momentarily in the elegant neoclassical facade of Boileau's poem.

Having disposed of the problem of Christian truth, Boileau continues with an expanded paraphrase of Horace's advice about writing an epic. Choose the plot well; be careful about beginnings (the first three lines of the *Aeneid* are translated to illustrate, ll. 705-7); vary your style; imitate Homer. Oddly, there is no explicit statement of the *in medias res* rule. Moving beyond Horace at the end, Boileau levels another volley at the poets of *préciosité*: "A poem where we all perfections find,/ Is not the work of a fantastic mind" (ll. 736-37). Fantastic poets claim their genius will be recognized by future generations; in fact, their manuscripts will remain "forgot, in dust and cobwebs" (l. 760).

Comedy is treated last. The transition in ancient Greek literature from Old to New Comedy is summarized. Comedy is a "glass" (mirror) in which each person can see his or her deformity. The master rule is "strive to be natural in all you write" (l. 796). The point is illustrated by character sketches of the three ages of man (ll. 804-17).

Boileau names Molière the paragon of French writers of comedy. Dryden names Ben Jonson. Jonson's problem was that he often sacrificed art for "the people's praise" (l. 824). Two of his plays are named: *The Fox* (*Volpone*) and *The Alchemist*. Comic style should sometimes be serious, an echo of Horace's *Art* (ll. 90-96), and pandering to the crowd through "bawdry" is fit only for the slums.

Canto IV of Boileau's *Art* begins with a satiric sketch of a physician so inept that he kills patients but then discovers that he is an excellent architect. Horace's observation that no one tolerates a mediocre poet is

repeated. Herringman, the bookseller, will throw a mediocre poet out
of his bookstall. Davenant's *Gondibert* and the plays of Thomas Shadwell (d. 1692) remain unsold.

Boileau returns to the subject of the concluding lines of Canto I—the
ideal critic. He then moves to the rules of poetic art. Poetry should instruct and delight (l. 946). The poet should be virtuous and should
write poems so that, for example, he does not ask us to sympathize
with a woman like Queen Dido of Carthage who foolishly gave her
love to Aeneas (ll. 959–60).

The poet's calling is noble. Poets can legitimately accept popular recognition, but the true reward of poetry is fame (l. 986). The value of
poetry is its civilizing power. Men were reclaimed from savagery by reason and "her all-conquering arts" (l. 995). The process is symbolized,
as in Horace (*Art*, ll. 391–407), by the myths of Orpheus and Amphion. These mythic poets were followed by Homer and Hesiod, but
eventually avarice tarnished the poet's trade.

On the other hand, exclaims Boileau, "an author cannot live on fame"
(l. 1035). This hard but inescapable fact leads to the final topic—
patronage. Here the triple image (Rome-France-England) that can be
seen so often in the Soames-Dryden translation is especially apparent.
Horace depended on the patronage of Maecenas and Augustus, Boileau
on Louis XIV, and Dryden on Charles II. In the case of Boileau and
Dryden the ideal answer to the question of how a poet can make a living is, "When a sharp-sighted prince, by early grants,/ Rewards your
merits and prevents your wants" (ll. 1048–49). The English version of
the poem lists several poets who benefited from patronage—Edmund
Spenser (parallel to Corneille in Boileau), Abraham Cowley, Sir John
Denham, and Edmund Waller (all three parallel to Racine), and last but
by no means least John Dryden himself, who promises to reform the
English stage if properly supported. Hints of an even more ambitious
plan are apparent in Dryden's list of the noble military exploits of
Charles II (parallel to exploits of Louis XIV related by Boileau) followed
by the "blessings of peace" (l. 1069), which Charles, like a second Augustus, has brought to England. Even if Dryden is unequal to writing an
epic, he promises to furnish those who are with lessons that his Muse
"Learnt, when she Horace for her guide did chuse" (l. 1085).

The point is nicely timed and would make an ideal ending. Boileau
and Dryden, however, prefer a problematized ending. The speaker will
wish all success to the hypothetical writer of epic, but will not sur-

render the critic's right to call attention to faults: "Apter to blame, than knowing how to mend;/ A sharp, but yet a necessary friend" (ll. 1092-3). This is Horatian, but it is something more. It is in some degree a recognition that the age of epic is over. Satire is inherently anti-epic. It does not elevate, it deflates. Criticism also tends to deflate. It is "finding fault," and Boileau and Dryden rationalize the stance of the fault-finder by equating the critic's work with thankless but necessary honesty.

L'Art poétique

Translated by Sir William Soames
(revised by John Dryden)

Canto I

Rash Author, tis a vain presumptuous Crime
To undertake the Sacred Art of Rhyme;
If at thy Birth the Stars that rul'd thy Sence
Shone not with a Poetic Influence:
In thy strait Genius thou wilt still be bound,
Find *Phoebus* deaf, and *Pegasus* unsound.
    You then, that burn with the desire to try
The dangerous Course of charming Poetry;
Forbear in fruitless Verse to lose your time,
Or take for Genius the desire of Rhyme: 10
Fear the allurements of a specious Bait,
And well consider your own Force and Weight.
    Nature abounds in Wits of every kind,
And for each Author can a Talent find:
One may in Verse describe an Amorous Flame,
Another sharpen a short Epigram:
Waller a Hero's mighty Acts extol;
Spencer Sing *Rosalind* in Pastoral:
But Authors that themselves too much esteem,
Lose their own Genius, and mistake their Theme;   20
Thus in times past *Dubartas* vainly Writ,
Allaying Sacred Truth with trifling Wit,
Impertinently, and without delight,
Describ'd the *Israelites* Triumphant Flight,
And following *Moses* o're the Sandy Plain,
Perish'd with *Pharaoh* in th'*Arabian* Main.

What-e're you write of Pleasant or Sublime,
Always let sence accompany your Rhyme:
Falsely they seem each other to oppose;
Rhyme must be made with Reason's Laws to close: 30
And when to conquer her you bend your force,
The Mind will Triumph in the Noble Course;
To Reason's yoke she quickly will incline,
Which, far from hurting, renders her Divine:
But, if neglected, will as easily stray,
And master Reason, which she should obey.
Love Reason then: and let what e're you Write
Borrow from her its Beauty, Force, and Light.
Most Writers, mounted on a resty Muse,
Extravagant and Senceless Objects chuse;   40
They Think they erre, if in their Verse they fall
On any thought that's Plain, or Natural:
Fly this excess; and let *Italians* be
Vain Authors of false glitt'ring Poetry.
All ought to aim at Sence; but most in vain
Strive the hard Pass, and slipp'ry Path to gain:
You drown, if to the right or left you stray;
Reason to go has often but one way.
Sometimes an Author, fond of his own Thought,
Pursues his Object till it's over-wrought: 50
If he describes a House, he shews the Face,
And after walks you round from place to place;
Here is a *Vista*, there the Doors unfold,
Balcone's here are Ballustred with Gold;
Then counts the Rounds and Ovals in the Halls,
The Festoons, Freezes, and the Astragals:
Tir'd with his tedious Pomp, away I run,
And skip o're twenty Pages to be gon.
Of such Descriptions the vain Folly see,
And shun their barren Superfluity.   60
All that is needless carefully avoid;
The Mind once satisfi'd is quickly cloy'd:
He cannot Write, who knows not to give o're;
To mend one Fault, he makes a hundred more:
A Verse was weak, you turn it much too strong,

And grow Obscure, for fear you should be Long.
Some are not Gaudy, but are Flat and Dry;
Not to be low, another soars too high.
Would you of every one deserve the Praise?
In Writing, vary your Discourse, and Phrase;   70
A frozen Stile, that neither Ebs or Flows,
Instead of pleasing, makes us gape and doze.
Those tedious Authors are esteem'd by none,
Who tire us, Humming the same heavy Tone.
Happy, who in his Verse can gently steer,
From Grave, to Light; from Pleasant, to Severe:
His Works will be admir'd where-ever found,
And oft with Buyers will be compass'd round.
In all you Write, be neither Low nor Vile:
The meanest Theme may have a proper Stile.   80
     The dull Burlesque appear'd with impudence,
And pleas'd by Novelty, in Spite of Sence.
All, except trivial points, grew out of date;
Parnassus spoke the Cant of *Belinsgate*:
Boundless and Mad, disorder'd Rhyme was seen:
Disguis'd *Apollo* chang'd to *Harlequin*.
This Plague, which first in Country Towns began,
Cities and Kingdoms quickly over-ran;
The dullest Scriblers some Admirers found,
And the *Mock-Tempest* was a while renown'd: 90
But this low stuff, the Town at last despis'd,
And scorn'd the Folly that they once had pris'd;
Distinguish'd Dull, from Natural and Plain,
And left the Villages to *Fleckno*'s Reign.
Let not so mean a Stile your Muse debase;
But learn from *Butler* the Buffooning grace:
And let Burlesque in Ballads be employ'd;
Yet noisy Bumbast carefully avoid,
Nor think to raise (tho' on *Pharsalia's* Plain)
Millions of mourning Mountains of the Slain: 100
Nor, with *Dubartas*, bridle up the Floods,
And Periwig with Wool the bald-pate Woods.
Chuse a just Stile; be Grave without constraint,
Great without Pride, and Lovely without Paint:

Write what your Reader may be pleas'd to hear;
And, for the Measure, have a careful Ear.
On easy Numbers fix your happy choice;
Of jarring Sounds avoid the odious noise:
The fullest Verse and the most labor'd Sence,
Displease us, if the Ear once take offence.   110
Our ancient Verse, (as homely as the Times,)
Was rude, unmeasur'd, only Tagg'd with Rhimes:
Number and Cadence, that have Since been Shown,
To those unpolish'd Writers were unknown.
Fairfax was He, who, in that Darker Age,
By his just Rules restrain'd Poetic Rage;
Spencer did next in Pastorals excel,
And taught the Noble Art of Writing well:
To stricter Rules the Stanza did restrain,
And found for Poetry a richer Veine.   120
Then *D'Avenant* came; who, with a new found Art,
Chang'd all, spoil'd all, and had his way apart:
His haughty Muse all others did despise,
And thought in Triumph to bear off the Prize,
Till the Sharp-sighted Critics of the Times
In their Mock-*Gondibert* expos'd his Rhimes;
The Lawrels he pretended did refuse,
And dash'd the hopes of his aspiring Muse.
This head-strong Writer, falling from on high,
Made following authors take less Liberty.   130
Waller came last, but was the first whose Art
Just Weight and Measure did to Verse impart;
That of a well-plac'd Word could teach the force,
And shew'd for Poetry a nobler Course:
His happy Genius did our Tongue Refine,
And easie Words with pleasing Numbers joyn:
His Verses to good method did apply,
And chang'd harsh Discord to Soft Harmony.
All own'd his Laws; which, long approv'd and try'd,
To present Authors now may be a Guide.   140
Tread boldly in his Steps, secure from Fear,
And be, like him, in your Expressions clear.
If in your Verse you drag, and Sence delay,

My Patience tires, my Fancy goes astray,
And from your vain Discourse I turn my mind,
Nor search an Author troublesom to find.
There is a kind of Writer pleas'd with Sound,
Whose Fustian head with clouds is compass'd round,
No Reason can disperse 'em with its Light:
Learn then to Think, e're you pretend to Write.   150
As your Idea's clear, or else obscure,
Th'Expression follows perfect, or impure:
What we conceive, with ease we can express;
Words to the Notions flow with readiness.
    Observe the Language well in all you Write,
And swerve not from it in your loftiest flight.
The smoothest Verse, and the exactest Sence
Displease us, if ill *English* give offence:
A barb'rous Phrase no Reader can approve;
Nor Bombast, Noise, or Affectation Love.   160
In short, without pure Language, what you Write,
Can never yield us Profit, or Delight.
Take time for thinking; never work in hast;
And value not your self for writing fast.
A rapid Poem, with such fury writ,
Shews want of Judgment, not abounding Wit.
More pleas'd we are to see a River lead
His gentle Streams along a flow'ry Mead,
Than from high Banks to hear loud Torrents roar,
With foamy Waters on a Muddy Shore.   170
Gently make haste, of Labour not afraid;
A hundred times consider what you've said:
Polish, repolish, every Colour lay,
And sometimes add; but oft'ner take away.
Tis not enough, when swarming Faults are writ,
That here and there are scattered Sparks of Wit;
Each Object must be fix'd in the due place,
And diff'ring parts have Corresponding Grace:
Till, by a curious Art dispos'd, we find
One perfect whole, of all the pieces join'd.   180
Keep to your Subject close, in all you say;
Nor for a sounding Sentence ever stray.

The publick Censure for your Writings fear,
And to your self be Critic most severe.
Fantastic Wits their darling Follies love;
But find You faithful Friends that will reprove,
That on your Works may look with careful Eyes,
And of you Faults be zealous Enemies:
Lay by an Author's Pride and Vanity,
And from a Friend a Flatterer descry,   190
Who seems to like, but means not what he says:
Embrace true Counsel, but suspect false Praise.
A Sycophant will every thing admire;
Each Verse, each Sentence sets his Soul on Fire:
All is Divine! there's not a Word amiss!
He shakes with Joy, and weeps with Tenderness;
He over-pow'rs you with his mighty Praise.
Truth never moves in those impetuous ways:
A Faithful Friend is careful of your Fame,
And freely will your heedless Errors blame;   200
He cannot pardon a neglected Line,
But Verse to Rule and Order will confine,
Reproves of words the too affected sound;
Here the Sence flags and your expression's round,
Your Fancy tires and your Discourse grows vain,
Your Terms improper make them just and plain.
Thus 'tis a faithful Friend will freedom use;
But Authors, partial to their Darling Muse,
Think to protect it they have just pretence,
And at your Friendly Counsel take offence.   210
Said you of this, that the Expression's flat?
Your Servant, Sir; you must excuse me that,
He answers you. This word has here no grace,
Pray leave it out: That, Sir,'s the proper'st place.
This Turn I like not: 'Tis approv'd by all.
Thus, resolute not from a fault to fall,
If there's a Syllable of which you doubt,
'Tis a sure Reason not to blot it out.
Yet still he says you may his Faults confute,
And over him your pow'r is absolute: 220
But of his feign'd Humility take heed;

'Tis a Bait lay'd, to make you hear him reed:
And when he leaves you, happy in his Muse,
Restless he runs some other to abuse,
And often finds; for in our scribling times
No Fool can want a Sot to praise his Rhymes:
The flattest work has ever, in the Court,
Met with some Zealous *Ass* for its support:
And in all times a forward, Scribling Fop
Has found some greater Fool to cry him up.   230

Canto II

Pastoral

As a fair Nymph, when Rising from her bed,
With sparkling Diamonds dresses not her head;
But, without Gold, or Pearl, or costly Scents,
Gathers from neighb'ring Fields her Ornaments:
Such, lovely in its dress, but plain withal,
Ought to appear a Perfect *Pastoral*:
Its humble method nothing has of fierce,
But hates the ratling of a lofty Verse:
There, Native beauty pleases, and excites,
And never with harsh Sounds the Ear affrights.   240
But in this stile a Poet often spent,
In rage throws by his Rural Instrument,
And vainly, when disorder'd thoughts abound,
Amid'st the Eclogue makes the Trumpet Sound:
Pan flyes, Alarm'd, into the neighb'ring Woods,
And frighted Nymphs dive down into the Floods.
Oppos'd to this another, low in stile,
Makes Shepherds speak a Language base and vile:
His Writings, flat and heavy, without Sound,
Kissing the Earth, and creeping on the ground;   250
You'd swear that *Randal*, in his Rustick Strains,
Again was quav'ring to the Country Swains,
And changing, without care of Sound or Dress,
Strephon and *Phyllis*, into *Tom* and *Bess*.
Twixt these extreams 'tis hard to keep the right;

For Guides take *Virgil*, and read *Theocrite*:
Be their just Writings, by the Gods inspir'd,
Your constant Pattern, practis'd and admir'd.
By them alone you'l easily comprehend
How Poets, without shame, may condescend   260
To sing of Gardens, Fields, of Flow'rs, and Fruit,
To stir up Shepherds, and to tune the Flute,
Of Love's rewards to tell the happy hour,
Daphne a Tree, *Narcissus* made a Flower,
And by what means the Eclogue yet has pow'r
To make the Woods worthy a Conqueror:
This of their Writings is the grace and flight;
Their risings lofty, yet not out of Sight.

Elegy

The *Elegy*, that loves a mournful stile,
With unbound hair weeps at a Funeral Pile,   270
It paints the Lovers Torments, and Delights,
A Mistress Flatters, Threatens, and Invites:
But well these Raptures if you'l make us see,
You must know Love, as well as Poetry.
I hate those Lukewarm Authors, whose forc'd Fire
In a cold stile described a hot Desire,
That sigh by Rule, and raging in cold blood
Their sluggish Muse whip to an Amorous mood:
Their feign'd Transports appear but flat and vain;
They always sigh, and always hug their Chain,   280
Adore their Prison, and their Suff'rings bless,
Make Sence and Reason quarrel as they please.
'Twas not of old in this affected Tone
That Smooth *Tibullus* made his Amorous moan;
Nor *Ovid*, when, Instructed from above,
By Nature's Rules he taught the Art of Love.
The Heart in Elegies forms the Discourse.

Ode

The Ode is bolder, and has greater force;
Mounting to Heav'n in her Ambitious flight,
Amongst the Gods and Heroes takes delight;   290

Of *Pisa*'s Wrestlers tells the Sin'ewy force,
And sings the dusty Conqueror's glorious Course:
To *Simois* streams does fierce *Achilles* bring,
And makes the *Ganges* bow to *Britain*'s King.
Sometimes she flies, like an Industrious Bee,
And robs the Flow'rs by Nature's Chymistry,
Describes the Shepherds Dances, Feasts, and Bliss,
And boasts from *Phyllis* to surprise a Kiss,
When gently she resists with feign'd remorse,
That what she grants may seem to be by force: 300
Her generous stile at random oft will part,
And by a brave disorder shows her Art.
Unlike those fearful Poets, whose cold Rhyme
In all their Raptures keep exactest time,
That sing th' Illustrious Hero's mighty praise
(Lean Writers!) by the terms of Weeks and Dayes;
And dare not from least Circumstances part,
But take all Towns by strictest Rules of Art:
Apollo drives those Fops from his abode;
And some have said, that once the humorous God   310
Resolving all such Scriblers to confound
For the short Sonnet order'd this strict bound:
Set Rules for the just Measure, and the Time,
The easy running, and alternate Rhyme;
But, above all, those Licences deny'd
Which in these Writings the lame Sence Supply'd;
Forbad an useless Line should find a place,
Or a repeated Word appear with grace.
A faultless Sonnet, finish'd thus, would be
Worth tedious Volumes of loose Poetry.   320
A hundred Scribling Authors, without ground
Believe they have this only Phoenix found:
When yet th'exactest scarce have two or three
Among whole Tomes, from Faults and Censure free.
The rest, but little read, regarded less,
Are shovel'd to the Pastry from the Press.
Closing the Sence within the measur'd time,
'Tis hard to fit the Reason to the Rhyme.

Epigram

The *Epigram*, with little art compos'd,
Is one good sentence in a Distich clos'd. 330
These points, that by *Italians* first were priz'd,
Our ancient Authors knew not, or despis'd:
The Vulgar, dazled with their glaring Light,
To their false pleasures quickly they invite;
But publick Favor so increas'd their pride,
They overwhelm'd *Parnassus* with their Tide.
The Madrigal at first was overcome,
And the proud Sonnet fell by the same Doom;
With these grave Tragedy adorn'd her flights,
And mournful Elegy her Funeral Rites: 340
A Hero never fail'd 'em on the Stage,
Without his point a Lover durst not rage;
The Amorous Shepherds took more care to prove
True to their Point, than Faithful to their Love.
Each word, like *Janus*, had a double face:
And Prose, as well as Verse allow'd it place:
The Lawyer with Conceits adorn'd his Speech,
The Parson without Quibling could not Preach,
At last affronted Reason look'd about,
And from all serious matters shut 'em out: 350
Declar'd that none should use 'em without Shame,
Except a scattering in the Epigram;
Provided that, by Art, and in due time
They turn'd upon the Thought, and not the Rhime.
Thus in all parts disorders did abate;
Yet Quiblers in the Court had leave to prate:
Insipid Jesters, and unpleasant Fools,
A Corporation of dull Punning Drolls.
'Tis not, but that sometimes a dextrous Muse
May with advantage a turn'd Sence abuse, 360
And, on a word, may trifle with address;
But above all avoid the fond excess,
And think not, when your Verse and Sence are lame,
With a dull Point to Tag your Epigram.

Each Poem his Perfection has apart;
The *Brittish* Round in plainness shows his Art;
The Ballad, tho the pride of Ancient time,
Has often nothing but his humorous Rhyme;
The Madrigal may softer Passions move,
And breath the tender Ecstasies of Love: 370
Desire to show it self, and not to wrong,
Arm'd Virtue first with Satyr in its Tongue.

Satyr

Lucilius was the man who bravely bold,
To *Roman* Vices did this Mirror hold,
Protected humble Goodness from reproach,
Show'd Worth on foot and Rascals in the Coach:
Horace his pleasing Wit to this did add,
And none uncensur'd could be Fool, or mad;
Unhappy was that Wretch, whose name might be
Squar'd to the Rules of their Sharp Poetry.   380
Persius, obscure, but full of Sence and Wit,
Affected brevity in all he writ:
And *Juvenal*, Learn'd as those times could be,
Too far did stretch his sharp Hyperbole;
Tho horrid Truths through all his labors shine,
In what he writes there's something of Divine:
Whether he blames the *Caprean* Debauch,
Or of *Sejanus* Fall tells the approach,
Or that he makes the trembling Senate come
To the stern Tyrant, to receive their Doom;   390
Or *Roman* Vice in coursest Habits shews,
And paints an Empress reeking from the Stews:
In all he Writes appears a noble Fire;
To follow such a Master then desire.
Chaucer alone, fix'd on this solid Base,
In his old Stile conserves a modern grace:
Too happy, if the freedom of his Rhymes
Offended not the method of our Times.
The *Latin* Writers, Decency neglect;
But modern Readers challenge our respect,   400

And at immodest Writings take offence,
If clean Expression cover not the Sence.
I love sharp Satyr, from obsceneness free;
Not Impudence, that Preaches Modesty:
Our *English*, who in Malice never fail,
Hence, in Lampoons and Libels, learnt to Rail;
Pleasant Detraction, that by Singing goes
From mouth to mouth, and as it marches grows!
Our freedom in our Poetry we see,
That Child of Joy, begot by Liberty.
But, vain Blasphemer, tremble, when you chuse   410
God for the Subject of your Impious Muse:
At last, those Jeasts which Libertines invent
Bring the lewd Author to just punishment,
Ev'n in a Song there must be Art, and Sence;
Yet sometimes we have seen, that Wine, or Chance
Have warm'd cold Brains, and given dull Writers Mettle,
And furnish'd out a Scene for Mr. Settle:
But for one lucky Hit, that made thee please,
Let not they Folly grow to a Disease,
Nor think thy self a Wit; for in our Age   420
If a warm Fancy does some Fop ingage;
He neither eats or sleeps, till he has Writ,
But plagues the World with his Adulterate Wit.
Nay, 'tis a wonder, if, in his dire rage,
He Prints not his dull Follies for the Stage;
And, in the Front of all his Senceless Plays,
Makes *David Logan* Crown his head with Bayes.

Canto III

Tragedy

There's not a Monster bred beneath the Sky
But, well dispos'd by Art, may please the Eye: 430
A curious Workman, by his Skill Divine,
From an ill Object makes a good Design.
Thus, to Delight us, Tragedy, in Tears

For *Oedipus*, provokes our Hopes, and Fears:
For Parricide *Orestes* asks relief;
And, to encrease our pleasure, causes grief.
You then, that in this noble Art would rise,
Come; and in lofty Verse dispute the Prize.
Would you upon the Stage acquire renown,
And for your Judges summon all the Town?   440
Would you your Works for ever should remain,
And, after Ages past, be sought again?
In all you Write, observe with Care and Art
To move the Passions, and incline the Heart.
If, in a labour'd Act, the pleasing Rage
Cannot our Hopes and Fears by turns ingage,
Nor in our mind a feeling Pity raise;
In vain with Learned Scenes you fill your Plays:
Your cold Discourse can never move the mind
Of a stern Critic, natu'rally unkind;   450
Who, justly tir'd with your Pedantic flight,
Or falls asleep, or censures all you Write.
The Secret is, Attention first to gain;
To move our minds, and then to entertain:
That, from the very op'ning of the Scenes,
The first may show us what the Author means.
I'm tir'd to see an Actor on the Stage
That knows not whether he's to Laugh, or Rage;
Who, an Intrigue unravelling in vain,
Instead of pleasing, keeps my mind in pain: 460
I'de rather much the nauseous Dunce should say
Downright, my name is *Hector* in the Play;
Than with a Mass of Miracles, ill joyn'd,
Confound my Ears, and not instruct my Mind.
The Subject's never soon enough exprest;
Your place of Action must be fix'd, and rest.
A *Spanish* Poet may, with good event,
In one day's space whole Ages represent;
There oft the Hero of a wandring Stage
Begins a Child, and ends the Play of Age: 470
But we, that are by Reason's Rules confin'd,

Will, that with Art the Poem be design'd,
That unity of Action, Time, and Place
Keep the Stage full, and all our Labors grace.
Write not what cannot be with ease conceiv'd;
Som Truths may be too strong to be believ'd.
A foolish Wonder cannot entertain:
My mind's not mov'd, if your Discourse be vain.
You may relate, what would offend the Eye:
Seeing, indeed, would better satisfy;   480
But there are objects, that a curious Art
Hides from the Eyes, yet offers to the Heart.
The mind is most agreably surpris'd,
When a well-woven Subject, long disguis'd,
You on a sudden artfully unfold,
And give the whole another face, and mould.
At first the Tragedy was void of Art;
A Song; where each man Danc'd, and Sung his Part,
And of God *Bacchus* roaring out the praise
Sought a good Vintage for their Jolly dayes: 490
Then Wine, and Joy, were seen in each man's Eyes,
And a fat Goat was the best Singer's prize.
Thespis was first, who, all besmear'd with Lee,
Began this pleasure for Posterity:
And, with his Carted Actors, and a Song,
Amus'd the People as he pass'd along.
Next, *Æschylus* the diff'rent Persons plac'd,
And with a better Masque his Players grac'd:
Upon a Theater his Verse express'd,
And show'd his Hero with a Buskin dress'd.   500
Then *Sophocles*, the Genius of his Age,
Increas'd the Pomp, and Beauty of the Stage,
Ingag'd the Chorus Song in every part,
And polish'd rugged Verse by Rules of Art:
He, in the *Greek*, did those perfections gain
Which the weak *Latin* never could attain.
Our pious Fathers, in their Priest-rid Age,
As Impious, and Prophane, abhorr'd the Stage:
A Troop of silly Pilgrims, as 'tis said,

Foolishly zealous, scandalously Play'd   510
(Instead of Heroes, and of Love's complaints)
The Angels, God, the Virgin, and the Saints.
At last, right Reason did his Laws reveal,
And show'd the Folly of their ill-plac'd Zeal,
Silenc'd those Nonconformists of the Age,
And rais'd the lawful Heroes of the Stage:
Only th'*Athenian* Masque was lay'd aside,
And Chorus by the Musick was supply'd.
Ingenious Love, inventive in new Arts,
Mingled in Playes, and quickly touch'd our Hearts: 520
This Passion never could resistance find,
But knows the shortest passage to the mind.
Paint then, I'm pleas'd my Hero be in Love;
But let him not like a tame Shepherd move:
Let not *Achilles* be like *Thyrsis* seen,
Or for a *Cyrus* show an *Artamen*;
That, strugling oft, his Passions we may find
The Frailty, not the Virtue of his mind.
Of Romance Heroes shun the low Design;
Yet to great Hearts some Human frailties joyn: 530
Achilles must with *Homer*'s heat ingage;
For an affront I'm pleas'd to see him rage.
Those little Failings in your Hero's heart
Show that of Man and Nature he has part:
To leave known Rules you cannot be allow'd;
Make *Agamemnon* covetous, and proud,
Æneas in Religious Rites austere,
Keep to each man his proper Character.
Of Countryes and of Times the humors know;
From diff'rent Climates, diff'ring Customs grow: 540
And strive to shun their fault, who vainly dress
An Antique Hero like some modern Ass;
Who make old *Romans* like our *English* move,
Show *Cato* Sparkish, or make *Brutus* Love.
In a Romance those errors are excus'd:
There 'tis enough that, Reading, we're amus'd:
Rules too severe would then be useless found;

But the strict Scene must have a juster bound:
Exact Decorum we must always find.
If then you form some Hero in your mind,   550
Be sure your Image with it self agree;
For what he first appears, he still must be.
Affected Wits will nat'urally incline
To paint their Figures by their own design:
Your Bully Poets, Bully Heroes write;
Chapman, in *Bussy D'Ambois* took delight,
And thought perfection was to Huff, and Fight.
Wise Nature by variety does please;
Cloath diff'ring Passions in a diff'ring Dress:
Bold Anger, in rough haughty words appears;   560
Sorrow is humble, and dissolves in Tears.
Make not your *Hecuba* with fury rage,
And show a Ranting grief upon the Stage;
Or tell in vain how the rough *Tanais* bore
His seven-fold Waters to the *Euxine* Shore:
These swoln expressions, this affected noise
Shows like some Pedant, that declaims to Boys.
In sorrow, you must softer methods keep;
And, to excite our tears, your self must weep:
Those noisy words with which ill Plays abound,   570
Come not from hearts that are in sadness drown'd.
    The Theatre for a young Poet's Rhymes
Is a bold venture in our knowing times:
An Author cannot eas'ly purchase Fame;
Critics are always apt to hiss, and blame:
You may be Judg'd by every Ass in Town,
The Priviledge is bought for half a Crown.
To please, you must a hundred Changes try;
Sometimes be humble, then must soar on high:
In noble thoughts must every where abound,   580
Be easy, pleasant, solid, and profound:
To these you must surprising Touches joyn,
And show us a new wonder in each Line;
That all in a just method well design'd,
May leave a strong Impression in the mind.

These are the Arts that Tragedy maintain.

The Epic

But the Heroic claims a Loftier Strain.
In the Narration of some great Design,
Invention, Art, and Fable all must joyn:
Here Fiction must employ its utmost grace;   590
All must assume a Body, Mind, and Face:
Each Virtue a Divinity is seen;
Prudence is *Pallas*, Beauty *Paphos* Queen.
'Tis not a Cloud from whence swift Lightnings fly;
But *Jupiter*, that thunders from the Sky:
Nor a rough Storm, that gives the Sailor pain;
But angry *Neptune*, plowing up the Main:
Echo's no more an empty Airy Sound;
But a fair Nymph that weeps, her Lover drown'd.
Thus in the endless Treasure of his mind,   600
The Poet does a thousand Figures find,
Around the work his Ornaments he pours,
And strows with lavish hand his op'ning Flow'rs.
'Tis not a wonder if a Tempest bore
The *Trojan* Fleet against the *Libyan* Shore;
From faithless Fortune this is no surprise,
For every day 'tis common to our eyes;
But angry *Juno*, that she might destroy,
And overwhelm the rest of ruin'd *Troy*;
That *Æolus* with the fierce Goddess joyn'd,   610
Op'ned the hollow Prisons of the Wind:
Till angry *Neptune*, looking o're the Main,
Rebukes the Tempest, calms the Waves again,
Their Vessels from the dang'rous quick-sands steers;
These are the Springs that move our hopes and fears.
Without these Ornaments before our Eyes,
Th' unsinew'd Poem languishes, and dyes:
Your Poet in his art will always fail,
And tell you but a dull insipid Tale.
In vain have our mistaken Authors try'd   620
These ancient Ornaments to lay aside,
Thinking our God, and Prophets that he sent,

Might Act like those the Poets did invent,
To fright poor Readers in each Line with Hell,
And talk of *Satan*, *Ashtaroth*, and *Bel*;
The Mysteries which Christians must believe,
Disdain such shifting Pageants to receive:
The Gospel offers nothing to our thoughts
But penitence, or punishment for faults;
And mingling falshoods with those Mysteries,   630
Would make our Sacred Truths appear like Lyes.
Besides, what pleasure can it be to hear,
The howlings of repining *Lucifer*,
Whose rage at your imagin'd Hero flyes,
And oft with God himself disputes the prize?
Tasso, you'l say, has done it with applause;
It is not here I mean to Judge his Cause:
Yet, tho our Age has so extoll'd his name,
His Works had never gain'd immortal Fame,
If holy *Godfrey* in his Ecstasies   640
Had only Conquer'd *Satan* on his knees:
If *Tancred*, and *Armida*'s pleasing form,
Did not his melancholy Theme adorn.
'Tis not, that Christian Poems ought to be
Fill'd with the Fictions of Idolatry;
But in a common Subject to reject
The Gods, and Heathen Ornaments neglect;
To banish Tritons who the Seas invade,
To take *Pan*'s Whistle, or the Fates degrade,
To hinder *Charon* in his leaky Boat   650
To pass the Shepherd with the Man of Note,
Is with vain Scruples to disturb your mind,
And search Perfection you can never find:
As well they may forbid us to present
Prudence or Justice for an Ornament,
To paint old *Janus* with his front of Brass,
And take from Time his Scythe, his Wings and Glass,
And every where, as 't were Idolatry,
Banish Descriptions from our Poetry.
Leave 'em their pious Follys to pursue;   660
But let our Reason such vain fears subdue:

And let us not, amongst our Vanities,
Of the true God create a God of Lyes.
In Fable we a thousand pleasures see,
And the smooth names seem made for Poetry;
As *Hector, Alexander, Helen, Phillis,*
Ulysses, Agamemnon, and *Achilles*:
In such a Crowd, the Poet were to blame
To chuse King *Chilp'eric* for his Hero's name.
Sometimes, the name being well or ill apply'd,   670
Will the whole Fortune of your Work decide.
Would you your Reader never should be tir'd?
Choose some great Hero, fit to be admir'd,
In Courage signal, and in Virtue bright,
Let ev'n his very failings give delight;
Let his great Actions our attention bind,
Like *Caesar,* or like *Scipio,* frame his mind,
And not like *Oedipus* his perjur'd Race;
A common Conqueror is a Theme too base.
Chuse not your Tale of Accidents too full;   680
Too much variety may make it dull:
Achilles rage alone, when wrought with skill,
Abundantly does a whole *Iliad* fill.
Be your Narrations likely, short, and smart;
In your Descriptions show your noblest Art:
There 'tis your Poetry may be employ'd;
Yet you must trivial Accidents avoid.
Nor imitate that Fool, who, to describe
The wondrous Marches of the Chosen Tribe,
Plac'd on the sides, to see their Armyes pass,   690
The Fishes staring through the liquid Glass;
Describ'd a Child, who with his little hand,
Pick'd up the shining Pebbles from the sand.
Such objects are too mean to stay our sight;
Allow your Work a just and nobler flight.
Be your beginning plain; and take good heed
Too soon you mount not on the Airy Steed:
Nor tell your Reader, in a Thund'ring Verse,
I sing the Conqueror of the Universe.
What can an Author after this produce?   700

The lab'ring Mountain must bring forth a Mouse.
Much better are we pleas'd with his Address
Who, without making such vast promises,
Sayes, in an easier Stile and plainer Sence,
"I Sing the Combats of that pious Prince
Who from the *Phrygian* Coast his Armies bore,
And landed first on the *Lavinian* shore."
His op'ning Muse sets not the World on fire,
And yet performs more than we can require:
Quickly you'l hear him celebrate the fame,   710
And future glory of the *Roman* Name;
Of *Styx* and *Acheron* describe the Floods,
And *Caesars* wandring in th' *Elysian* Woods:
With Figures numberless his Story grace,
And every thing in beauteous Colours trace.
At once you may be pleasing, and sublime;
I hate a heavy melancholy Rhyme:
I'de rather read *Orlando*'s Comic Tale,
Than a dull Author always stiff and stale,
Who thinks himself dishonour'd in his stile,   720
If on his Works the Graces do but smile.
'Tis said, that *Homer*, Matchless in his Art,
Stole *Venus* Girdle, to ingage the Heart:
His Works indeed vast Treasures do unfold,
And whatsoe're he touches, turns to Gold:
All in his hands new beauty does acquire;
He always pleases, and can never tire.
A happy Warmth he every where may boast;
Nor is he in too long Digressions lost:
His Verses without Rule a method find,   730
And of themselves appear in order joyn'd:
All without trouble answers his intent;
Each Syllable is tending to th' Event.
Let his example your indeavours raise:
To love his Writings, is a kind of praise.
  A Poem, where we all perfections find,
Is not the work of a Fantastick mind:
There must be Care, and Time, and Skill, and Pains;
Not the first heat of unexperienc'd Brains.

Yet sometimes Artless Poets, when the rage   740
Of a warm Fancy does their minds ingage,
Puff'd with vain pride, presume they understand,
And boldly take the Trumpet in their hand;
Their Fustian Muse each Accident confounds;
Nor can she fly, but rise by leaps and bounds,
Till, their small stock of Learning quickly spent,
Their Poem dyes for want of nourishment:
In vain Mankind the hot-brain'd fools decryes,
No branding Censures can unveil their eyes;
With Impudence the Laurel they invade,   750
Resolv'd to like the Monsters they have made.
Virgil, compar'd to them, is flat and dry;
And *Homer* understood not Poetry:
Against their merit if this Age Rebel,
To future times for Justice they appeal.
But waiting till Mankind shall do 'em right,
And bring their Works Triumphantly to Light;
Neglected heaps we in by-corners lay,
Where they become to Worms and Moths a prey;
Forgot, in Dust and Cobwebs let 'em rest,   760
Whilst we return from whence we first digrest.
   The great Success which Tragic Writers found,
In *Athens* first the Comedy renown'd,
Th' abusive *Grecian* there, by pleasing wayes,
Dispers'd his natu'ral malice in his Playes:
Wisdom, and Virtue, Honor, Wit, and Sence,
Were Subject to Buffooning insolence:
Poets were publickly approv'd, and sought,
That Vice extol'd, and Virtue set at naught;
And *Socrates* himself, in that loose Age,   770
Was made the Pastime of a Scoffing Stage.
At last the Public took in hand the Cause,
And cur'd this Madness by the pow'r of Laws;
Forbad at any time, or any place,
To name the Person, or describe the Face.
The Stage its ancient Fury thus let fall,
And Comedy diverted without Gall:
By mild reproofs, recover'd minds diseas'd,

And, sparing Persons, innocently pleas'd.
Each one was nicely shown in this new Glass,   780
And smil'd to think He was not meant the Ass:
A Miser oft would laugh the first, to find
A faithful Draught of his own sordid mind;
And Fops were with such care and cunning writ,
They lik'd the Piece for which themselves did sit.
You then, that would the Comic Lawrels wear,
To study Nature be your only care:
Who e're knows man, and by a curious art
Discerns the hidden secrets of the heart;
He who observes, and naturally can Paint   790
The Jealous Fool, the fawning Sycophant,
A Sober Wit, an enterprising Ass,
A humorous *Otter*, or a *Hudibras*;
May safely in these noble Lists ingage,
And make 'em Act and Speak upon the Stage:
Strive to be natural in all you Write,
And paint with Colours that may please the Sight.
Nature in various Figures does abound;
And in each mind are diff'rent Humors found:
A glance, a touch, discovers to the wise;   800
But every man has not discerning eyes.
All-changing Time does also change the mind;
And diff'rent Ages, diff'rent pleasures find:
Youth, hot and furious, cannot brook delay,
By flattering Vice is eas'ly led away;
Vain in discourse, inconstant in desire,
In Censure, rash; in pleasure, all on fire.
The Manly age does steadier thoughts enjoy;
Pow'r, and Ambition do his Soul employ:
Against the turns of Fate he sets his mind;   810
And by the past the future hopes to find.
Decrepit Age, still adding to his Stores,
For others heaps the Treasure he adores;
In all his actions keeps a frozen pace;
Past Times extols, the present to debase:
Incapable of pleasures Youth abuse,
In others blames, what age does him refuse.

Your Actors must by Reason be control'd;
Let young men speak like young, old men like old:
Observe the Town, and study well the Court;   820
For thither various Characters resort:
Thus 'twas great *Jonson* purchas'd his renown,
And in his Art had born away the Crown;
If, less desirous of the People's praise,
He had not with low Farce debas'd his Playes;
Mixing dull Buffoonry with Wit refin'd,
And *Harlequin* with noble *Terence* joyn'd.
When in the *Fox* I see the Tortois hist,
I lose the Author of the *Alchymist.*
The Comic Wit, born with a smiling Air,   830
Must Tragic grief and pompous Verse forbear;
Yet may he not, as on a Market-place,
With Baudy jests amuse the Populace:
With well-bred Conversation you must please,
And your Intrigue unravel'd be with ease:
Your Action still should Reason's Rules obey,
Nor in an empty Scene may lose its way.
Your humble Stile must sometimes gently rise;
And your Discourse Sententious be, and Wise:
The Passions must to Nature be confin'd,   840
And Scenes to Scenes with Artful weaving joyn'd:
Your Wit must not unseasonably play;
But follow Bus'ness, never lead the way.
Observe how *Terence* does this error shun;
A careful Father chides his Am'orous Son:
Then see that Son, whom no advice can move,
Forget those Orders, and pursue his Love:
'Tis not a well-drawn Picture we discover;
'Tis a true son, a Father, and a Lover.
I like an Author that Reforms the Age;   850
And keeps the right Decorum of the Stage,
That always pleases by just Reason's Rule:
But for a tedious Droll, a Quibling Fool,
Who with low nauseous Baudry fills his Plays;
Let him be gon and on two Tressels raise

Some *Smithfield* Stage, where he may act his Pranks,
And make *Jack Puddings* speak to Mountebanks.

Canto IV

   In *Florence* dwelt a Doctor of Renown,
The Scourge of God, and Terror of the Town,
Who all the Cant of Physick had by heart,   860
And never Murder'd but by rules of Art.
The Public mischief was his Private gain;
Children their slaughter'd Parents sought in vain:
A brother here his poyson'd Brother wept;
Some bloodless dy'd, and some by *Opium* slept.
Colds, at his presence, would to Frenzies turn;
And Agues, like Malignant Fevers, burn.
Hated, at last, his Practice gives him o'er:
One Friend, unkill'd by Drugs, of all his Store,
In his new Country-house affords him place,   870
'Twas a rich Abbot, and a Building Ass:
Here first the Doctor's Talent came in play,
He seems Inspir'd, and talks like *Wren* or *May*:
Of this new Portico condemns the Face,
And turns the Entrance to a better place;
Designs the Stair-case at the other end.
His Friend approves, does for his Mason send,
He comes; the Doctor's Arguments prevail.
In short, to finish this our hum'rous Tale,
He *Galen*'s dang'rous Science does reject,   880
And from ill Doctor turns good Architect.
   In this Example we may have our part:
Rather be Mason, ('tis an useful Art!)
Than a dull Poet; for that Trade accurst,
Admits no mean betwixt the Best and Worst.
In other Sciences, without disgrace
A Candidate may fill a second place;
But Poetry no Medium can admit,
No Reader suffers an indiff'rent Wit:
The ruin'd Stationers against him baul,   890

And *Herringman* degrades him from his Stall.
Burlesque, at least our Laughter may excite;
But a cold Writer never can delight.
The *Counter-Scuffle* has more Wit and Art,
Than the stiff Formal Stile of *Gondibert*.
Be not affected with that empty praise
Which your vain Flatterers will sometimes raise,
And when you read, with Ecstasie will say,
The finish'd Piece! *The admirable Play*!
Which, when expos'd to Censure and to Light,   900
Cannot indure a Critic's piercing sight.
A hundred Authors' Fates have been foretold,
And *Shadwell*'s Works are Printed, but not Sold.
Hear all the world; consider every Thought;
A Fool by chance may stumble on a Fault:
Yet, when *Apollo* does your Muse inspire,
Be not impatient to expose your Fire;
Nor imitate the *Settles* of our Times,
Those Tuneful Readers of their own dull Rhymes,
Who seize on all th' Acquaintance they can meet,   910
And stop the Passengers that walk the Street;
There is no Sanctuary you can chuse
For a Defence from their pursuing Muse.
I've said before, Be patient when they blame;
To alter for the better is no shame.
Yet yield not to a Fool's Impertinence:
Sometimes conceited Sceptics void of Sence,
By their false taste condemn some finish'd part,
And blame the noblest flights of Wit and Art.
In vain their fond Opinions you deride,   920
With their lov'd Follies they are satisfy'd;
And their weak Judgment, void of Sence and Light,
Thinks nothing can escape their feeble sight:
Their dang'rous Counsels do not cure, but wound;
To shun the Storm, they run your Verse aground,
And thinking to escape a Rock, are drown'd.
Chuse a sure Judge to Censure what you Write,
Whose Reason leads, & Knowledge gives you light,
Whose steady hand will prove your Faithful Guide,

And touch the darling follies you would hide: 930
He, in your doubts, will carefully advise,
And clear the Mist before your feeble eyes.
'Tis he will tell you, to what noble height
A generous Muse may sometimes take her flight;
When, too much fetter'd with the Rules of Art,
May from her stricter Bounds and Limits part:
But such a perfect Judge is hard to see,
And every Rhymer knows not Poetry;
Nay some there are, for Writing Verse extol'd,
Who know not *Lucan*'s Dross from *Virgil*'s Gold.   940
    Would you in this great Art acquire Renown?
Authors, observe the Rules I here lay down.
In prudent Lessons every where abound;
With pleasant, joyn the useful and the sound:
A Sober Reader, a vain Tale will slight;
He seeks as well Instruction, as Delight.
Let all your Thoughts to Virtue be confin'd,
Still off'ring noble Figures to our Mind:
I like not those loose Writers, who employ
Their guilty Muse, good Manners to destroy;   950
Who with false Colours still deceive our Eyes,
And show us Vice dress'd in a fair Disguise.
Yet do I not their sullen Muse approve
Who from all modest Writings banish Love;
That strip the Play-house of its chief Intrigue,
And make a Murderer of *Roderigue*:
The lightest Love, if decently exprest,
Will raise no Vitious motions in our brest.
Dido in vain may weep, and ask relief;
I blame her Folly, whil'st I share her Grief.   960
A Virtuous Author, in his Charming Art,
To please the Sense needs not corrupt the Heart;
His heat will never cause a guilty Fire:
To follow Virtue then be your desire.
In vain your Art and Vigor are exprest;
Th' obscene expression shows th' Infected breast.
But above all, base Jealousies avoid,
In which detracting Poets are employ'd:

A noble Wit dares lib'rally commend;
And scorns to grudge at his deserving Friend.   970
Base Rivals, who true Wit and Merit hate,
Caballing still against it with the Great,
Maliciously aspire to gain Renown
By standing up, and pulling others down.
Never debase your self by Treacherous ways,
Nor by such abject methods seek for praise:
Let not your only bus'ness be to Write;
Be Virtuous, Just, and in your Friends delight.
'Tis not enough your Poems be admir'd;
But strive your Conversation be desir'd: 980
Write for immortal Fame; nor ever chuse
Gold for the object of a gen'erous Muse.
I know a noble Wit may, without Crime,
Receive a lawful Tribute for his time:
Yet I abhor those Writers, who despise
Their Honor; and alone their Profit prize;
Who their *Apollo* basely will degrade,
And of a noble Science, make a Trade.
Before kind Reason did her Light display,
And Government taught Mortals to obey,   990
Men, like wild Beasts, did Nature's Laws pursue,
They fed on Herbs, and drink from Rivers drew;
Their Brutal force, on Lust and Rapine bent,
Committed Murders without Punishment:
Reason at last, by her all-conquering Arts,
Reduc'd these Savages, and Tun'd their hearts;
Mankind from Bogs, and Woods, and Caverns calls,
And Towns and Cities fortifies with Walls:
Thus fear of Justice made proud Rapine cease,
And shelter'd Innocence by Laws and Peace.   1000
    These benefits from Poets we receiv'd,
From whence are rais'd those Fictions since believ'd,
That *Orpheus*, by his soft Harmonious strains
Tam'd the fierce Tigers of the *Thracian* Plains;
Amphion's Notes, by their melodious pow'rs,
Drew Rocks & Woods, and rais'd the *Theban* Tow'rs:
These Miracles from numbers did arise,

Since which, in Verse Heav'n taught his Mysteries,
And by a Priest, possess'd with rage Divine,
Apollo spoke from his Prophetick Shrine.   1010
Soon after, *Homer* the old Heroes prais'd,
And noble minds by great Examples rais'd;
Then *Hesiod* did his *Graecian* Swains incline
To till the Fields, and prune the bounteous Vine.
Thus useful Rules were by the Poets' aid,
In easy numbers, to rude men convey'd,
And pleasingly their Precepts did impart;
First Charm'd the Ear, and then ingag'd the Heart:
The Muses thus their Reputation rais'd,
And with just Gratitude in *Greece* were prais'd.   1020
With pleasure Mortals did their Wonders see,
And Sacrific'd to their Divinity:
But Want, at last base Flatt'ry entertain'd,
And old *Parnassus* with this Vice was stain'd:
Desire of gain dazling the Poets' Eyes,
Their Works were fill'd with fulsome flatteries.
Thus needy Wits a vile revenue made,
And Verse became a mercenary Trade.
Debase not with so mean a Vice thy Art:
If Gold must be the Idol of thy heart,   1030
Fly, fly th' unfruitful *Heliconian* strand,
Those streams are not inrich'd with Golden Sand:
Great Wits, as well as Warriors, only gain
Laurels and Honors for their Toyl and Pain:
But, what? an Author cannot live on Fame,
Or pay a Reck'ning with a lofty Name:
A Poet to whom Fortune is unkind,
Who when he goes to bed has hardly din'd;
Takes little pleasure in *Parnassus* Dreams,
Or relishes the *Heliconian* streams.   1040
Horace had Ease and Plenty when he writ,
And free from cares for money or for meat,
Did not expect his dinner from his wit.
'Tis true; but Verse is cherish'd by the Great,
And now none famish who deserve to eat:
What can we fear, when Virtue, Arts, and Sence,

Receive the Stars propitious Influence;
When a sharp-sighted Prince, by early Grants
Rewards your Merits, and prevents your Wants?
Sing then his Glory, Celebrate his Fame;   1050
Your noblest Theme is his immortal Name.
Let mighty *Spencer* raise his reverend head,
Cowley and *Denham* start up from the dead;
Waller his age renew, and Off'rings bring,
Our Monarch's praise let bright-ey'd Virgins sing;
Let *Dryden* with new Rules our Stage refine,
And his great Models form by this Design:
But where's a Second *Virgil*, to Rehearse
Our Hero's Glories in his Epic Verse?
What *Orpheus* sing his Triumphs o'er the Main,   1060
And make the Hills and Forests move again;
Show his bold Fleet on the *Batavian* shore,
And *Holland* trembling as his Canons roar;
Paint *Europe*'s Balance in his steady hand,
Whilst the two Worlds in expectation stand
Of Peace or War, that wait on his Command?
But, as I speak, new Glories strike my Eyes,
Glories, which Heav'n it Self does give, and prize,
Blessings of Peace; that with their milder Rayes
Adorn his Reign, and bring *Saturnian* Dayes: 1070
Now let Rebellion, Discord, Vice, and Rage,
That have in Patriots Forms debauch'd our Age,
Vanish, with all the Ministers of Hell;
His Rayes their poys'nous Vapors shall dispel:
'Tis He alone our safety did create,
His own firm Soul secur'd the Nation's Fate,
Oppos'd to all the *boutefeus* of the State.
Authors, for Him your great indeavours raise;
The loftiest Numbers will but reach his praise.
For me, whose Verse in Satyr has been bred,   1080
And never durst Heroic Measures tread;
Yet you shall see me, in that famous Field
With Eyes and Voice, my best assistance yield;
Offer you Lessons, that my Infant Muse
Learnt, when she *Horace* for her Guide did chuse:

Second your Zeal with Wishes, Heart, and Eyes,
And afar off hold up the glorious Prize.
But pardon too, if, Zealous for the Right,
A strict observer of each Noble flight,
From the fine Gold I separate th' Allay,   1090
And show how hasty Writers sometimes stray:
Apter to blame, than knowing how to mend;
A sharp, but yet a necessary Friend.

IV

~~~~~~~~~~

An Essay on Criticism
by
Alexander Pope

Introduction and Commentary

Alexander Pope and the English Tradition

The concept of criticism as finding fault is based on a confidence in critical standards combined with an equal confidence in the integrity of the critic. The questions it raises are first, what if the standards are wrong, and second, what if the critic is not an incorruptible source of truth?

These are exactly the questions posed by Pope's *Essay on Criticism* (1711), which begins with the observation that a single poet begets large numbers of wrong-minded critics: "Some few in that, but numbers err in this,/ Ten censure wrong for one who writes amiss" (ll. 5–6).

Pope's *Essay* is a youthful work, completed when he was barely twenty-one. Its most striking feature is its decision to turn the focus of the Horatian "poem about poetry" from rules for writing verse to standards of criticism. The latter subject is important in the *Art* and is included in most imitations of it, but Pope makes it the central concern of the entire work.

Of almost equal interest is the fact that having taken criticism as his subject, Pope offers a series of qualifications of the neoclassical position. He begins, as has been noted, with a warning that negative criticism is even more common than bad poetry. Among the factors that undermine the validity of criticism are subjective judgments, overly rational analysis, and the fact that many critics are failed poets. Emotion is recognized as a decisive element in critical judgments. The position sounds almost modern. Reason and nature soon return, however. The need to base critical judgments on nature, the fact that rules are nature methodized, and the value of the classics as models of imitation of nature are presented in a lively if predictable way. The fact that great poets "snatch a grace beyond the reach of art" (l. 155) is less predictable. The line may owe something to Boileau and also to Rapin's theory of the *je ne sais quoi*. Later (ll. 169–80), the possibility of objective standards is brought into question: Horace's *ut pictura poesis* passage (*Art*, ll. 361–65) leads to an explicit statement that judgments are relative to the perspective of the reader. In part II of the *Essay* the emphasis is not on the soundness of the critic's judgments but on the motives that may lead him astray, including vanity and too little learning. These are subjecive motives, and they call into question the second fundamental assumption of the neoclassical view of the critic—the critic's integrity.

Pope now offers advice about judging faulty works:

> A perfect judge will read each work of wit
> With the same spirit that the author writ;
> Survey the WHOLE, nor seek slight faults to find
> Where nature moves, and rapture warms the mind. (ll. 233–36)

This is a significant adaptation of Horace's concept of wholeness (*Art*, l. 23), and, if elaborated, it could be read as an anticipation of the romantic theory of "genial criticism." It is considerably more generous than Pope was to prove in many of the literary quarrels he entered into later in life. At any rate, from this point on, the essay tends to conform to expectations. Faults are enumerated on the assumption that the critic must be alert to them. Some are pardonable, but no pardon is possible for the poet who is corrupted by a corrupt age (ll. 526–59).

Part III of the *Essay* continues along the path already marked out. It includes definitions of the bad and the good critic and a still interesting thumbnail history of criticism that begins with Aristotle, continues to the fall of Rome, skips the Middle Ages, and then moves from Erasmus to the Rome of Girolamo Vida to the France of Boileau and finally to the England of William Walsh, one of Pope's early mentors.

Pope's ideal critic would be less uncompromising and more human—because less self-assured—than Boileau's. However, the limits of toleration are evidently narrow. Pope assumes that his standards are basically sound and have to be adjusted only to recognize that "even Homer nods" and that occasionally what may seem a blemish is actually a virtue, so that "it is [not] Homer nods but we that dream" (l. 180).

What if things are much worse than Pope imagined? What if the standards themselves are wrong and the critic turns out to be an egotistical prig or a sadist determined to use his power to crush all dissenting opinion? Neoclassical criticism was a synthesis intended to reconcile many conflicting seventeenth-century trends and suppress others, including the idea of inspiration and the vogue of conceits. It was always vulnerable, and by the mid-eighteenth century new trends were emerging that would require a radical shift of standards rather than a recognition that poetry can sometimes rise "beyond the reach of art."

An Essay on Criticism

'Tis hard to say, if greater want of skill
Appear in writing or in judging ill;
But, of the two, less dang'rous is th' offence
To tire our patience, than mislead our sense.
Some few in that, but numbers err in this,
Ten censure wrong for one who writes amiss;
A fool might once himself alone expose,
Now one in verse makes many more in prose.
   'Tis with our judgments as our watches, none
Go just alike, yet each believes his own.   10
In poets as true genius is but rare,
True taste as seldom is the critic's share;
Both must alike from heav'n derive their light,
These born to judge, as well as those to write.
Let such teach others who themselves excel,
And censure freely, who have written well.
Authors are partial to their wit, 'tis true,
But are not critics to their judgment too?
   Yet, if we look more closely, we shall find
Most have the seeds of judgment in their mind: 20
Nature affords at least a glimm'ring light,
The lines, though touched but faintly, are drawn right;
But as the slightest sketch, if justly traced,
Is by ill-colouring but the more disgraced,
So by false learning is good sense defaced:
Some are bewildered in the maze of schools,
And some made coxcombs nature meant but fools.
In search of wit, these lose their common sense,
And then turn critics in their own defense:

Each burns alike, who can, or cannot write, 30
Or with a rival's, or an eunuch's spite.
All fools have still an itching to deride,
And fain would be upon the laughing side.
If Maevius scribble in Apollo's spite,
There are who judge still worse than he can write.
  Some have at first for wits, then poets passed,
Turned critics next, and proved plain fools at last.
Some neither can for wits nor critics pass,
As heavy mules are neither horse nor ass.
Those half-learned witlings, num'rous in our isle, 40
As half-formed insects on the banks of Nile;
Unfinished things, one knows not what to call,
Their generation's so equivocal:
To tell 'em would a hundred tongues require,
Or one vain wit's, that might a hundred tire.
  But you who seek to give and merit fame,
And justly bear a critic's noble name,
Be sure yourself and your own reach to know,
How far your genius, taste, and learning go;
Launch not beyond your depth, but be discreet, 50
And mark that point where sense and dulness meet.
  Nature to all things fixed the limits fit,
And wisely curbed proud man's pretending wit.
As on the land while here the ocean gains,
In other parts it leaves wide sandy plains;
Thus in the soul while memory prevails,
The solid pow'r of understanding fails;
Where beams of warm imagination play,
The memory's soft figures melt away.
One science only will one genius fit; 60
So vast is art, so narrow human wit:
Not only bounded to peculiar arts,
But oft in those confined to single parts.
Like kings we lose the conquests gained before,
By vain ambition still to make them more
Each might his sev'ral province well command,
Would all but stoop to what they understand.
  First follow nature, and your judgment frame

By her just standard, which is still the same:
Unerring nature, still divinely bright,   70
One clear, unchanged, and universal light,
Life, force, and beauty, must to all impart,
At once the source, and end, and test of art.
Art from that fund each just supply provides;
Works without show, and without pomp presides:
In some fair body thus th' informing soul
With spirits feeds, with vigour fills the whole,
Each motion guides, and ev'ry nerve sustains;
Itself unseen, but in th' effects remains.
Some, to whom heav'n in wit has been profuse,   80
Want as much more, to turn it to its use;
For wit and judgment often are at strife,
Though meant each other's aid, like man and wife.
'Tis more to guide, than spur the muse's steed;
Restrain his fury, than provoke his speed;
The winged courser, like a gen'rous horse,
Shows most true mettle when you check his course.
    Those rules of old discovered, not devised,
Are nature still, but nature methodised;
Nature, like liberty, is but restrained   90
By the same laws which first herself ordained.
    Hear how learn'd Greece her useful rules indites,
When to repress, and when indulge our flights:
High on Parnassus' top her sons she showed,
And pointed out those arduous paths they trod;
Held from afar, aloft, th' immortal prize,
And urged the rest by equal steps to rise.
Just precepts thus from great examples giv'n,
She drew from them what they derived from heav'n.
The gen'rous critic fanned the poet's fire,   100
And taught the world with reason to admire
Then criticism the muse's handmaid proved,
To dress her charms, and make her more beloved:
But following wits from that intention strayed,
Who could not win the mistress, wooed the maid;
Against the poets their own arms they turned,
Sure to hate most the men from whom they learned.

So modern 'pothecaries, taught the art
By doctors' bills to play the doctor's part,
Bold in the practice of mistaken rules,   110
Prescribe, apply, and call their masters fools.
Some on the leaves of ancient authors prey,
Nor time nor moths e'er spoiled so much as they;
Some dryly plain, without invention's aid,
Write dull receipts how poems may be made;
These leave the sense, their learning to display,
And those explain the meaning quite away.
   You then whose judgment the right course would steer,
Know well each ancient's proper character;
His fable, subject, scope in ev'ry page;   120
Religion, country, genius of his age:
Without all these at once before your eyes,
Cavil you may, but never criticise.
Be Homer's works your study and delight,
Read them by day, and meditate by night;
Thence form your judgment, thence your maxims bring,
And trace the muses upward to their spring.
Still with itself compared, his text peruse;
And let your comment be the Mantuan muse.
   When first young Maro in his boundless mind   130
A work t' outlast immortal Rome designed,
Perhaps he seemed above the critic's law,
And but from nature's fountain scorned to draw:
But when t' examine ev'ry part he came,
Nature and Homer were, he found, the same.
Convinced, amazed, he checks the bold design:
And rules as strict his laboured work confine,
As if the Stagyrite o'erlooked each line.
Learn hence for ancient rules a just esteem;
To copy nature is to copy them.   140
   Some beauties yet no precepts can declare,
For there's a happiness as well as care.
Music resembles poetry; in each
Are nameless graces which no methods teach,
And which a master hand alone can reach.
If, where the rules not far enough extend,

(Since rules were made but to promote their end,)
Some lucky licence answer to the full
Th' intent proposed, that licence is a rule.
Thus Pegasus, a nearer way to take,   150
May boldly deviate from the common track.
Great wits sometimes may gloriously offend,
And rise to faults true critics dare not mend;
From vulgar bounds with brave disorder part,
And snatch a grace beyond the reach of art,
Which, without passing through the judgment, gains
The heart, and all its end at once attains.
In prospects, thus, some objects please our eyes,
Which out of nature's common order rise,
The shapeless rock, or hanging precipice.   160
But though the ancients thus their rules invade,
(As kings dispense with laws themselves have made,)
Moderns, beware! or if you must offend
Against the precept, ne'er transgress its end;
Let it be seldom, and compelled by need;
And have, at least, their precedent to plead.
The critic else proceeds without remorse,
Seizes your fame, and puts his laws in force.
    I know there are, to whose presumptuous thoughts
Those freer beauties, ev'n in them, seem faults.   170
Some figures monstrous and mis-shaped appear,
Considered singly, or beheld too near,
Which, but proportioned to their light, or place,
Due distance reconciles to form and grace.
A prudent chief not always must display
His pow'rs in equal rank, and fair array,
But with th' occasion and the place comply,
Conceal his force, nay, seem sometimes to fly.
Those oft are stratagems which errors seem,
Nor is it Homer nods but we that dream.   180
    Still green with bays each ancient altar stands,
Above the reach of sacrilegious hands;
Secure from flames, from envy's fiercer rage,
Destructive war, and all-involving age.
See, from each clime, the learn'd their incense bring;

Hear, in all tongues consenting Paeans ring!
In praise so just let ev'ry voice be joined,
And fill the gen'ral chorus of mankind.
Hail, bards triumphant! born in happier days;
Immortal heirs of universal praise!   190
Whose honours with increase of ages grow,
As streams roll down, enlarging as they flow;
Nations unborn your mighty names shall sound,
And worlds applaud, that must not yet be found!
O may some spark of your celestial fire,
The last, the meanest of your sons inspire,
(That on weak wings, from far, pursues your flights;
Glows while he reads, but trembles as he writes,)
To teach vain wits a science little known,
T' admire superior sense, and doubt their own!   200

II

Of all the causes which conspire to blind
Man's erring judgment, and misguide the mind,
What the weak head with strongest bias rules,
Is pride, the never-failing vice of fools.
Whatever nature has in worth denied,
She gives in large recruits of needful pride;
For as in bodies, thus in souls, we find
What wants in blood and spirits, swelled with wind:
Pride, where wit fails, steps in to our defence,
And fills up all the mighty void of sense.   210
If once right reason drives that cloud away,
Truth breaks upon us with resistless day.
Trust not yourself; but your defects to know,
Make use of ev'ry friend and ev'ry foe.
A little learning is a dang'rous thing;
Drink deep, or taste not the Pierian spring:
There shallow draughts intoxicate the brain,
And drinking largely sobers us again.
Fired at first sight with what the muse imparts,
In fearless youth we tempt the heights of arts,   220
While from the bounded level of our mind,

Short views we take, nor see the lengths behind;
But more advanced, behold with strange surprise,
New distant scenes of endless science rise!
So pleased at first the tow'ring Alps we try,
Mount o'er the vales, and seem to tread the sky,
Th' eternal snows appear already past,
And the first clouds and mountains seem the last:
But those attained, we tremble to survey
The growing labours of the lengthened way,   230
Th' increasing prospect tires our wand'ring eyes,
Hills peep o'er hills, and Alps on Alps arise!
    A perfect judge will read each work of wit
With the same spirit that its author writ:
Survey the whole, nor seek slight faults to find
Where nature moves, and rapture warms the mind;
Nor lose for that malignant dull delight,
The gen'rous pleasure to be charmed with wit.
But in such lays as neither ebb nor flow,
Correctly cold, and regularly low,   240
That, shunning faults, one quiet tenour keep,
We cannot blame indeed, but we may sleep.
In wit, as nature, what affects our hearts
Is not th' exactness of peculiar parts;
'Tis not a lip, or eye, we beauty call,
But the joint force and full result of all.
Thus when we view some well-proportioned dome,
(The world's just wonder, and ev'n thine, O Rome!)
No single parts unequally surprise,
All comes united to th' admiring eyes;   250
No monstrous height, or breadth, or length, appear;
The whole at once is bold, and regular.
    Whoever thinks a faultless piece to see,
Thinks what ne'er was, nor is, nor e'er shall be.
In ev'ry work regard the writer's end,
Since none can compass more than they intend;
And if the means be just, the conduct true,
Applause, in spite of trivial faults, is due.
As men of breeding, sometimes men of wit,
T' avoid great errors, must the less commit: 260

Neglect the rules each verbal critic lays,
For not to know some trifles is a praise.
Most critics, fond of some subservient art,
Still make the whole depend upon a part:
They talk of principles, but notions prize,
And all to one loved folly sacrifice.
    Once on a time, La Mancha's knight, they say,
A certain bard encount'ring on the way,
Discoursed in terms as just, with looks as sage,
As e'er could Dennis, of the Grecian stage;   270
Concluding all were desp'rate sots and fools,
Who durst depart from Aristotle's rules.
Our author, happy in a judge so nice,
Produced his play, and begged the knight's advice;
Made him observe the subject, and the plot,
The manners, passions, unities, what not,
All which, exact to rule, were brought about,
Were but a combat in the lists left out.
"What! leave the combat out!" exclaims the knight;
Yes, or we must renounce the Stagyrite.   280
"Not so, by heav'n!" he answers in a rage,
"Knights, squires, and steeds, must enter on the stage."
So vast a throng the stage can ne'er contain.
"Then build a new, or act it in a plain."
    Thus critics of less judgment than caprice,
Curious not knowing, not exact but nice,
Form short ideas; and offend in arts,
As most in manners, by a love to parts.
    Some to conceit alone their taste confine,
And glitt'ring thoughts struck out at ev'ry line;   290
Pleased with a work where nothing's just or fit;
One glaring chaos and wild heap of wit.
Poets, like painters, thus unskilled to trace
The naked nature, and the living grace,
With gold and jewels cover ev'ry part,
And hide with ornaments their want of art.
True wit is nature to advantage dressed;
What oft was thought, but ne'er so well expressed;
Something, whose truth convinced at sight we find,

That gives us back the image of our mind.   300
As shades more sweetly recommend the light,
So modest plainness sets off sprightly wit;
For works may have more wit than does 'em good,
As bodies perish through excess of blood.
  Others for language all their care express,
And value books, as women men, for dress:
Their praise is still,—the style is excellent;
The sense, they humbly take upon content.
Words are like leaves; and where they most abound,
Much fruit of sense beneath is rarely found: 310
False eloquence like the prismatic glass,
Its gaudy colours spreads on ev'ry place;
The face of nature we no more survey,
All glares alike, without distinction gay:
But true expression, like th' unchanging sun,
Clears and improves whate'er it shines upon,
It gilds all objects, but it alters none.
Expression is the dress of thought, and still
Appears more decent, as more suitable:
A vile conceit in pompous words expressed   320
Is like a clown in regal purple dressed:
For diff'rent styles with diff'rent subjects sort
As sev'ral garbs with country, town, and court.
Some by old words to fame have made pretence,
Ancients in phrase, mere moderns in their sense;
Such laboured nothings, in so strange a style,
Amaze th' unlearn'd, and make the learned smile.
Unlucky, as Fungoso in the play,
These sparks with awkward vanity display
What the fine gentleman wore yesterday;   330
And but so mimic ancient wits at best,
As apes our grandsires, in their doublets drest.
In words, as fashions, the same rule will hold;
Alike fantastic, if too new, or old:
Be not the first by whom the new are tried,
Nor yet the last to lay the old aside.
  But most by numbers judge a poet's song,
And smooth or rough, with them, is right or wrong:

In the bright muse, though thousand charms conspire,
Her voice is all these tuneful fools admire;   340
Who haunt Parnassus but to please their ear,
Not mend their minds; as some to church repair,
Not for the doctrine, but the music there.
These equal syllables alone require,
Tho' oft the ear the open vowels tire;
While expletives their feeble aid do join;
And ten low words oft creep in one dull line:
While they ring round the same unvaried chimes,
With sure returns of still expected rhymes;
Where'er you find "the cooling western breeze,"   350
In the next line, it "whispers through the trees":
If crystal streams "with pleasing murmurs creep,"
The reader's threatened, not in vain, with "sleep":
Then, at the last and only couplet fraught
With some unmeaning thing they call a thought,
A needless Alexandrine ends the song,
That, like a wounded snake, drags its slow length along.
Leave such to tune their own dull rhymes, and know
What's roundly smooth, or languishingly slow;
And praise the easy vigour of a line,   360
Where Denham's strength, and Waller's sweetness join.
True ease in writing comes from art, not chance,
As those move easiest who have learned to dance.
'Tis not enough no harshness gives offense,
The sound must seem an echo to the sense.
Soft is the strain when zephyr gently blows,
And the smooth stream in smoother numbers flows;
But when loud surges lash the sounding shore,
The hoarse, rough verse should like the torrent roar:
When Ajax strives some rock's vast weight to throw,   370
The line too labours, and the words move slow:
Not so, when swift Camilla scours the plain,
Flies o'er th' unbending corn, and skims along the main.
Hear how Timotheus' varied lays surprise,
And bid alternate passions fall and rise!
While at each change, the son of Libyan Jove
Now burns with glory, and then melts with love;

Now his fierce eyes with sparkling fury glow,
Now sighs steal out, and tears begin to flow:
Persians and Greeks like turns of nature found,   380
And the world's victor stood subdued by sound!
The pow'r of music all our hearts allow,
And what Timotheus was, is Dryden now.
    Avoid extremes; and shun the fault of such,
Who still are pleased too little or too much.
At ev'ry trifle scorn to take offense,
That always shows great pride, or little sense:
Those heads, as stomachs, are not sure the best,
Which nauseate all, and nothing can digest.
Yet let not each gay turn thy rapture move;   390
For fools admire, but men of sense approve:
As things seem large which we through mists descry,
Dulness is ever apt to magnify.
    Some foreign writers, some our own despise;
The ancients only, or the moderns prize.
Thus wit, like faith, by each man is applied
To one small sect, and all are damned beside.
Meanly they seek the blessing to confine,
And force that sun but on a part to shine,
Which not alone the southern wit sublimes,   400
But ripens spirits in cold northern climes;
Which, from the first has shone on ages past,
Enlights the present, and shall warm the last;
Though each may feel increases and decays,
And see now clearer and now darker days:
Regard not then if wit be old or new,
But blame the false, and value still the true.
    Some ne'er advance a judgment of their own,
But catch the spreading notion of the town:
They reason and conclude by precedent,   410
And own stale nonsense which they ne'er invent.
Some judge of authors' names, not works, and then
Nor praise nor blame the writings, but the men.
Of all this servile herd, the worst is he
That in proud dulness joins with quality,
A constant critic at the great man's board,

To fetch and carry nonsense for my lord.
What woeful stuff this madrigal would be,
In some starved hackney sonneteer, or me!
But let a lord once own the happy lines,   420
How the wit brightens! how the style refines!
Before his sacred name flies ev'ry fault,
And each exalted stanza teems with thought!
　　The vulgar thus through imitation err;
As oft the learn'd by being singular;
So much they scorn the crowd, that if the throng
By chance go right, they purposely go wrong:
So schismatics the plain believers quit,
And are but damned for having too much wit.
Some praise at morning what they blame at night;   430
But always think the last opinion right.
A muse by these is like a mistress used,
This hour she's idolised, the next abused;
While their weak heads, like towns unfortified,
'Twixt sense and nonsense daily change their side.
Ask them the cause; they're wiser still they say;
And still to-morrow's wiser than to-day.
We think our fathers fools, so wise we grow;
Our wiser sons, no doubt, will think us so.
Once school divines this zealous isle o'erspread;   440
Who knew most Sentences, was deepest read;
Faith, gospel, all, seemed made to be disputed,
And none had sense enough to be confuted:
Scotists and Thomists, now, in peace remain,
Amidst their kindred cobwebs in Duck-lane.
If faith itself has diff'rent dresses worn,
What wonder modes in wit should take their turn?
Oft, leaving what is natural and fit,
The current folly proves the ready wit;
And authors think their reputation safe,   450
Which lives as long as fools are pleased to laugh.
　　Some valuing those of their own side or mind,
Still make themselves the measure of mankind:
Fondly we think we honour merit then,
When we but praise ourselves in other men.

Parties in wit attend on those of state,
And public faction doubles private hate.
Pride, malice, folly, against Dryden rose,
In various shapes of parsons, critics, beaus;
But sense survived when merry jests were past;   460
For rising merit will buoy up at last.
Might he return, and bless once more our eyes,
New Blackmores and new Milbournes must arise:
Nay, should great Homer lift his awful head,
Zoilus again would start up from the dead.
Envy will merit, as its shade, pursue;
But like a shadow, proves the substance true:
For envied wit, like Sol eclipsed, makes known
Th' opposing body's grossness, not its own.
When first that sun too pow'rful beams displays,   470
It draws up vapours which obscure its rays;
But ev'n those clouds at last adorn its way,
Reflect new glories, and augment the day.
  Be thou the first true merit to befriend;
His praise is lost, who stays till all commend.
Short is the date, alas! of modern rhymes,
And 'tis but just to let them live betimes.
No longer now that golden age appears,
When patriarch wits survived a thousand years:
Now length of fame (our second life) is lost,   480
And bare threescore is all ev'n that can boast;
Our sons their fathers' failing language see,
And such as Chaucer is, shall Dryden be.
So when the faithful pencil has designed
Some bright idea of the master's mind,
Where a new world leaps out at his command,
And ready nature waits upon his hand;
When the ripe colours soften and unite,
And sweetly melt into just shade and light;
When mellowing years their full perfection give,   490
And each bold figure just begins to live,
The treach'rous colours the fair art betray,
And all the bright creation fades away!
  Unhappy wit, like most mistaken things,

Atones not for that envy which it brings.
In youth alone its empty praise we boast,
But soon the short-lived vanity is lost:
Like some fair flow'r the early spring supplies,
That gaily blooms, but ev'n in blooming dies.
What is this wit, which must our cares employ?   500
The owner's wife, that other men enjoy;
Then most our trouble still when most admired,
And still the more we give, the more required;
Whose fame with pains we guard, but lose with ease,
Sure some to vex, but never all to please;
'Tis what the vicious fear, the virtuous shun,
By fools 'tis hated, and by knaves undone!
    If wit so much from ign'rance undergo,
Ah let not learning too commence its foe!
Of old, those met rewards who could excel,   510
And such were praised who but endeavour'd well:
Though triumphs were to gen'rals only due,
Crowns were reserved to grace the soldiers too.
Now, they who reach Parnassus' lofty crown,
Employ their pains to spurn some others down;
And while self-love each jealous writer rules,
Contending wits become the sport of fools:
But still the worst with most regret commend,
For each ill author is as bad a friend.
To what base ends, and by what abject ways,   520
Are mortals urged through sacred lust of praise!
Ah ne'er so dire a thirst of glory boast,
Nor in the critic let the man be lost.
Good-nature and good sense must ever join;
To err is human, to forgive, divine.
    But if in noble minds some dregs remain
Not yet purged off, of spleen and sour disdain;
Discharge that rage on more provoking crimes,
Nor fear a dearth in these flagitious times.
No pardon vile obscenity should find,   530
Though wit and art conspire to move your mind;
But dulness with obscenity must prove
As shameful sure as impotence in love.

In the fat age of pleasure, wealth, and ease,
Sprung the rank weed, and thrived with large increase:
When love was all an easy monarch's care;
Seldom at council, never in a war:
Jilts ruled the state, and statesmen farces writ:
Nay, wits had pensions, and young lords had wit:
The fair sat panting at a courtier's play,   540
And not a mask went unimproved away:
The modest fan was lifted up no more,
And virgins smiled at what they blushed before.
The following license of a foreign reign
Did all the dregs of bold Socinus drain;
Then unbelieving priests reformed the nation,
And taught more pleasant methods of salvation;
Where heaven's free subjects might their rights dispute,
Lest God himself should seem too absolute:
Pulpits their sacred satire learned to spare,   550
And vice admired to find a flatt'rer there!
Encouraged thus, wit's Titans braved the skies,
And the press groaned with licensed blasphemies.
These monsters, critics! with your darts engage,
Here point your thunder, and exhaust your rage!
Yet shun their fault, who, scandalously nice,
Will needs mistake an author into vice;
All seems infected that th' infected spy,
As all looks yellow to the jaundiced eye.

III

Learn then what morals critics ought to show,   560
For 'tis but half a judge's task, to know.
'Tis not enough, taste, judgment, learning, join;
In all you speak, let truth and candour shine,
That not alone what to your sense is due
All may allow, but seek your friendship too.
Be silent always when you doubt your sense;
And speak, though sure, with seeming diffidence:
Some positive, persisting fops we know,

Who, if once wrong, will needs be always so;
But you with pleasure own your errors past,   570
And make each day a critique on the last.
  'Tis not enough your counsel still be true;
Blunt truths more mischief than nice falsehoods do;
Men must be taught as if you taught them not,
And things unknown proposed as things forgot.
Without good-breeding truth is disapproved;
That only makes superior sense beloved.
  Be niggards of advice on no pretense:
For the worst avarice is that of sense.
With mean complaisance ne'er betray your trust,   580
Nor be so civil as to prove unjust.
Fear not the anger of the wise to raise;
Those best can bear reproof, who merit praise.
  'Twere well might critics still this freedom take,
But Appius reddens at each word you speak,
And stares, tremendous, with a threat'ning eye,
Like some fierce tyrant in old tapestry.
Fear most to tax an Honourable fool,
Whose right it is, uncensured, to be dull;
Such, without wit, are poets when they please,   590
As without learning they can take degrees.
Leave dang'rous truths to unsuccessful satires,
And flattery to fulsome dedicators,
Whom, when they praise, the world believes no more,
Than when they promise to give scribbling o'er.
'Tis best sometimes your censure to restrain,
And charitably let the dull be vain:
Your silence there is better than your spite,
For who can rail so long as they can write?
Still humming on, their drowsy course they keep,   600
And lashed so long, like tops, are lashed asleep.
False steps but help them to renew the race,
As, after stumbling, jades will mend their pace.
What crowds of these, impenitently bold,
In sounds and jingling syllables grown old,
Still run on poets in a raging vein,

Ev'n to the dregs and squeezing of the brain,
Strain out the last dull droppings of their sense,
And rhyme with all the rage of impotence.
    Such shameless bards we have; and yet, 'tis true,   610
There are as mad, abandoned critics too.
The bookful blockhead, ignorantly read,
With loads of learned lumber in his head,
With his own tongue still edifies his ears,
And always list'ning to himself appears.
All books he reads, and all he reads assails,
From Dryden's Fables down to Durfey's Tales.
With him most authors steal their works, or buy;
Garth did not write his own Dispensary.
Name a new play, and he's the poet's friend,   620
Nay, showed his faults—but when would poets mend?
No place so sacred from such fops is barred,
Nor is Paul's church more safe than Paul's churchyard:
Nay, fly to altars; there they'll talk you dead;
For fools rush in where angels fear to tread.
Distrustful sense with modest caution speaks,
It still looks home, and short excursions makes;
But rattling nonsense in full volleys breaks,
And never shocked, and never turned aside,
Bursts out, resistless, with a thund'ring tide.   630
    But where's the man, who counsel can bestow,
Still pleased to teach, and yet not proud to know?
Unbiassed, or by favour, or by spite;
Not dully prepossessed, nor blindly right;
Though learn'd, well-bred; and though well-bred, sincere;
Modestly bold, and humanly severe;
Who to a friend his faults can freely show,
And gladly praise the merit of a foe?
Blest with a taste exact, yet unconfined;
A knowledge both of books and human kind;   640
Gen'rous converse; a soul exempt from pride;
And love to praise, with reason on his side?
    Such once were critics; such the happy few,
Athens and Rome in better ages knew.
The mighty Stagyrite first left the shore,

Spread all his sails, and durst the deeps explore;
He steered securely, and discovered far,
Led by the light of the Maeonian star.
Poets, a race long unconfined, and free,
Still fond and proud of savage liberty,   650
Received his laws; and stood convinced 'twas fit,
Who conquered nature, should preside o'er wit.
    Horace still charms with graceful negligence,
And without method talks us into sense;
Will, like a friend, familiarly convey
The truest notions in the easiest way.
He, who supreme in judgment, as in wit,
Might boldly censure, as he boldly writ,
Yet judged with coolness, though he sung with fire;
His precepts teach but what his works inspire.   660
Our critics take a contrary extreme,
They judge with fury, but they write with phlegm:
Nor suffers Horace more in wrong translations
By wits, than critics in as wrong quotations.
    See Dionysius Homer's thoughts refine,
And call new beauties forth from ev'ry line!
    Fancy and art in gay Petronius please,
The scholar's learning, with the courtier's ease.
    In grave Quintilian's copious work, we find
The justest rules, and clearest method joined: 670
Thus useful arms in magazines we place,
All ranged in order, and disposed with grace,
But less to please the eye, than arm the hand,
Still fit for use, and ready at command.
    Thee, bold Longinus! all the Nine inspire,
And bless their critic with a poet's fire.
An ardent judge, who, zealous in his trust,
With warmth gives sentence, yet is always just:
Whose own example strengthens all his laws;
And is himself that great sublime he draws.   680
    Thus long succeeding critics justly reigned,
Licence repressed, and useful laws ordained.
Learning and Rome alike in empire grew;
And arts still followed where her eagles flew;

From the same foes, at last, both felt their doom,
And the same age saw learning fall and Rome.
With tyranny, then superstition joined,
As that the body, this enslaved the mind;
Much was believed, but little understood,
And to be dull was construed to be good; 690
A second deluge learning thus o'er-run,
And the monks finished what the Goths begun.
   At length Erasmus, that great injured name,
(The glory of the priesthood and the shame!)
Stemmed the wild torrent of a barb'rous age,
And drove those holy Vandals off the stage.
   But see! each muse, in Leo's golden days,
Starts from her trance, and trims her withered bays,
Rome's ancient genius, o'er its ruins spread,
Shakes off the dust, and rears his rev'rend head. 700
Then sculpture and her sister-arts revive;
Stones leaped to form, and rocks began to live;
With sweeter notes each rising temple rung;
A Raphael painted, and a Vida sung.
Immortal Vida: on whose honoured brow
The poet's bays and critic's ivy grow:
Cremona now shall ever boast thy name,
As next in place to Mantua, next in fame!
But soon by impious arms from Latium chased,
Their ancient bounds the banished Muses passed. 710
Thence arts o'er all the northern world advance,
But critic-learning flourished most in France;
The rules a nation, born to serve, obeys;
And Boileau still in right of Horace sways.
But we, brave Britons, foreign laws despised,
And kept unconquered, and uncivilized;
Fierce for the liberties of wit, and bold,
We still defied the Romans, as of old.
Yet some there were, among the sounder few
Of those who less presumed, and better knew, 720
Who durst assert the juster ancient cause,
And here restored wit's fundamental laws.
Such was the Muse, whose rules and practice tell

"Nature's chief master-piece is writing well."
Such was Roscommon, not more learn'd than good,
With manners gen'rous as his noble blood;
To him the wit of Greece and Rome was known,
And ev'ry author's merit, but his own.
Such late was Walsh, the muse's judge and friend,
Who justly knew to blame or to commend: 730
To failings mild, but zealous for desert;
The clearest head, and the sincerest heart.
This humble praise, lamented shade! receive,
This praise at least a grateful muse may give:
The muse, whose early voice you taught to sing,
Prescribed her heights, and pruned her tender wing,
(Her guide now lost) no more attempts to rise,
But in low numbers short excursions tries;
Content, if hence th' unlearn'd their wants may view,
The learn'd reflect on what before they knew: 740
Careless of censure, nor too fond of fame;
Still pleased to praise, yet not afraid to blame;
Averse alike to flatter, or offend;
Not free from faults, nor yet too vain to mend.

New Standards

During his *Conversations with Eckermann* in 1830, Goethe recalled the enormous change that had occurred in European taste during his younger years:

> The idea of the distinction between classical and romantic poetry, which is now spread over the whole world, and occasions so many quarrels and divisions, came originally from Schiller and myself. I laid down the maxim of objective treatment in poetry . . . but Schiller, who worked quite in the subjective way, deemed his own fashion the right one, and to defend himself against me, wrote the treatise upon *Naive and Sentimental Poetry*. He proved to me that I, myself, against my will, was romantic, and that my [tragedy] *Iphigenia*, through the predominance of sentiment, was by no means so classical and so much in the antique spirit as some people had supposed.
>
> The Schlegels took up this idea and carried it further, so that it has now been diffused over the whole world; and every one talks about classicism and romanticism—of which nobody thought fifty years ago.
>
> (Goethe, cited in O.B. Hardison, ed.,
Modern Continental Literary Criticism [1962], 54)

There is no basis for Goethe's claim to have originated the distinction between classical and romantic, although he was influential in popularizing it and in providing literary models of both kinds of writing. Goethe is correct, however, in recognizing that there had been a fundamental change in the European literary climate around the middle of the eighteenth century. The harsher doctrines of neoclassicism were already softening in one of its apparently classic statements—Pope's *Essay on Criticism*, published in 1711. With the softening came a new relationship between *The Art of Poetry* and the literary world. Some of the changes are evident in the way the *Art* was presented to readers. Some are evident in new literary treatments of themes that the prestige of the *Art* had made traditional. And some are corollaries of social and intellectual changes that shaped the contest within which the *Art* was read.

Scholarship: The *Art* Problematized

The *Poetria Nova* of Geoffrey of Vinsauf and the 1503 edition of the *Art* by Badius Ascensius have a common function. Both of them are grammar textbooks. In the schools of the thirteenth century and in the classrooms occupied by the "excellent boys" (*adulescenti*) of the academy at Lyons the focus was on writing rather than on literary appreciation. Horace's *Art* was understood in the most direct way. It was a mine of rules and suggestions that aspiring authors should follow if they wanted to succeed.

Poems about poetry like Girolamo Vida's *De arte poetica*, Jacques Peletier's *L'Art poétique*, Boileau's *L'Art poétique*, and Pope's *Essay on Criticism* are also testimony to the vital relationship between Horace's *Art* and contemporary society. They are not intended for schoolboys, but they *are* intended for practicing authors and for readers interested in the theory underlying artistic creation.

For the most part, sixteenth-century commentaries on Horace's *Art* follow the lead of Badius Ascensius. They are learned, but their learning has a practical aim. The commentators seek answers to important literary questions of their own day in Horace's *Art*. Inevitably, however, as the century progressed, commentators began to quarrel with one another and the discussion became more technical. Among the technical issues were variant readings in early manuscripts of the *Art*, the line-order of the work, and Horace's sources. These issues are of interest to scholars but have limited relevance to the task of the poet. Daniel Heinsius began his career as a believer in the power of inspiration and of the power of poetry to change society. At Leiden, under the influence of Joseph Scaliger, son of the great Italian critic and scholar, and other distinguished professors, he was exposed to the most sophisticated scholarship being practiced in Europe. It was, however, a scholarship turned inward on itself that had surrendered the sense of engagement in great public issues characteristic of the earlier phases of humanism. J.H. Meter (*Heinsius*, 16–17) argues that the retreat of the scholars and the marginalizing of their work came in response to religious warfare and spreading political absolutism: "The possibility of actualizing the Humanistic ideal had

been completely shaken, so that scholars tended to withdraw into thei
ivory towers. . . . The rise of Humanism to a higher scholarly leve
and its decline in social function went hand in hand."

Heinsius published an edition of the *Art* in 1610 and reissued it i
augmented form in 1612. Although he remains ambivalent about th
separation of scholarship, the emphasis in his edition is on craftsman
ship rather than inspiration. More significant, he treats the *Art* as
scholar or a philologist rather than a poet. The text has become a suc
cession of questions to be solved by the application of learning and rig
orous editorial principles, and it gives the impression of being intende
for those who are interested in the *Art* as a philological problem rathe
than as a guide to making poetry.

The tendency evident in the edition of Heinsius becomes unambigu
ous in the edition of the great English classical scholar Richard Bentley
Bentley's edition of Horace was published in 1711, the year of Pope'
Essay on Criticism. He quotes the Horatian phrase *sapere aude* (*Epistle*
I.2.40)—"dare to know"—in his *Preface.* His daring, however, is evi
dent chiefly in his proposed emendations of the text. Most of these hav
been rejected, although they continue to be cited in modern editions
Alexander Pope considered the edition absurd and felt the same wa
about Bentley's later edition of Milton. His reaction neatly defines th
argument between those who considered Horace a living influence an
those who considered him a philologist's puzzle. Bentley appears in Boo
IV of the *Dunciad* as Aristarchus. His address to the goddess Dullness i
a litany of the abuses and stupidities of scholarship:

> . . . is Aristarchus yet unknown?
> Thy mighty Scholiast, whose unwearied pains
> Made Horace dull, and humbled Milton's strains.
> Turn what they will to Verse, their toil is vain,
> Critics like me shall make it Prose again . . .
> For Attic phrase in Plato let [others] seek,
> I poach in Suidas for unlicensed Greek.
> In ancient Sense if any needs will deal,
> Be sure I give them Fragments, not a Meal;
> What Gellius or Stobaeus hashed before,
> Or chew'd by blind old Scholiasts o'er and o'er . . .
> For thee we dim the eyes, and stuff the head
> With all such reading as was never read:

For thee explain a thing till all men doubt it,
And write about it, Goddess, and about it . . .
With the same CEMENT, ever sure to bind,
We bring to one dead level every mind. (ll. 210-68)

Pope speaks for humanists who want classical poetry to be a living influence on modern authors. Bentley is treated as representative of the scholars—the "blind old Scholiasts"—who are killing classical poetry with pedantry, bringing it "to one dead level." Pope was in the minority, and the future of the classics was in the hands of the scholars. This is not because of a plot or a failure of vision. It is the inevitable result of larger changes. As knowledge grew in the seventeenth and eighteenth centuries, learning inevitably became more specialized. Classical scholarship illustrates the trend. During the eighteenth and nineteenth centuries classical scholars became increasingly isolated from the rest of society by their specialized knowledge. The classics were still read in the schoolroom, but they ceased to have a vital relationship to the mainstream of literature.

Many scholarly editions of the *Art* have been published since Bentley's. In general, they have become ever more sophisticated from the point of view of scholars and ever more inconsequential from the point of view of poets. The most recent full-scale treatment is the first and second volume (1963, 1971) of C. O. Brink's *Horace on Poetry*. Brink seeks to provide the best possible text of the *Art* and to explain it in terms of the best current theories. He includes a meticulous review of prior scholarship and learned notes on all difficult passages—sometimes two pages of fine print are used to explain a single difficult line. Brink also recognizes that the *Art* is a poem. He devotes considerable space to explaining the conventions and qualities of a poetic epistle in contrast to an "art," and he ridicules those who are so poetically insensitive that they look to the *Art* for straightforward exposition. In all this elaborate discussion, however, there is hardly a single comment to explain why a contemporary poet or reader of modern poetry should read the *Art*.

The commentaries and scholarly monographs that have been written about the *Art* since the seventeenth century have the same tendencies as the editions. In fact, in many cases, commentary and edition have been combined, as is the case for Brink's *Horace on Poetry*. The German scholar Johannes Vahlen is notable for having suggested (1867) that the best approach to the *Art* is via the topics of classical rhetoric and for having identified decorum as the dominant theme of the *Art*. Properly speaking, this is a revival of a sixteenth-century line of analysis. It was destined to have considerable influence. Eduard Norden (1905) supplemented Vahlen's ideas with the notion that a typical classical "art" is divided into two large topics—*ars* and *artifex*. He complemented this insight with an extended analysis of rhetorical topics used in the *Art*.

The pace of analysis of the *Art* picked up in 1918, when Christen Jensen published fragments of the poetic theories of Neoptolemus of Parium. His discovery gave scholars of the *Art* what were to be some of the central themes of the next sixty years: the three-part organization of the work, the question of whether *poesis* or *poeta* should be the first of the three parts, the question of where the dividing lines between part one and part two come, the question of how each of the major sections should be subdivided, the question of how much influence reached Horace from Aristotle's *Rhetoric* and *Poetics*, the question of how much the Aristotelian influence was diluted by "Alexandrian" critical theory, and the question of whether there were original "Alexandrian" doctrines and if so, what they were.

Four major commentaries have been published in the twentieth century: Augusto Rostagni (1930), Otto Immisch (1932), Charles Brink (1963, 1971), and Niall Rudd (1989). All of them deal with Neoptolemus, and they all treat rhetorical topics used in the *Art*. None of them is any more successful than Brink in suggesting why the *Art* might be of interest to a modern poet. This does not mean that the *Art* lacks such interest. It means only that one of the effects of cultural change since the seventeenth century has been the separation of the *Art* from the audience for which it was originally intended.

The Romantic Aesthetic
(The Place of the Critic; The Power of Art)

The romantic aesthetic that was emerging in the eighteenth century had a different but equally pronounced effect on the fortunes of Horace's *Art*. Two ways in which the effect manifested itself were a decisive broadening of the Horatian understanding of the responsibilities of the critic and a naturalizing of the Horatian idea of the civilizing power of poetry.

Dr. Samuel Johnson (d. 1784) was the dominant English critic of the mid-eighteenth century. He honored many of the ideals of neoclassicism, especially the norm of nature and the rule of reason, but he also admired, with reservations, the accomplishments of English authors like Shakespeare and Milton who violated the neoclassical rules. In a prologue written to mark the opening of the Theatre Royal in Drury Lane in 1747, Dr. Johnson celebrated Shakespeare for his vivid depiction of "life" and "passion." Shakespeare wrote without benefit of "art" in the sense of knowing the rules. Conversely, Ben Jonson was "instructed from the school,/ To please in method and invent by rule." All he gained by his correctness was "cold Approbation." Dr. Johnson then considers the decline in the quality of English drama after the Restoration of 1660. Restoration dramatists had too much method and too little nature. The poem moves to a passionate denunciation of the "rules":

> . . . crush'd by rules, and weakn'd as refin'd,
> For years the power of tragedy declin'd;
> From bard to bard the frigid caution crept,
> Till Declamation roar'd whilst Passion slept. (ll. 29–32)

Dr. Johnson asks where a better form of drama will come from but has no answer. He knows only that the old tradition is dead. From the vantage point of the later twentieth century it is possible to answer his question. There could be no renewal of English drama until there was a renewal of relations between drama and the society around it. Richard Sheridan and Oliver Goldsmith are more skillful than their contemporaries, but they have nothing really new to offer. The new drama that Dr. Johnson desired would not appear until the later nineteenth century; when it did appear, it would do so first in translations of the work of Ibsen and Strindberg.

Shakespeare provided a substitute in the eighteenth century for a genuinely new drama. In addition to offering powerful moments of "life" and "passion," his plays made a mockery of the neoclassical aesthetic. Voltaire had called them barbaric and crude. They had multiple plots, their actions often extended over several years, and their scenes wandered with abandon from city to city and country to country. They included magic and the supernatural, they mixed noble and crudely comic characters, they depicted violence onstage, their language was sometimes obscene and often obscure, and they failed to observe poetic justice. In the "Preface" to his edition of Shakespeare's *Works* (1765) Dr. Johnson tried to balance his love of Shakespeare with a frank recognition that all too often Shakespeare nods. It is clear, however, that Dr. Johnson is on Shakespeare's side in spite of himself. He has been subverted by Shakespeare. Other writers of the period embraced Shakespeare specifically because he represented everything in art that the age of reason rejected. In short, to admire Shakespeare in the eighteenth century was to join the romantic conspiracy against neoclassicism.

The English transmitted this view of Shakespeare to the Germans, who were struggling in the mid-eighteenth century to escape almost total cultural domination by France. Shakespeare became, in effect, a German national poet. He demonstrated the possibility of a robust "Germanic" or "Gothic" kind of art in contrast to the effete and timid regularity of the French.

Treatises began to be written about Shakespeare that greatly enlarge the Horatian concept of criticism. Among the topics examined were the nature of art, primitive versus sophisticated art, the beauties of medieval romances and "Gothic" stories, national literature and national identity, nature and genius versus reason and art, and the supreme value of emotion (pathos) in tragedy. Among English critics who used Shakespeare as a means of enlarging the scope of criticism were Lord Kames, Richard Framer, Lady Montague, and Maurice Morgann, whose *Essay on the Dramatic Character of Sir John Falstaff* (1777) looks forward to the romantic criticism of authors like Hazlitt and Lamb. In spite of their movement away from the neoclassical aesthetic, however, all of these authors have a conservative side. They use a traditional critical terminology, and they seek to broaden the understanding of poetry rather than to develop radically new approaches.

The situation was quite different in Germany. There Shakespeare became a prime literary exhibit of philosophers and critics who were applying formal philosophy to the business of understanding art. These German critics shifted the discussion of poetry from Horatian ideas like talent, nature, "art," character, and diction to topics like epistemology, imagination, form and substance, reconciliation of opposites, and organic unity. G. E. Lessing, C. M. Wieland, and Goethe are important as popularizers and imitators of Shakespeare in Germany; Friedrich Schiller and August and Friedrich Schlegel are especially important for combining Shakespeare with criticism and philosophical theorizing.

Whatever the variations in Shakespeare's fortunes, his presence at the center of much eighteenth-century literary controversy consistently helped to broaden understanding of the responsibilities of criticism. The absurdity of trying to cope with a play like *King Lear* by making out a list of "faults and virtues" was obvious. What, then, *was* the responsibility of the critic? Pope had focused on precisely this question in his *Essay on Criticism*. He had accepted the ideas that the critic is essentially a giver of rules and a judge of errors, but he softened them by acknowledging the importance of taste and the need to base critical judgments on an understanding of the whole work of art. German philosophical criticism showed how far beyond Pope criticism had to move in order to be current with the best thinking of the age.

A second theme prominent in Horace's *Art* and given new forms in the eighteenth century is the civilizing power of poetry. The theme forms the basis of Thomas Gray's *The Progress of Poesy* (1757). Gray's poem is a Pindaric, a lyric using heightened language and a stylized three-part stanza. It contrasts strikingly with the colloquial tone and uniform hexameter of Horace's "conversation poem" (*sermo*) technique in the *Art*.

Gray begins by equating the arrival of poetry among men with the beginning of social harmony. In other words, Gray attributes the same effect to poetry that is described in Horace's passage about Orpheus and Amphion (*Art*, ll. 391–407):

> In climes beyond the solar road,
> Where shaggy forms o'er ice-built mountains roam,
>   The Muse has broke the twilight-gloom
> To cheer the shiv'ring native's dull abode.
>   And oft, beneath the od'rous shade
>   Of Chili's boundless forests laid,
> She deigns to hear the savage youth repeat
>   In loose numbers wildly sweet
> Their feather-cinctured chiefs and dusky loves.
>   Her track, where'er the goddess roves,
>   Glory pursue, and generous Shame.
> Th'unconquerable Mind, and Freedom's holy flame. (ll. 54–65)

The contrasts with Horace are as important as the similarities. In Gray's *Progress* the civilizing effect of poetry is not something that occurred in a remote past described in myths but is going on as the poet writes. Horace concentrates on actions (roaming, taming, building, rule-giving, etc.); Gray concentrates on details of the scenery (ice-built mountains, shaggy forms, od'rous shade, etc.). In general Horace narrates while Gray describes. Like many eighteenth-century poets he interprets the phrase *ut pictura poesis* as advice to write poetry as though painting a picture. Gray is also interested in realism. He has read accounts of the exploration of South America. The "ice-bound mountains" are the Andes; the Indian tribes are specifically located in Chile. The reference to the chiefs as "feather-cinctured" is an especially nice touch. Once the scene has been painted, the moral is drawn. Even in savage conditions poetry cheers depressed souls and provides words for lovers. It also stirs higher emotions—glory, modesty, the "unconquerable mind," and "freedom," the last two items being reminiscences of Satan's speech in Hell in *Paradise Lost* (I.106). Notably different from Horace is Gray's suggestion that true poetry comes from nature rather than from the imitation of literary models. In sum, the theme of Gray's poem is Horatian but the treatment is immediate and contemporary and stresses originality rather than learning from earlier poets.

In *The Minstrel; or, The Progress of Genius* (1771) James Beattie enlarges on the theme of nature as the teacher of true poetry. Horace touched on this theme whenever he celebrated the delights of his Sabine farm. It is part of the nostalgia of Augustan Romans for an earlier, simpler life. Horace describes the delights of his Sabine farm. In the *Art* the speaker praises the rustics who formed the first audiences for tragedy (*Art*, ll. 202-11) and condemns those who are more in love with money than art (*Art*, ll. 323-32). *The Minstrel* is also about the way a poet is shaped by life in a natural environment. The poet's name is Edwin, and his parents were simple Scottish shepherds, not too different, one imagines, from the freedman-farmer who was Horace's father.

Edwin is nurtured by the sublimities of the natural landscape, which Beattie describes at some length. His moral education begins when he recognizes the brevity of beauty. A tear rolls down his cheek, and he breaks into a spontaneous lament: "O ye wild groves, O where is now your bloom" (l. 199). It is a Horatian theme, but Edwin does not conclude, as did Horace, that the solution to the brevity of things is wine and love. Instead he is moved to poetry. Later he draws another conclusion from nature: even as the seasons return, "man's majesty beauty [will] bloom again" (l. 242).

On a summer evening Edwin dreams of fairies dancing and jousting. He learns poetic harmony from the music of wild brooks and shepherd pipes and the whirring of partridge wings. The village Beldam tells him folk tales and chants "heroic ditties." Nature is not something Edwin imitates. Instead she is his teacher:

Thus Heaven enlarg'd his soul in riper years,
For Nature gave him strength, and fire, to soar,
On Fancy's wing above this vale of tears;
Where dark cold-hearted skeptics, creeping, pore
Through microscope of metaphysic lore:
And much they grope for truth but never hit. (ll. 451–56)

Edwin has grown up in a natural world that is opposed to the heartless world of the city. Like Horace's speaker he is a character as well as a means of presenting ideas, and as a character he is an outsider. Like the theme of country versus city, the theme of the poet as outsider is genuinely Horatian. The difference is that Horace's outsider at least pretends that he is criticizing society in order to improve it. Gray's outsider is simply an outsider—isolated from the larger world by his rural habitat as well as by his moral attitudes. The isolation of the artist became a dominant theme in later romantic poetry. It was eventually exaggerated to the point of presenting the artist as an alien, an exile, a half-crazed mariner, a perpetual wanderer, a social misfit—in Kafka, a cockroach.

There, of course, the similarities between Horace and Beattie end. Officially, at least, Horace approves his life as a confidants of Augustus. When he advises the poet to follow nature he means "the real world," not "the kind of nature you find in the remote countryside." He believes nature is something objective that can be imitated or at least that nature reveals principles of art that can be followed. Beattie's Nature has two faces. On the one hand it is the scenery described at such length in *The Minstrel*. It is the charming nature of murmuring streams and summer evenings and the sublime nature of storms and mountain peaks. On the other hand, Nature is a moral force that shapes Edwin's soul and eventually turns him into a poet. Edwin does not imitate nature in the sense of describing it. His poetry expresses emotions aroused by nature like sorrow over the shortness of natural beauty, or it is a poetry of fantasy symbolized by visions of dancing and jousting fairies. Finally, Horace had reservations about city life, but he was always enthusiastic about the study of philosophy. For Beattie (and presumably Edwin) Nature and philosophy are antagonists. The two poles are symbolized by the opposition between "Fancy's wing" and "microscopes of metaphysic lore." The microscope image is all the more powerful because it combines a general allusion to philosophy with a specific allusion to natural philosophy, or science.

Beattie's true mentor is Rousseau, not Horace. Man was born free, and everywhere he is in bondage. Nature liberates, human society corrupts. It is a prophecy of things to come. Wordsworth's *Prelude*, subtitled "The Growth of a Poet's Mind," traces the way nature gradually shaped Wordsworth's mental outlook. Many of the experiences are remarkably like Edwin's:

> . . . to the open fields I told
> A prophecy: poetic numbers came
> Spontaneously to clothe in priestly robe
> A renovated spirit singled out (ll. 50–53)

A more sensational English version of the theme of nature as a teacher of poetry is found in another romantic pageant of a sensitive (if dissolute) soul, written, as it happens, in the same Spenserian stanza used by Beattie in *The Minstrel*. Byron's *Childe Harold's Pilgrimage* traces the journey of an alienated protagonist through many kingdoms and diverse morals of men. Harold is more than an outsider, he is a pariah, exiled by his own countrymen. It takes a while for him to discover that the true moral life is in nature, but discover it he does in the third Canto:

> The desert, forest, cavern, breaker's foam,
> Were unto him companionship; they spake
> A mutual language, clearer than the tome
> Of his land's tongue, which he would oft forsake
> For Nature's pages glass'd by sunbeams on the lake. (Stanza 13)

Childe Harold develops the Horatian theme of the outsider as social critic. Horace's speaker knows the simpler life of the Romans of Cato's age and of the honest farmers who can be found in the countryside even of Augustan Rome. His knowledge gives him license to chastise the sins of the age in the *Satires* and the inadequacies of Roman poetry in *The Art of Poetry*. The romantic critic tended to equate society itself with moral corruption. In the first discourse *Discours sur les sciences et les arts* (1750) Rousseau remarks that the pleasantries that make society run so smoothly are actually hypocrisies and lies—"in a word, the appearance of virtues without there being any." The motto of this discourse is taken from Horace's *Art*: "we are deceived by the appearance of truth" (l. 25). In the third canto of *Childe Harold* Byron writes:

I have not loved the world, nor the world me;
I have not flatter'd its rank breath, nor bow'd
To its idolatries a patient knee,
Nor coin'd my cheek to smiles, nor cried aloud
In worship of an echo; in the crowd
They could not deem me one of such: I stood
Among them, but not of them (Stanza 113)

A final example of the transposition of Horatian themes in romantic poetry is provided by Goethe's *Natur und Kunst*. The title is best translated "Nature and Art," for this is the opposition that Goethe intends. It is an explicitly Horatian contrast. Many romantics sided unhesitatingly with nature. Goethe is not sure. Unlike his friend Schiller, he was never entirely satisfied with romanticism, and he admired what he considered the objectivity of classical art. In *Nature and Art* the two concepts are opposed at first, but by the end of the poem art is in the ascendency:

Nature and Art—they seem to fly apart.
And yet before you think, they've found each other;
My own antipathy is also gone,
And both seem equally important to me.
And that means we must feel a real tension!
And as we first in nicely measured hours
With mind and will commit ourselves to Art.
Let freest Nature blaze up in our hearts.
That's the way it is for all creation:
In vain will minds that have no discipline
Seek the perfection of the purest heights.
Who seeks great things must pull himself together;
Accepting limits shows the Master first,
And only the law can give our freedom to us.

In Horace the tension between nature and art emerges in the image of the mad poet, who is all nature (in the sense of *ingenium*) and no art. Horace does not explicitly consider the other side of the equation—the poet who is all art and no talent, although that possibility is surely implicit in the flat rejection of the possibility of a mediocre poet. In Goethe not only is the tension overt, but it is objectified in a sonnet that concludes, "He who wishes to achieve great things must combine; the mas-

ter artist first shows himself in limits, and only the law can give us
freedom."

Nature and Art is an echo at the beginning of the full tide of the romantic era of a genuinely Horatian theme.

Standards, Social and Philosophical

The clearest of the many underlying causes for social change in the
eighteenth century is expansion of commerce encouraged by the development of colonialism and the emergence of a powerful middle class.
England was in the forefront of the expansion because of a relatively
progressive political system and a positive climate for enterprise and in-
vestment. Population growth was another factor, although it was as
much a symptom of change as a cause. The Industrial Revolution, the
appearance of the first modern factories, the beginning of the age of
steam, and the rise of the coal industry all contributed to the result. In
France social change was frustrated by the monarchy. Eventually the
pressure for change became revolutionary. In Germany change was also
in the air, but because Germany was a mosaic of principalities and city-
states rather than a unified country the changes had fewer immediate
consequences than in England or France.

Changing social economic conditions were complemented by changes
in the way literature was produced and the nature of the reading public.
The first great wave of change was a by-product of the Reformation: the
combination of small, cheap books and literate citizens interested in religious issues created the possibility of mass production of books. Drama
created another sort of literary market. The popular theaters of the later
sixteenth century in England and Spain had audiences large enough to
support companies of players, and Shakespeare, among others, became
moderately wealthy through a career in the popular theater.

In the seventeenth and eighteenth century a large market developed
for popular literature ranging from self-help manuals to sermons to romantic fiction. In England printers and booksellers flourished. For the
authors of the new literature, however, the rewards were uncertain. Patronage was the order of the day, and with it, dominance of literary
taste by an upper-class elite. This is another way of saying that in some
important ways the system of producing and consuming literature in
late seventeenth-century Europe would have seemed familiar to Horace
because it was not very different from the system of Augustan Rome.

Alexander Pope stands on the margin of this tradition. His work is definitely an extension of the older order, although, as has been noted, the order is softened in it. But Pope was also a contemporary of Daniel Defoe, Joseph Addison, and Richard Steele, who were part of the new order of things.

In England the novel gained a broad middle-class audience, which continued to grow throughout the eighteenth century. Readership of newspapers and journals also grew, in part because of increasing involvement of the middle class in politics. The *Tatler* and the *Spectator* are early examples of a large and varied group of general-interest journals published during the eighteenth century, another being *The Rambler* published 1750–52 by Dr. Johnson. In the wake of such developments it became possible to eke out a living as a professional writer. Dr. Johnson chronicled the precarious, often tragic lives of many authors who attempted to live by their writing, and he himself is a prominent example of an author who tried and succeeded.

The heritage of the old, aristocratically dominated period of literature was such, however, that even as they tried to make a living, authors who sought independence by the sort of writing for which there was a public market were derided as mercenary, unprincipled, and crude. They were called "Grub Street hacks," "hack" being a term for an unprincipled journalist and Grub Street, the location of the offices of many of the journals. The class-labeling would continue through much of the nineteenth century, but during this period the literature was continuously professionalized, and by the end of it the aristocratic amateur had become the exception rather than the rule. In Byron's *English Bards and Scotch Reviewers* the obvious tensions are between the creative artist and the critic, but the submerged tensions are between Byron, who upholds the aristocratic tradition of literature, and Francis Jeffrey, editor of the *Edinburgh Review*, who represents the new, professional literary class.

Changes in literary forms and thematics are complemented in the eighteenth century by changes in the production and consumption of literature. These are most obvious in the case of the bourgeois novel, but they are also evident in poetry. Classicizing forms like ode, pastoral, and elegy give way during the period to meditative poems and lyric imitations of folk ballads. Nature poetry begins to describe nature rather than imitate ancient descriptions of rural Sicily. The public topics examined in epic and formal verse satire give way to poetry that traces the "progress" of the poet's soul or moments of inspired insight. Characters in poetic narratives no longer come from Greek mythology. Increasingly they are figures from a romanticized "Gothic" past or simple country folk who presumably exhibit in their lives the shaping power of life close to nature. Diction changes. The stylized language of eighteenth-century poetry, shaped by the same rhetorical treatises that shaped the discussion of diction in Horace's *Art*, gives way to "imitations" of the speech of real people. Rustics are especially popular since their speech is thought to be close to "natural" language uncorrupted by sophisticated society. "Humble and rustic life was generally chosen," says Wordsworth in the "Preface" to *Lyrical Ballads* (1798), "because in that condition, the essential passions of the heart find a better soil in which they can attain their maturity, are under less restraint, and speak a plainer and more emphatic language." And again: "My purpose was to imitate, and, as far as possible, to adopt the very language of men."

In France the chief prophet of the new movement was Jean Jacques Rousseau (d. 1778), whose celebration of man in a state of nature and belief that society inevitably corrupts original innocence would influence European thought for the next century. However, in spite of Rousseau and other pioneers, French cultural developments remained strongly colored by the bias of patronage and court-centered elitism. When the old regime went up in the fires of the French Revolution literary standards changed abruptly and permanently.

In Germany yet another scenario developed. Originally dominated by France, German intellectuals began to turn in the second half of the eighteenth century to England. Shakespeare became a German culture hero, Milton was venerated and imitated, and eighteenth-century English authors were read almost as enthusiastically as in England. Goethe and Schiller are the foremost representatives of the large and talented group of writers who transformed German literature in the last quarter of the eighteenth century

This is not the place for a detailed review of the shift from the neoclassical to the romantic aesthetic, but even a summary comment helps to place Byron's *English Bards and Scotch Reviewers* in perspective. Byron's speaker is an aristocrat indignant because commoners are presuming to write and judge poetry. From his perspective, the new poetic is not a welcome opening up of poetic horizons but a betrayal of literary standards. The worst feature of the new literature is that it is prosy. It lacks the fine wit of the heroic couplet, and its themes are as banal as the middle-class poets who create it. Byron became more receptive to the romantic aesthetic as he matured, but he never fully endorsed it. He admired Goethe so highly that he dedicated his tragedy *Werner* to him, but he remained ambivalent about the English romantics. In 1821 he complained, "Those poor idiots of the Lakes . . . are diluting our literature as much as they can." He was positively ferocious on the subject of Keats, who had dared criticize Pope and whose writing, he announced, is "a sort of mental masturbation." "I look upon a proper appreciation of Pope," he remarked to Octavius Gilchrist in 1821, "as a touchstone of taste."

The question of literary standards involves changes in philosophical outlook as well as social changes. Anticipations of the philosophical developments at the end of the eighteenth century can be found with the aid of hindsight, but any view of the period that tries to see things historically will recognize that the decisive event was the publication of Immanuel Kant's three critiques of *Pure Reason* (1781), *Practical Reason* (1788), and *Judgment* (1790). Kant referred to his writings as a "Copernican revolution" in philosophy, and there is no reason to disagree with this appraisal. Kant was not interested in literary criticism, but his *Critique of Judgment* establishes a powerful philosophical basis for aesthetics, and several German critics immediately set about using its insights to develop radically new theories of literature.

Schiller's *Letters on the Aesthetic Education of Man* (*Briefe über die ästhetische Erziehung des Menschen*, 1795) is solidly grounded on Kantian principles. Literature is like play (*Spiel*). It is governed by rules that are as demanding—and as arbitrary—as the rules of a game, and, like a game, it is undertaken for enjoyment rather than for practical or useful ends. An art work combines form and material, spirit and substance, mind and nature. Art, including literature, benefits mankind by gradually humanizing society. This is exactly what Horace claims in *The Art of Poetry* when he cites the examples of Orpheus and Amphion. For Schiller the humanizing effect of art was vitally important. He had seen during the Reign of Terror how the effort to legislate freedom politically could lead to new kinds of tyranny. The history of Greek art as Schiller knew it seemed to confirm the idea that art humanizes, and although Schiller did not cite Horace, there is a similar view of the effect of art on the Greeks in *The Art of Poetry* (ll. 323-24; 391-407).

After Schiller several German philosopher-critics developed Kantian theories of literature. Kant argued that we can never know nature in itself (the *Ding an sich*); we can only know the phenomenal world our imagination makes of it. Friedrich Schelling (d. 1854) based his theory on the idea that the artist can penetrate intuitively past the barrier that Kant erected between man and nature. For Kant art is always a combination of opposed elements and thus, by implication, a tension. August von Schlegel (d. 1845) translated the works of Shakespeare into German and delivered a series of lectures on dramatic art in 1808 that define the tragic experience as the tension between "inward liberty and external necessity." In the process he attacks the tradition of criticism as faultfinding and the theory of the three dramatic unities, and explores the idea of national literatures. Friedrich von Schlegel, August's brother, deepened the theory of national literature in a course of lectures (1815) that extended from Greece to modern Germany.

The transformation of standards that occurred in Germany between 1790 and 1820 was not long in arriving in England. Samuel Taylor Coleridge had met William Wordsworth in the 1790s and had collaborated with him in *Lyrical Ballads* (1798), which is generally considered the manifesto of English romanticism. In 1798 Coleridge traveled to Germany, where he absorbed the new Kantian philosophy. Kant took hold of him, he says, as though by a "giant hand." He soon developed his own synthesis from Kant, Schelling, the Schlegels, and others, and applied it to literature in several series of lectures on Shakespeare and other English poets (1808, 1811-12, 1813-14, 1818, etc.). His great work of criticism is the *Biographia Literaria* (1817), which outlines the Kantian basis of aesthetics and then applies it to various questions of English literature including the differences between his own kind of art and Wordsworth's.

Coleridge's lectures contain the germs of the theory of organic unity and the technique of reading a literary work in terms of its unifying principle rather than formal rules and conventions of diction or religious or political motives. The "Definition of Poetry" that prefaces the lectures of 1818 distinguishes between science, which seeks truth, and poetry, which exists purely for the pleasure it gives. The pleasure is, in turn, "a pleasure from the whole consistent with a consciousness of pleasure from the component parts;—and the perfection of which is, to communicate from each part the . . . pleasure compatible with the largest sum of pleasure on the whole." The success of the poem depends on the imagination of the poet, which produces "the balancing and reconciling of opposite or discordant qualities, sameness with difference, a

sense of novelty and freshness with old or customary objects. . . ."
Together with the *Biographia* the lectures form the most important single statement of critical theory in English between 1800 and 1900.
They announce precisely that change of philosophical standards that altered the context within which literature was understood. As such they
announce that Horace's *Art* can no longer be read in the old way. It is
no longer the hub of a wheel from which various specific literary doctrines extend like so many spokes. Its relevance to living art must be
found in a new understanding of what Horace was attempting.

V

English Bards and Scotch Reviewers and *Hints from Horace*
by
Lord Byron

Introduction and Commentary

In 1807, at the age of nineteen, Byron published a collection of lyrics titled *Hours of Idleness*. It caused a modest stir, and Byron was encouraged to begin a sustained work to be titled *The British Bards: A Satire* in the tradition of Alexander Pope's *Essay on Criticism*. Byron had looked at the poetical landscape and discovered all too many poets who failed to measure up. Many of them are forgotten today, but Byron included several who were highly regarded at the time and others whose reputations were destined to eclipse his. In 1808, shortly after he finished his first draft he read a devastating anonymous review of *Hours of Idleness* in the *Edinburgh Review*. Byron had included the information that he was a "minor" on the title page of *Hours*, and the reviewer, now known to be Henry Brougham (d. 1868) used the opportunity to make a pun on a famous observation in *The Art of Poetry*, "Neither gods nor the booksellers allow a poet to be mediocre" (l. 371; the pun is *minor = mediocribus*): "The poesy of this young lord belongs to the class which neither gods nor men are said to permit. Indeed, we do not recollect to have seen such a quantity of verse with so few deviations in either direction from that exact standard. His effusions are spread over a dead flat, and can no more get above or below that level than if they were so much stagnant water" (*Edinburgh Review*, 9 [January 1808]: 285).

The tone of the review is familiar. It is the tone of the amused, superior Horatian critic, for whom the highest critical task is the identification of errors. "If you read anything to Quintilius," writes Horace, "he would say, 'Please. Correct this and this.' If after two or three unsuccessful attempts you said you couldn't improve, he would tell you to blot it out and start hammering out the verses all over again" (ll. 438–41). Byron had used the same tone in *English Bards*, but he was deeply upset. He would remark later, on hearing about critical attacks

on Keats, that "A savage review is like Hemlock to a sucking author.
. . . The one on me . . . knocked me down—but I got up again."
Instead of retiring to lick his wounds, he feverishly revised *English Bards*.
The finished poem would be two-edged. He would retain the attacks on
contemporary poets, and he would add an equally—as it turned out,
even more—savage attack on modern critics. The title of the work was
changed to *English Bards and Scotch Reviewers*. A first edition of some
696 lines was published in March 1809, and a second edition of some
1,050 lines in May 1809.

The poem shows the way it was composed. The first draft was essentially a group of satirical sketches of English poets in the manner of
Pope's *Dunciad* and nineteenth-century imitators of Pope like William
Gifford and Thomas Mathias. The enlarged work added satirical sketches
of reviewers. But Byron did not simply add the new material to the end
of the earlier poem. Instead he tried to interweave the two, and the
seams between them show.

The oddest paradox in the poem is the conflict of themes. When reviewing contemporary poets Byron is the critic whose task is to find
faults, and he is nastier than Horace ever was. Horace associated the
satire of named individuals with Old Comedy and Lucilius and explicitly
rejected it. Like Pope and Gifford, Byron names names. He seldom
praises but he damns at great length. His sketches begin with poetic
errors, but they often trail off into abuse pure and simple. Although the
abuse is often amusing at this remove in time, it must have seemed
cruel when the poem was published. At any rate, as a critic of poets
Byron is the honest outsider who sits in judgment on the poetic establishment. Byron asserts that his censure is even more necessary for talented than for untalented poets: "The unquestionable possession of considerable genius by several of the writers here censured renders their
mental prostitution the more to be regretted. Imbecility may be pitied,
or, at worst, laughed at and forgotten: perverted powers demand the
most decided reprehension."

The sections dealing with reviewers introduce a new tone, which some
readers have felt closer to Juvenal's bitter and abusive satire than to
Horace. It attacks "Scotch reviewers" for precisely the obsession with
fault-finding that Byron himself exhibits. Reviewers, he complains, are
bloated with egotism and corrupted by avarice and traitors to the muse.
In 1791 Thomas Thorild had condemned the same tendency in *A Critique of the Critics*. Criticism, he complained, should be "far above those

wild incursions in literature worthy only of Cossacks . . . who seek merely what might be robbed and ravaged, and above the low, rude mocker which ought to belong only to the Hottentots. And yet, one of these is what criticism has always been." (*Literary Criticism*, ed. Allen and Clark [1941], 119).

Wild incursions and rude mockery described by Thorild are, of course, not Horace but what doctrinaire neoclassicism and the demands of the popular press had increasingly made of criticism. Byron questions this kind of criticism not because he disapproves it in the abstract but because he has directly experienced the pain it causes. Coleridge and Keats, among others, would experience the same kind of pain and propose the same sort of change in critical methods.

English Bards and Scotch Reviewers is filled with the names of forgotten minor literati of the early nineteenth century. They are identified in the notes. Most can be ignored. The few who became famous are immediately recognizable. The initial section establishes the speaker as a critic and poet. Horace had not commented on the eagerness of critics to criticize; Byron remedies the deficiency with an especially nasty generalization:

> A man must serve his time to ev'ry trade
> Save censure—critics all are ready made.
> Take hackney'd jokes from Miller, got by rote,
> With just enough of learning to misquote. (ll. 63–66)

The passage is directed at Francis Jeffrey (d. 1850), editor of the *Edinburgh Review* from 1803 to 1829 and the man whom Byron erroneously believed to be the author of the review of *Hours of Idleness*. "Fear not to lie," says Byron, "'twill seem a sharper hit;/ Shrink not from blasphemy, 'twill pass for wit" (ll. 71–72).

A tirade against corrupt criticism begins, only to turn suddenly into an attack on modern English poets. Southey is pilloried for the first but by no means the last time. More interesting is the association of the new poetry with the profusion of technical innovations: "The cow-pox, tractors, galvanism, and gas,/ In turns appear to make the vulgar stare" (ll. 132–33). The root cause of Byron's irritation is that literature is no longer the possession of the elite. It has been democratized by the marketplace so that "Each country book-club bows the knee to Baal" (l. 138). The romantic revival of the folk ballad appealed to many readers for whom the classical forms of neoclassical poetry seemed elitist and irrelevant. The fake ballads in Sir Walter Scott's *Lay of the Last Minstrel* were hugely popular, and therefore Byron considers them especially pernicious. Corrupt poetry is a by-product of the corruption of writing for money: "Let such forego the poet's sacred name,/ Who rack their brains for lucre, not for fame:/ Still for stern Mammon may they toil in vain" (ll. 177–79). The theme is Horatian (*Art*, ll. 325–32). As an aristocrat (and a moderately wealthy one) writing in an aristocratic medium, Byron claims to be shocked that anyone would consider poetry a way to make a living.

Southey is attacked again. He writes too much. Byron would use him repeatedly as an example of the false poet. He eventually became the subject of Byron's most devastating personal satire, *The Vision of Judgment* (1821). Of greater interest is the attack on Wordsworth. Byron eventually came to appreciate Wordsworth, with qualifications, but here he is described as a poet "Who, both by precept and example, shows/ That prose is verse, and verse is merely prose" (ll. 241–42). This is a neoclassical comment on the romantic ideal of simple, direct poetic diction and one more instance of the shift from neoclassical to romantic. Within a few years Byron was ready to acknowledge that at its best Wordsworth's diction is sublime, although Byron, himself, never aspired to Wordsworthian plainness.

By 1811 Coleridge had already delivered lectures that incorporated German philosophical theory with practical criticism and had contributed *The Rime of the Ancient Mariner* and *Kubla Khan* to *Lyrical Ballads*. To the young Byron he is the author of "turgid ode and tumid stanza" (l. 256).

Other authors pass in review. William Bowles (d. 1860) wrote fourteen sentimental sonnets (1789) much admired by Coleridge and considered the epitome of sloppy sentimentalism by Byron. Bowles was no poetic genius, but Byron's satirical remarks are simply an extension of his partisan attack on the romantic school. Notable in this and other criticisms of the new school is aristocratic contempt—perhaps also a fear—of the appeal of sentimental poetry to the great book-buying public. Byron calls this appeal worship of Mammon; the romantics considered it evidence that their program to return poetry to the people was succceeding.

Jeffrey now returns to center stage (ll. 438–559). The tirade is the centerpiece of Byron's poem and reaches its own ferocious climax when

Byron suggests that the "evening sweets" of the Edina—namely the sewage poured into it—will shower "their odours on thy candid sheets,/ Whose hue and fragrance to thy work adhere—/This scents its pages, and that gilds its rear" (ll. 533-35).

There is a long section (ll. 560-740) on drama that complains of the glut of translated German tragedies and the vogue of Italian comedy, which, Byron intimates, is half erotic peepshow. More poets are attacked (ll. 741-948), with further shots at Wordsworth, Coleridge, and Walter Scott. The poem ends in mock despair. Like a proper Horatian critic, Byron claims that all has been done out of "zeal" for his country's honor (l. 992). The concluding farewell is a real one. As he wrote it, Byron was preparing to leave England for the grand tour that provided the substance of *Childe Harold*. As though anticipating that poem, he vows solemnly that if he returns "no tempting press/ Shall drag my journal from the desk's recess" (l. 1024). In spite of his vow, the poem was published immediately after his return in 1812.

Byron published a specifically Horatian critical work. *Hints from Horace* is an imitation, complete with updatings from English literature, of Horace's *Art of Poetry*. He was so proud of his creative adaptation that he printed Horace's Latin text beside his English. There are many virtues to the translation, and it will repay anyone interested in the history of Horace's influence. It is polished, even elegant, compared to the messy, poorly organized, and sometimes incoherent *English Bards and Scotch Reviewers*. At the same time, however, it strikes the reader as clever and cold—a performance piece.

Byron's whole personality was involved in *English Bards*. He could not, like Pope at the time of the *Essay on Criticism*, find guidance in a well-established tradition. His revisions show that he was making the work up as he went along. For all its faults, it is a living piece of writing and a living imitation of Horace's *Art*. It brings us into the hot, uncomfortable, intensely competitive, and endlessly fascinating literary world of English romanticism. Who can forget the "evening sweets" that Edina will bring to Jeffrey, even though Jeffrey was, historically, a cultivated and witty man who consistently furthered the cause of literature in his *Review*. Who can forget Wordsworth "Convincing all, by demonstration plain,/ Poetic souls delight in prose insane" (ll. 243-44)? And who can forget Coleridge, of whom "none in lofty numbers can surpass/ The bard who soars to elegize an ass" (ll. 261-62)? This is true although Wordsworth and Coleridge are better poets than Byron and Coleridge had a view of art that made Byron's clever couplets and elegantly snide judgments irrelevant to the future of critical theory.

English Bards and Scotch Reviewers is the last significant poem on poetry to be written, in English at least, in the Horatian mode. The future lay with a different kind of criticism and different kinds of poems on poetry. The basis of these poems would not be commonplaces inherited from Rome's Augustan age but the separation, announced by Kant, between the mind and the world.

English Bards and Scotch Reviewers

Still must I hear?—shall hoarse Fitzgerald bawl
His creaking couplets in a tavern hall,
And I not sing, lest, haply, Scotch Reviews
Should dub me scribbler, and denounce my Muse?
Prepare for rhyme—I'll publish, right or wrong:
Fools are my theme, Let Satire be my song.
    Oh! Nature's noblest gift—my grey goose-quill!
Slave of my thoughts, obedient to my will,
Torn from thy parent bird to form a pen,
That mighty instrument of little men!   10
The pen! foredoomed to aid the mental throes
Of brains that labour, big with Verse or Prose;
Though Nymphs forsake, and Critics may deride,
The Lover's solace, and the Author's pride.
What Wits! what Poets dost thou daily raise!
How frequent is thy use, how small thy praise!
Condemned at length to be forgotten quite,
With all the pages which 'twas thine to write.
But thou, at least, mine own especial pen!
Once laid aside, but now assumed again,   20
Our task complete, like Hamet's shall be free;
Though spurned by others, yet beloved by me:
Then let us soar to-day; no common theme,
No Eastern vision, no distempered dream
Inspires—our path, though full of thorns, is plain;
Smooth be the verse, and easy be the strain.
    When Vice triumphant holds her sov'reign sway,
Obey'd by all who nought beside obey;
When Folly, frequent harbinger of crime,

Bedecks her cap with bells of every Clime;   30
When knaves and fools combined o'er all prevail,
And weigh their Justice in a Golden Scale;
E'en then the boldest start from public sneers,
Afraid of Shame, unknown to other fears,
More darkly sin, by Satire kept in awe,
And shrink from Ridicule, though not from Law.
    Such is the force of Wit! but not belong
To me the arrows of satiric song;
The royal vices of our age demand
A keener weapon, and a mightier hand.   40
Still there are follies, e'en for me to chase,
And yield at least amusement in the race:
Laugh when I laugh, I see no other fame,
The cry is up, and scribblers are my game:
Speed, Pegasus!—ye strains of great and small,
Ode! Epic! Elegy!—have at you all!
I, too, can scrawl, and once upon a time
I poured along the town a flood of rhyme,
A schoolboy freak, unworthy praise or blame;
I printed—older children do the same.   50
'Tis pleasant, sure, to see one's name in print;
A Book's a Book, altho' there's nothing in't.
Not that a Title's sounding charm can save
Or scrawl or scribbler from an equal grave:
This Lamb must own, since his patrician name
Failed to preserve the spurious Farce from shame.
No matter, George continues still to write,
Tho' now the name is veiled from public sight.
Moved by the great example, I pursue
The self-same road, but make my own review: 60
Not seek great Jeffrey's, yet like him will be
Self-constituted Judge of Poesy.
    A man must serve his time to every trade
Save Censure—Critics all are ready made.
Take hackneyed jokes from Miller, got by rote,
With just enough of learning to misquote;
A man well skilled to find, or forge a fault;
A turn for punning—call it Attic salt;

To Jeffrey go, be silent and discreet,
His pay is just ten sterling pounds per sheet: 70
Fear not to lie, 'twill seem a *sharper* hit;
Shrink not from blasphemy, 'twill pass for wit;
Care not for feeling—pass your proper jest,
And stand a Critic, hated yet caress'd.
    And shall we own such judgment? no—as soon
Seek roses in December—ice in June;
Hope constancy in wind, or corn in chaff,
Believe a woman or an epitaph,
Or any other thing that's false, before
You trust in Critics, who themselves are sore;   80
Or yield one single thought to be misled
By Jeffrey's heart, or Lamb's Boeotian head.
To these young tyrants, by themselves misplaced,
Combined usurpers on the Throne of Taste;
To these, when Authors bend in humble awe,
And hail their voice as Truth, their word as Law;
While these are Censors, 'twould be sin to spare;
While such are Critics, why should I forbear?
But yet, so near all modern worthies run,
'Tis doubtful whom to seek, or whom to shun;   90
Nor know we when to spare, or where to strike,
Our Bards and Censors are so much alike.
    Then should you ask me, why I venture o'er
The path which Pope and Gifford trod before;
If not yet sickened, you can still proceed;
Go on; my rhyme will tell you as you read.
"But hold!" exclaims a friend,—"here's some neglect:
This—that—and t'other line seems incorrect."
What then? the self-same blunder Pope has got,
And careless Dryden—"Aye, but Pye has not":—   100
Indeed!—'tis granted, faith!—but what care I?
Better to err with Pope, than shine with Pye.
    Time was, ere yet in these degenerate days
Ignoble themes obtained mistaken praise,
When Sense and Wit with Poesy allied,
No fabled Graces, flourished side by side,
From the same fount their inspiration drew,

And, reared by Taste, bloomed fairer as they grew.
Then, in this happy Isle, a Pope's pure strain
Sought the rapt soul to charm, nor sought in vain;   110
A polished nation's praise aspired to claim,
And raised the people's, as the poet's fame.
Like him great Dryden poured the tide of song,
In stream less smooth, indeed, yet doubly strong.
Then Congreve's scenes could cheer, or Otway's melt;
For Nature then an English audience felt—
But why these names, or greater still, retrace,
When all to feebler Bards resign their place?
Yet to such times our lingering looks are cast,
When taste and reason with those times are past.   120
Now look around, and turn each trifling page,
Survey the precious works that please the age;
This truth at least let Satire's self allow,
No dearth of Bards can be complained of now.
The loaded Press beneath her labour groans,
And Printers' devils shake their weary bones;
While Southey's Epics cram the creaking shelves,
And Little's Lyrics shine in hot-pressed twelves.
Thus saith the Preacher: "Nought beneath the sun
Is new," yet still from change to change we run.   130
What varied wonders tempt us as they pass!
The Cow-pox, Tractors, Galvanism, and Gas,
In turns appear, to make the vulgar stare,
Till the swoln bubble bursts—and all is air!
Nor less new schools of Poetry arise,
Where dull pretenders grapple for the prize:
O'er Taste a while these Pseudo-bards prevail;
Each country Book-club bows the knee to Baal,
And, hurling lawful Genius from the throne,
Erects a shrine and idol of its own;   140
Some leaden calf—but whom it matters not,
From soaring Southey, down to groveling Stott.
　　Behold! in various throngs the scribbling crew,
For notice eager, pass in long review:
Each spurs his jaded Pegasus apace,
And Rhyme and Blank maintain an equal race;

Sonnets on sonnets crowd, and ode on ode;
And Tales of Terror jostle on the road;
Immeasurable measures move along;
For simpering Folly loves a varied song,   150
To strange, mysterious Dulness still the friend,
Admires the strain she cannot comprehend.
Thus Lays of Minstrels—may they be the last!—
On half-strung harps whine mournful to the blast.
While mountain spirits prate to river sprites,
That dames may listen to the sound at nights;
And goblin brats, of Gilpin Horner's brood
Decoy young Border-nobles through the wood,
And skip at every step, Lord knows how high,
And frighten foolish babes, the Lord knows why;   160
While high-born ladies in their magic cell,
Forbidding Knights to read who cannot spell,
Despatch a courier to a wizard's grave,
And fight with honest men to shield a knave.
   Next view in state, proud prancing on his roan,
The golden-crested haughty Marmion,
Now forging scrolls, now foremost in the fight,
Not quite a Felon, yet but half a Knight,
The gibbet or the field prepared to grace;
A mighty mixture of the great and base.   170
And think'st thou, Scott! by vain conceit perchance,
On public taste to foist thy stale romance,
Though Murray with his Miller may combine
To yield thy muse just half-a-crown per line?
No! when the sons of song descend to trade,
Their bays are sear, their former laurels fade,
Let such forego the poet's sacred name,
Who rack their brains for lucre, not for fame:
Still for stern Mammon may they toil in vain!
And sadly gaze on Gold they cannot gain!   180
Such be their meed, such still the just reward
Of prostituted Muse and hireling bard!
For this we spurn Apollo's venal son,
And bid a long "good night" to Marmion.
   These are the themes that claim our plaudits now;

These are the Bards to whom the Muse must bow;
While Milton, Dryden, Pope, alike forgot,
Resign their hallowed Bays to Walter Scott.
  The time has been, when yet the Muse was young,
When Homer swept the lyre, and Maro sung,   190
An Epic scarce ten centuries could claim,
While awe-struck nations hailed the magic name:
The work of each immortal Bard appears
The single wonder of a thousand years.
Empires have mouldered from the face of earth,
Tongues have expired with those who gave them birth,
Without the glory such a strain can give,
As even in ruin bids the language live.
Not so with us, though minor Bards, content,
On one great work a life of labour spent: 200
With eagle pinion soaring to the skies,
Behold the Ballad-monger Southey rise!
To him let Camoëns, Milton, Tasso yield,
Whose annual strains, like armies, take the field.
First in the ranks see Joan of Arc advance,
The scourge of England and the boast of France!
Though burnt by wicked Bedford for a witch,
Behold her statue placed in Glory's niche;
Her fetters burst, and just released from prison,
A virgin Phoenix from her ashes risen.   210
Next see tremendous Thalaba come on,
Arabia's monstrous, wild, and wond'rous son;
Domdaniel's dread destroyer, who o'erthrew
More mad magicians than the world e'er knew.
Immortal Hero! all thy foes o'ercome,
For ever reign—the rival of Tom Thumb!
Since startled Metre fled before thy face,
Well wert thou doomed the last of all thy race!
Well might triumphant Genii bear thee hence,
Illustrious conqueror of common sense!   220
Now, last and greatest, Madoc spreads his sails,
Cacique in Mexico, and Prince in Wales;
Tells us strange tales, as other travellers do,

More old than Mandeville's, and not so true.
Oh, Southey! Southey! cease thy varied song!
A bard may chant too often and too long:
As thou art strong in verse, in mercy, spare!
A fourth, alas! were more than we could bear.
But if, in spite of all the world can say,
Thou still wilt verseward plod thy weary way;   230
If still in Berkeley-Ballads most uncivil,
Thou wilt devote old women to the devil,
The babe unborn thy dread intent may rue:
"God help thee," Southey, and thy readers too.
  Next comes the dull disciple of thy school,
That mild apostate from poetic rule,
The simple Wordsworth, framer of a lay
As soft as evening in his favourite May,
Who warns his friend "to shake off toil and trouble,
And quit his books, for fear of growing double";   240
Who, both by precept and example, shows
That prose is verse, and verse is merely prose;
Convincing all, by demonstration plain,
Poetic souls delight in prose insane;
And Christmas stories tortured into rhyme
Contain the essence of the true sublime.
Thus, when he tells the tale of Betty Foy,
The idiot mother of "an idiot Boy";
A moon-struck, silly lad, who lost his way,
And, like his bard, confounded night with day;   250
So close on each pathetic part he dwells,
And each adventure so sublimely tells,
That all who view the "idiot in his glory"
Conceive the Bard the hero of the story.
  Shall gentle Coleridge pass unnoticed here,
To turgid ode and tumid stanza dear?
Though themes of innocence amuse him best,
Yet still Obscurity's a welcome guest.
If Inspiration should her aid refuse
To him who takes a Pixy for a muse,   260
Yet none in lofty numbers can surpass

The bard who soars to elegize an ass:
So well the subject suits his noble mind,
He brays, the Laureate of the long-eared kind.
   Oh! wonder-working Lewis! Monk, or Bard,
Who fain would make Parnassus a church-yard!
Lo! wreaths of yew, not laurel, bind thy brow,
Thy Muse a Sprite, Apollo's sexton thou!
Whether on ancient tombs thou tak'st thy stand,
By gibb'ring spectres hailed, thy kindred band;   270
Or tracest chaste descriptions on thy page,
To please the females of our modest age;
All hail, M.P.! from whose infernal brain
Thin-sheeted phantoms glide, a grisly train;
At whose command "grim women" throng in crowds,
And kings of fire, of water, and of clouds,
With "small grey men,"—"wild yagers," and what not,
To crown with honour thee and Walter Scott:
Again, all hail! if tales like thine may please,
St. Luke alone can vanquish the disease: 280
Even Satan's self with thee might dread to dwell,
And in thy skull discern a deeper Hell.
   Who in soft guise, surrounded by a choir
Of virgins melting, not to Vesta's fire,
With sparkling eyes, and cheek by passion flushed
Strikes his wild lyre, whilst listening dames are hushed?
'Tis Little! young Catullus of his day,
As sweet, but as immoral, in his Lay!
Grieved to condemn, the Muse must still be just,
Nor spare melodious advocates of lust.   290
Pure is the flame which o'er her altar burns;
From grosser incense with disgust she turns
Yet kind to youth, this expiation o'er,
She bids thee "mend thy line, and sin no more."
   For thee, translator of the tinsel song,
To whom such glittering ornaments belong,
Hibernian Strangford! with thine eyes of blue,
And boasted locks of red or auburn hue,
Whose plaintive strain each love-sick Miss admires,
And o'er harmonious fustian half expires,   300

Learn, if thou canst, to yield thine author's sense,
Nor vend thy sonnets on a false pretense.
Think'st thou to gain thy verse a higher place,
By dressing Camoëns in a suit of lace?
Mend, Strangford! mend thy morals and thy taste;
Be warm, but pure; be amorous, but be chaste:
Cease to deceive; thy pilfered harp restore,
Nor teach the Lusian Bard to copy Moore.
    Behold—Ye Tarts!—one moment spare the text!—
Hayley's last work, and worst—until his next;   310
Whether he spin poor couplets into plays,
Or damn the dead with purgatorial praise,
His style in youth or age is still the same,
For ever feeble and for ever tame.
Triumphant first see "Temper's Triumphs" shine!
At least I'm sure they triumphed over mine.
Of "Music's Triumphs," all who read may swear
That luckless Music never triumph'd there.
    Moravians, rise! bestow some meet reward
On dull devotion—Lo! the Sabbath Bard,   320
Sepulchral Grahame, pours his notes sublimes
In mangled prose, nor e'en aspires to rhyme;
Breaks into blank the Gospel of St. Luke,
And boldly pilfers from the Pentateuch;
And, undisturbed by conscientious qualms,
Perverts the Prophets, and purloins the Psalms.
    Hail, Sympathy! thy soft idea brings
A thousand visions of a thousand things,
And shows, still whimpering thro' threescore of years,
The maudlin prince of mournful sonneteers.   330
And art thou not their prince, harmonious Bowles!
Thou first, great oracle of tender souls?
Whether thou sing'st with equal ease, and grief,
The fall of empires, or a yellow leaf;
Whether thy muse most lamentably tells
What merry sounds proceed from Oxford bells,
Or, still in bells delighting, finds a friend
In every chime that jingled from Ostend;
Ah! how much juster were thy Muse's hap,

If to thy bells thou would'st but add a cap!   340
Delightful Bowles! still blessing and still blest,
All love thy strain, but children like it best.
'Tis thine, with gentle Little's moral song,
To soothe the mania of the amorous throng!
With thee our nursery damsels shed their tears,
Ere Miss as yet completes her infant years:
But in her teens thy whining powers are vain;
She quits poor Bowles for Little's purer strain.
Now to soft themes thou scornest to confine
The lofty numbers of a harp like thine;   350
"Awake a louder and a loftier strain,"
Such as none heard before, or will again!
Where all discoveries jumbled from the flood,
Since first the leaky ark reposed in mud,
By more or less, are sung in every book,
From Captain Noah down to Captain Cook.
Nor this alone—but, pausing on the road,
The Bard sighs forth a gentle episode,
And gravely tells—attend, each beauteous Miss!—
When first Madeira trembled to a kiss.   360
Bowles! in thy memory let this precept dwell,
Stick to thy Sonnets, Man!—at least they sell.
But if some new-born whim, or larger bribe,
Prompt thy crude brain, and claim thee for a scribe:
If 'chance some bard, though once by dunces feared,
Now, prone in dust, can only be revered;
If Pope, whose fame and genius, from the first,
Have foiled the best of critics, needs the worst,
Do thou essay: each fault, each failing scan;
The first of poets was, alas! but man.   370
Rake from each ancient dunghill ev'ry pearl,
Consult Lord Fanny, and confide in Curll;
Let all the scandals of a former age
Perch on thy pen, and flutter o'er thy page;
Affect a candour which thou canst not feel,
Clothe envy in a garb of honest zeal;
Write, as if St. John's soul could still inspire,
And do from hate what Mallet did for hire.

Oh! hadst thou lived in that congenial time,
To rave with Dennis, and with Ralph to rhyme;   380
Thronged with the rest around his living head,
Not raised thy hoof against the lion dead,
A meet reward had crowned thy glorious gains,
And linked thee to the Dunciad for thy pains.
   Another Epic! Who inflicts again
More books of blank upon the sons of men?
Boeotian Cottle, rich Bristowa's boast,
Imports old stories from the Cambrian coast,
And sends his goods to market—all alive!
Lines forty thousand, Cantos twenty-five!   390
Fresh fish from Hippocrene! who'll buy? who'll buy?
The precious bargain's cheap—in faith, not I.
Your turtle-feeder's verse must needs be flat,
Though Bristol bloat him with the verdant fat;
If Commerce fills the purse, she clogs the brain,
And Amos Cottle strikes the Lyre in vain.
In him an author's luckless lot behold!
Condemned to make the books which once he sold.
Oh, Amos Cottle!—Phoebus! what a name
To fill the speaking-trump of future fame!—   400
Oh, Amos Cottle! for a moment think
What meagre profits spring from pen and ink!
When thus devoted to poetic dreams,
Who will peruse thy prostituted reams?
Oh! pen perverted! paper misapplied!
Had Cottle still adorned the counter's side,
Bent o'er the desk, or, born to useful toils,
Been taught to make the paper which he soils,
Ploughed, delved, or plied the oar with lusty limb,
He had not sung of Wales, nor I of him.   410
   As Sisyphus against the infernal steep
Rolls the huge rock whose motions ne'er may sleep,
So up thy hill, ambrosial Richmond! heaves
Dull Maurice all his granite weight of leaves:
Smooth, solid monuments of mental pain!
The petrifactions of a plodding brain,
That, ere they reach the top, fall lumbering back again.

With broken lyre and cheek serenely pale,
Lo! sad Alcaeus wanders down the vale;
Though fair they rose, and might have bloomed at last,   420
His hopes have perished by the northern blast:
Nipped in the bud by Caledonian gales,
His blossoms wither as the blast prevails!
O'er his lost works let *classic* Sheffield weep;
May no rude hand disturb their early sleep!
   Yet say! why should the Bard, at once, resign
His claim to favour from the sacred Nine?
For ever startled by the mingled howl
Of Northern Wolves, that still in darkness prowl;
A coward Brood, which mangle as they prey,   430
By hellish instinct, all that cross their way;
Aged or young, the living or the dead,
No mercy find—these harpies must be fed.
Why do the injured unresisting yield
The calm possession of their native field?
Why tamely thus before their fangs retreat,
Nor hunt the blood-hounds back to Arthur's Seat?
   Health to immortal Jeffrey! once, in name,
England could boast a judge almost the same;
In soul so like, so merciful, yet just,   440
Some think that Satan has resigned his trust,
And given the Spirit to the world again,
To sentence Letters, as he sentenced men.
With hand less mighty, but with heart as black,
With voice as willing to decree the rack;
Bred in the Courts betimes, though all that law
As yet hath taught him is to find a flaw,—
Since well instructed in the patriot school
To rail at party, though a party tool—
Who knows? if chance his patrons should restore   450
Back to the sway they forfeited before,
His scribbling toils some recompense may meet,
And raise this Daniel to the Judgment-Seat.
Let Jeffrey's shade indulge the pious hope,
And greeting thus, present him with a rope:
"Heir to my virtues! man of equal mind!

Skilled to condemn as to traduce mankind,
This cord receive! for thee reserved with care,
To wield in judgment, and at length to wear."
  Health to great Jeffrey! Heaven preserve his life,   460
To flourish on the fertile shores of Fife,
And guard it sacred in its future wars,
Since authors sometimes seek the field of Mars!
Can none remember that eventful day,
That ever-glorious, almost fatal fray,
When Little's leadless pistol met his eye,
And Bow-street Myrmidons stood laughing by?
Oh, day disastrous! on her firm-set rock,
Dunedin's castle felt a secret shock;
Dark rolled the sympathetic waves of Forth,   470
Low groaned the startled whirlwinds of the north;
Tweed ruffled half his waves to form a tear,
The other half pursued his calm career;
Arthur's steep summit nodded to its base,
The surly Tolbooth scarcely kept her place.
The Tolbooth felt—for marble sometimes can,
On such occasions, feel as much as man—
The Tolbooth felt defrauded of his charms,
If Jeffrey died, except within her arms:
Nay last, not least, on that portentous morn,   480
The sixteenth story, where himself was born,
His patrimonial garret, fell to ground,
And pale Edina shuddered at the sound:
Strewed were the streets around with milk-white reams,
Flowed all the Canongate with inky streams;
This of his candour seemed the sable dew,
That of his valour showed the bloodless hue;
And all with justice deemed the two combined
The mingled emblems of his mighty mind.
But Caledonia's goddess hovered o'er   490
The field, and saved him from the wrath of Moore;
From either pistol snatched the vengeful lead,
And straight restored it to her favourite's head;
That head, with greater than magnetic power,
Caught it, as Danaë caught the golden shower,

And, though the thickening dross will scarce refine,
Augments its ore, and is itself a mine.
"My son," she cried, "ne'er thirst for gore again,
Resign the pistol and resume the pen;
O'er politics and poesy preside,   500
Boast of thy country, and Britannia's guide!
For long as Albion's heedless sons submit,
Or Scottish taste decides on English wit,
So long shall last thine unmolested reign,
Nor any dare to take thy name in vain.
Behold, a chosen band shall aid thy plan,
And own thee chieftain of the critic clan.
First in the oat-fed phalanx shall be seen
The travelled Thane, Athenian Aberdeen.
Herbert shall wield Thor's hammer, and sometimes   510
In gratitude, thou'lt praise his rugged rhymes.
Smug Sydney too thy bitter page shall seek,
And classic Hallam, much renowned for Greek;
Scott may perchance his name and influence lend,
And paltry Pillans shall traduce his friend;
While gay Thalia's luckless votary, Lamb,
Damned like the Devil—Devil-like will damn.
Known be thy name! unbounded be thy sway!
Thy Holland's banquets shall each toil repay!
While grateful Britain yields the praise she owes   520
To Holland's hirelings and to Learning's foes.
Yet mark one caution ere thy next Review
Spread its light wings of Saffron and of Blue,
Beware lest blundering Brougham destroy the sale,
Turn Beef to Bannocks, Cauliflowers to Kail."
Thus having said, the kilted Goddess kist
Her son, and vanished in a Scottish mist.
    Then prosper, Jeffrey! pertest of the train
Whom Scotland pampers with her fiery grain!
Whatever blessing waits a genuine Scot,   530
In double portion swells thy glorious lot;
For thee Edina culls her evening sweets,
And showers their odours on thy candid sheets,
Whose Hue and Fragrance to thy work adhere—

This scents its pages, and that gilds its rear.
Lo! blushing Itch, coy nymph, enamoured grown,
Forsakes the rest, and cleaves to thee alone,
And, too unjust to other Pictish men,
Enjoys thy person, and inspires thy pen!
    Illustrious Holland! hard would be his lot,   540
His hirelings mentioned, and himself forgot!
Holland, with Henry Petty at his back,
The whipper-in and huntsman of the pack.
Blest be the banquets spread at Holland House,
Where Scotchmen feed, and Critics may carouse!
Long, long beneath that hospitable roof
Shall Grub-Street dine, while duns are kept aloof.
See honest Hallam lay aside his fork,
Resume his pen, review his Lordship's work,
And, grateful for the dainties on his plate,   550
Declare his landlord can at least translate!
Dunedin! view thy children with delight,
They write for food—and feed because they write:
And lest, when heated with the unusual grape,
Some glowing thoughts should to the press escape,
And tinge with red the female reader's cheek,
My lady skims the cream of each critique;
Breathes o'er the page her purity of soul,
Reforms each error, and refines the whole.
    Now to the Drama turn—Oh! motley sight!   560
What precious scenes the wondering eyes invite:
Puns, and a Prince within a barrel pent,
And Dibdin's nonsense yield complete content.
Though now, thank Heaven! the Rosciomania's o'er.
And full-grown actors are endured once more;
Yet what avail their vain attempts to please,
While British critics suffer scenes like these;
While Reynolds vents his *"dammes!"* "poohs!" and
    "zounds!"
And common-place and common sense confounds?
While Kenney's "World"—ah! where is Kenney's wit?—   570
Tires the sad gallery, lulls the listless Pit;
And Beaumont's pilfered Caratach affords

A tragedy complete in all but words?
Who but must mourn, while these are all the rage
The degradation of our vaunted stage?
Heavens! is all sense of shame and talent gone?
Have we no living Bard of merit?—none?
Awake, George Colman! Cumberland, awake!
Ring the alarum bell! let folly quake!
Oh! Sheridan! if aught can move thy pen,   580
Let Comedy assume her throne again;
Abjure the mummery of German schools;
Leave new Pizarros to translating fools;
Give, as thy last memorial to the age,
One classic drama, and reform the stage.
Gods! o'er those boards shall Folly rear her head,
Where Garrick trod, and Siddons lives to tread?
On those shall Farce display buffoonery's mask,
And Hook conceal his heroes in a cask?
Shall sapient managers new scenes produce   590
From Cherry, Skeffington, and Mother Goose?
While Shakespeare, Otway, Massinger, forgot,
On stalls must moulder, or in closets rot?
Lo! with what pomp the daily prints proclaim
The rival candidates for Attic fame!
In grim array though Lewis' spectres rise,
Still Skeffington and Goose divide the prize.
And sure *great* Skeffington must claim our praise,
For skirtless coats and skeletons of plays
Renowned alike; whose genius ne'er confines   600
Her flight to garnish Greenwood's gay designs;
Nor sleeps with "Sleeping Beauties," but anon
In five facetious acts comes thundering on.
While poor John Bull, bewildered with the scene,
Stares, wondering what the devil it can mean;
But as some hands applaud, a venal few!
Rather than sleep, why John applauds it too.
    Such are we now. Ah! wherefore should we turn
To what our fathers were, unless to mourn?
Degenerate Britons! are ye dead to shame,   610
Or, kind to dulness, do you fear to blame?

Well may the nobles of our present race
Watch each distortion of a Naldi's face;
Well may they smile on Italy's buffoons,
And worship Catalani's pantaloons,
Since their own Drama yields no fairer trace
Of wit than puns, of humour than grimace.
   Then let Ausonia, skill'd in every art
To soften manners, but corrupt the heart,
Pour her exotic follies o'er the town,   620
To sanction Vice, and hunt Decorum down:
Let wedded strumpets languish o'er Deshayes,
And bless the promise which his form displays;
While Gayton bounds before th' enraptured looks
Of hoary Marquises, and stripling Dukes:
Let high-born lechers eye the lively Presle
Twirl her light limbs, that spurn the needless veil;
Let Angiolini bare her breast of snow,
Wave the white arm, and point the pliant toe;
Collini trill her love-inspiring song,   630
Strain her fair neck, and charm the listening throng!
Whet not your scythe, Suppressors of our Vice!
Reforming Saints! too delicately nice!
By whose decrees, our sinful souls to save,
No Sunday tankards foam, no barbers shave;
And beer undrawn, and bears unmown, display
Your holy reverence for the Sabbath-day.
   Or hail at once the patron and the pile
Of vice and folly, Greville and Argyle!
Where yon proud palace, Fashion's hallow'd fane,   640
Spreads wide her portals for the motley train,
Behold the new Petronius of the day,
Our arbiter of pleasure and of play!
There the hired eunuch, the Hesperian choir,
The melting lute, the soft lascivious lyre,
The song from Italy, the step from France,
The midnight orgy, and the mazy dance,
The smile of beauty, and the flush of wine,
For fops, fools, gamesters, knaves, and Lords combine:
Each to his humour—Comus all allows;   650

Champaign, dice, music, or your neighbour's spouse.
Talk not to us, ye starving sons of trade!
Of piteous ruin, which ourselves have made;
In Plenty's sunshine Fortune's minions bask,
Nor think of Poverty, except "en masque,"
When for the night some lately titled ass
Appears the beggar which his grandsire was,
The curtain dropped, the gay Burletta o'er,
The audience take their turn upon the floor:
Now round the room the circling dow'gers sweep,   660
Now in loose waltz the thin-clad daughters leap;
The first in lengthened line majestic swim,
The last display the free unfettered limb!
Those for Hibernia's lusty sons repair
With art the charms which Nature could not spare;
These after husbands wing their eager flight,
Nor leave much mystery for the nuptial night.
     Oh! blest retreats of infamy and ease,
Where, all forgotten but the power to please,
Each maid may give a loose to genial thought,   670
Each swain may teach new systems, or be taught:
There the blithe youngster, just returned from Spain,
Cuts the light pack, or calls the rattling main;
The jovial Caster's set, and seven's the Nick,
Or—done!—a thousand on the coming trick!
If, mad with loss, existence 'gins to tire,
And all your hope or wish is to expire,
Here's Powell's pistol ready for your life,
And, kinder still, two Pagets for your wife:
Fit consummation of an earthly race   680
Begun in folly, ended in disgrace,
While none but menials o'er the bed of death,
Wash thy red wounds, or watch thy wavering breath;
Traduced by liars, and forgot by all,
The mangled victim of a drunken brawl,
To live like Clodius, and like Falkland fall.
     Truth! rouse some genuine Bard, and guide his hand
To drive this pestilence from out the land.
E'en I—least thinking of a thoughtless throng,

Just skilled to know the right and choose the wrong,   690
Freed at that age when Reason's shield is lost,
To fight my course through Passion's countless host,
Whom every path of Pleasure's flow'ry way
Has lured in turn, and all have led astray—
E'en I must raise my voice, e'en I must feel
Such scenes, such men, destroy the public weal:
Altho' some kind, censorious friend will say,
"What art thou better, meddling fool, than they?"
And every Brother Rake will smile to see
That miracle, a Moralist in me.   700
No matter—when some Bard in virtue strong,
Gifford perchance, shall raise the chastening song,
Then sleep my pen for ever! and my voice
Be only heard to hail him, and rejoice,
Rejoice, and yield my feeble praise, though I
May feel the lash that Virtue must apply.
    As for the smaller fry, who swarm in shoals
From silly Hafiz up to simple Bowles,
Why should we call them from their dark abode,
In Broad St. Giles's or Tottenham-Road?   710
Or (since some men of fashion nobly dare
To scrawl in verse) from Bond-Street or the Square?
If things of Ton their harmless lays indite,
Most wisely doomed to shun the public sight,
What harm? in spite of every critic elf,
Sir T. may read his stanzas to himself;
Miles Andrews still his strength in couplets try,
And live in prologues, though his dramas die.
Lords too are Bards: such things at times befall,
And 'tis some praise in Peers to write at all.   720
Yet, did or Taste or Reason sway the times,
Ah! who would take their titles with their rhymes?
Roscommon! Sheffield! with your spirits fled,
No future laurels deck a noble head;
No Muse will cheer, with renovating smile,
The paralytic puling of Carlisle.
The puny schoolboy and his early lay
Men pardon, if his follies pass away;

But who forgives the Senior's ceaseless verse,
Whose hairs grow hoary as his rhymes grow worse?   730
What heterogeneous honours deck the Peer!
Lord, rhymester, petit-maitre, pamphleteer!
So dull in youth, so drivelling in his age,
His scenes alone had damned our sinking stage;
But Managers for once cried, "Hold, enough!"
Nor drugged their audience with the tragic stuff.
Yet at their judgment let his Lordship laugh,
And case his volumes in congenial calf;
Yes! doff that covering, where Morocco shines,
And hang a calf-skin on those recreant lines.   740
    With you, ye Druids! rich in native lead,
Who daily scribble for your daily bread:
With you I war not: Gifford's heavy hand
Has crushed, without remorse, your numerous band.
On "All the Talents" vent your venal spleen;
Want is your plea, let Pity be your screen.
Let Monodies on Fox regale your crew,
And Melville's Mantle prove a Blanket too!
One common Lethe waits each hapless Bard,
And, peace be with you! 'tis your best reward.   750
Such damning fame; as Dunciads only give
Could bid your lines beyond a morning live;
But now at once your fleeting labours close,
With names of greater note in blest repose.
Far be't from me unkindly to upbraid
The lovely Rosa's prose in masquerade,
Whose strains, the faithful echoes of her mind,
Leave wondering comprehension far behind.
Though Crusca's bards no more our journals fill,
Some stragglers skirmish round the columns still;   760
Last of the howling host which once was Bell's,
Matilda snivels yet, and Hafiz yells;
And Merry's metaphors appear anew,
Chained to the signature of O. P. Q.
    When some brisk youth, the tenant of a stall,
Employs a pen less pointed than his awl,
Leaves his snug shop, forsakes his store of shoes,

St. Crispin quits, and cobbles for the Muse,
Heavens! how the vulgar stare! how crowds applaud!
How ladies read, and Literati laud!   770
If chance some wicked wag should pass his jest,
'Tis sheer ill-nature—don't the world know best?
Genius must guide when wits admire the rhyme,
And Capel Lofft declares 'tis quite sublime.
Hear, then, ye happy sons of needless trade!
Swains! quit the plough, resign the useless spade!
Lo! Burns and Bloomfield, nay, a greater far,
Gifford was born beneath an adverse star,
Forsook the labours of a servile state,
Stemmed the rude storm, and triumphed over Fate: 780
Then why no more? if Phoebus smiled on you,
Bloomfield! why not on brother Nathan too?
Him too the Mania, not the Muse, has seized;
Not inspiration, but a mind diseased:
And now no Boor can seek his last abode,
No common be inclosed without an ode.
Oh! since increased refinement deigns to smile
On Britain's sons, and bless our genial Isle,
Let Poesy go forth, pervade the whole,
Alike the rustic, and mechanic soul!   .   790
Ye tuneful cobblers! still your notes prolong,
Compose at once a slipper and a song;
So shall the fair your handywork peruse,
Your sonnets sure shall please—perhaps your shoes.
May Moorland weavers boast Pindaric skill,
And tailors' lays be longer than their bill!
While punctual beaux reward the grateful notes,
And pay for poems—when they pay for coats.
    To the famed throng now paid the tribute due,
Neglected Genius! let me turn to you.   800
Come forth, oh Campbell! give thy talents scope;
Who dares aspire if thou must cease to hope?
And thou, melodious Rogers! rise at last,
Recall the pleasing memory of the past;
Arise! let blest remembrance still inspire,
And strike to wonted tones thy hallowed lyre;

Restore Apollo to his vacant throne,
Assert thy country's honour and thine own.
What! must deserted Poesy still weep
Where her last hopes with pious Cowper sleep?   810
Unless, perchance, from his cold bier she turns,
To deck the turf that wraps her minstrel, Burns!
No! though contempt hath marked the spurious brood,
The race who rhyme from folly, or for food,
Yet still some genuine sons 'tis hers to boast,
Who, least affecting, still affect the most:
Feel as they write, and write but as they feel—
Bear witness Gifford, Sotheby, Macneil.
  "Why slumbers Gifford?" once was asked in vain;
Why slumbers Gifford? let us ask again.   820
Are there no follies for his pen to purge?
Are there no fools whose backs demand the scourge?
Are there no sins for Satire's Bard to greet?
Stalks not gigantic Vice in every street?
Shall Peers or Princes tread pollution's path,
And 'scape alike the Laws and Muse's wrath?
Nor blaze with guilty glare through future time,
Eternal beacons of consummate crime?
Arouse thee, Gifford! be thy promise claimed,
Make bad men better, or at least ashamed.   830
  Unhappy White! while life was in its spring,
And thy young Muse just waved her joyous wing,
The Spoiler swept that soaring Lyre away,
Which else had sounded an immortal lay.
Oh! what a noble heart was here undone,
When Science' self destroyed her favourite son!
Yes, she too much indulged thy fond pursuit,
She sowed the seeds, but Death has reaped the fruit.
'Twas thine own Genius gave the final blow,
And helped to plant the wound that laid thee low: 840
So the struck Eagle, stretched upon the plain,
No more through rolling clouds to soar again,
Viewed his own feather on the fatal dart,
And winged the shaft that quivered in his heart;
Keen were his pangs, but keener far to feel

He nursed the pinion which impelled the steel;
While the same plumage that had warmed his nest
Drank the last life-drop of his bleeding breast.
    There be who say, in these enlightened days,
That splendid lies are all the poet's praise;   850
That strained Invention, ever on the wing,
Alone impels the modern Bard to sing:
'Tis true, that all who rhyme—nay, all who write,
Shrink from that fatal word to Genius—Trite;
Yet Truth sometimes will lend her noblest fires,
And decorate the verse herself inspires:
This fact in Virtue's name let Crabbe attest;
Though Nature's sternest Painter, yet the best.
    And here let Shee and Genius find a place,
Whose pen and pencil yield an equal grace;   860
To guide whose hand the sister Arts combine,
And trace the Poet's or the Painter's line;
Whose magic touch can bid the canvas glow,
Or pour the easy rhyme's harmonious flow;
While honours, doubly merited, attend
The Poet's rival, but the Painter's friend.
    Blest is the man who dares approach the bower
Where dwelt the Muses at their natal hour;
Whose steps have pressed, whose eye has marked afar,
The clime that nursed the sons of song and war,   870
The scenes which Glory still must hover o'er,
Her place of birth, her own Achaian shore.
But doubly blest is he whose heart expands
With hallowed feelings for those classic lands;
Who rends the veil of ages long gone by,
And views their remnants with a poet's eye!
Wright! 'twas thy happy lot at once to view
Those shores of glory, and to sing them too;
And sure no common Muse inspired thy pen
To hail the land of Gods and Godlike men.   880
    And you, associate Bards! who snatched to light
Those gems too long withheld from modern sight;
Whose mingling taste combined to cull the wreath
While Attic flowers Aonian odours breathe,

And all their renovated fragrance flung,
To grace the beauties of your native tongue;
Now let those minds, that nobly could transfuse
The glorious Spirit of the Grecian Muse,
Though soft the echo, scorn a borrowed tone:
Resign Achaia's lyre, and strike your own.   890
    Let these, or such as these, with just applause,
Restore the Muse's violated laws;
But not in flimsy Darwin's pompous chime,
That mighty master of unmeaning rhyme,
Whose gilded cymbals, more adorned than clear,
The eye delighted, but fatigued the ear,
In show the simple lyre could once surpass,
But now, worn down, appear in native brass;
While all his train of hovering sylphs around
Evaporate in similes and sound: 900
Him let them shun, with him let tinsel die:
False glare attracts, but more offends the eye.
    Yet let them not to vulgar Wordsworth stoop,
The meanest object of the lowly group,
Whose verse, of all but childish prattle void,
Seems blessed harmony to Lamb and Lloyd:
Let them—but hold, my Muse, nor dare to teach
A strain far, far beyond thy humble reach:
The native genius with their being given
Will point the path, and peal their notes to heaven.   910
    And thou, too, Scott! resign to minstrels rude
The wilder Slogan of a Border feud:
Let others spin their meagre lines for hire;
Enough for Genius, if itself inspire!
Let Southey sing, altho' his teeming muse,
Prolific every spring, be too profuse;
Let simple Wordsworth chime his childish verse,
And brother Coleridge lull the babe at nurse;
Let Spectre-mongering Lewis aim, at most,
To rouse the Galleries, or to raise a ghost;   920
Let Moore still sigh; let Strangford steal from Moore,
And swear that Camoëns sang such notes of yore;
Let Hayley hobble on, Montgomery rave,

And godly Grahame chant a stupid stave;
Let sonneteering Bowles his strains refine,
And whine and whimper to the fourteenth line;
Let Stott, Carlisle, Matilda, and the rest
Of Grub Street, and of Grosvenor Place the best,
Scrawl on, 'till death release us from the strain,
Or Common Sense assert her rights again;   930
But Thou, with powers that mock the aid of praise,
Should'st leave to humbler Bards ignoble lays:
Thy country's voice, the voice of all the Nine,
Demand a hallowed harp—that harp is thine.
Say! will not Caledonia's annals yield
The glorious record of some nobler field,
Than the vile foray of a plundering clan,
Whose proudest deeds disgrace the name of man?
Or Marmion's acts of darkness, fitter food
For Sherwood's outlaw tales of Robin Hood?   940
Scotland! still proudly claim thy native Bard,
And be thy praise his first, his best reward!
Yet not with thee alone his name should live,
But own the vast renown a world can give;
Be known, perchance, when Albion is no more,
And tell the tale of what she was before;
To future times her faded fame recall,
And save her glory, though his country fall.
     Yet what avails the sanguine Poet's hope,
To conquer ages, and with time to cope?   950
New eras spread their wings, new nations rise,
And other Victors fill th' applauding skies;
A few brief generations fleet along,
Whose sons forget the Poet and his song:
E'en now, what once-loved Minstrels scarce may claim
The transient mention of a dubious name!
When Fame's loud trump hath blown its noblest blast,
Though long the sound, the echo sleeps at last;
And glory, like the Phoenix midst her fires,
Exhales her odours, blazes, and expires.   960
     Shall hoary Granta call her sable sons,
Expert in science, more expert at puns?

Shall these approach the Muse? ah, no! she flies,
Even from the tempting ore of Seaton's prize;
Though Printers condescend the press to soil
With rhyme by Hoare, and epic blank by Hoyle:
Not him whose page, if still upheld by whist,
Requires no sacred theme to bid us list.
Ye! who in Granta's honours would surpass,
Must mount her Pegasus, a full-grown ass;   970
A foal well worthy of her ancient Dam,
Whose Helicon is duller than her Cam.
   There Clarke, still striving piteously "to please,"
Forgetting doggerel leads not to degrees,
A would-be satirist, a hired Buffoon,
A monthly scribbler of some low Lampoon,
Condemned to drudge, the meanest of the mean,
And furbish falsehoods for a magazine,
Devotes to scandal his congenial mind;
Himself a living libel on mankind.   980
   Oh! dark asylum of a Vandal race!
At once the boast of learning, and disgrace!
So lost to Phoebus, that nor Hodgson's verse
Can make thee better, nor poor Hewson's worse.
But where fair Isis rolls her purer wave,
The partial Muse delighted loves to lave;
On her green banks a greener wreath she wove,
To crown the Bards that haunt her classic grove;
Where Richards wakes a genuine poet's fires,
And modern Britons glory in their Sires.   990
   For me, who, thus unasked, have dared to tell
My country, what her sons should know too well,
Zeal for her honour bade me here engage
The host of idiots that infest her age;
No just applause her honoured name shall lose,
As first in freedom, dearest to the Muse.
Oh! would thy bards but emulate thy fame,
And rise more worthy, Albion, of thy name!
What Athens was in science, Rome in power,
What Tyre appeared in her meridian hour,   1000
'Tis thine at once, fair Albion! to have been—

Earth's chief Dictatress, Ocean's lovely Queen:
But Rome decayed, and Athens strewed the plain,
And Tyre's proud piers lie shattered in the main;
Like these, thy strength may sink, in ruin hurled,
And Britain fall, but bulwark of the world.
But let me cease, and dread Cassandra's fate,
With warning ever scoffed at, till too late;
To themes less lofty still my lay confine,
And urge thy Bards to gain a name like thine.   1010
    Then, hapless Britain! be thy rulers blest,
The senate's oracles, the people's jest!
Still hear thy motley orators dispense
The flowers of rhetoric, though not of sense,
While Canning's colleagues hate him for his wit,
And old dame Portland fills the place of Pitt.
    Yet once again, adieu! ere this the sail
That wafts me hence is shivering in the gale;
And Afric's coast and Calpe's adverse height,
And Stamboul's minarets must greet my sight: 1020
Thence shall I stray through Beauty's native clime,
Where Kaff is clad in rocks, and crowned with snows
        sublime.
But should I back return, no tempting press
Shall drag my Journal from the desk's recess;
Let coxcombs, printing as they come from far,
Snatch his own wreath of Ridicule from Carr;
Let Aberdeen and Elgin still pursue
The shade of fame through regions of Virtú;
Waste useless thousands on their Phidian freaks,
Misshapen monuments and maimed antiques;   1030
And make their grand saloons a general mart
For all the mutilated blocks of art:
Of Dardan tours let Dilettanti tell,
I leave topography to rapid Gell;
And, quite content, no more shall interpose
To stun the public ear—at least with Prose.
    Thus far I've held my undisturbed career,
Prepared for rancour, steeled 'gainst selfish fear;
This thing of rhyme I ne'er disdained to own—

Though not obtrusive, yet not quite unknown: 1040
My voice was heard again, though not so loud,
My page, though nameless, never disavowed;
And now at once I tear the veil away:—
Cheer on the pack! the Quarry stands at bay,
Unscared by all the din of Melbourne house,
By Lamb's resentment, or by Holland's spouse,
By Jeffrey's harmless pistol, Hallam's rage,
Edina's brawny sons and brimstone page.
Our men in buckram shall have blows enough,
And feel they too are "penetrable stuff":   1050
And though I hope not hence unscathed to go,
Who conquers me shall find a stubborn foe.
The time hath been, when no harsh sound would fall
From lips that now may seem imbued with gall;
Nor fools nor follies tempt me to despise
The meanest thing that crawled beneath my eyes:
But now, so callous grown, so changed since youth,
I've learned to think, and sternly speak the truth;
Learned to deride the critic's starch decree,
And break him on the wheel he meant for me;   1060
To spurn the rod a scribbler bids me kiss,
Nor care if courts and crowds applaud or hiss:
Nay more, though all my rival rhymesters frown,
I too can hunt a Poetaster down;
And, armed in proof, the gauntlet cast at once
To Scotch marauder, and to Southern dunce.
Thus much I've dared; if my incondite lay
Hath wronged these righteous times, let others say:
This, let the world, which knows not how to spare,
Yet rarely blames unjustly, now declare.   1070

Hints from Horace

Who would not laugh, if Lawrence, hired to grace
His costly canvas with each flattered face,
Abused his art, till Nature, with a blush,
Saw cits grow Centaurs underneath his brush?
Or, should some limner join, for show or sale,
A Maid of Honour to a Mermaid's tail?
Or low Dubost—as once the world has seen—
Degrade God's creatures in his graphic spleen?
Not all that forced politeness, which defends
Fools in their faults, could gag his grinning friends.   10
Believe me, Moschus, like that picture seems
The book which, sillier than a sick man's dreams,
Displays a crowd of figures incomplete,
Poetic Nightmares, without head or feet.
    Poets and painters, as all artists know,
May shoot a little with a lengthened bow;
We claim this mutual mercy for our task,
And grant in turn the pardon which we ask;
But make not monsters spring from gentle dams—
Birds breed not vipers, tigers nurse not lambs.   20
    A laboured, long Exordium, sometimes tends
(Like patriot speeches) but to paltry ends;
And nonsense in a lofty note goes down,
As Pertness passes with a legal gown:
Thus many a Bard describes in pompous strain
The clear brook babbling through the goodly plain:
The groves of Granta, and her Gothic halls,
King's Coll—Cam's stream—stained windows, and old
    walls:

Or, in adventurous numbers, neatly aims
To paint a rainbow, or—the river Thames.   30
    You sketch a tree, and so perhaps may shine—
But daub a shipwreck like an alehouse sign;
You plan a *vase*—it dwindles to a *pot*;
Then glide down Grub Street—fasting and forgot;
Laughed into Lethe by some quaint Review,
Whose wit is never troublesome till—true.
    In fine, to whatsoever you aspire,
Let it at least be simple and entire.
    The greater portion of the rhyming tribe
(Give ear, my friend, for thou hast been a scribe)   40
Are led astray by some peculiar lure.
I labour to be brief—become obscure;
One falls while following Elegance too fast;
Another soars, inflated with Bombast;
Too low a third crawls on, afraid to fly,
He spins his subject to Satiety;
Absurdly varying, he at last engraves
Fish in the woods, and boars beneath the waves!
    Unless your care's exact, your judgment nice,
The flight from Folly leads but into Vice;   50
None are complete, all wanting in some part,
Like certain tailors, limited in art.
For galligaskins Slowshears is your man
But coats must claim another artisan.
Now this to me, I own, seems much the same
As Vulcan's feet to bear Apollo's frame;
Or, with a fair complexion, to expose
Black eyes, black ringlets, but—a bottle nose!
    Dear Authors! suit your topics to your strength,
And ponder well your subject, and its length;   60
Nor lift your load, before you're quite aware
What weight your shoulders will, or will not, bear.
But lucid Order, and Wit's siren voice,
Await the Poet, skilful in his choice;
With native Eloquence he soars along,
Grace in his thoughts, and Music in his song.
    Let Judgment teach him wisely to combine

With future parts the now omitted line:
This shall the Author choose, or that reject,
Precise in style, and cautious to select;   70
Nor slight applause will candid pens afford
To him who furnishes a wanting word.
Then fear not, if 'tis needful, to produce
Some term unknown, or obsolete in use,
(As Pitt has furnished us a word or two,
Which Lexicographers declined to do;)
So you indeed, with care,—(but be content
To take this license rarely)—may invent.
New words find credit in these latter days,
If neatly grafted on a Gallic phrase;   80
What Chaucer, Spenser did, we scarce refuse
To Dryden's or to Pope's maturer Muse.
If you can add a little, say why not,
As well as William Pitt, and Walter Scott?
Since they, by force of rhyme and force of lungs,
Enriched our Island's ill-united tongues;
'Tis then—and shall be—lawful to present
Reform in writing, as in Parliament.
    As forests shed their foliage by degrees,
So fade expressions which in season please;   90
And we and ours, alas! are due to Fate,
And works and words but dwindle to a date.
Though as a Monarch nods, and Commerce calls,
Impetuous rivers stagnate in canals;
Though swamps subdued, and marshes drained, sustain
The heavy ploughshare and the yellow grain,
And rising ports along the busy shore
Protect the vessel from old Ocean's roar,
All, all, must perish; but, surviving last,
The love of Letters half preserves the past.   100
True, some decay, yet not a few revive;
Though those shall sink, which now appear to thrive,
As Custom arbitrates, whose shifting sway
Our life and language must alike obey.
    The immortal wars which Gods and Angels wage,
Are they not shown in Milton's sacred page?

His strain will teach what numbers best belong
To themes celestial told in Epic song.
The slow, sad stanza will correctly paint
The Lover's anguish, or the Friend's complaint.   110
But which deserves the Laurel—Rhyme or Blank?
Which holds on Helicon the higher rank?
Let squabbling critics by themselves dispute
This point, as puzzling as a Chancery suit.
    Satiric rhyme first sprang from selfish spleen.
You doubt—see Dryden, Pope, St. Patrick's Dean.
    Blank verse is now, with one consent, allied
To tragedy, and rarely quits her side.
Though mad Almanzor rhymed in Dryden's days,
No sing-song Hero rants in modern plays;   120
Whilst modest Comedy her verse foregoes
For jest and *pun* in very middling prose.
Not that our Bens or Beaumonts show the worse,
Or lose one point, because they wrote in verse.
But so Thalia pleases to appear,
Poor Virgin! damned some twenty times a year!
    Whate'er the scene, let this advice have weight:—
Adapt your language to your Hero's state.
At times Melpomene forgets to groan,
And brisk Thalia takes a serious tone;   130
Nor unregarded will the act pass by
Where angry Townly "lifts his voice on high."
Again, our Shakespeare limits verse to Kings,
When common prose will serve for common things;
And lively Hal resigns heroic ire,
To "hollaing Hotspur" and his sceptred sire.
    'Tis not enough, ye Bards, with all your art,
To polish poems; they must touch the heart:
Where'er the scene be laid, whate'er the song,
Still let it bear the hearer's soul along;   140
Command your audience or to smile or weep,
Whiche'er may please you—anything but sleep.
The Poet claims our tears; but, by his leave,
Before I shed them, let me see *him* grieve.
    If banished Romeo feigned nor sigh nor tear,

Lulled by his langour, I could sleep or sneer.
Sad words, no doubt, become a serious face,
And men look angry in the proper place.
At double meanings folks seem wondrous sly,
And sentiment prescribes a pensive eye;   150
For nature formed at first the inward man,
And actors copy nature—when they can.
She bids the beating heart with rapture bound,
Raised to the stars, or levelled with the ground;
And for expression's aid, 't is said, or sung,
She gave our mind's interpreter—the tongue,
Who, worn with use, of late would fain dispense
(At least in theatres) with common sense:
O'erwhelm with sound the boxes, gallery, pit
And raise a laugh with anything—but wit.   160
    To skilful writers it will much import,
Whence spring their scenes, from common life or court;
Whether they seek applause by smile or tear,
To draw a Lying Valet, or a Lear,
A sage, or rakish youngster wild from school,
A wandering Peregrine, or plain John Bull;
All persons please when nature's voice prevails,
Scottish or Irish, born in Wilts or Wales.
    Or follow common fame, or forge a plot.
Who cares if mimic heroes lived or not?   170
One precept serves to regulate the scene:—
Make it appear as if it *might* have *been.*
    If some Drawcansir you aspire to draw,
Present him raving and above all law:
If female furies in your scheme are plann'd,
Macbeth's fierce dame is ready to your hand;
For tears and treachery, for good and evil,
Constance, King Richard, Hamlet, and the Devil!
But if a new design you dare essay,
And freely wander from the beaten way,   180
True to your characters, till all be pass'd,
Preserve consistency from first to last.
    'T is hard to venture where our betters fail,
Or lend fresh interest to a twice-told tale;

And yet, perchance, 't is wiser to prefer
A hackneyed plot, than choose a new, and err.
Yet copy not too closely, but record,
More justly, thought for thought than word for word;
Nor trace your prototype through narrow ways,
But only follow where he merits praise.   190
    For you, young bard! whom luckless fate may lead
To tremble on the nod of all who read,
Ere your first score of cantos time unrolls,
Beware—for God's sake, don't begin like Bowles!
"Awake a louder and a loftier strain,"—
And pray, what follows from his boiling brain?
He winks to Southey's level in a trice,
Whose epic mountains never fail in mice!
Not so of yore awoke your mighty sire
The tempered warblings of his master-lyre;   200
Soft as the gentler breathing of the lute,
"Of man's first disobedience and the fruit"
He speaks, but, as his subject swells along,
Earth, heaven, and Hades echo with the song.
Still to the "midst of things" he hastens on,
As if we witnessed all already done;
Leaves on his path whatever seems too mean
To raise the subject, or adorn the scene;
Gives, as each page improves upon the sight,
Not smoke from brightness, but from darkness—light;   210
And truth and fiction with such art compounds,
We know not where to fix their several bounds.
    If you would please the public, deign to hear
What soothes the many-headed monster's ear;
If your heart triumph when the hands of all
Applaud in thunder at the curtain's fall,
Deserve those plaudits—study nature's page,
And sketch the striking traits of every age;
While varying man and varying years unfold
Life's little tale, so oft, so vainly told.   220
Observe his simple childhood's dawning days,
His pranks, his prate, his playmates, and his plays;

Till time at length the mannish tyro weans,
And prurient vice outstrips his tardy teens!
  Behold him Freshman! forced no more to groan
O'er Virgil's devilish verses and—his own;
Prayers are too tedious, lectures too abstruse,
He flies from Tavell's frown to "Fordham's Mews"
(Unlucky Tavell! doom'd to daily cares
By pugilistic pupils, and by bears);   230
Fines, tutors, tasks, conventions threat in vain,
Before hounds, hunters, and Newmarket plain.
Rough with his elders, with his equals rash,
Civil to sharpers, prodigal of cash;
Constant to nought—save hazard and a whore,
Yet cursing both—for both have made him sore;
Unread (unless, since books beguile disease,
The p–x becomes his passage to degrees);
Fooled, pillaged, dunned, he wastes his terms away,
And, unexpelled perhaps, retires M.A.;   240
Master of arts! as *hells* and *clubs* proclaim,
Where scarce a blackleg bears a brighter name!
  Launched into life, extinct his early fire,
He apes the selfish prudence of his sire;
Marries for money, chooses friends for rank,
Buys land, and shrewdly trusts not to the Bank;
Sits in the Senate; gets a son and heir;
Sends him to Harrow, for himself was there.
Mute, though he votes, unless when called to cheer,
His son's so sharp—he'll see the dog a peer!   250
  Manhood declines—age palsies every limb;
He quits the scene—or else the scene quits him;
Scrapes wealth, o'er each departing penny grieves,
And avarice seizes all ambition leaves;
Counts cent per cent, and smiles, or vainly frets,
O'er hoards diminished by young Hopeful's debts;
Weighs well and wisely what to sell or buy,
Complete in all life's lessons—but to die;
Peevish and spiteful, doting, hard to please,
Commending every time, save times like these;   260

Crazed, querulous, forsaken, half forgot,
Expires unwept—is buried—let him rot!
　But from the Drama let me not digress,
Nor spare my precepts, though they please you less.
Though woman weep, and hardest hearts are stirred,
When what is done is rather seen than heard,
Yet many deeds preserved in history's page
Are better told than acted on the stage;
The ear sustains what shocks the timid eye,
And horror thus subsides to sympathy.   270
True Briton all beside, I here am French—
Bloodshed 't is surely better to retrench:
The gladiatorial gore we teach to flow
In tragic scene disgusts, though but in show;
We hate the carnage while we see the trick,
And find small sympathy in being sick.
Not on the stage the regicide Macbeth
Appals an audience with a monarch's death;
To gaze when sable Hubert threats to sear
Young Arthur's eyes, can *ours* or *nature* bear?   280
A halter'd heroine Johnson sought to slay—
We saved Irene, but half damned the play,
And (Heaven be praised!) our tolerating times
Stint metamorphoses to pantomimes;
And Lewis' self, with all his sprites, would quake
To change Earl Osmond's negro to a snake!
Because, in scenes exciting joy or grief,
We loathe the action which exceeds belief
And yet, God knows! what may not authors do,
Whose postscripts prate of dyeing "heroines blue?"   290
　Above all things *Dan* Poet, if you can,
Eke out your acts, I pray, with mortal man;
Nor call a ghost, unless some cursed scrape
Must open ten trap-doors for your escape.
Of all the monstrous things I'd fain forbid,
I loathe an opera worse than Dennis did;
Where good and evil persons, right or wrong,
Rage, love, and aught but moralize, in song.
Hail, last memorial of our foreign friends,

Which Gaul allows and still Hesperia lends!   300
Napoleon's edicts no embargo lay
On whores, spies, singers wisely shipp'd away.
Our giant capital, whose squares are spread
Where rustics earned, and now may beg, their bread,
In all iniquity is grown so nice,
It scorns amusements which are not of price.
Hence the pert shopkeeper, whose throbbing ear
Aches with orchestras which he pays to hear,
Whom shame, not sympathy, forbids to snore,
His anguish doubling by his own "encore";   310
Squeezed in "Fop's Alley," jostled by the beaux,
Teased with his hat, and trembling for his toes;
Scarce wrestles through the night, nor tastes of ease
Till the dropped curtain gives a glad release:
Why this, and more, he suffers—can ye guess?—
Because it costs him dear, and makes him dress!
    So prosper eunuchs from Etruscan schools;
Give us but fiddlers, and they're sure of fools!
Ere scenes were played by many a reverend clerk
(What harm, if David danced before the ark?),   320
In Christmas revels, simple country folks
Were pleased with morrice-mumm'ry and coarse jokes.
Improving years, with things no longer known,
Produced blithe Punch and merry Madame Joan,
Who still frisk on with feats so lewdly low,
'T is strange Benvolio suffers such a show;
Suppressing peer! to whom each vice gives place,
Oaths, boxing, begging,—all, save rout and race.
    Farce follow'd Comedy, and reach'd her prime,
In ever-laughing Foote's fantastic time: 330
Mad wag! who pardoned none, nor spared the best,
And turn'd some very serious things to jest.
Nor church nor state escaped his public sneers,
Arms nor the gown, priests, lawyers, volunteers:
"Alas, poor Yorick!" now forever mute!
Whoever loves a laugh must sigh for Foote.
    We smile, perforce, when histrionic scenes
Ape the swoln dialogue of kings and queens,

When "Chrononhotonthologos must die,"
And Arthur struts in mimic majesty.   340
    Moschus! with whom once more I hope to sit,
And smile at folly, if we can't at wit;
Yes friend! for thee I'll quit my cynic cell,
And bear Swift's motto, "Vive la bagatelle!"
Which charmed our days in each Aegean clime,
As oft at home, with revelry and rhyme.
Then may Euphrosyne, who sped the past,
Soothe thy life's scenes, nor leave thee in the last;
But find in thine, like pagan Plato's bed,
Some merry manuscript of mimes, when dead.   350
    Now to the Drama let us bend our eyes,
Where fettered by whig Walpole low she lies;
Corruption foil'd her, for she feared her glance;
Decorum left her for an opera dance!
Yet Chesterfield, whose polished pen inveighs
'Gainst laughter, fought for freedom to our plays;
Unchecked by megrims of patrician brains,
And damning dulness of lord chamberlains.
Repeat that act! again let Humour roam
Wild o'er the stage—we've time for tears at home;   360
Let Archer plant the horns on Sullen's brows,
And Estifania gull her "Copper" spouse;
The moral's scant—but that may be excused,
Men go not to be lectured, but amused.
He whom our plays dispose to good or ill
Must wear a head in want of Willis' skill;
Ay, but Macheath's example—psha!—no more!
It formed no thieves—the thief was form'd before;
And, spite of puritans and Collier's curse,
Plays make mankind no better, and no worse.   370
Then spare our stage, ye methodistic men;
Nor burn damned Drury if it rise again.
But why to brain-scorched bigots thus appeal?
Can heavenly mercy dwell with earthly zeal?
For times of fire and faggot let them hope!
Times dear alike to puritan or pope.
As pious Calvin saw Servetus blaze,

So would new sects on newer victims gaze.
E'en now the songs of Solyma begin;
Faith cants, perplexed apologist of sin!   380
While the Lord's servant chastens whom he loves,
And Simeon kicks, where Baxter only "shoves."
    Whom nature guides so writes that every dunce,
Enraptured, thinks to do the same at once;
But after inky thumbs and bitten nails,
And twenty scattered quires, the coxcomb fails.
    Let Pastoral be dumb; for who can hope
To match the youthful eclogues of our Pope!
Yet his and Phillips' faults, of different kind,
For art too rude, for nature too refined,   390
Instruct how hard the medium 't is to hit
'Twixt too much polish and too coarse a wit.
    A vulgar scribbler, certes, stands disgraced
In this nice age, when all aspire to taste;
The dirty language and the noisome jest,
Which pleased in Swift of yore, we now detest;
Proscribed not only in the world polite,
But even too nasty for a city knight!
    Peace to Swift's faults! his wit hath made them pass,
Unmatch'd by all save matchless Hudibras!   400
Whose author is perhaps the first we meet,
Who from our couplet lopped two final feet;
Nor less in merit than the longer line,
This measure moves a favourite of the Nine.
Though at first view eight feet may seem in vain
Formed, save in ode, to bear a serious strain,
Yet Scott has shown our wondering isle of late
This measure shrinks not from a theme of weight,
And, varied skilfully, surpasses far
Heroic rhyme, but most in love and war,   410
Whose fluctuations, tender or sublime,
Are curbed too much by long-recurring rhyme.
    But many a skilful judge abhors to see,
What few admire—irregularity.
This some vouchsafe to pardon; but 't is hard
When such a word contents a British bard.

And must the bard his glowing thoughts confine,
Lest censure hover o'er some faulty line?
Remove whate'er a critic may suspect,
To gain the paltry suffrage of *"correct"*?   420
Or prune the spirit of each daring phrase,
To fly from error, not to merit praise!
   Ye, who seek finished models, never cease
By day and night to read the works of Greece.
But our good fathers never bent their brains
To heathen Greek, content with native strains.
The few who read a page, or used a pen,
Were satisfied with Chaucer and old Ben;
The jokes and numbers suited to their taste
Were quaint and careless, anything but chaste;   430
Yet whether right or wrong the ancient rules,
It will not do to call our fathers fools!
Though you and I, who eruditely know
To separate the elegant and low,
Can also, when a hobbling line appears,
Detect with fingers, in default of ears.
   In sooth I do not know, or greatly care
To learn, who our first English strollers were;
Or if, till roofs received the vagrant art,
Our Muse, like that of Thespis, kept a cart;   440
But this is certain, since our Shakspeare's days,
There's pomp enough, if little else, in plays;
Nor will Melpomene ascend her throne
Without high heels, white plume, and Bristol stone.
   Old comedies still meet with much applause,
Though too licentious for dramatic laws:
At least, we moderns, wisely 't is confest,
Curtail or silence the lascivious jest.
   Whate'er their follies, and their faults beside,
Our enterprising bards pass nought untried;   450
Nor do they merit slight applause who choose
An English subject for an English muse,
And leave to minds which never dare invent
French flippancy and German sentiment.
Where is that living language which could claim

Poetic more, as philosophic, fame,
If all our bards, more patient of delay,
Would stop like Pope to polish by the way?
    Lords of the quill, whose critical assaults
O'erthrow whole quartos with their quires of faults,   460
Who soon detect, and mark where'er we fail,
And prove our marble with too nice a nail!
Democritus himself was not so bad;
He only *thought*, but *you* would make, us mad!
    But truth to say, most rhymers rarely guard
Against that ridicule they deem so hard;
In person negligent, they wear, from sloth,
Beards of a week and nails of annual growth;
Reside in garrets, fly from those they meet,
And walk in alleys rather than the street.   470
    With little rhyme, less reason, if you please,
The name of poet may be got with ease,
So that not tuns of helleboric juice
Shall ever turn your head to any use;
Write but like Wordsworth, live beside a lake,
And keep your bushy locks a year from Blake;
Then print your book, once more return to town,
And boys shall hunt your bardship up and down.
    Am I not wise, if such some poets' plight,
To purge in spring—like Bayes—before I write?   480
If this precaution soften'd not my bile,
I know no scribbler with a madder style;
But since (perhaps my feelings are too nice)
I cannot purchase fame at such a price,
I'll labour gratis as a grinder's wheel,
And, blunt myself, give edge to others' steel,
Nor write at all, unless to teach the art
To those rehearsing for the poet's part;
From Horace show the pleasing paths of song,
And from my own example—what is wrong.   490
    Though modern practice sometimes differs quite,
'T is just as well to think before you write;
Let every book that suits your theme be read,
So shall you trace it to the fountain-head.

He who has learned the duty which he owes
To friends and country, and to pardon foes;
Who models his deportment as may best
Accord with brother, sire, or stranger guest;
Who takes our laws and worship as they are,
Nor roars reform for senate, church, and bar;   500
In practice, rather than loud precept, wise,
Bids not his tongue, but heart, philosophise;—
Such is the man the poet should rehearse,
As joint exemplar of his life and verse.
　　Sometimes a sprightly wit, and tale well told,
Without much grace or weight or art, will hold
A longer empire o'er the public mind
Than sounding trifles, empty, though refined.
　　Unhappy Greece! thy sons of ancient days
The muse may celebrate with perfect praise,   510
Whose generous children narrow'd not their hearts
With commerce, given alone to arms and arts.
Our boys (save those whom public schools compel
To "long and short" before they're taught to spell)
From frugal fathers soon imbibe by rote,
"A penny saved, my lad, 's a penny got."
Babe of a city birth! from sixpence take
The third, how much will the remainder make?—
"A groat."—"Ah bravo! Dick hath done the sum!
He'll swell my fifth thousand to a plum."   520
　　They whose young souls receive this rust betimes,
'T is clear, are fit for anything but rhymes;
And Locke will tell you, that the father's right
Who hides all verses from his children's sight;
For poets (says this sage and many more)
Make sad mechanics with their lyric lore;
And Delphi now, however rich of old,
Discovers little silver and less gold,
Because Parnassus, though a mount divine,
Is poor as Irus or an Irish mine.   530
　　Two objects always should the poet move,
Or one or both,—to please or to improve.
Whate'er you teach, be brief, if you design

For our remembrance your didactic line;
Redundance places memory on the rack,
For brains may be o'erloaded, like the back.
   Fiction does best when taught to look like truth,
And fairy fables bubble none but youth:
Expect no credit for too wondrous tales,
Since Jonas only springs alive from whales!   540
   Young men with aught but elegance dispense;
Maturer years require a little sense.
To end at once:—that bard for all is fit
Who mingles well instruction with his wit;
For him reviews shall smile, for him o'erflow
The patronage of Paternoster-row;
His book, with Longman's liberal aid, shall pass
(Who ne'er despises books that bring him brass);
Through three long weeks the taste of London lead,
And cross St. George's Channel and the Tweed.   550
   But everything has faults, nor is 't unknown
That harps and fiddles often lose their tone,
And wayward voices, at their owner's call,
With all his best endeavours, only squall;
Dogs blink their covey, flints withhold the spark,
And double-barrels (damn them!) miss their mark.
   Where frequent beauties strike the reader's view,
We must not quarrel for a blot or two;
But pardon equally to books or men
The slips of human nature and the pen.   560
   Yet if an author, spite of foe or friend,
Despises all advice too much to mend,
But ever twangs the same discordant string,
Give him no quarter howsoe'er he sing.
Let Havard's fate o'ertake him, who, for once,
Produced a play too dashing for a dunce:
At first none deem'd it his; but when his name
Announced the fact—what then?—it lost its fame.
Though all deplore when Milton deigns to doze,
In a long work 't is fair to steal repose.   570
   As pictures, so shall poems be; some stand
The critic eye, and please when near at hand;

But others at a distance strike the sight;
This seeks the shade, but that demands the light,
Nor dreads the connoisseur's fastidious view,
But, ten times scrutinised, is ten times new.
    Parnassian pilgrims! ye whom chance or choice
Hath led to listen to the Muse's voice,
Receive this counsel, and be timely wise;
Few reach the summit which before you lies.   580
Our church and state, our courts and camps, concede
Reward to very moderate heads indeed!
In these plain common sense will travel far;
All are not Erskines who mislead the bar.
But poesy between the best and worst
No medium knows; you must be last or first;
For middling poets' miserable volumes
Are damned alike by gods and men and columns.
    Again, my Jeffrey!—as that sound inspires
How wakes my bosom to its wonted fires!   590
Fires, such as gentle Caledonians feel
When Southrons writhe upon their critic wheel,
Or mild Eclectics, when some, worse than Turks,
Would rob poor Faith to decorate "good works."
Such are the genial feelings thou canst claim—
My falcon flies not at ignoble game.
Mightiest of all Dunedin's beasts of chase!
For thee my Pegasus would mend his pace.
Arise, my Jeffrey! or my inkless pen
Shall never blunt its edge on meaner men;   600
Till thee or thine mine evil eye discerns,
Alas! I cannot "strike at wretched kernes."
Inhuman Saxon! wilt thou then resign
A muse and heart by choice so wholly thine?
Dear, d—d contemner of my schoolboy songs,
Hast thou no vengeance for my manhood's wrongs?
If unprovoked thou once could bid me bleed,
Hast thou no weapon for my daring deed?
What!—not a word!—and am I then so low?
Wilt thou forbear, who never spared a foe?   610
Hast thou no wrath, or wish to give it vent?

No wit for nobles, dunces by descent?
No jest on "minors," quibbles on a name,
Nor one facetious paragraph of blame?
Is it for this on Ilion I have stood,
And thought of Homer less than Holyrood?
On shore of Euxine or Aegean sea,
My hate, untravelled, fondly turn'd to thee.
Ah! let me cease; in vain my bosom burns,
From Corydon unkind Alexis turns: 620
Thy rhymes are vain; thy Jeffrey then forego,
Nor woo that anger which he will not show.
What then?—Edina starves some lanker son,
To write an article thou canst not shun;
Some less fastidious Scotchman shall be found,
As bold in Billingsgate, though less renowned.
    As if at table some discordant dish
Should shock our optics, such as frogs for fish;
As oil in lieu of butter men decry,
And poppies please not in a modern pie;   630
If all such mixtures then be half a crime,
We must have excellence to relish rhyme.
Mere roast and boil'd no epicure invites;
Thus poetry disgusts, or else delights.
    Who shoot not flying rarely touch a gun:
Will he who swims not to the river run?
And men unpractised in exchanging knocks
Must go to Jackson ere they dare to box.
Whate'er the weapon, cudgel, fist, or foil,
None reach expertness without years of toil;   640
But fifty dunces can, with perfect ease,
Tag twenty thousand couplets when they please.
Why not?—shall I, thus qualified to sit
For rotten boroughs, never show my wit?
Shall I, whose fathers with the quorum sate,
And lived in freedom on a fair estate;
Who left me heir, with stables, kennels, packs.
To *all* their income, and to—*twice* its tax;
Whose form and pedigree have scarce a fault,—
Shall I, I say, suppress my Attic salt?   650

Thus think "the mob of gentlemen"; but you,
Besides all this, must have some genius too.
Be this your sober judgment, and a rule,
And print not piping hot from Southey's school,
Who (ere another Thalaba appears),
I trust, will spare us for at least nine years.
And hark ye, Southey! pray—but don't be vex'd—
Burn all your last three works—and half the next.
But why this vain advice? once publish'd, books
Can never be recalled—from pastry-cooks!   660
Though *Madoc*, with *Pucelle*, instead of punk,
May travel back to Quito—on a trunk.
    Orpheus, we learn from Ovid and Lempriere,
Led all wild beasts but women by the ear;
And had he fiddled at the present hour,
We'd seen the lions waltzing in the Tower;
And old Amphion, such were minstrels then,
Had built St. Paul's without the aid of Wren.
Verse too was justice, and the bards of Greece
Did more than constables to keep the peace;   670
Abolish'd cuckoldom with much applause,
Call'd county meetings, and enforced the laws,
Cut down crown influence with reforming scythes,
And served the church—without demanding tithes;
And hence, throughout all Hellas and the East,
Each poet was a prophet and a priest,
Whose old-established board of joint controls
Included kingdoms in the cure of souls.
    Next rose the martial Homer, Epic's prince,
And fighting's been in fashion ever since;   680
And old Tyrtaeus, when the Spartans warr'd
(A limping leader, but a lofty bard),
Though walled Ithome had resisted long,
Reduced the fortress by the force of song.
    When oracles prevail'd, in times of old,
In song alone Apollo's will was told.
Then if your verse is what all verse should be,
And gods were not ashamed on 't, why should we?
The Muse, like mortal females, may be wooed;

In turns she'll seem a Paphian, or a prude; 690
Fierce as a bride when first she feels affright,
Mild as the same upon the second night;
Wild as the wife of alderman or peer,
Now for his grace, and now a grenadier!
Her eyes beseem, her heart belies, her zone,
Ice in a crowd and lava when alone.

    If verse be studied with some show of art,
Kind Nature always will perform her part;
Though without genius and a native vein
Of wit, we loathe an artificial strain— 700
Yet art and nature join'd will win the prize,
Unless they act like us and our allies.

    The youth who trains to ride or run a race,
Must bear privations with unruffled face,
Be called to labour when he thinks to dine,
And, harder still, leave wenching and his wine.
Ladies who sing, at least who sing at sight,
Have followed music through her farthest flight;
But rhymers tell you neither more nor less,
"I've got a pretty poem for the press"; 710
And that's enough; then write and print so fast;—
If Satan take the hindmost, who'd be last?
They storm the types, they publish, one and all,
They leap the counter, and they leave the stall.
Provincial maidens, men of high command,
Yea, baronets have ink'd the bloody hand!
Cash cannot quell them; Pollio played this prank
(Then Phoebus first found credit in a bank!)
Not all the living only, but the dead,
Fool on, as fluent as an Orpheus' head; 720
Damned all their days, they posthumously thrive—
Dug up from dust, though buried when alive!
Reviews record this epidemic crime,
Those Books of Martyrs to the rage for rhyme.
Alas! woe worth the scribbler! often seen
In Morning Post, or Monthly Magazine.
There lurk his earlier lays; but soon, hot-pressed,
Behold a quarto!—Tarts must tell the rest.

Then leave, ye wise, the lyre's precarious chords
To muse-mad baronets or madder lords,   730
Or country Crispins, now grown somewhat stale,
Twin Doric minstrels, drunk with Doric ale!
Hark to those notes, narcotically soft,
The cobbler-laureats sing to Capel Lofft!
Till, lo! that modern Midas, as he hears,
Adds an ell growth to his egregious ears!
    There lives one druid, who prepares in time
'Gainst future feuds his poor revenge of rhyme;
Racks his dull memory and his duller muse,
To publish faults which friendship should excuse.   740
If friendship's nothing, self-regard might teach
More polish'd usage of his parts of speech.
But what is shame, or what is aught to him?
He vents his spleen, or gratifies his whim.
Some fancied slight has roused his lurking hate,
Some folly crossed, some jest, or some debate;
Up to his den Sir Scribbler hies, and soon
The gather'd gall is voided in lampoon.
Perhaps at some pert speech you've dared to frown,
Perhaps your poem may have pleased the town: 750
If so, alas! 't is nature in the man—
May Heaven forgive you, for he never can!
Then be it so; and may his withering bays
Bloom fresh in satire, though they fade in praise!
While his lost songs no more shall steep and stink,
The dullest, fattest weeds on the Lethe's brink,
But springing upwards from the sluggish mould,
Be (what they never were before) be—sold!
Should some rich bard (but such a monster now,
In modern physics, we can scarce allow),   760
Should some pretending scribbler of the court,
Some rhyming peer—there's plenty of the sort—
All but one poor dependent priest withdrawn
(Ah! too regardless of his chaplain's yawn!),
Condemn the unlucky curate to recite
Their last dramatic work by candle-light,
How would the preacher turn each rueful leaf,

Dull as his sermons, but not half so brief!
Yet, since 't is promised at the rector's death,
He'll risk no living for a little breath.   770
Then spouts and foams, and cries at every line
(The Lord forgive him!), "Bravo! grand! divine!"
Hoarse with those praises (which, by flatt'ry fed,
Dependence barters for her bitter bread),
He strides and stamps along with creaking boot,
Till the floor echoes his emphatic foot;
Then sits again, then rolls his pious eye,
As when the dying vicar will not die!
Nor feels, forsooth, emotion at his heart;—
But all dissemblers overact their part.   780
    Ye, who aspire to "build the lofty rhyme,"
Believe not all who laud your false "sublime";
But if some friend shall hear your work, and say,
"Expunge that stanza, lop that line away,"
And, after fruitless efforts, you return
Without amendment, and he answers, "Burn!"
That instant throw your paper in the fire,
Ask not his thoughts, or follow his desire;
But if (true bard!) you scorn to condescend,
And will not alter what you can't defend,   790
If you will breed this bastard of your brains,—
We'll have no words—I've only lost my pains.
    Yet, if you only prize your favourite thought,
As critics kindly do, and authors ought;
If your cool friend annoy you now and then,
And cross whole pages with his plaguy pen
No matter, throw your ornaments aside,—
Better let him than all the world deride.
Give light to passages too much in shade,
Nor let a doubt obscure one verse you've made;   800
Your friend's a "Johnson," not to leave one word,
However trifling, which may seem absurd;
Such erring trifles lead to serious ills,
And furnish food for critics, or their quills.
    As the Scotch fiddle, with its touching tune,
Or the sad influence of the angry moon

All men avoid bad writers' ready tongues,
As yawning waiters fly Fitzscribble's lungs;
Yet on he mouths—ten minutes—tedious each
As prelate's homily or placeman's speech;   810
Long as the last years of a lingering lease,
When riot pauses until rents increase.
While such a minstrel, muttering fustian, strays
O'er hedge and ditch, through unfrequented ways,
If by some chance he walks into a well,
And shouts for succour with stentorian yell,
"A rope! help, Christians, as ye hope for grace!"
Nor woman, man, nor child will stir a pace;
For there his carcass he might freely fling,
From frenzy or the humour of the thing.   820
Though this has happen'd to more bards than one;
I'll tell you Budgell's story,—and have done.
    Budgell, a rogue and rhymester, for no good
(Unless his case be much misunderstood),
When teased with creditors' continual claims,
"To die like Cato," leapt into the Thames!
And therefore be it lawful through the town
For any bard to poison, hang, or drown.
Who saves the intended suicide receives
Small thanks from him who loathes the life he leaves;   830
And, sooth to say, mad poets must not lose
The glory of that death they freely choose.
    Nor is it certain that some sorts of verse
Prick not the poet's conscience as a curse;
Dosed with vile drams on Sunday he was found,
Or got a child on consecrated ground!
And hence is haunted with a rhyming rage—
Feared like a bear just bursting from his cage.
If free, all fly his versifying fit,
Fatal at once to simpleton or wit: 840
But *him*, unhappy! whom he seizes,—*him*
He flays with recitation limb by limb;
Probes to the quick where'er he makes his breach,
And gorges like a lawyer—or a leech.

The Kantian Revolution

One emphatic consequence of Kantian theory was the separation of art and social utility, or, in Horatian terms, teaching from delight. Kant did this in his *Critique of Judgment* (1790) by extending his analysis from scientific and moral judgments to aesthetic ones. He had already established that intuitions can be understood in relation either to causality or to freedom. To relate an intuition to a system based on causality is to relate it to pure reason. To relate it to a system based on the idea of freedom is to relate it to practical reason. In either case, the intuition is treated "as though" it illustrates the system to which it is related. In Kantian terms, it is treated as though it had a purpose—in German, a *Zweck*. The intuition can, however, be treated as though it is its own reason for being or its own purpose. In this case, Kant argues, it has "purposiveness without purpose" (*Zweckmässigkeit ohne Zweck*).

What is an intuition? Is it a representation of a pre-existing reality? The traditions that art should imitate nature and is a "mirror" held up to life—which are the traditions within which Horace's *Art* was understood for most of the eighteenth century and probably the traditions that Horace, himself, had in mind—assume that the mind simply receives images from the surrounding world (that is, "nature"). Poetic imitation is the process of representing the images in words, hence complementary to the idea that poetry is essentially verbal description and that poets are like painters. Rejecting this theory, Kant pointed out that to be intelligible an intuition must be a combination of data from the outside and categories contributed to it by the mind. The faculty that does the contributing is imagination (*Einbildungskraft*). Imagination is not a passive faculty that produces mental images but an active one that combines inner and outer materials to create the world as we know it. If "reality" means the source of the external data of perception, it is forever beyond human knowledge—a "thing in itself" (*Ding an sich*).

Meanwhile, the world humans *can* know has a dual aspect. To perceive, say, a tree is to become aware of something that seems exterior to the observer and thus to have an "objective" existence of its own. At the same time, the act of perception makes the observer aware of an inner, "subjective" realm, an "I" that does the perceiving.

The Greek source of the word "aesthetic" is *aisthanomai*, meaning "to perceive." In the Kantian formulation delight in art arises from contemplation of the perception considered as its own purpose. Since this sort of contemplation has no ulterior motive, it is "disinterested." If, for example, the perception of an apple or the picture of an apple arouses hunger, the response is not disinterested. The pleasure caused by the perception is related to a human motive that is extraneous to the image itself. If, on the other hand, an apple—or a picture of an apple— is admired simply for its beauty, the response is disinterested and, in Kant's terms, truly aesthetic. A painting of an apple is explicitly aesthetic because everyone knows from the beginning that it cannot be eaten.

Art that argues for or against some pre-estabished value like "home-land" or "divine love" or "courage" or "ambition" is not disinterested. This sort of art was generally admired during the Renaissance and the Enlightenment and was equated with the "profit" part of the Horatian "profit-delight" formula. From a Kantian point of view it is impure art. On the other hand, art that presents moral ideas without reference to pre-established values is in the aesthetic mode. The contrast is illustrated by the difference between "The Star Spangled Banner," which is a summons to patriotism, and the poems celebrating American experience in Walt Whitman's *Leaves of Grass*. In some post-Kantian formulations, the direct representation of the idea or object is understood as representation of the thing "as it exists." In this formulation, aesthetic representation is "ontological" since it presents ideas and objects according to their mode of being. Hence the often-quoted lines of Archibald MacLeish's poem *Ars poetica*, "A poem should be palpable and mute/ As a globed fruit . . . A poem should not mean/ But be."

The difference between interested and disinterested modes of creating art leads to different modes of criticism. For example, a reader or critic can approach *Macbeth* as though it is a warning against ambition, thus attributing an exterior purpose to it. Conversely, an aesthetic critic might interpret *Macbeth* as a study in human relations that does not need to be forced into the shape of a moral allegory to be appreciated.

In fact, it can be argued that to force *Macbeth* into the shape of a moral allegory is to falsify it and thus to rob it of its interest as a work of art, which is the source of its "delight" in the Horatian sense and its "purpose" in the Kantian one.

Kant himself and a good many followers regarded aesthetic as that inner coherence produced by imagination when it combines mental (or spiritual) categories with data from the *Ding an sich*. In much Kantian criticism "unity" and "organic unity" are synonyms for this inner coherence. A variant Kantian position regards the work as a "reconciliation of opposites" or the holding of opposing elements in a synthesis or "tension," a quality that can also be interpreted as a form of irony. Both "organic unity" and "reconciliation of opposites" imply conscious artistry. The artist is considered a craftsman who uses his skills to create the unity or reconcile the divergent elements in the art work. The idea of art as craftsmanship is, of course, emphatic in Horace's *Art of Poetry*. It recurs in the nineteenth century in the theories of the creative process of Edgar Allen Poe and the symbolists, beginning with Baudelaire, in France. It is also found in criticism that focuses on the "artistry" that the art work exhibits. The "new critical" technique of the 1940s and 1950s, for example, attempted to show the value of poems as art either by showing how the parts of the poem being examined all relate to a central intuition or by demonstrating how the poem holds diverse elements in tension. Two apparent Horatian intimations of this view are Horace's insistence on the overriding importance of making the work "simple and unified" and his fascination with the "coming together" of diverse elements in the finished work. In both cases, however, Horace's understanding is rhetorical rather than aesthetic.

In his *Letters on the Aesthetic Education of Man* (1795) Schiller applied Kantian theory to history. He was motivated in part by his distress at the way that the political goals of the French Revolution had ended in the bloodbath known as the Reign of Terror.

Schiller believed he had found a better and more certain path to reform, which he called "aesthetic education." He also believed that he had found in a treatise by Johann Wincklemann titled *Reflections on the Painting and Sculpture of the Greeks: With . . . an Essay on Grace in Works of Art* (Eng. tr., 1787) an empirical demonstration of the effectiveness of aesthetic education. Over the centuries Greek art humanized Greek culture. It did not do this with propaganda. Rather, the art of each generation became a little more human and graceful because of the examples provided by earlier artists. As art became more human and graceful, the society that was exposed to the art became more humane and civil.

This is a dynamic interpretation of Kantian ideas. Schiller rejected the essentially aesthetic content inherent in concepts like "organic unity" and "irony" and "tension," and substituted for it the idea of beauty as something that is constantly changing and evolving and, in the process, becoming more and more human. His view of the power of art to civilize is similar to and entirely compatible with Horace's remarks in the *Art* about the benign effects of poetry on Greek culture.

Armed, as he believed, with empirical evidence, Schiller devoted his *Letters* to showing that modern art can gradually civilize and humanize modern European culture. But—and the point cannot be emphasized too strongly—it can perform this function only in a condition of freedom. To compel it to create examples of virtue being rewarded and vice being punished is to make it into propaganda and to rob it of its civilizing power. Art for art's sake is therefore the condition that allows art to be something more than a trivial recreation or a tool for social manipulation. The freedom of art contributes in a very specific way to social progress by contributing to the spread of the idea of freedom. The argument has persuaded many lovers of art, but it is also frequently (and violently) rejected. Many of its opponents argue that art should be "engaged" in the sense of actively promoting worthy causes. By the same token artists should be prevented by law from exploring improper subjects.

The apparent separation created by Kantian theory between the world as we can know it and "reality" in the sense of the *Ding an sich* leads to another controversy. Although Schiller was willing to accept this sort of exile from the real, a great many later philosophers, critics, and artists were not. A recurrent theme of nineteenth-century poetry is the desire to return to "nature"—interpreted as an otherwise unknowable reality—through intuitive artistic experiences called, in Wordsworth's phrase, "spots of time," or, in Joyce's phrase, "epiphanies." Without such experiences, is not man condemned to live in a world of fictions and masks?

Many other questions can be raised about the Kantian aesthetic, but it refuses to go away. It has, in fact, permanently changed the terms in which critical issues are framed. Much twentieth-century critical theory can be traced to continuing attempts to refine Kant or revise him or find an alternative theory that answers the questions he raises.

The Palace of Art

The *Poetria Nova* of Geoffrey of Vinsauf begins with the image of the poet as architect. The image glances in two directions—at the poet as a master craftsman and at the poet as a minor god engaged in a miniature version of Genesis. Alfred Tennyson begins his *Palace of Art* (1832) with the same image:

> I built myself a lordly pleasure-house,
>   Wherein at ease for aye to dwell.
> I said, "O Soul, make merry and carouse,
>   Dear Soul, for all is well."

Tennyson's palace is the work of a master craftsman but it is not a miniature version of the world of divine creation. Instead it is a refuge from the world—a symbol of the isolation of the artist implicit in the philosophy of art for art's sake as Tennyson understood it. Keats put the idea of art for art's sake in a much quoted aphorism in *Endymion*: "Beauty is truth, truth beauty. That is all/ You know on earth, and all you need to know." Is it? Tennyson suggests that by rejecting "purpose" and requiring that the pursuit of beauty be disinterested, the artist builds what looks like a palace but is actually a prison.

Much of the poem expresses the pride of the poet-architect in workmanship: "I built it firm" (l. 9). There are loving descriptions of dragon fountains, galleries opening on distant views, stained glass windows, pleasantly gloomy corridors, a picture gallery, and the like. The imagery is specific and sensuous. Tennyson's palace contains symbols and representations of every possible human activity, including several "wise men" who turn out to be poets: Milton, Shakespeare, Dante, Homer. It is a little world but it is a dead world, a triumph of "art" in the Horatian sense of being the result of conscious artistic technique.

The Lady of Tennyson's palace is identified as the poet's soul. She will live "apart" in her palace while the world "runs round and round." She is pleased: "Trust me, in bliss I shall abide/ In this great mansion" (ll. 18–19). Later she revels in her "godlike isolation" (l. 197). Eventually, however, the delights of isolation fade. After three years the Lady feels "exiled from eternal God" (l. 263) and "utterly confused with fears" (l. 269). At the end of the fourth year,

> She threw her royal robes away.
> "Make me a cottage in the vale," she said,
> "Where I may mourn and pray." (l. 290–92)

Keats's *Ode on a Grecian Urn* contrasts the cold immortality of art with the passion of human love, and his *Eve of St. Agnes* tells the story of how two lovers escape from a castle that looks suspiciously like an earlier version of Tennson's palace. Tennyson's palace, however, is explicitly concerned with art, and the message it ultimately delivers is that art for art's sake leads to spiritual death. Or is the Palace of Art the imagination itself, trapped in its fictions and forever separated from reality? Evidently not. Tennyson was not much of a philosopher, and he strongly endorsed the hardy nineteenth-century credo that "the Godlike life is with man and for man." No escape is possible from the world created by the Kantian imagination. It is the only world there is. However, Tennyson's Lady is not hopelessly trapped in the palace; she proves this by escaping from it. The palace is definitely "of art" not "of imagination," and escaping from it is a good thing. Yes, but . . . The escape has just a hint of ambivalence. In the last stanza of the poem, in spite of the fact that the Lady has taken up residence in "a cottage in the vale," she commands, "pull not down my palace towers . . . perchance I may return" (ll. 293–96).

There are no direct Horatian reminiscences in *The Palace of Art*, but there are Horatian themes. The artist as craftsman is both Horatian and central to nineteenth-century American and French strains of symbolism. The Horatian requirement that poetry delight is honored by Tennyson's varied and sensual descriptions of the palace and its furnishings. The central argument of the poem is also Horatian: delight cannot be separated from profit. Schiller felt that art becomes socially useful because it is delightful in itself, like a game. Tennyson felt that delighting and profiting are separate activities. In *The Palace of Art* delight for its own sake is associated with enervating self-indulgence, profit with human contact and "mourning and praying."

Are delighting and profiting complementary or separate and to a degree antithetical? The answer suggested by Horace's story of how Amphion and Orpheus charmed the savage world with beautiful songs might justify arguing that Schiller is closer to Horace than Tennyson. On the other hand, Tennyson's robust emphasis on life "with man and for man" seems close to the frank desire for social reform that runs through Horatian satire, and Tennyson's celebration of England's past and Victoria's reign has obvious resemblances to Horace's celebration of Rome and Augustus. The fact is that in the nineteenth century the Horatian formula can be interpreted in quite different ways with equal validity, which is another way of saying that modern difficulties in interpreting the *Art* arise partly because readers understand it in the only way they can—in the context of their own theories of art.

Paul Verlaine's *Art poétique* (1874) announces its parallel to Horace's *Art* in its title. It is short enough to be quoted in full:

> Music before everything,
> And for music use the uneven number of syllables,
> Vaguer than other rhymes, more subtle in air,
> And nothing in it that weighs down or alights.
>   Moreover, you must not go
> Choosing your words without some scorn:
> Nothing is dearer than the gray song
> Where the Imprecise and the Precise are joined.
>   It is like fair eyes behind veils,
> Or the great trembling light of noon,
> Or, in a warm autumn sky,
> The blue confusion of clear stars.
>   For we still want Nuance,
> Not color, only Nuance!
> Oh! Nuance alone links
> The dream to the dream and the flute to the horn.
>   Flee far away from murderous Jest.
> Cruel wit and the impure laugh
> That makes the eyes of the Azure weep
> —And all such low-kitchen garlic.
>   Take eloquence and wring its neck!
> You will do well, while you are about it,
> To tame rhyme a little:
> Without some control, where won't it go.
>   O who will tell the wrongs done to Rhyme!

What heedless child, or what wild, black savage
Has forged for us this penny gem
That sounds false and hollow under the file?
Music again and always!
And let your verse be the thing in flight
That one senses fleeing from a soul as it goes
Toward other skies to other loves.
Let your verse be the lucky find
Scattered on the crisp wind of morning
That goes stirring the scent of mint and thyme . . .
And all the rest is literature.

(Verlaine, cited in O.B. Hardison, Jr., ed.,
Modern Continental Literary Criticism
[New York, 1962], 175-76)

Like Horace, Verlaine uses a speaker who sets out rules for poetry. Poetry is described in the Horatian manner—which is also the manner of the symbolists—as a precise craft. Horace associates music with lyric and drama. Verlaine also considers musicality a fundamental value in poetry. Horace explains how certain meters were associated with certain genres. Verlaine explains that musicality is produced in French poetry by lines with an uneven syllable count such as seven or nine, which happens to be the syllable count of the line used in *L'Art poétique*. Later, Verlaine comments on a prosodic element unknown to Horace— rhyme. His comments emphasize the fact that the music of verse comes from language and not from the trivial device ("penny gem") of rhyme. Although rhyme is associated with barbarism because it was invented during the middle ages, French poets generally use it—in fact, *L'Art poétique* has an "a-b-b-a" rhyme scheme. The solution is given in a Horatian metaphor: eliminate whatever sounds "hollow and false under the file." In all these respects, Verlaine's poem is remarkably close to the model announced by its title. The poem might be called "notes taken while reading Horace."

There are also differences. When Horace discusses diction the emphasis is on *Latinitas*—clear and graceful Latin. Although his odes are often suggestive in almost the manner outlined by Verlaine, his rules for the Pisos emphasize clarity. Verlaine, on the other hand, wants the poet's language to strike a balance between the precise and the suggestive like the eyes of a woman behind a veil. Horace would, however, have approved of Verlaine's prohibition of coarse language and low humor—he said much the same thing about the Satyr Play.

The famous advice "Take eloquence and wring its neck!" ("Prends l'éloquence et tords-lui son cou!") refers to conventional poetic style. "Eloquence" is a reminder that the romantics considered rhetoric a prime source of arbitrary rules and conventions of language. Eloquence is its highest goal. Horace would not have understood Verlaine's line for the simple reason that he thought of rhetoric not as the art of inflated language but the art of speaking well. Eloquence is a term of praise, not abuse. Beyond the term, however, it is clear that Horace objected to formulas and clichés in writing. That is why he advises against purple patches, elegant but digressive descriptions, and bombastic dialogue (ll. 97-98).

Finally, Horace's artist works for every effect achieved, and no "lucky finds" are mentioned in the *Art*. Verlaine is closer in his comments on serendipity in writing to Longinus than to Horace. Verlaine's parting shot is both ironic and truly Horatian. Only the very best poetry merits being called poetry. The rest is classified with those dreary and forgotten works called "literature" that gather dust on library shelves. The terms are different but the message is the same: "Neither men nor gods nor booksellers allow poets to be mediocre" (ll. 372-73).

VI

୨୦୯୦୯୦୨

Notes Toward a Supreme Fiction
by
Wallace Stevens

Introduction and Commentary

Wallace Stevens and Twentieth-Century Aesthetic

For Wallace Stevens (1879–1955), the issues raised by Kantian aesthetic were not only the basis for understanding the nature of poetry and the poet's function, they were the proper subject of poetry itself. His early poetry enacts the flamboyant play of the imagination, and it creates its baroque palaces of art. Time and time again the poems celebrate themselves in much the same way that a fugue is, above all, a celebration of the possibilities of the fugue form.

During the 1930s many critics wondered aloud if Stevens had not cut himself off from the grim political realities of his age. The criticism was particularly strong from the political left, but even mainstream critics were often uncomfortable. Stevens published little between 1935 and 1942. The Second World War began in 1939, and America entered the war on December 7, 1941. The world had suddenly plunged into an enormous war over moral values. Was there a place at such a time for "art for art's sake"? Stevens insisted that there was. Replying to a question from his friend Hi Simons in a letter written in February 1942 he wrote: "About social obligation: It is simply a question of whether poetry is a thing in itself, or whether it is not. I think it is. I don't think it is if it is detached from reality, but it has a free choice, or should have. There is no obligation that it shall attach itself to a political reality, social or sociological reality, etc." (*Letters*, ed. Holly Stevens [1966], 403).

Stevens means that the poet is most responsible—most himself—when he is making the best art he can. He has no obligation to write propaganda for or against any political or social or religious group. If doing so requires that he falsify his direct intuitions of the way things are, then instead of being responsible he is betraying his art. To extend the

point a little, since it is difficult—especially in wartime—to resist the
pressure to support urgent political and social issues, resistance takes
courage. The poet who resists is, in a sense, heroic. Since by resisting,
he is committing himself to the best understanding he can have of things
as they are, he can be considered a hero of the real.

Notes Toward a Supreme Fiction was written in the spring of 1942.
As far as the war was concerned 1942 was bloody and uncertain, although in retrospect it can be seen as the turning point for the allied
cause. *Notes* makes only the most general references to the war but
must be read with this background in mind. It brings together many of
the tensions that Stevens was feeling about the role of the poet, and it
attempts to resolve them by reaffirming the independence of the poet
even in time of war. Does the independence serve any useful purpose?
Here the idea of aesthetic education first proposed in Schiller's *Letters
on the Aesthetic Education of Man* becomes relevant. Poetry is a powerful civilizing force—an alternative to the doomed efforts of politics to
impose freedom on man by force. However, it cannot do its work if it
sells out to politics or becomes just another kind of politics. This position is the basis of Stevens's defense of poetry in *Notes*.

Whether or not the use of a persona was suggested by Horace's *Art*,
Notes demonstrates the continuing vitality of the most basic Horatian
tradition, the idea that the best way to write about poetry is in verse.
Writing in a poetic rather than a discursive form allows Stevens to be
playful, oblique, apparently contradictory, epigrammatic, pungent, and
objective and personal by turns. Released in the discussion of poetry
from the rigid logical organization of the *techne* or "treatise," the comment can be as tentative and challenging as poetry itself. Stevens wrote
several essays on poetry and the imagination. The best are readily available in his collection titled *The Necessary Angel* (1951). All his essays
are suggestive and associative. Although they are "essays," they want to
be poems. *Notes Toward a Supreme Fiction* is their fulfillment. It is
what they all aspire to and would be if they were not hostages to the
circumstances under which they were written. In this sense, *Notes* is
more truly in the Horatian tradition than the poems on poetry of Geoffrey of Vinsauf or Boileau or Pope, all of which are essentially well organized essays or *technai* in verse. It is also more Horatian than Byron's
English Bards, which is closer to a tirade of abuse than a poetic meditation on poetry. Byron has all the answers. Like Horace's speaker, the
speaker in *Notes* is genuinely in search of answers to his questions.

Notes is a difficult poem and a complete reading cannot be offered here. The present emphasis will be on basic themes and on points of contact and divergence from Horace's *Art*. There are numerous aids for the reader who wants to explore it further. To begin with, Stevens himself wrote more about its contents than about any of his other poems. Five long letters to Hi Simons explain its images and symbolism (*Letters*, 426–27, 430, 433–34, 437–38, 444–45). There are also numerous "readings" of the poem in books that have been written about Stevens's poetry. A good introduction is provided by Ronald Sukenick in *Wallace Stevens: Musing the Obscure* [1967], 136–63), which should be supplemented by the chapter on *Notes* in Helen Vendler's *On Extended Wings* [1969], 168–205). Several other, more recent readings are listed in the Bibliography at the end of this volume.

The difficulties of *Notes* recall the difficulties of Horace's *Art*. First among these is the problem of organization. Horace's *Art* looks simple at first glance; the more it is examined, the more perplexing the organization (if one exists) becomes. In the same way *Notes* looks at first like a paragon of organization. In fact, the organization is an allusion to Dante's hyper-organized *Divine Comedy*. *Notes* is in three parts, each part having ten stanzas and each stanza having three lines. There is also an epilogue, so that the sum is 31 units rather than 30. The *Divine Comedy* has an introductory canto plus three books of 33 cantos each, making 100 rather than 99 (3 × 33 + 1).

Stevens was, among other things, a very playful poet, and he was doubtless pleased with the playful contrast between Dante's celebration of eternal verities and his own comment on man's all-too-human limitations. *Notes* intentionally parodies the hyper-organization suggested by its numerology. Dante's tercets are in *terza rima*; Stevens's are almost, but not quite, unrhymed. "Not quite" is part of the game. There is a slovenly memory of Dante in occasional lines that rhyme in the form "a-b-a." Slovenly rhyme is complemented by the slovenly wilderness of themes that Stevens emphasizes by the word *Notes*. He explained to Hi Simons, "It is only when you try to systematize the poems in the NOTES that you conclude that it is not the statement of a philosophic theory. A philosopher is never at rest unless he is systematizing: constructing a theory. But these are Notes; the nucleus of the matter is contained in the title. It is implicit in the title that there can be no such thing as a supreme fiction. . . . The NOTES are a miscellany" (*Letters*, 430).

Notes are notes, the reverse of system. But the mere fact that they are notes means that they have been noted. They are fragments of the world brought together in an apparently elegantly organized form called "development" by Stevens that turns out on inspection to be closer to a bag for scraps. This is not accidental but the condition of the poem's success: "The first step toward a supreme fiction would be to get rid of all existing fictions. . . . But I very soon found out that, if I stuck closely to a development, I should lose all of the qualities that I really wanted to get into the thing" (*Letters*, 431).

The parallel to Horace's *Art* has the effect of making Horace more interesting. His rejection of the neat organization of the standard "art," or *techne*, can be understood as the strategy of a skeptic for whom the traditional verities have lost their certainty. It is the strategy of a poet disillusioned with the official culture of Augustan Rome and aware that the old pieties had been radically undercut by an academic skepticism according to which nothing is true and everything is a fiction to be evaluated in terms of its probability. In Stevens's *Notes* it is the strategy of a poet who rejects even the possibility of a supreme truth so that a supreme fiction is all that is left. The strategy of the earlier work is clarified by the strategies of the later.

R. P. Blackmur equates the idea of a supreme fiction with Platonic ideas (*Wallace Stevens: The Critical Heritage*, ed. Charles Doyle [1985], 218). In the *Republic* divine ideas are real. Their material embodiments in the world are imitations of ideas and hence less real, and artistic imitations of material embodiments are more unreal still. They fully merit being described as fictions—even, as Socrates has it, as lies of the sort poets tell. Stevens offers a more severe idealism. Although Stevens refers the idealism to Descartes, it is a Kantian sort of idealism, according to which the very act of imagination that makes the world possible makes it a fiction. There are no Platonic ideas in this system and consequently no possibility of a "real" world behind the actual one. The world is a fiction, but it is a necessary fiction because we cannot get along without it. Is there a supreme fiction, a fiction more fundamental, deeper, more essential than other fictions? Is the idea of God a supreme fiction? *Notes* raises these questions and answers them almost—but not quite—in the negative.

One of the things *Notes* is "about" is the constant grasping of the mind for a supreme fiction, only to be forced by its own success into accepting a present fiction. We seek the ultimate, and find ourselves watching an ordinary sunset in New Haven at 6:00 P.M. or a blackbird, or one of thirteen (or two hundred) possible blackbirds. Stevens wrote to Hi Simons in 1940, "If one no longer believes in God (as truth), it is not possible merely to disbelieve; it becomes necessary to believe in something else. Logically, I ought to believe in essential imagination, but that has its difficulties. It is easier to believe in a thing created by the imagination. A good deal of my poetry recently has been concerned with an identity for that thing. . . . In one of my poems ['Asides on the Oboe'] I say that one's final belief must be in a fiction. I think that the history of belief will show that it has always been a fiction" (*Letters*, 370). A useful parallel to this idea is Edward Harrison's *Masks of the Universe* (1984), which is the meditation of a physicist on the fact that each age "explains" the world by draping it with a different mask. Each of the masks is thought to be the revelation of the truth behind the appearance of things but each is discarded as science progresses.

Mythological astronomy (Apollo, the sun god; the zodiac) gives way to Ptolemaic astronomy (earth at the center, the sun and the planets rotating in spheres around it), which gives way to the Copernican system (the sun at the center, earth and the planets in orbit around it), which gives way to the open, galactic universe, which gives way to cosmos bounded by curved space-time, which . . . And so forth. Harrison's conclusion is that man never knows anything but masks, and that is remarkably close to a scientist's version of Stevens's concept of necessary fictions.

Stevens's determination to imitate nature in the sense of the truth of the human situation as far as it is known contributes to the difficulty of *Notes*, just as the determination to imitate the ways people speak and think in real life makes James Joyce's *Ulysses* difficult. But it is nature that is the object of art in general and the object of Stevens's poem in particular. The speaker uses the fragment, the occasional opaque symbol, the enigmatic statement to suggest the elusiveness of nature. If some things in the poem baffle, some things in nature are also baffling. Nature is the "fat girl" and the "mondo" of the poem and is larger than all theories of nature.

The headings of the poem's three sections are useful signposts in the same way that names on a map—"Carson City" or "Mobile"—are useful. They say where, in general, a place is, but they give no idea of what is in the place. Part I claims that "It must be abstract." The statement is an assertion of fact, not an exhortation: "A supreme fiction can only be abstract." That is, the original, ur-conception of the world must have been a conception created by combining the most primitive and undifferentiated data—an objective concept with almost no spiritual element—with the categories of an imagination that still has no sense of self or of prior experience. The speaker symbolizes the first experiences of nature with images that are primitive in their simplicity and materiality: the sun or a rock on the one hand; a "major man"—that is, the idea of a god like the sun-god Phoebus Apollo—on the other.

As ever richer streams of data are absorbed by the imagination from Stevens's equivalent to the *Ding an sich*, the world and the perceiver both become more complex. They "change." Just as part I of the poem recalls the static polarities of Kant, part II recalls the dynamic operation of these polarities in history as explained by Schiller. Hence the title of the second section, "It [the supreme fiction] must change." Like designs seen in a child's kaleidoscope, the change is inherently pleasing. This leads to part III, "It must please." The phrase does not mean "It should please," but "Of necessity, it pleases." "It" pleases because it is the variety and color and life in the world. It is a necessary fiction, and perhaps it is also the supreme fiction since it is the only fiction there is.

Stevens's persona is unlike the abusive speaker of Byron's *English Bards* but strikingly like the speaker of Horace's *Art.* In the first section he is quietly superior. He speaks like a teacher and addresses a listener whom he calls "ephebe," meaning "learner" or "apprentice"—especially an apprentice-soldier. Like Horace's comments to the Pisos, his comments tend to be in the third person, to things and events that are safely contained in the objective world.

In part II the tone becomes more autobiographical and engaged. The "he" often seems to be a fictional version of the speaker. Little narratives are offered—the story of the statue of General Du Puy, the sparrow's cry, the marriage preparations of Nanzia Nunzio. The listener is no longer an ephebe but "my companion, my fellow, my self" (II.4).

In part III the tone changes again. The speaker shifts to the first person ("We drank Meursault," III.5; "What am I to believe?" III.8; "I can do," III.9; "I find . . . I am . . . I think . . . I call," III.10). The speaker is no longer giving a lecture but sharing his own thoughts and emotions. The listener is not referred to or else has become equated, in the last canto, with the "you" of "I call you by name, my fluent mundo" (III.10).

In the third section of the *Art* Horace's speaker also drops the mask of impersonality to announce that he has given up poetry, and the *Art* ends with the speaker trying to escape a leechlike poet. In the epilogue of *Notes* the ephebe, the apprentice-soldier, has become a real soldier fighting a real war. The speaker no longer lectures him but asks for his understanding. The speaker is a poet who must fight an endless war of his own. Poet and soldier are in a sense engaged in the same struggle. It is not necessarily a happy view of the world, but it is a more affirmative one than the one offered at the end of Horace's *Art*.

Abstraction—Change—Pleasure

The poem begins with a dedication to Henry Church. Church was a friend of many years and publisher of the French journal *Mesures*, in which Stevens published translations of several of his poems. At the beginning of the Second World War, Church and his wife were in the United States. Church corresponded at length with Stevens about beginning an American journal comparable to *Mesures*, or supporting an existing journal like John Crowe Ransom's *Kenyon Review*, or supporting a lecture series. He eventually chose the last alternative and invited Stevens to present a lecture—which turned out to be *The Noble Rider and the Sound of Words*. Stevens insisted that the lines following the dedication do *not* refer to Church. If not, they must refer to "the supreme fiction." It is the idea of a supreme fiction for which Stevens or the speaker of the poem feels "love" and with which he communes "for a moment in the central of our being."

The first section of the poem is "It Must Be Abstract." For all its complexities, the section is based on the opposition of objective and subjective. Stevens begins with the objective side of the equation. How might we imagine the first intuition of the world to a mind that has no preconceptions? As the sun, Stevens decides. He is recalling the near-universality of sun-worship in primitive religion; also the appropriateness of the sun—burning, brilliant, simple, absolute—as a symbol of the real before the complexity of reality can be imagined.

Whether his skepticism comes from Lucretius or Nietzsche, the speaker is convinced that god is dead: "Phoebus is dead, ephebe. But Phoebus was/ A name for something that never could be named." That leaves the sun, which has no name, even though, with sly irony, the speaker names it: "gold flourisher." The second canto turns from the world to the mind. Does the act of naming banish truth, making it "The hermit in the poet's metaphors"? The axioms of the first part of *Notes* have now been laid down. Comments on the tension between the mind and the world follow. According to Genesis, Adam named the animals with divine aid: "The first idea was not our own," says the speaker. Adam was inspired by God. But to name is to falsify. Adam is thus "the father of Descartes"; that is, the father of the philosopher who split experience into subject and object, mind and world. The central cantos of the poem explore the middle ground between the objective and the subjective. Animals symbolize the raw vitality of the objective, while the ephebe, clutching a pillow under a mansard roof, struggles to control the world in the sense of imitating it in art. The effort is "heroic"—an anticipation of the theme of the poet as hero in Stevens's epilogue.

The focus of the first part changes with canto VI from the "objective" to the subjective. The idea of a larger order of things, which is associated with "giants" and gods, is contrasted with human experience, which is associated with being mesmerized by the charm of the everyday world. During "moments of awakening"—that is, moments of extremely clear perception—theories about the order of things become irrelevant, like academies dissolving into mist. What Stevens calls "moments" resemble Wordsworth's "spots of time" and Joyce's "epiphanies."

In canto VIII Viollet-le-Duc, a famous designer of fake Gothic churches, is associated with a "castle-fortress-home." The parallel to Tennyson's *Palace of Art* may be unintentional, but it is illuminating. Stevens is talking about the palace of art created by the imagination.

Can we create such an imposing fake building, Stevens asks, and put somebody named MacCullough into it? That is, can we imagine that this wonderful Gothic cathedral of a world was created by ordinary people? Isn't something higher required? This leads to an exploration of the human and subjective side of experience. The speaker imagines two MacCulloughs. One is an ordinary man; the other is a "major man" who is venerated as though he were a kind of deity enshrined in the cathedral. Stevens disliked the philosophy that makes man the measure of all things—what he calls "humanism." Humanism elevates man to godlike status, the status of "major man." Stevens explains in one of his letters, "MacCullough is any name, any man. The trouble with humanism is that man as God remains man, but there is an extension of man, the leaner being, in fiction" (*Letters*, 434). The enshrined Mac-

Cullough is less interesting ("leaner") than the real MacCullough "loung-ing by the sea,/ Drowned in its washes" (I.8).

Is the idea of god the result of self-deification ("apotheosis," I.9)? The speaker rejects the suggestion. The origin of religion is more com-plicated than the neat equations of humanism and "reasons click-clack." Stevens's term for god is "Major man." Major man rises out of history, "the foundling of the infected past." Stevens seems to have Christ and the doctrine of original sin ("infected past") in mind. Whether or not this is the case, major man is the product of man's deepest emotions: "the hot of him is purest in the heart."

As true religion is exiled from modern society by humanism, "Major man" is forced to become an outsider in "slouching pantaloons, beyond the town." In spite of being exiled, he remains powerful. "It is of him, ephebe, to confect/ The final elegance." "Major man" is also the artist in a society contemptuous of the values of art. Reduced to a parody in clown's clothes, "The man/ in that old coat" still produces the ulti-mate elegance, the world. He does not explain so much as present it: "Not to console/ Nor sanctify, but plainly to propound."

The second section of Notes sets the polarities of the part I in mo-tion. Subjective and objective constantly interact in the mind. There is a festive air, because the interaction has the fascination of a game. There are Italian girls with "jonquils in their hair," bees happily occu-pied with the business of be-ing. Contrasts are set up between figures who connote permanence and figures who ignore it—the president who ordains (II.2), the statue of General Du Puy, who was "rubbish in the end" (II.3), man and woman, north and south (II.4). The imagery turns from dominance and permanence to wild orange trees, scraggy trees weighted with "garbled green," a pineapple "pungent as Cuban sum-mer" (II.5).

Efforts to exert control over all this are as silly as the chatter of wrens asserting control of the real ("bethou me in my glade"). All such efforts fail. Assertions of control are "minstrels lacking minstrelsy" (II.6). They give way to images of love. The mind is more than a frame for the world, it is a lover of the world, perhaps a lover of the nature that is beyond the world. This is what gives the ignorant man "courage" and the scholar "heat" (II.7). The world appears in canto 8 as a bride trem-bling with passion for the lover who will be "precious" for the lover's perfecting (II.8). Ozymandias, whose statue symbolizes efforts to con-trol the world, becomes a symbol of impermanence.

The world is concealed under human motives. In spite of the passion of her lovers, "The bride/ Is never naked" (II.8). We come to poetry. Poetry seeks to represent the real in all its unimaginable variety. It tries to compound "the imagination's Latin," which is the theory of the real, with "the lingua franca et jocundissima," which is the "gibberish"—the outrageous and slovenly language of the everyday world—that overwhelms all efforts to understand it. For those who accept the limits of understanding, the world becomes music, a gathering of saints, a brilliant, always changing mosaic. The images that seem to rise out of it are reflections of the imagination that finds them:

> The freshness of the world. It is our own,
> It is ourselves, the freshness of ourselves,
> And that necessity and that presentation
>   Are rubbings of a glass in which we peer. (II.10)

Finally "It must give pleasure." The third section of *Notes* is filled with playful and outrageous imagery. As Kantian theory argues, the pleasure of art consists in our discovery in it of what was put there in the process of imagining it. This section of *Notes* enacts the process of pleasurable discovery. It is an effort to see and "to catch from that/ Irrational moment its unreasoning" (III.1). The "blue woman" is identified by Stevens in his *Letters* (444) as "probably the weather of a Sunday morning early last April when I wrote this." She casts a lacy, bluish shade on everything around her just as the light of a Paris evening affects the human figures in an Impressionist painting.

Bawda and the Captain are opposites, like world and imagination. Their wedding expresses contentment with where they are: "The marriage-place/ Was what they loved. It was neither heaven nor hell./ They were love's characters come face to face" (III.4). The emphasis is on uncomplicated pleasure in the here and now. Canon Aspirin, "the man who has explored all projections of the mind" (*Letters*, 445), abandons his theories to feast on lobster Bombay with mango chutney. His delight in his sister and her two daughters emerges as music—"a fugue of praise." When the Canon sleeps he dreams of children and stars and finally reaches the end of thought. He could choose nothingness, but he chooses "the whole/ The complicate, the amassing harmony." In his dream he recreates the world in a more seemly order (III.5–7). Yet the act is an imposing of order, and imposing is a kind of exclusion: "To impose is not to discover." The world should not mean but be. Ideally, we should happen on it without having thought about it and thus distorted it:

> Not to impose, not to have reasoned at all,
> Out of nothing to have come on major weather,
>   It is possible, possible, possible. It must
> Be possible. It must be that in time
> The real will from its crude compoundings come. (III.7)

The yearning for an impossible real-ization of the world pushes the speaker toward the idea of a divine view of the world. The speaker imagines an angel "serenely gazing at the violent abyss" (III.8). The image is one of many references in the poem to religious faith. Is there a higher knowledge of the world, a supreme truth in contrast to a supreme fiction? The speaker remains skeptical. The angel is a product of imagination, not a separate being but a part of him: "Is it he or is it I that experience this?" (III.8). Whatever the answer, the angel experiences bliss contemplating the world, and the speaker shares that bliss: "I can/ Do all that angels can. I enjoy like them" (III.9).

The title of the third section of *Notes* is "It Must Give Pleasure." The passage on the angel enacts the process of deriving pleasure from the highest fiction that the mind can make of the world. Even this fiction, however, is not a supreme fiction. The section ends with a hymn to a world that is always larger than the imagination can imagine. It is a "fat girl" who should be named "flatly" (the pun is part of the general playfulness of this section of the poem) but who remains "more than a natural figure." The speaker comes back to the questions of how the world is created in the imagination and why it is so beguiling. He thinks for a moment that there may be an explanation: "They will get it straight one day at the Sorbonne," and when that happens the irrational will be rational. The contradiction is ironic. Adam's naming of things in the Garden of Eden is recalled throughout the poem. It is an attempt to fix the eternal change of nature. When the irrational is rational, says the speaker, he will be able to name the "green . . . fluent mundo" like a second Adam. It is an ambivalent miracle. Once it is named, the world will stop changing and be dead: "You will have stopped revolving except in crystal" (III.10).

The epilogue to *Notes* seems to be in a key different from that of the poem itself. According to Helen Vendler it is "something of an anticlimax" (*On Extended Wings*, 205). That is true only if the context of the poem is ignored. *Notes* was written by a poet concerned about the ideal of pure poetry at a time when voices on every side were insisting that the poet in general, and Stevens in particular, should be committed to a cause. Stevens had to ask himself whether the profession of poetry was still a worthy one in view of the sacrifice being made by soldiers who were fighting with guns and lives rather than words.

The epilogue is spoken to the ephebe, who has grown up and become a soldier. It is an apologia and also an affirmation. The poet's profession has its own risks and its own heroism and makes its own contribution to the social order. Stevens is concerned here with the profit side of Horace's formula, and he takes a position like that taken by Schiller in his *Letters on the Aesthetic Education of Man*. Poetry does not support established values. Rather, it creates values, and these values give meaning to life. The creation is a kind of war between mind and sky, world and imagination. It never ends because conditions are always changing. Stevens asserts that the poet and the soldier are alike. Both are fighting to preserve civilization. The soldier encounters the poet's words "in a book in a barrack, a letter from Malay" ("Epilogue"). The words help the soldier understand his war and define for him the meaning of heroism. By creating necessary fictions, the poet creates the possibility of nobility:

> How simply the fictive hero becomes the real;
> How gladly with proper words the soldier dies,
> If he must, or lives on the bread of faithful speech.
>
> ("Epilogue")

The mood recalls one of Horace's best-known lines: "It is sweet and proper to die for one's country" (Dulce et decorum est/ pro patria more). In both Horace and Stevens the idea of decorum unites political values and lyric poetry; but Stevens has the benefit of a more powerful symbol. Horace would have understood "Vergilian cadences," but he would have been baffled by Stevens's concluding image because it refers to the Eucharist. In addition to the reality of an honorable death, the poet's words lead to the communion of citizens in "the bread of faithful speech."

Notes Toward a Supreme Fiction

To Henry Church

And for what, except for you, do I feel love?
Do I press the extremest book of the wisest man
Close to me, hidden in me day and night?
In the uncertain light of single, certain truth,
Equal in living changingness to the light
In which I meet you, in which we sit at rest,
For a moment in the central of our being,
The vivid transparence that you bring is peace.

I. *It Must Be Abstract*

I.1.

Begin, ephebe, by perceiving the idea
Of this invention, this invented world,
The inconceivable idea of the sun.
      You must become an ignorant man again
And see the sun again with an ignorant eye
And see it clearly in the idea of it.
      Never suppose an inventing mind as source
Of this idea nor for that mind compose
A voluminous master folded in his fire.
      How clean the sun when seen in its idea,   10
Washed in the remotest cleanliness of a heaven
That has expelled us and our images . . .
      The death of one god is the death of all.
Let purple Phoebus lie in umber harvest,
Let Phoebus slumber and die in autumn umber,
      Phoebus is dead, ephebe. But Phoebus was
A name for something that never could be named.

There was a project for the sun and is.
    There is a project for the sun. The sun
Must bear no name, gold flourisher, but be   20
In the difficulty of what it is to be.

I.2.

    It is the celestial ennui of apartments
That sends us back to the first idea, the quick
Of this invention; and yet so poisonous
    Are the ravishments of truth, so fatal to
The truth itself, the first idea becomes
The hermit in a poet's metaphors,
    Who comes and goes and comes and goes all day.
May there be an ennui of the first idea?
What else, prodigious scholar, should there be?
    The monastic man is an artist. The philosopher   10
Appoints man's place in music, say, today.
But the priest desires. The philosopher desires.
    And not to have is the beginning of desire.
To have what is not is its ancient cycle.
It is desire at the end of winter, when
    It observes the effortless weather turning blue
And sees the myosotis on its bush.
Being virile, it hears the calendar hymn.
    It knows that what it has is what is not
And throws it away like a thing of another time,   20
As morning throws off stale moonlight and shabby sleep.

I.3.

    The poem refreshes life so that we share,
For a moment, the first idea . . . It satisfies
Belief in an immaculate beginning
    And sends us, winged by an unconscious will,
To an immaculate end. We move between these points:
From that ever-early candor to its late plural
    And the candor of them is the strong exhilaration
Of what we feel from what we think, of thought
Beating in the heart, as if blood newly came,
    An elixir, an excitation, a pure power.   10

The poem, through candor, brings back a power again
That gives a candid kind to everything.
    We say: At night an Arabian in my room,
With his damned hoobla-hoobla-hoobla-how,
Inscribes a primitive astronomy
    Across the unscrawled fores the future casts
And throws his stars around the floor. By day
The wood-dove used to chant his hoobla-hoo
    And still the grossest iridescence of ocean
Howls hoo and rises and howls hoo and falls.   20
Life's nonsense pierces us with strange relation.

I.4.

    The first idea was not our own. Adam
In Eden was the father of Descartes
And Eve made air the mirror of herself,
    Of her sons and of her daughters. They found themselves
In heaven as in a glass; a second earth;
And in the earth itself they found a green—
    The inhabitants of a very varnished green.
But the first idea was not to shape the clouds
In imitation. The clouds preceded us
    There was a muddy centre before we breathed.   10
There was a myth before the myth began,
Venerable and articulate and complete.
    From this the poem springs: that we live in a place
That is not our own and, much more, not ourselves
And hard it is in spite of blazoned days.
    We are the mimics. Clouds are pedagogues
The air is not a mirror but bare board,
Coulisse bright-dark, tragic chiaroscuro
    And comic color of the rose, in which
Abysmal instruments make sounds like pips   20
Of the sweeping meanings that we add to them.

I.5.

    The lion roars at the enraging desert,
Reddens the sand with his red-colored noise,
Defies red emptiness to evolve his match,

Master by foot and jaws and by the mane,
Most supple challenger. The elephant
Breaches the darkness of Ceylon with blares,
   The glitter-goes on surfaces of tanks,
Shattering velvetest far-away. The bear,
The ponderous cinnamon, snarls in his mountain
   At summer thunder and sleeps through winter snow.   10
But you, ephebe, look from your attic window,
Your mansard with a rented piano. You lie
   In silence upon your bed. You clutch the corner
Of the pillow in your hand. You writhe and press
A bitter utterance from your writhing, dumb,
   Yet voluble dumb violence. You look
Across the roofs as sigil and as ward
And in your centre mark them and are cowed . . .
   These are the heroic children whom time breeds
Against the first idea—to lash the lion,   20
Caparison elephants, teach bears to juggle.

I.6.

   Not to be realized because not to
Be seen, not to be loved nor hated because
Not to be realized. Weather by Franz Hals,
   Brushed up by brushy winds in brushy clouds,
Wetted by blue, colder for white. Not to
Be spoken to, without a roof, without
   First fruits, without the virginal of birds,
The dark-blown ceinture loosened, not relinquished.
Gay is, gay was, the gay forsythia
   And yellow, yellow thins the Northern blue.   10
Without a name and nothing to be desired,
If only imagined but imagined well.
   My house has changed a little in the sun.
The fragrance of the magnolias comes close,
False flick, false form, but falseness close to kin.
   It must be visible or invisible,
Invisible or visible or both:
A seeing and unseeing in the eye.
   The weather and the giant of the weather,

Say the weather, the mere weather, the mere air: 20
An abstraction blooded, as a man by thought.

I.7.

It feels good as it is without the giant,
A thinker of the first idea. Perhaps
The truth depends on a walk around a lake,
    A composing as the body tires, a stop
To see hepatica, a stop to watch
A definition growing certain and
    A wait within that certainty, a rest
In the swags of pine-trees bordering the lake.
Perhaps there are times of inherent excellence,
    As when the cock crows on the left and all   10
Is well, incalculable balances,
At which a kind of Swiss perfection comes
    And a familiar music of the machine
Sets up its Schwärmerei, not balances
That we achieve but balances that happen,
    As a man and woman meet and love forthwith.
Perhaps there are moments of awakening,
Extreme, fortuitous, personal, in which
    We more than awaken, sit on the edge of sleep,
As on an elevation, and behold   20
The academies like structures in a mist.

I.8.

Can we compose a castle-fortress-home,
Even with the help of Viollet-le-Duc,
And set the MacCullough there as major man?
    The first idea is an imagined thing.
The pensive giant prone in violet space
May be the MacCullough, an expedient,
    Logos and logic, crystal hypothesis,
Incipit and a form to speak the word
And every latent double in the word,
    Beau linguist. But the MacCullough is MacCullough.   10
It does not follow that major man is man.
If MacCullough himself lay lounging by the sea,

Drowned in its washes, reading in the sound,
About the thinker of the first idea,
He might take habit, whether from wave or phrase,
   Or power of the wave, or deepened speech,
Or a leaner being, moving in on him,
Of greater aptitude and apprehension,
   As if the waves at last were never broken,
As if the language suddenly, with ease,   20
Said things it had laboriously spoken.

I.9.

The romantic intoning, the declaimed clairvoyance
Are parts of apotheosis, appropriate
And of its nature, the idiom thereof.
   They differ from reason's click-clack, its applied
Enflashings. But apotheosis is not
The origin of the major man. He comes,
   Compact in invincible foils, from reason,
Lighted at midnight by the studious eye,
Swaddled in revery, the object of
   The hum of thoughts evaded in the mind,   10
Hidden from other thoughts, he that reposes
On a breast forever precious for that touch,
   For whom the good of April falls tenderly,
Falls down, the cock-birds calling at the time.
My dame, sing for this person accurate songs.
   He is and may be but oh! he is, he is,
This foundling of the infected past, so bright,
So moving in the manner of his hand.
   Yet look not at his colored eyes. Give him
No names. Dismiss him from your images.   20
The hot of him is purest in the heart.

I.10.

The major abstraction is the idea of man
And major man is its exponent, abler
In the abstract than in his singular,
   More fecund as principle than particle,
Happy fecundity, flor-abundant force,

In being more than an exception, part,
  Though an heroic part, of the commonal.
The major abstraction is the commonal,
The inanimate, difficult visage. Who is it?
  What rabbi, grown furious with human wish,   10
What chieftain, walking by himself, crying
Most miserable, most victorious,
  Does not see these separate figures one by one,
And yet see only one, in his old coat,
His slouching pantaloons, beyond the town,
  Looking for what was, where it used to be?
Cloudless the morning. It is he. The man
In that old coat, those sagging pantaloons,
  It is of him, ephebe, to make, to confect
The final elegance, not to console   20
Nor sanctify, but plainly to propound.

II. *It Must Change*

II.1.

The old seraph, parcel-gilded, among violets
Inhaled the appointed odor, while the doves
Rose up like phantoms from chronologies.
  The Italian girls wore jonquils in their hair
And these the seraph saw, had seen long since,
In the bandeaux of the mothers, would see again.
  The bees came booming as if they had never gone,
As if hyacinths had never gone. We say
This changes and that changes. Thus the constant
  Violets, doves, girls, bees and hyacinths   10
Are inconstant objects of inconstant cause
In a universe of inconstancy. This means
  Night-blue is an inconstant thing. The seraph
Is satyr in Saturn, according to his thoughts.
It means the distaste we feel for this withered scene
  Is that it has not changed enough. It remains,
It is a repetition. The bees come booming
As if—The pigeons clatter in the air.

An erotic perfume, half of the body, half
Of an obvious acid is sure what it intends   20
And the booming is blunt, not broken in subtleties.

II.2.

The President ordains the bee to be
Immortal. The President ordains. But does
The body lift its heavy wing, take up,
    Again, an inexhaustible being, rise
Over the loftiest antagonist
To drone the green phrases of its juvenal?
    Why should the bee recapture a lost blague,
Find a deep echo in a horn and buzz
The bottomless trophy, new hornsman after old?
    The President has apples on the table   10
And barefoot servants round him, who adjust
The curtains to a metaphysical t
    And the banners of the nation flutter, burst
On the flag-poles in a red-blue dazzle, whack
At the halyards. Why, then, when in golden fury
    Spring vanishes the scraps of winter, why
Should there be a question of returning or
Of death in memory's dream? Is spring a sleep?
    This warmth is for lovers at last accomplishing
Their love, this beginning, not resuming, this   20
Booming and booming of the new-come bee.

II.3.

    The great statue of the General Du Puy
Rested immobile, though neighboring catafalques
Bore off the residents of its noble Place.
    The right, uplifted foreleg of the horse
Suggested that, at the final funeral,
The music halted and the horse stood still.
    On Sundays, lawyers in their promenades
Approached this strongly-heightened effigy
To study the past, and doctors, having bathed
    Themselves with care, sought out the nerveless frame   10
Of a suspension, a permanence, so rigid

That it made the General a bit absurd,
  Changed his true flesh to an inhuman bronze.
There never had been, never could be, such
A man. The lawyers disbelieved, the doctors
  Said that as keen, illustrious ornament,
As a setting for geraniums, the General,
The very Place Du Puy, in fact, belonged
  Among our more vestigial states of mind.
Nothing had happened because nothing had changed.   20
Yet the General was rubbish in the end.

II.4.

  Two things of opposite natures seem to depend
On one another, as a man depends
On a woman, day on night, the imagined
  On the real. This is the origin of change.
Winter and spring, cold copulars, embrace
And forth the particulars of rapture come.
  Music falls on the silence like a sense,
A passion that we feel, not understand.
Morning and afternoon are clasped together
  And North and South are an intrinsic couple   10
And sun and rain a plural, like two lovers
That walk away as one in the greenest body.

  In solitude the trumpets of solitude
Are not of another solitude resounding;
A little string speaks for a crowd of voices.
  The partaker partakes of that which changes him.
The child that touches takes character from the thing,
The body, it touches. The captain and his men
  Are one and the sailor and the sea are one.
Follow after, O my companion, my fellow, my self,   20
Sister and solace, brother and delight.

II.5.

  On a blue island in a sky-wide water
The wild orange trees continued to bloom and to bear,
Long after the planter's death. A few limes remained,
  Where his house had fallen, three scraggy trees weighted

With garbled green. These were the planter's turquoise
And his orange blotches, these were his zero green,
   A green baked greener in the greenest sun.
These were his beaches, his sea-myrtles in
White sand, his patter of the long sea-slushes.

   There was an island beyond him on which rested,   10
An island to the South, on which rested like
A mountain, a pineapple pungent as Cuban summer.

   And là-bas, là-bas, the cool bananas grew,
Hung heavily on the great banana tree,
Which pierces clouds and bends on half the world.

   He thought often of the land from which he came,
How that whole country was a melon, pink
If seen rightly and yet a possible red.

   An unaffected man in a negative light
Could not have borne his labor nor have died   20
Sighing that he should leave the banjo's twang.

II.6.

   Bethou me, said sparrow, to the crackled blade,
And you, and you, bethou me as you blow,
When in my coppice you behold me be.

   Ah, ké! the bloody wren, the felon jay,
Ké-ké, the jug-throated robin pouring out,
Bethou, bethou, bethou me in my glade.

   There was such idiot minstrelsy in rain,
So many clappers going without bells,
That these bethous compose a heavenly gong.

   One voice repeating, one tireless chorister,   10
The phrases of a single phrase, ké-ké,
A single text, granite monotony,

   One sole face, like a photograph of fate,
Glass-blower's destiny, bloodless episcopus,
Eye without lid, mind without any dream—

   These are of minstrels lacking minstrelsy,
Of an earth in which the first leaf is the tale
Of leaves, in which the sparrow is a bird

   Of stone, that never changes. Bethou him, you

And you, bethou him and bethou. It is   20
A sound like any other. It will end.

II.7.

After a lustre of the moon, we say
We have not the need of any paradise,
We have not the need of any seducing hymn.
    It is true. Tonight the lilacs magnify
The easy passion, the ever-ready love
Of the lover that lies within us and we breathe
    An odor evoking nothing, absolute.
We encounter in the dead middle of the night
The purple odor, the abundant bloom.
    The lover sighs as for accessible bliss,   10
Which he can take within him on his breath,
Possess in his heart, conceal and nothing known.
    For easy passion and ever-ready love
Are of our earthy birth and here and now
And where we live and everywhere we live,
    As in the top-cloud of a May night-evening,
As in the courage of the ignorant man,
Who chants by book, in the heat of the scholar, who writes
    The book, hot for another accessible bliss:
The fluctuations of certainty, the change   20
Of degrees of perception in the scholar's dark.

II.8.

On her trip around the world, Nanzia Nunzio
Confronted Ozymandias. She went
Alone and like a vestal long-prepared.
    I am the spouse. She took her necklace off
And laid it in the sand. As I am, I am
The spouse. She opened her stone-studded belt.
    I am the spouse, divested of bright gold
The spouse beyond emerald or amethyst,
Beyond the burning body that I bear.
    I am the woman stripped more nakedly   10
Than nakedness, standing before an inflexible

Order, saying I am the contemplated spouse.
  Speak to me that, which spoken, will array me
In its own only precious ornament.
Set on me the spirit's diamond coronal.
  Clothe me entire in the final filament,
So that I tremble with such love so known
And myself am precious for your perfecting.
  Then Ozymandias said the spouse, the bride
Is never naked. A fictive covering   20
Weaves always glistening from the heart and mind.

II.9.

  The poem goes from the poet's gibberish to
The gibberish of the vulgate and back again.
Does it move to and fro or is it of both
  At once? Is it a luminous flittering
Or the concentration of a cloudy day?
Is there a poem that never reaches words
  And one that chaffers the time away?
Is the poem both peculiar and general?
There's a meditation there, in which there seems
  To be an evasion, a thing not apprehended or   10
Not apprehended well. Does the poet
Evade us, as in a senseless element?
  Evade, this hot, dependent orator,
The spokesman at our bluntest barriers,
Exponent by a form of speech, the speaker
  Of a speech only a little of the tongue?
It is the gibberish of the vulgate that he seeks.
He tries by a peculiar speech to speak
  The peculiar potency of the general,
To compound the imagination's Latin with   20
The lingua franca et jocundissima.

II.10.

  A bench was his catalepsy, Theatre
Of Trope. He sat in the park. The water of
The lake was full of artificial things,
  Like a page of music, like an upper air,

Like a momentary color, in which swans
Were seraphs, were saints, were changing essences.
  The west wind was the music, the motion, the force
To which the swans curveted, a will to change,
A will to make iris frettings on the blank.
  There was a will to change, a necessitous   10
And present way, a presentation, a kind
Of volatile world, too constant to be denied,
  The eye of a vagabond in metaphor
That catches our own. The casual is not
Enough. The freshness of transformation is
  The freshness of a world. It is our own,
It is ourselves, the freshness of ourselves,
And that necessity and that presentation
  Are rubbings of a glass in which we peer.
Of these beginnings, gay and green, propose   20
The suitable amours. Time will write them down.

III. *It Must Give Pleasure*

III.1.

  To sing jubilas at exact, accustomed times,
To be crested and wear the mane of a multitude
And so, as part, to exult with its great throat,
  To speak of joy and to sing of it, borne on
The shoulders of joyous men, to feel the heart
That is the common, the bravest fundament,
  This is a facile exercise. Jerome
Begat the tubas and the fire-wind strings,
The golden fingers picking dark-blue air:
  For companies of voices moving there,   10
To find of sound the bleakest ancestor,
To find of light a music issuing
  Whereon it falls in more than sensual mode.
But the difficultest rigor is forthwith,
On the image of what we see, to catch from that
  Irrational moment its unreasoning,
As when the sun comes rising, when the sea

Clears deeply, when the moon hangs on the wall
    Of heaven-haven. These are not things transformed.
Yet we are shaken by them as if they were.   20
We reason about them with a later reason.

III.2.

The blue woman, linked and lacquered, at her window
Did not desire that feathery argentines
Should be cold silver, neither that frothy clouds
    Should foam, be foamy waves, should move like them,
Nor that the sexual blossoms should repose
Without their fierce addictions, nor that the heat
    Of summer, growing fragrant in the night,
Should strengthen her abortive dreams and take
In sleep its natural form. It was enough
    For her that she remembered: the argentines   10
Of spring come to their places in the grape leaves
To cool their ruddy pulses; the frothy clouds
    Are nothing but frothy clouds; the frothy blooms
Waste without puberty; and afterward,
When the harmonious heat of August pines
    Enters the room, it drowses and is the night.
It was enough for her that she remembered.
The blue woman looked and from her window named
    The corals of the dogwood, cold and clear,
Cold, coldly delineating, being real,   20
Clear and, except for the eye, without intrusion.

III.3.

A lasting visage in a lasting bush,
A face of stone in an unending red,
Red-emerald, red-slitted-blue, a face of slate,
    An ancient forehead hung with heavy hair,
The channel slots of rain, the red-rose-red
And weathered and the ruby-water-worn,
    The vines around the throat, the shapeless lips,
The frown like serpents basking on the brow,
The spent feeling leaving nothing of itself,
    Red-in-red repetitions never going   10

Away, a little rusty, a little rouged,
A little roughened and ruder, a crown
    The eye could not escape, a red renown
Blowing itself upon the tedious ear.
An effulgence faded, dull cornelian
    Too venerably used. That might have been.
It might and might have been. But as it was,
A dead shepherd brought tremendous chords from hell
    And bade the sheep carouse. Or so they said.
Children in love with them brought early flowers   20
And scattered them about, no two alike.

III.4.

We reason of these things with later reason
And we make of what we see, what we see clearly
And have seen, a place dependent on ourselves.
    There was a mystic marriage in Catawba,
At noon it was on the mid-day of the year
Between a great captain and the maiden Bawda.
    This was their ceremonial hymn: Anon
We loved but would no marriage make. Anon
The one refused the other one to take,
    Foreswore the sipping of the marriage wine.   10
Each must the other take not for his high,
His puissant front nor for her subtle sound,
    The shoo-shoo-shoo of secret cymbals round.
Each must the other take as sign, short sign
To stop the whirlwind, balk the elements.
    The great captain loved the ever-hill Catawba
And therefore married Bawda, whom he found there,
And Bawda loved the captain as she loved the sun.
    They married well because the marriage-place
Was what they loved. It was neither heaven nor hell.   20
They were love's characters come face to face.

III.5.

We drank Meursault, ate lobster Bombay with mango
Chutney. Then the Canon Aspirin declaimed
Of his sister, in what a sensible ecstasy

She lived in her house. She had two daughters, one
Of four, and one of seven, whom she dressed
The way a painter of pauvred color paints.

But still she painted them, appropriate to
Their poverty, a gray-blue yellowed out
With ribbon, a rigid statement of them, white,

With Sunday pearls, her widow's gayety.   10
She hid them under simple names. She held
Them closelier to her by rejecting dreams.

The words they spoke were voices that she heard.
She looked at them and saw them as they were
And what she felt fought off the barest phrase.

The Canon Aspirin, having said these things,
Reflected, humming an outline of a fugue
Of praise, a conjugation done by choirs.

Yet when her children slept, his sister herself
Demanded of sleep, in the excitements of silence   20
Only the unmuddled self of sleep, for them.

III.6.

When at long midnight the Canon came to sleep
And normal things had yawned themselves away,
The nothingness was a nakedness, a point,

Beyond which fact could not progress as fact.
Thereon the learning of the man conceived
Once more night's pale illuminations, gold

Beneath, far underneath, the surface of
His eye and audible in the mountain of
His ear, the very material of his mind.

So that he was the ascending wings he saw   10
And moved on them in orbits' outer stars
Descending to the children's bed, on which

They lay. Forth then with huge pathetic force
Straight to the utmost crown of night he flew.
The nothingness was a nakedness, a point

Beyond which thought could not progress as thought.
He had to choose. But it was not a choice
Between excluding things. It was not a choice

Between, but of. He chose to include the things

That in each other are included, the whole,   20
The complicate, the amassing harmony.

III.7.

He imposes orders as he thinks of them,
As the fox and snake do. It is a brave affair.
Next he builds capitols and in their corridors,
    Whiter than wax, sonorous, fame as it is,
He establishes statues of reasonable men,
Who surpassed the most literate owl, the most erudite
    Of elephants. But to impose is not
To discover. To discover an order as of
A season, to discover summer and know it,
    To discover winter and know it well, to find,   10
Not to impose, not to have reasoned at all,
Out of nothing to have come on major weather,
    It is possible, possible, possible. It must
Be possible. It must be that in time
The real will from its crude compoundings come,
    Seeming, at first, a beast disgorged, unlike,
Warmed by a desperate milk. To find the real,
To be stripped of every fiction except one,
    The fiction of an absolute—Angel,
Be silent in your luminous cloud and hear   20
The luminous melody of proper sound.

III.8.

What am I to believe? If the angel in his cloud,
Serenely gazing at the violent abyss,
Plucks on his strings to pluck abysmal glory,
    Leaps downward through evening's revelations, and
On his spredden wings, needs nothing but deep space,
Forgets the gold centre, the golden destiny.
    Grows warm in the motionless motion of his flight,
Am I that imagine this angel less satisfied?
Are the wings his, the lapis-haunted air?
    Is it he or is it I that experience this?   10
Is it I then that keep saying there is an hour
Filled with expressible bliss, in which I have

No need, am happy, forget need's golden hand,
Am satisfied without solacing majesty,
And if there is an hour there is a day,
    There is a month, a year, there is a time
In which majesty is a mirror of the self:
I have not but I am and as I am, I am.
    These external regions, what do we fill them with
Except reflections, the escapades of death,   20
Cinderella fulfilling herself beneath the roof?

III.9.

Whistle aloud, too weedy wren. I can
Do all that angels can. I enjoy like them,
Like men besides, like men in light secluded,
    Enjoying angels. Whistle, forced bugler,
That bugles for the mate, nearby the nest,
Cock bugler, whistle and bugle and stop just short,
    Red robin, stop in your preludes, practicing
Mere repetitions. These things at least comprise
An occupation, an exercise, a work,
    A thing final in itself and, therefore, good: 10
One of the vast repetitions final in
Themselves and, therefore, good, the going round
    And round and round, the merely going round,
Until merely going round is a final good,
The way wine comes at a table in a wood.
    And we enjoy like men, the way a leaf
Above the table spins its constant spin,
So that we look at it with pleasure, look
    At it spinning its eccentric measure. Perhaps,
The man-hero is not the exceptional monster,   20
But he that of repetition is most master.

III.10.

Fat girl, terrestrial, my summer, my night,
How is it I find you in difference, see you there
In a moving contour, a change not quite completed?
    You are familiar yet an aberration.
Civil, madam, I am, but underneath

A tree, this unprovoked sensation requires
　　That I should name you flatly, waste no words,
Check your evasions, hold you to yourself.
Even so when I think of you as strong or tired,
　　Bent over work, anxious, content, alone,   10
You remain the more than natural figure. You
Become the soft-footed phantom, the irrational
　　Distortion, however fragrant, however dear.
That's it: the more than rational distortion,
The fiction that results from feeling. Yes, that.
　　They will get it straight one day at the Sorbonne.
We shall return at twilight from the lecture
Pleased that the irrational is rational,
　　Until flicked by feeling, in a gildered street,
I call you by name, my green, my fluent mundo.   20
You will have stopped revolving except in crystal.

*   *   *

　　Soldier, there is a war between the mind
And sky, between thought and day and night. It is
For that the poet is always in the sun,
　　Patches the moon together in his room
To his Virgilian cadences, up down,
Up down. It is a war that never ends.
　　Yet it depends on yours. The two are one.
They are a plural, a right and left, a pair,
Two parallels that meet if only in
　　The meeting of their shadows or that meet
In a book in a barrack, a letter from Malay.
But your war ends. And after it you return
　　With six meats and twelve wines or else without
To walk another room . . . Monsieur and comrade,
The soldier is poor without the poet's lines,
　　His petty syllabi, the sounds that stick,
Inevitably modulating, in the blood.
And war for war, each has its gallant kind.
　　How simply the fictive hero becomes the real;
How gladly with proper words the soldier dies,
If he must, or lives on the bread of faithful speech.

Notes

I. *Ars Poetica* by Horace

1. This translation has been significantly influenced by the excellent edition and commentary of N. Rudd, *Horace: Epistles Book II and Epistle to the Pisones ("Ars Poetica")* (Cambridge, 1989). I have followed a number of Rudd's textual emendations and interpretations of passages.

2. Horace's complaint here is that a former Roman tolerance for the invention of new terms no longer appears to be extended to more recent writers. M. Cornelius Cethegus (d. 196 B.C.) and Marcus Porcius Cato (234–149 B.C.) were important political leaders and renowned orators of an earlier period. Caecilius (ca. 220–168 B.C.) and Plautus (d. circa 184 B.C.) were comic poets of a former time. Ennius (239–169 B.C.) was an early poet who wrote in several genres. Vergil (70–19 B.C.) and Varius were poets who were contemporary with Horace (65–8 B.C.)

3. Bentley, followed by Rudd, read *"adflent"* here in place of the *"adsunt"* of the manuscripts. I follow this emendation.

4. "Cavalry" and "infantry" refer to social and economic classes in the audience; the "cavalry" being wealthier and socially superior to the "infantry."

5. I follow Rudd in referring the Latin term *"vaga"* (translated "wanderer") both to Io's physical and mental condition.

6. Rudd, *Horace*, 172, interprets this line to be a critical comment on the epic cycle of poems as "something trite and vulgar."

7. Here I follow Rudd's emendation *"concipit"* in place of the manuscript reading, *"colligit."*

8. In the above passage I follow Rudd, who prints Bentley's conjectures *"lentus"* (translated "apathetic") in place of *"longus"* in the manuscripts and *"pavidusque"* (translated "fearful") in place of *"avidusque"* in the manuscripts. I also adopt Rudd's emendation *"moraberis"* (translated "you shall spend time") in place of *"morabimur"* and *"morabitur,"* which are found in the manuscripts.

9. Here I follow Rudd's reading *"urbem"* (translated "city") in place of *"urbes"* in the manuscripts.

10. The Latin for "guardian spirit" is "Genius." Rudd (98) suggests this translation of the term.

11. Davus, Pythias, and Simo are comic characters while the satyr, Silenus, is the guardian of the god Dionysus. Horace advises aspiring poets to avoid confusing comic, tragic, and satyric diction.

12. Rudd (191) suggests the translation "wanton" here.

13. Pompilius is the ancestor of the clan to which the family of the Pisones belonged. Rudd refers the "test of the well-trimmed nail" to the use by the sculptor or carpenter of his fingernail to test the joints of the work he is constructing.

14. Rudd, citing the use of the drug, hellebore, to treat insanity, suggests the rendering "three times Anticyra's output of hellebore" adopted in the translation. Some have supposed the line to refer to the production of hellebore in three actual cities named Anticyra. C. O. Brink, *Horace on Poetry: The "Ars Poetica"* (Cambridge, 1971), 331-32, recognizes the medicinal use of hellebore as a purgative to treat insanity but he comments further (333) that hellebore also "was supposed to render the mind alert and inventive."

15. Scholars have found this passage difficult to interpret. Rudd suggests that Horace welcomes here a medical treatment, the purging of bile, which will transform him from a mad poet into a rational critic. I do not believe that Horace ever suggests that criticism is a superior activity to poetry. I think that Brink, *Horace on Poetry*, 333-34, offers a much better interpretation when he suggests that Horace is speaking sarcastically here in desiring to be cured of the "melancholia of genius." We have noted in the previous footnote that purgation by hellebore could be used both to cure madness and to stimulate creativity. By emphasizing the role of hellebore in fostering creativity we have, I think, a still better interpretation available for this troubled passage. Horace first denounces the poets who rely only on their madness, their "inspiration," and pay no attention to art. At this point he sarcastically and ironically comments that he undergoes the purgative stimulus for creativity each spring, but he concludes, also sarcastically and ironically, that the creative process involving "madness" or inspiration isn't worth the effort and that it is better just to be a critic, an uninspired student of the art of poetry, who gives instructions to other poets. The lines make good sense only when full value is given to their ironic and sarcastic elevation of criticism over poetry.

16. The "centuries of elders" refers to a subdivision of the comitia centuriata, an important political institution in Rome. Its members were all over 45 years old and as "elders" were specifically interested in the benefits conferred by poetry. "The high and mighty Ramnes" refer to a military and political division of younger men (under 30) who are of great wealth and prestige and who can be presumed, on the basis of their youth, to be interested in the pleasure which poetry affords. The Sosii were brothers and very well known booksellers.

17. An epic poet in the retinue of Alexander the Great whose achievements he celebrated in his work. Here he is a symbol for poetic mediocrity.

18. Messala (64 B.C.–A.D. 8) was a political leader, orator, author, solider, and a patron of the arts. Cascellius (born c. 104 B.C.) was a political leader and a distinguished jurist.

19. Maecius refers most probably to the person who in 55 B.C. selected the plays to be performed in Pompey's theater.

20. Pieria was a region in Macedonia that was associated with the muses. Here it refers to the genre of lyric poetry.

21. Rudd suggests the need to add the phrase "I say this" at this point.

22. The "Pythian piece" is a composition performed at the Pythian games either in honor of Apollo's victory over the Python or in general association with the games.

23. We are unable to make a precise identification of this Quintilius but he was obviously admired as a strict and perceptive critic.

24. Rudd persuasively suggests that the "black line" was the obelus used by critics and scholars such as Aristarchus to mark lines in poetry they deemed spurious. Aristarchus (216–145 B.C.) was head of the library at Alexandria and a scholar of enormous reputation who produced important editions of a number of Greek authors.

II. *Poetria Nova* by Geoffrey of Vinsauf

Dedication: Innocent III. Pope from 1198 to 1216. Innocent had stormy relations with England during Geoffrey's lifetime. There is no evidence that Geoffrey had met or corresponded with him.

47 "The mind's hand." For other metaphors based on parts of the body, see ll. 55, 111, 721, 778, 1062, 1225, 1615.

56 "Order." Like Horace, Geoffrey uses the Latin *ordo* rather than the more common *dispositio*.

57 "Cadiz." "Limit." To the Greeks and Romans Cadiz (ancient Gades) was long the westernmost point of the known world.

80 "Path." That is, natural or artificial order.

285 "The serpent." Vergil, *Eclogues*, III, 93.

296. "Lighter burdens." Cf. Horace. *Ars Poetica*, l. 40.

368ff. Cf. Chaucer, *Nun's Priest's Tale*, ll. 527-31.

377-78 Richard was wounded on a Friday (March 26, 1100) and died on April 6.

515-26 Probably a reference to Chateau-Gaillard, completed by Richard in 1198.

747 "Picture." Cf. Horace, *Ars Poetica*, ll. 360ff.

949-1060 Based on *Rhetorica ad Herennium*, IV.42-46.

1098ff. Based on *Rhetorica ad Herennium*, IV.18–41.

1251 "Cicero." Cicero was thought to be the author of the *Ad Herennium* throughout the Middle Ages.

1327–44 *Rhetorica ad Herennium*, V.56–57.

1588–1841 The section on conversions and determinations has no counterpart in the *Ad Herennium* and is a by-product of medieval grammatical theory.

1820 "Sidonius." The late Latin Christian poet Sidonius Apollinaris (fl. A.D. 470). The lines are an imitation of a description by Sidonius of the Gothic king Theodoric. *Epistles*, 1.2.7ff.

1843 Geoffrey uses *proprie* here and *proprietas* in line 1846. The terms are related to Horace's idea of decorum.

1867 Aulus Gellius, *Noctes Atticae*, 1.7.20.

1928 *"Tu, Tite . . ."* Very close to a famous line by Ennius quoted in *Ad Herennium*, IV.18.

1969ff. For memory, see *Ad Herennium*, III.29–40.

1986 Quoted from Sidonius, *Epistles*, 1.2.6.

2031ff. For delivery, see *Ad Herennium*, III.19–27.

2100 "William." Possibly William Wrotham, administrator of the Navy and holder of other important posts between 1204 and 1215. Another possibility is the William who was Bishop of London from 1199 to 1221.

III. *L'Art poétique* by Boileau (tr. Soames-Dryden)

17 "Waller." English poet substituted by Dryden for Malherbe. François de Malherbe (d. 1628) was the supreme mentor of French neoclassical decorum. Edmund Waller (d. 1687) sided with both the royalists and the puritans. He was considered by the generation of poets that followed him to have been a pioneer in the light and graceful style that they admired.

21 "Dubartas." Guillaume de Salluste Dubartas (d. 1590), author of a paraphrase of Genesis translated into English by Joshua Sylvester (d. 1618). The translation influenced Milton's *Paradise Lost*. This is the first of several references that question the mingling of Christian subjects and fiction.

94 "Fleckno." *Mac Flecknoe* (1678), a satiric poem by John Dryden.

96 "Butler." Samuel Butler (d. 1680), author of *Hudibras*, a hugely successful mock epic.

115 "Fairfax." Edward Fairfax (d. 1635). Translator of Torquato Tasso's romance *Jerusalem Liberated*. Used here as the equivalent of François Villon (d. ?1464), the French author named here by Boileau. The parallel is strained since Villon was a medieval poet, while Fairfax wrote during the "golden age" of English Renaissance literature.

117 "Spencer." Edmund Spenser (d. 1599). Parallel here to Boileau's citation of Pierre de Ronsard (d. 1585), the most famous of the group of French Renaissance poets who called themselves the Pléiade.

121 "D'Avenant." Sir William Davenant (d. 1668), author of the epic *Gondibert* and of the first English opera, *The Siege of Rhodes* (1656).

131 "Waller." Edmund Waller again. Here the French line is famous: "Enfin Malherbe vint"—"Finally Malherbe came."

256 "Theocrite." Theocritus (fl. 270 B.C.). The inventor of pastoral, imitated in Vergil's *Eclogues*.

284 "Tibullus." Albius Tibullus (d. 19 B.C.). Latin elegiac poet whose principal theme was love.

285 "Ovid." P. Ovidius Naso (d. A.D. 18). Author of a mythological poem, *Metamorphoses*. Here referred to because of his *Amores*, poems about love.

312 "Sonnet." This is one of relatively few references in the *Art* to modern European, as against classical, poetic forms. Others are musical forms: the madrigal (l. 337), the round (French *rondeau*, l. 367), and ballad (French *ballade*, l. 368).

373 "Lucilius." Gaius Lucilius (d. 102 B.C.). Horace's chief guide and model in the art of Roman satire.

381 "Persius." Aulus Persius Flaccus (d. A.D. 62). Roman satirist influenced by Lucilius and Horace.

383 "Juvenal." Decius Junius Juvenalis (d. second century A.D.). Roman satirist especially bitter in his denunciations of city life and of women.

387 "Caprean debauch." The debaucheries of Tiberius on the island of Capri.

388 "Sejanus." Lucius Aelius Sejanus, sentenced to death A.D. 31 by the Roman Senate after being denounced by Tiberius.

418 "Mr. Settle." Elkanah Settle (d. 1724), pilloried as Doeg by Dryden in *Absalom and Achitophel*. Author of several plays between 1666 and 1718.

428 "David Logan." Should be spelled David Loggan, an English engraver of the seventeenth century.

525 "Thyrsis." A generic name for a simple shepherd lad.

526 "Artamen." A base character—in contrast to Cyrus the Great, King of Persia (d. 529 B.C.).

544 "Cato." Probably Marcus Porcius Cato (d. 46 B.C.), a patriot of unbending integrity who upheld Pompey in the civil wars and committed suicide when he saw that his cause was hopeless.

544 "Brutus." Marcus Junius Brutus (d. 42 B.C.), the noble leader of the republican cause and assassin of Caesar.

556 "Chapman." George Chapman (d. 1634), a distinguished tragedian and translator of Homer. Chapman's popular tragedy *Bussy D'Ambois* was about royal intrigues in sixteenth-century France.

565 "Euxine." The Black Sea.

636 "Tasso." Torquato Tasso (d. 1595), author of the romance *Jerusalemme Liberata*, the story of the liberation of Jerusalem by the knights who followed

Godfrey of Bologna, and ornamented by digressions, fabulous adventures, and the love story of Tancred and Armida.

640 "Godfrey." See line 636.

642 "Tancred and Armida." See line 636.

669 "Chilp'eric." Frankish King of Neustria (d. 584).

677 "Scipio." Scipio Africanus (d. 183 B.C.), great Roman general during the Punic War.

705-7 Translated from the first three lines of Vergil's *Aeneid*. "Lavinian shore": "Italian shore."

718 "Orlando." The hero of *Orlando Furioso* by Ariosto and *Orlando Innamorato* by Boiardo, both Italian Renaissance romances with a strong comic element.

770 "Socrates." Satirized by Aristophanes in *The Clouds* (423 B.C.).

793 "Hudibras." See line 96.

822 "Jonson." Ben Jonson (d. 1637). The great English writer of comedies and the prophet of English neoclassicism. The French parallel here is Jean Baptiste Molière (d. 1673), the greatest of the French seventeenth-century writers of comedy.

827 "Harlequin." Stock clown in Italian-derived farces.

828 "Fox." Ben Jonson's comedy *Volpone, or the Fox*. "Alchemist." Ben Jonson's *The Alchemist*. These titles are substituted for titles of plays by Molière.

856 "Smithfield stage." Equivalent to "slum stage."

857 "Jack Puddings." A stock comic character.

873 "Wren." Sir Christopher Wren (d. 1723), architect of St. Paul's Cathedral in London.

880 "Galen." Galen (d. A.D. 199), Greek physician whose medical works were still influential in the sixteenth century.

891 "Herringman." Seventeenth-century London bookseller.

895 "Gondibert." See line 121.

903 "Shadwell." Thomas Shadwell (d. 1692), dramatist and poet. Attacked Dryden as John Bayes in a satire and was himself travestied by Dryden as Og in *Absalom and Achitophel*. He succeeded Dryden as Poet Laureate.

908 "Settle." See line 418.

940 "Lucan." Marcus Annaeus Lucanus (d. A.D. 65), author of an epic on the Roman civil wars titled *Pharsalia*.

1053 "Cowley." Abraham Cowley (d. 1667), author of pindarics and a Christian epic *Davideis*. "Denham." Sir John Denham (d. 1669), author of a landscape poem *Cooper's Hill*, much admired during the Restoration.

1054 "Waller." See line 17.

1059 "Our hero." Charles II in the English version, Louis XIV in the French of Boileau.

1070 "Saturnian." A golden age like the age during which Saturn reigned.

1077 "Boutefeus." Incendiaries.

IV. *An Essay on Criticism* by Pope

34 "Maevius." Inferior Roman poet who attacked the work of Horace and Vergil.

41 "Half-formed insects." According to legend, the sun bred insects in the muddy banks of the Nile.

48ff. Cf. *Ars Poetica*, 38–41.

53 Cf. Boileau, *L'Art poétique*, ll. 13–41.

68–76 "Nature" here reflects the eighteenth-century sense that through Newton and others, science had demonstrated the profound regularity and order of natural law. "Rules" in art are like "laws" in Nature. Cf. also ll. 89, 243, 297.

129 "Mantuan muse." Vergil was born near Mantua.

138 "Stagirite." Aristotle was born in Macedonia, in the town of Stagira.

141–57 These lines echo the theory of Longinus that the rarest poetic beauties are produced by flashes of insight rather than conscious "art."

144 "Nameless Graces." Suggestive of the French *je ne sais quoi*—"I don't know what"—that is, the quality that is essential to successful art but eludes neat formulation.

150 "Pegasus." The winged horse, symbolizing poetic inspiration.

181 "Bays." Bay leaves used in antiquity to crown great poets.

186 "Paeans." Songs of triumph.

216 "Pierian Spring." A spring sacred to the Muses ("Pierides").

233–41 A contrast is established here between "nature" (cf. Latin *natura*; sometimes *ingenium*) and "art" (cf. *techne, ars*). As Horace argues, both are needed. However, it was common to contrast artists who relied on one more than the other. Shakespeare was a prime example in English literature of the poet who had little learning but made up for it by natural genius. Hence Milton's famous description of "Sweetest Shakespeare, fancy's child,/ warbling his woodnotes wild." If nature without art was "warm" and "gen'rous," art without nature was "cold" and "dull."

254 Cf. Horace, *Ars Poetica*, ll. 347–53.

267 "La Mancha." Don Quixote de la Mancha, in *Don Quixote* by Cervantes (d. 1616).

270 "Dennis." John Dennis (d. 1734), dramatist and critic who attacked Pope and was therefore satirized in Pope's *Dunciad*.

289 "Conceit." A reference to "witty figures of speech" of the sort admired by the metaphysical poets in England, the *concettisti* in Italy, and the French poets of *préciocité*.

328 "Fungoso." A poor scholar satirized in Ben Jonson's *Every Man out of His Humour.*

344-61 A passage famous for its imitation in verse of the sound effects it describes.

356 "Alexandrine." French twelve-syllable line. Used by Edmund Spenser as the concluding line of the "Spenserian stanza."

361 "Denham." Sir John Denham (d. 1669), dramatist and author of the much admired landscape poem *Cooper's Hill.* "Waller." Edmund Waller (d. 1687), poet considered a forerunner of Restoration style for his simple but elegantly turned lyrics.

372 "Camilla." One of Diana's attendants in Vergil's *Aeneid,* VII.808-11.

374 "Timotheus." Poet who charms Alexander the Great in Dryden's elaborate lyric poem *Alexander's Feast.*

395 Note the reference to the quarrel between the ancients and moderns.

420-23 Cf. Horace, *Ars Poetica,* ll. 382-84.

441 "Sentences." Scholastic propositions. Especially the *Sentences* of Peter Lombard.

444 "Scotists." Followers of Duns Scotus (d. 1308), nominalist and opponent of Thomism. "Thomists." Followers of St. Thomas Aquinas (d. 1274).

445 "Duck Lane." Location of many secondhand bookstalls.

463 "Blackmore." Sir Richard Blackmore (d. 1729), physician and minor poet who criticized Dryden. "Milbourne." Rev. Luke Milbourne (d. 1668), another critic of Dryden.

465 "Zoilus." A legendary fault-finder of Homer's poems, proverbial as the type of the sour critic.

480-93 Cf. Horace's remarks on changing language, *Ars Poetica,* ll. 60-72.

536 "Monarch's care." A reference to the dissolute quality of the reign of Charles II (1660-85).

538 "Jilts." Kept mistresses.

544 "Foreign reign." The reign of William III (1689-1702), of the Dutch House of Orange.

545 "Socinus." Laelius Socinus (d. 1562), Italian religious reformer who professed to be a follower of Calvin but was, in fact, more rationalistic and is often considered a prophet of Deism. His position implied denial of the divinity of Christ, of the trinity, and of Christ's atonement for man's sin. It attracted a wide following in several European countries, including England, in the seventeenth century.

585 "Appius." A reference to John Dennis's tragedy *Appius and Virginia* (1709).

617 "Durfey." Thomas D'Urfey (d. 1723), dramatist and song-writer. Many of his poems are semi-pornographic.

619 "Garth." Sir Samuel Garth (d. 1719), author of *The Dispensary*, a popular satire.

623 "Paul's churchyard." Location of many London bookstalls.

665 "Dionysius." Dionysius of Halicarnassus, Greek rhetorician and critic, 1st c. B.C.

667 "Petronius." Gaius Petronius Arbiter (d. A.D. 65), author of the comic novel *The Satyricon*.

669 "Quintilian." Marcus Fabius Quintilianus (d. A.D. 95), author of the most elaborate surviving Roman rhetoric, the *Institute of Oratory* in twelve books.

675 "Longinus." Dionysius Longinus, possibly 1st c. B.C., reputed author of the essay *On the Sublime*.

693 "Erasmus." Desiderius Erasmus (d. 1536), Dutch humanist and author of *The Praise of Folly*, "injured" because in spite of the fact that he refused to endorse the anti-Catholic position of Martin Luther, he was considered suspect by Catholic authorities and his works were eventually placed on the Index. Erasmus was especially influential in the development of English humanism.

697 "Leo." Pope Leo X, whose papacy (1513-21) is often considered the "golden age" of the Renaissance in Rome.

704 "Vida." Girolamo Vida (d. 1566), author of the verse essay imitating Horace titled *De arte poetica*. From Cremona.

724 "Nature's . . ." The line is quoted from *An Essay on Poetry* (1682) by John Sheffield, Earl of Mulgrave (d. 1721).

725 "Roscommon." Wentworth Dillon, Earl of Roscommon (d. 1685), author of a much admired essay *On Translated Verse* and a translation of Horace's *Art of Poetry*.

726 "Walsh." William Walsh (d. 1708), friend and mentor of the young Alexander Pope.

V. *English Bards and Scotch Reviewers* by Byron

[For complete annotation plus textual notes, see *Lord Byron: The Complete Poetical Works* (Oxford University Press, 1980), I, 227-64 and 393-419.]

Preface. The *Preface* first appeared in the 5th (1811) edition.

"Bowles." Rev. William Lisle Bowles (d. 1850), friend of Coleridge and author of fourteen sonnets (1789) anticipating the tone of romantic lyric. His remarks about Pope's character in his edition of the *Works* (10 vols., 1807) was attacked by Byron and others for its critical comments on that author's probity.

"Mr. Gifford." William Gifford (d. 1826) lived in the romantic era but his sympathies were with the age of Pope and Dr. Johnson. His verse satires *The Baviad* and *The Maeviad* imitated Pope and were much admired by Byron. His translation of Juvenal (1802) may have influenced the tone of Byron's revisions of *English Bards*. Gifford was also a keen and frequently devastating critic as editor of two journals *The Anti-Jacobin* and *The Quarterly Review*. He edited several Elizabethan dramatists, including Philip Massinger and Ben Jonson. Byron refers to him several times in *English Bards*.

"Edinburgh Reviewers." Established in 1802, the *Edinburgh Review* was one of the most energetic and influential of the journals that followed literary events in England in the early nineteenth century. It was generally hostile to the romantics, and its reviews were often savagely cutting. Its anonymous review of *Hours of Idleness* led Byron to revise *English Bards* by incorporating denunciations of "Scotch reviewers."

1 "Fitzgerald." William Fitzgerald (d. 1829), a minor poet of the period. The opening line echoes the opening line of Juvenal's first satire.

3-4 "Scotch Reviews." An allusion to the anonymous review of *Hours of Idleness*. Byron attributed the review (incorrectly) to Francis Jeffrey. In fact, it was written by Henry Brougham.

21 "Hamet." Cid Hamet Benengeli promises to lay down his pen in the last chapter of *Don Quixote*.

55 "Lamb." William Lamb (d. 1848), later prime minister. See below, ll. 516-17.

57 "George." George Lamb (d. 1834), a contributor to the *Edinburgh Review*.

61 "Jeffrey." Francis Jeffrey (d. 1850), editor of the *Edinburgh Review* (1802-29), and, as a reviewer, the chief target of Byron's scorn in *English Bards*. He was, in fact, a man of considerable breadth and talent and a witty conversationalist. As noted above, Brougham rather than Jeffrey was the reviewer of *Hours of Idleness*.

65 "Miller." Joe Miller (d. 1738), reputed author of the famous collection of jokes.

68 "Attic." Greek.

82 "Boeotian." Greek.

94 "Gifford." See *Preface*.

100 "Pye." Henry James Pye (d. 1813), translated Aristotle's *Poetics* and, as poet laureate (1790-1813), wrote ludicrously dull official poetry.

115 "Congreve." William Congreve (d. 1729), brilliant Restoration writer of comedies, the most famous being *The Way of the World*. "Otway." Thomas Otway (d. 1685), author of heroic plays of which *Venice Preserved* is the most famous, since it established the style for Restoration heroic drama. Famous for the tearful pathos of his scenes.

127 "Southey." Robert Southey (d. 1843), friend of Wordsworth and Coleridge and with them a pioneer of the new romantic style. He was poet laureate

from 1813. He published voluminously and unwisely. Eventually he became a favorite target for romantics who believed that he had sold out both poetically and politically.

128 "Little." Pseudonymous poet of *Poems of the Late Thomas Little, Esq.* (1801) by Thomas Moore. Classical in style.

132 "Galvanism." An allusion to early nineteenth-century experiments in electricity.

142 "Stott." Robert Stott, a minor literary figure who wrote for the *Morning Post.* Byron recalls that he wrote "a Sonnet to Rats."

153 "Lays of Minstrels." A reference to *The Lay of the Last Minstrel* by Sir Walter Scott (d. 1832), novelist, ballad collector, and poet. Byron said of the *Lay*, "Never was any plan so incongruous and absurd," but the work was broadly popular.

157 "Gilpin Horner." One of Scott's characters.

166 "Marmion." Scott's *Marmion* was published in 1808 and was even more popular than *The Lay of the Last Minstrel.*

173 "Murray with his Miller." Booksellers.

176 "Bays." Bay-leaves, symbols of poetic achievement.

190 "Maro." Vergil (Publius Vergilius Maro).

203 "Camoëns." Luis de Camoëns (d. 1580), Portuguese poet and author of the epic *The Lusiads,* celebrating the voyages of Vasco da Gama. "Tasso." Torquato Tasso (d. 1595), author of *Jerusalem Liberated.*

207 "Bedford." The Duke of Bedford, who burned Joan of Arc at the stake. Southey wrote a *Joan of Arc.*

211, 13 "Thalaba." *Thalaba* (1801), one of Southey's poems. "Domdaniel." A character in *Thalaba.*

216 "Tom Thumb." A reference to the mock tragic farce (1730) by Henry Fielding.

221 "Madoc." Another of Southey's poems.

223 "Mandeville." Sir John Mandeville, ostensible author of a journal of fabulous travels popular in the fourteenth century.

231 "Berkeley Ballads." "The Old Woman of Berkeley," a ballad by Southey, tells of an old lady carried away on a horse by Beelzebub.

240 Byron cites Wordsworth's "The Tables Turned": "Up, up, my Friend, and quit your books;/ Or surely you'll grow double."

247-48 "Betty Foy." A reference to Wordsworth's "The Idiot Boy." Betty Foy is the boy's mother.

262 "Ass." Cf. Coleridge's "Lines to a Young Ass."

265 "Lewis." Matthew Gregory Lewis (d. 1818), author of a famous gothic novel *The Monk* (1795). The genre was filled with romantic ruins, graveyards, and wild adventures, and was thought to be especially admired by ladies.

287 "Little." See line 128; also line 308.

297 "Hibernian Strangford." Irish Strangford, translator of *The Lusiads* by Camoens.

308 "Moore." Thomas Moore (d. 1852), Irish author, writer of ballads. His best known book is *Irish Melodies*. He published a controversial *Life* of Byron in 1830.

310 "Hayley." William Hayley (d. 1820), author of "The Triumph of Temper" (1781) and "The Triumph of Music" (1804) and other prosy poems. Even Southey remarked "Everything about that man is good except his poetry."

321 "Grahame." James Grahame (d. 1811), writer of devotional poetry; e.g., *Sabbath Walks* (1804).

331 "Bowles." See *Preface.*

338 "Ostend." In Flanders.

340 "Cap." Clowns and court fools wore a cap and bells.

351 "Awake . . ." First line of Bowles's *The Spirit of Discovery by Sea* (1805).

356 "Captain Cook." The famous eighteenth-century south-sea explorer.

372 "Lord Fanny, and . . . Curll." John Lord Hervey (d. 1743), author of "Lines to the Imitator of Horace," was dubbed "Lord Fanny" and "Sporus" by Pope. Edmund Curll (d. 1747), one of the characters in Pope's *Dunciad*, was a bookseller.

378 "Mallet." David Mallet (or Malloch, d. 1765), hired by Bolingbroke to attack Pope after his death.

380 "Dennis." John Dennis (d. 1734), critic satirized by Pope in the *Dunciad*. "Ralph." James Ralph (d. 1762), satirized by Pope in the *Dunciad*.

387 "Cottle." Amos and Joseph Cottle were Bristol booksellers. Byron remarks "I don't know which" is intended here. Later, the emphasis is on Amos.

388 "Cambrian." Welsh.

413-14 "Richmond . . . Maurice." *Richmond Hill* (1807) is the title of Maurice's long descriptive poem.

419 "Alcaeus." Greek lyric poet (sixth c. B.C.); a name for the Scotch poet James Montgomery (d. 1854).

422 "Caledonian." Scotch.

424 "Sheffield." Scottish town. For James Montgomery (d. 1854), poet and divine. He was much admired and Byron says that "his *Wanderer of Switzerland* is worth a thousand *Lyrical Ballads.*"

437 "Arthur's Seat." Name of a hill outside Edinburgh.

439 "Judge." George Jefferies (d. 1689), a famous hanging judge.

464-511 Mock-heroic description of a challenge to a duel issued by Thomas Moore to Jeffrey in 1806 after the *Edinburgh Review* had attacked one of Moore's volumes of poetry. The duel was stopped by authorities, and when the pistols were examined, it was found that they had not been loaded with bullets.

468 "Dunedin." Another name for Edinburgh.

472 "Tweed." Scottish river.

475 "Tolbooth." The principal prison in Edinburgh.

483 "Edina." River in Edinburgh.

485 "Canongate." A district of Edinburgh.

490 "Caledonia's goddess." Byron says that he has invented this goddess because she was needed for the machinery of the poem and Scottish "kelpies" and "brownies" were not dignified enough.

495 "Danaë." A maiden loved by Jove, who seduced her by appearing as a shower of gold.

498–525 Addressed to Jeffrey by "Caledonia's goddess."

509 "Travelled Thane . . ." George Hamilton Gordon.

510 "Herbert." William Herbert (d. 1847), author of *Select Icelandic Poetry* (1804).

512 "Sidney." Sydney Smith (d. 1845), assisted the founding of the *Edinburgh Review* and advocated Catholic emancipation in the *Pymley Letters* (1807–8).

513 "Hallam." Henry Hallam (d. 1859), learned and penetrating historian known especially for his study of the middle ages.

515 "Pillans." James Pillans (d. 1864), a tutor at Eton.

516 "Lamb." See line 57.

519 "Holland." Holland House, the London residence of Henry Richard, Lord Holland (d. 1840), patron of letters and center of a brilliant literary salon. Byron is snide. Elsewhere (ll. 540–45) he makes disparaging remarks about Holland's translations from Lope de Vega.

524 "Brougham." Henry, 1st Lord Brougham and Vaux (d. 1868), was one of the founders of the *Edinburgh Review* and a frequent contributor. He had an abrasive personality but acquired great prestige for political, educational, and scientific activities. It was Brougham who anonymously reviewed Byron's *Hours of Idleness*.

532 "Evening sweets." Sewage.

535 "Rear." In a note Byron calls attention to the color of the back cover of the *Review*.

538 "Pictish." Related to the ancient Scottish race of Picts.

540–5 "Holland." See line 519.

562 "Dibdin." Charles Dibdin (d. 1841), dramatist and writer of sea-songs. His *History of the Stage* (1795) is a significant contribution to the subject. Cf. line 591, which refers to his pantomime on Mother Goose.

564 "Rosciomania." Roscius was a famous Roman actor. "Rosciomania" refers to adulation of actors.

565 "Full-grown actors." William Betty (d. 1874), who enjoyed a vogue as a boy actor in 1804.

568 "Reynolds." Minor English writer of comedies.

570 "Kenney." Minor dramatist.

572 "Beaumont." The tragedy *Bonduca* by Francis Beaumont, the English Renaissance dramatist, was stripped of its dialogue by Thomas Sheridan, son of the great dramatist, and presented as a mime called *Caractacus* at Drury Lane Theater in 1808.

577 "Colman." George Colman (d. 1836), a minor dramatist of the period. "Cumberland." Richard Cumberland (d. 1811), a dramatist whose best play is *The West Indian.*

580 "Sheridan." Richard Brinsley Sheridan, author of *The School for Scandal* (1777), among other plays. He abandoned playwriting after writing *Pizarro* in 1799.

582 "German schools." Especially the plays of August Kotzebue (d. 1819), who had a long vogue in English translation. Coleridge translated Schiller's *Wallenstein* and Sir Walter Scott Goethe's *Götz von Berlichingen*. These are representative of a large number of dramatic translations during the romantic period.

587 "Garrick." David Garrick (d. 1779), the famous eighteenth-century actor. "Siddons." Sarah Siddons (d. 1831), who dominated the Drury Lane stage after 1782. She was the sister of Charles Kemble the actor (d. 1854) and John Philip Kemble, manager of Drury Lane after 1788.

589 "Hook." Theodore Edward Hook (d. 1841), minor dramatist and later editor and novelist.

591 "Cherry." Andrew Cherry (d. 1812), a minor dramatist, actor, and bookseller. "Skeffington." Sir Lumley Skeffington (d. 1850), minor writer of comedies. "Mother Goose." A pantomime by Thomas Dibdin (see line 563). *Mother Goose's Melody*, the primary collection of Mother Goose rhymes, was first published in 1760.

601 "Greenwood." Scene painter at Drury Lane Theater.

602 "Sleeping Beauties." *Sleeping Beauty* is the title of one of Skeffington's dramatic pieces.

604 "John Bull." The typical Englishman.

613-17 Giuseppi Naldi (d. 1820) and Angelica Catalani (d. 1849) were popular performers of Italian farce. Catalani created a sensation by performing in trousers ("pantaloons").

618 "Ausonia." Italy.

618-37 A comment on the seductive charms of actors—Deshayes [Andre des Hayes] (l. 622)—and actresses—Gayton (l. 624), Angiolini (l. 628), and Collini (l. 630). Byron includes an ironic dig at sabbatarians, who have managed to have laws passed against such Sunday entertainments as beer drinking and such professions as barbering, but ignore the erotic enticements of the stage.

639 "Greville and Argyle." The Argyle Rooms were for gambling and musical entertainments described ll. 640-67.

642 "Petronius." Arbiter of Elegance (d. A.D. 65) and of decadence.

650 "Comus." God of revelry.

655 "En masque." Think of poverty only when wealthy patrons are in the costume of beggars.

658 "Burletta." Comic opera.

678-79 "Powell." Sir Arthur Powell, who mortally wounded Lord Charles Cary, Viscount Falkland, in a duel in 1809; the "two Pagets" are Sir Arthur Paget and his brother, both of whom eloped.

686 "Clodius." Clodius Pulcher, defamer of the gods, enemy of Cicero, lover of Caesar's wife Pompeia and a bully who led street gangs. "Falkland." See lines 678-79.

702 "Gifford." See *Preface*.

708 "Hafiz." Name of a famous Persian poet. Used by a minor English journalist (Robert Stott) as a pseudonym. "Bowles." See *Preface*.

707-818 "Smaller fry." There follows a listing of various now forgotten poets, some of them female, and many from the working class. "Roscommon." Wentworth Dillon, Earl of Roscommon (d. 1685). Poet and translator of Horace.

726 "Carlisle." Frederick Howard, Earl of Carlisle (d. 1825), who was Byron's guardian and to whom Byron had dedicated the volume *Hours of Idleness*. See also line 927.

759-64 "Crusca's bards." An attack on the so-called "Della Cruscan" poets, who followed in the path of Robert Merry (d. 1798) and were roundly satirized by William Gifford in *The Maeviad* (1795). References to Merry, John Bell the publisher, Charlotte Dacre ("Rosa Matilda"), and Robert Stott ("Hafiz"). The "Della Cruscans" typically published their poems in the *World*, a newspaper.

764 "O.P.Q." Abbreviated signatures of various contributors to "poetical columns" of newspapers.

768 "St. Crispin." Patron saint of shoemakers. See line 777.

774 "Capel Lofft" (d. 1824). Literary patron of Robert Bloomfield. Byron scornfully calls him "the Maecenas of shoemakers." See line 777.

777 (and elsewhere below) "Gifford." See *Preface*. "Bloomfield." Robert Bloomfield (d. 1823), a shoemaker. He worked under conditions of extreme poverty. His best-known poem is *The Farmer's Boy*. The manuscript came to the attention of Chapel Lofft, a Suffolk squire, who had it published in 1800. It sold 26,000 copies in three years. After various other publications and efforts to establish a business, he died in great poverty.

795 "Moorland." A weavers' district.

801 "Campbell." Thomas Campbell (d. 1844), Scottish poet, author of *The Pleasures of Hope* (1700) and *Gertrude of Wyoming* (1809).

803 "Rogers." Samuel Rogers (d. 1855), British poet, author of *The Plea-*

sures of Memory (1792), which Byron coupled with *The Pleasures of Hope* (see line 810) as "the most beautiful didactic poems in our language." Also wrote *Columbus* (1810). He was offered, but declined, the laureateship.

810 "Cowper." William Cowper (d. 1800), co-author of *Olney Hymns* and author of *The Task* (1785).

812 "Burns." Robert Burns (d. 1796), the Scottish national poet.

818 "Sotheby." William Sotheby (d. 1833), translator of German authors, e.g. Wieland's *Oberon*, and of Vergil—especially the *Georgics*. "Macneil." Hector Macneil (d. 1818), Scottish poet, author of *The Harp* (1789) and songs and ballads.

831 "White." Henry Kirke White (d. 1806), who died prematurely but had, Byron feels, great promise.

857 "Crabbe." George Crabbe (d. 1832), author of *The Village* (1783). Sometimes called "the poet of the poor" for his sympathetic, often somber descriptions of the life of simple people.

859 "Shee." Martin Shee (d. 1850), president of the Royal Academy of Art and author of "Rhymes on Art" and *Elements of Art*.

872 "Achaian." Greek.

877 "Wright." Thomas Rodwell Wright, consul-general in the Greek isles and author of *Horae Ionicae* (1809) describing the islands and coast of Greece.

893 "Darwin." Erasmus Darwin (d. 1802), author of long botanical poems— *The Loves of the Plants* (1789) and *The Economy of Vegetables* (1792).

906 "Lamb." Charles Lamb (d. 1834), essayist, poet, and supporter of the romantic poets. "Lloyd." Charles Lloyd (d. 1839).

911-40 A summary, mentioning several poets who have been cited earlier and identified in earlier notes.

961 "Granta." Another name for the river Cam, which flows past Cambridge.

966 "Hoare." Rev. Charles Hoare (d. 1865), author of a poem about *The Shipwreck of St. Paul* (1807). "Hoyle." Rev. Charles Hoyle (d. 1848), the author of a poem about *Moses Viewing the Promised Land* (1804); explicitly differentiated by Byron from the author of *Hoyles Games*, containing rules for domestic games, from which "according to Hoyle."

973 "Clarke." Hewson Clarke (d. ?1832). A sizer of Emanuel College, Cambridge. Author of a poem titled *The Art of Pleasing*. He was paid to collect sensational items for a journal called *The Satirist*. Clarke satirized Byron— hence his indignation.

981 "Vandal." According to Gibbon the Emperor Probus sent many members of the Vandal tribe to Cambridgeshire. Byron observes, "There is no reason to doubt this assertion; the breed is still in high perfection."

983-84 "Hodgson . . . Hewson." Examples of promising and wretched poets. Hewson is Hewson Clarke. See line 973.

985 "Isis." The Thames River is often called "Isis" in its upper reaches, including Oxford. Byron turns from Cambridge to Oxford poets.

989 "Richards." Rev. George Richards (d. 1837), author of the poem Aboriginal *Britons* (1792).

1014 "Flowers of rhetoric." Compare *Poetria Nova*. The old labels persist.

1016 "Portland." William Henry Portland (d. 1809), who was prime minister briefly before Pitt and at the time of the writing of *English Bards* was once again prime minister (1807–9), thus occupying the position occupied by William Pitt (d. 1806). Byron's contempt is suggested by the epithet "old dame portland."

1017 "The sail." Byron left on a "grand tour" lasting two years immediately after completing the 1809 edition of *English Bards*. This tour provided much of the substance of *Childe Harold*.

1019 "Calpe." Ancient name for Gibraltar.

1022 "Kaff." Mount Caucasus.

1027 "Elgin." Thomas Bruce, Lord Elgin (d. 1841), diplomat and antiquary. He brought the Elgin marbles from the Parthenon in Athens to England in 1806. He was proud of the collection of ancient marbles in his "stoneshop," as Byron puts it.

1029 "Phidian." Attributed to the Greek sculptor Phidias (fifth c. B.C.)

1034 "Gell." William Gell (d. 1836), author of a *Topography of Troy* (1804).

1046 "Lamb." See line 55. "Holland." See line 519.

1047 "Hallam." See line 513.

1048 "Edina." See line 483.

VI. *Notes Toward a Supreme Fiction* by Stevens

Dedication. "Henry Church." Stevens became acquainted with Church when Church was publishing the journal *Mesures* in France before World War II. Later Church came to America and Stevens became caught up on Church's effort to found an American version of *Mesures*. Eventually he settled for an endowed lecture series at Princeton. Stevens gave a lecture at the first session of the series. His lecture was *The Noble Rider and the Sound of Words*. In the *Letters*, edited by Holly Stevens, there are many letters from Stevens to Church and Mrs. Church.

"And for what . . ." Stevens wanted this poem separated from the dedication to Church. See *Letters*, 409. It is thus improperly presented in the *Collected Poems*. The point is not that Stevens feels love for Church but that he feels love for the world.

I.1.1 "Ephebe." A young citizen preparing for garrison duty. The point is important. World War II casts a shadow over the entire *Notes*. More generally, however, a young person preparing for full citizenship, an apprentice.

I.1.14 "Phoebus." Apollo, the sun god.

I.3.13 "Arabian." "The Arabian is the moon." *Letters*, 433.

I.4.2 "Descartes." "Descartes is a symbol of the reason." *Letters*, 433. René Descartes (d. 1650). Father of dualism, according to which there is an inner world of freedom and an outer world of scientific law. The problem in this case becomes how, if at all, the inner and the outer can interact. It would become a preoccupation of philosophers up to and including Immanuel Kant.

I.5.6 "Ceylon." Stevens corresponded extensively with Leonard C. van Geyzel, who lived in Ceylon.

I.5.7 "Tanks." According to Stevens, Ceylonese reservoirs for water. *Letters*, 434.

I.5.12 "Mansard." A sloping roof.

I.6.3 "Franz Hals." Dutch painter (d. 1666).

I.7.5 "Hepatica." A houseplant with liver-shaped leaves.

I.7.14 "Schwärmerei." German for rapture or ecstasy.

I.8.2 "Viollet-le-Duc." French architect (d. 1849) at the forefront of the revival of Gothic architecture, especially as a purely aesthetic enterprise. Thus a representative of the aesthetic and the engaged view of religious faith.

I.8.3 "MacCullough." Both a man and a "major man." See *Letters*, 434, 448.

I.9.2 "Apotheosis." Deification.

II.1.1 "Seraph." An angel.

II.2.7 "Blague." Falsehood, lies.

II.2.15 "Halyards." Ropes controlling sails on a ship.

II.3.1 "Du Puy." French war hero, located on its own street ("Place Du Puy").

II.3.2 "Catafalques." Hearses.

II.5.13 "Là-bas." Down there.

II.6.4 "Ké-ké." The song of the sparrow. See *Letters*, 438.

II.6.5 "Bethou." Stevens simply equates this with the bird's song. *Letters*, 435. A slightly different account is given *Letters*, 438. "Bethou" is related by William van O'Connor to Shelley's "Ode to the West Wind": "Be thou, Spirit fierce,/ My spirit! Be thou me, impetuous one!" The point of the reference by Stevens is the imperialist mode of the imagination seeking to reduce the diversity of things to itself.

II.8.1 "Nanzia Nunzio." A colorful name.

II.8.2 "Ozymandias." The ruler commemorated in the ruined statue found by Shelley's traveler in the sonnet "Ozymandias." The statue is all but ruined but preserves an inscription: "Look on my works, ye Mighty, and despair."

II.9.21 "Lingua franca." The common language. "Jocundissima." Jolliest.

II.10.1 "Catalepsy." A trance-like seizure.

II.10.2 "Trope." A figure of speech, a metaphor, Latin *transformation*.

III.1.1 "Jubilas." Religious songs of praise, related here to the celebration of the services of the canonical Hours ("at exact, accustomed times").

III.1.7 "Jerome." St. Jerome (d. A.D. 420), translator of the Bible into Latin, who thus "began the tubas." See *Letters*, 435.

III.1.19 "Heaven-haven." Cf. Gerard Manley Hopkins's poem "Heaven-Haven: A Nun Takes the Veil" (1864).

III.2.1 "Blue woman." Probably, the weather when the poem was being written. See *Letters*, 444.

III.3.15 "Cornelian." Deep red.

III.4.4 "Catawba." Town in North Carolina.

III.4.6. "Bawda." The meaning is suggested by the sound—"bawd."

III.5.1 "Meursault." A French wine.

III.5.2 "Canon Aspirin." A sophisticated man. See *Letters*, 445, 427.

III.5.6 "Pauvred." Made poor, drained of color.

III.8.10 "Lapis-haunted." Air tinged with the deep blue color of lapis-lazuli. The mineral was often used for mosaics.

III.10.16 "Sorbonne." The University of Paris.

III.10.20. "Mundo." World.

Bibliography

Note: Because of the extent of the materials available, background and collateral studies have been omitted for the nineteenth and twentieth centuries.

Horace

Brink, C.O. *Horace on Poetry I, II, III*. Cambridge: Cambridge University Press, 1963, 1971, 1982.

Fraenkel, E. *Horace*. Oxford: Oxford University Press, 1957.

Griffin, J. "Augustus and the Poets: *Caesar qui cogere posset*." In *Caesar Augustus: Seven Aspects*, edited by F. Millar and E. Segal. Oxford: Oxford University Press, 1984.

Herrick, M.T. *The Fusion of Horatian and Aristotelian Literary Criticism, 1531–1555*. Urbana, IL: University of Illinois Press, 1946.

Kilpatrick, R. *The Poetry of Criticism: Horace, Epistles II*. University of Alberta Press, 1986.

Rudd, N. *Horace: Epistles Book II and Epistle to the Pisones ("Ars Poetica")*. Cambridge University Press, 1989.

Weinberg, B. *A History of Literary Criticism in the Italian Renaissance*. 2 vols. Chicago: University of Chicago Press, 1961.

West, D.A. *Reading Horace*. Edinburgh University Press, 1966.

Wood, A.G. *Literary Satire and Theory: A Study of Horace, Boileau, and Pope*. Garland, 1985.

Medieval: General

Baldwin, C.S. *Medieval Rhetoric and Poetic*. New York: Macmillan, 1928.

Bolgar, R.R. *The Classical Heritage and Its Beneficiaries: From the Carolinian Age to the End of the Renaissance*. New York: Harper & Row, 1964.

Buttenwieser, H. "Popular Authors of the Middle Ages: The Testimony of the Manuscripts." *Speculum* 17 (1942): 54.

Faral, E. *Les Arts poétiques du XIIe et du XIIIe siècle* (Paris: Champion, rpt. 1958). [Includes a Latin text of Geoffrey of Vinsauf, *Poetria Nova*, 194–262.]

Hardison, O.B., Jr., ed. *Medieval Literary Criticism: Translations and Interpretations*. New York: Ungar, 1985.

Huygens, R. B. C. *Conrad of Hirsau, "Dialogus super Auctores."* Brussels, 1955.

Kelly, D. "The Scope of the Treatment of Composition in the Twelfth- and Thirteenth-Century Arts of Poetry." *Speculum* 41 (1966): 261–78.

Lawlor, T., ed. *The Parisiana poetria of John of Garland.* New Haven: Yale University Press, 1974. [Includes translation.]

Manitius, M. *Analekten zur Geschichte des Horaz im Mittelalter bis 1300.* Göttingen, 1893.

Minnis, A. J., and A. B. Scott, eds. *Medieval Literary Theory and Criticism, c. 1100–c. 1375: The Commentary Tradition.* Oxford University Press, 1988. [Does not treat the *artes poeticae*, but is extremely useful as a general introduction to medieval critical theory.]

Murphy, J. J., ed. *Three Medieval Rhetorical Arts.* Berkeley: University of California Press, 1971. [Includes a translation of Geoffrey of Vinsauf's *Poetria Nova* and two other "arts."]

Robins, R. M. *Ancient and Medieval Grammatical Theory in Europe.* London, 1951.

Stock, B. *Myth and Science in the Twelfth Century: A Study of Bernard Silvestris.* Princeton: University Press, 1972.

Vickers, B., ed. *Rhetoric Revalued.* Birmingham: Medieval and Renaissance Texts and Studies, 1982. [Collection of articles.]

Wright, T., ed. *Anglo-Latin Satirical Poets of the Twelfth Century.* 2 vols. London, 1872.

Zechmeister, J. *Scholia Vindobonensia ad Horatii Artem Poeticam.* Vienna, 1877.

Geoffrey of Vinsauf

Bagni, P. "L'Inventio nell'ars poetica Latina-medievale," In *Rhetoric Revalued*, edited by B. Vickers, 99–114. Birmingham: Medieval and Renaissance Texts and Studies, 1982.

Geoffrey of Vinsauf. For text see Margaret F. Nims, Roger P. Parr.

Murphy, J. J. "A New Look at Chaucer and the Rhetoricians." *Review of English Studies* 15 (1964): 1–20.

Nims, M. F., tr. *The Poetria nova of Geoffrey of Vinsauf.* Toronto: Pontifical Institute of Medieval Studies, 1967.

Parr, R. P. *Geoffrey of Vinsauf: Documentum de modo et arte dictandi et versificandi Translated from the Latin with an Introduction.* Milwaukee, WI: University Press, 1968.

Showerman, G. *Horace and his Influence.* New York: Longsman, Green, 1922.

Renaissance to Eighteenth Century: General

Atkins, J. W. H. *English Literary Criticism: The Seventeenth and Eighteenth Centuries.* New York: Barnes and Noble, 1966.

Garcia-Berrio, A. *La Formacion de la teoria literaria moderna: La topica horatiana en Europa.* Madrid, 1977.

Herrick, M.T. *The Fusion of Horatian and Aristotelian Criticism, 1531–1555.* Urbana: University of Illinois Press, 1946.

Kern, E. *The Influence of Heinsius and Vossius upon French Dramatic Theory.* Baltimore: Johns Hopkins University Press, 1949.

Meter, J.H. *The Literary Theories of Daniel Heinsius.* Assen, The Netherlands: Van Gorcum, 1984.

Patterson, W.F. *Three Centuries of French Poetic Theory, 1328–1630.* 3 vols. New York: Russell and Russell, 1966.

Sellin, P. *Daniel Heinsius and Stuart England.* Leiden: Leiden University Press, 1968.

Weinberg, B. "Badius Ascensius and the Transmission of Medieval Literary Criticism." *Romance Philology* 9 (1956): 209–16.

———. *A History of Literary Criticism in the Italian Renaissance.* 2 vols. Chicago: University of Chicago Press, 1961. [Esp. I, Chaps. III–VI, which trace the influence of Horace's *Ars Poetica* in the earlier sixteenth century.]

Boileau

Boileau (Nicolas Boileau-Despréaux). For text, see Dilworth, Escal.

Brody, J. *Boileau and Longinus.* Geneva: Groz, 1958.

Clark, A. *Boileau and the French Classical Critics in England.* Paris: Champion, 1925.

Dilworth, E., tr. *Selected Criticism of Boileau.* Indianapolis: Bobbs-Merrill, 1965.

Escal, F., ed. *Oeuvres complètes de Boileau.* Paris: Gallimard, 1966.

Alexander Pope

Aden, J. "First Follow Nature: Strategy and Stratification in *Essay on Criticism.*" *Journal of English and Germanic Philology* 55 (1956): 604–17.

Audra, E., and A. Williams, eds. *Pastoral Poetry and "An Essay on Criticism."* The Yale Edition of The Poems of Alexander Pope. New Haven: Yale University Press, 1961. ["An Essay on Criticism," 195–326.]

Empson, W. "Wit in *An Essay on Criticism,*" In *Pope: Essential Articles,* edited by M. Mack, 208–26. Hamden, CT: Archon Books, 1968.

Fogel, R.H. "Metaphors of Organic Form in Pope's *An Essay on Criticism.*" *Tulane Studies in English* 13 (1963): 51–58.

Hotch, R. "Pope Surveys his Kingdom: *An Essay on Criticism.*" *Studies in English Literature* 13 (1973): 470–85.

Mack, M. *Alexander Pope: A Life.* New Haven: Yale University Press, 1986.

———, ed. *Pope: Essential Articles* (rev. ed.). Hamden, CT: Archon Books, 1968.

————, ed. *Pope: Recent Essays by Several Hands* (2nd ed.). Hamden, CT: Archon Books, 1980.

Morris, D. S. *Alexander Pope.* Cambridge: Harvard University Press, 1984. [The "Essay on Criticism" is discussed in Chapter II, 47–74.]

Pope (Alexander Pope). For text see E. Audra and A. Williams.

Quennell, P. *Alexander Pope: The Education of Genius, 1688–1728.* New York: Stein and Day, 1968.

Reverand, C., II. "*Ut pictura poesis,* and Pope's Satire II, i." In *Pope: Recent Essays,* edited by M. Mack, 373–91.

Sherburn, G. W. *The Early Career of Alexander Pope.* Oxford: Clarendon Press, 1934.

Spacks, P. "Imagery and Method in *An Essay on Criticism,*" In *Pope: Recent Essays,* edited by M. Mack, 106–30.

Nineteenth Century: George Gordon, Lord Byron

Clearman, M. "A Blueprint for *English Bards and Scotch Reviewers: The First Satire of Juvenal.*" *Keats-Shelley Journal* 19 (1970): 87–99.

Maurois, A. *Byron,* tr. Hamish Miles. New York: Grossett and Dunlop, 1930.

Marchand, L. *Byron: A Bibliography.* 3 vols. New York: Knopf, 1957.

McGann, J. J., ed. *Lord Byron: The Complete Poetical Works.* Oxford: Oxford University Press. *English Bards and Scotch Reviewers* is in Vol. I (1980): 227–64.

Mellown, M. J. "Francis Jeffrey, Lord Byron, and *English Bards and Scotch Reviewers.*" *Studies in Scottish Literature* 16 (1981): 80–90.

Sargent, M. G. "*English Bards* and Afterwards: Byron as a Critic of his Contemporaries." In *Byron,* edited by J. Hogg, 64–83. Salzburg: University of Salzburg, 1982.

van Rennes, J. J. *Bowles, Byron and the Pope Controversey.* New York: Haskell House, 1966. [Re. 11. 327–84 of *English Bards.*]

Twentieth Century: Wallace Stevens

Bloom, H. *Wallace Stevens: The Poems of Our Climate.* Ithaca: Cornell University Press, 1976. [*Notes,* Chap. VIII, 167–218.]

Cook, E. *Poetry, Word-Play, and Word-War in Wallace Stevens.* Princeton: Princeton University Press, 1988. [*Notes,* Chap. XI, 214–66.]

Carroll, J. *Wallace Stevens' Supreme Fiction: A New Romanticism.* Baton Rouge: Louisiana State University Press, 1987.

Doyle, C., ed. *Wallace Stevens: The Critical Heritage.* London: Routledge & Kegan Paul, 1985.

Hines, T. J. *The Later Poetry of Wallace Stevens: Phenomenological Parallels with Husserl and Heidegger.* Lewisburg, PA: Bucknell University Press, 1976. [*Notes,* Chap. VI, 138–212.]

Peterson, M. *Wallace Stevens and the Idealist Tradition.* Ann Arbor: UMI Research Press, 1983. [*Notes*, Chap. VI, 143-63.]

Stevens, H., ed. *Letters of Wallace Stevens.* New York: Knopf, 1961.

Stevens, W. *The Collected Poems of Wallace Stevens.* New York: Knopf, 1961.

Sukenick, R. *Wallace Stevens: Musing the Obscure.* New York: New York University Press, 1967. [*Notes*, 136-62.]

Vendler, H. *On Extended Wings: Wallace Stevens' Longer Poems.* Cambridge: Harvard University Press, 1969. [*Notes*, Chap. VII, 168-205.]

Weston, S. B. *Wallace Stevens: An Introduction to the Poetry.* New York: Columbia University Press, 1977. [*Notes*, Chap. V, 83-110.]

General Index

Index of Foreign Terms

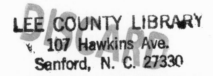